Economic Issues of Social Entrepreneurship

Elena G. Popkova · Bruno S. Sergi
Editors

Economic Issues of Social Entrepreneurship

Editors
Elena G. Popkova
MGIMO University
Moscow, Russia

Bruno S. Sergi
University of Messina
Messina, Italy

ISBN 978-3-030-77290-1 ISBN 978-3-030-77291-8 (eBook)
https://doi.org/10.1007/978-3-030-77291-8

© The Editor(s) (if applicable) and The Author(s), under exclusive license to Springer Nature Switzerland AG 2021
This work is subject to copyright. All rights are solely and exclusively licensed by the Publisher, whether the whole or part of the material is concerned, specifically the rights of translation, reprinting, reuse of illustrations, recitation, broadcasting, reproduction on microfilms or in any other physical way, and transmission or information storage and retrieval, electronic adaptation, computer software, or by similar or dissimilar methodology now known or hereafter developed.
The use of general descriptive names, registered names, trademarks, service marks, etc. in this publication does not imply, even in the absence of a specific statement, that such names are exempt from the relevant protective laws and regulations and therefore free for general use.
The publisher, the authors and the editors are safe to assume that the advice and information in this book are believed to be true and accurate at the date of publication. Neither the publisher nor the authors or the editors give a warranty, expressed or implied, with respect to the material contained herein or for any errors or omissions that may have been made. The publisher remains neutral with regard to jurisdictional claims in published maps and institutional affiliations.

This Palgrave Macmillan imprint is published by the registered company Springer Nature Switzerland AG
The registered company address is: Gewerbestrasse 11, 6330 Cham, Switzerland

Introduction: Social Entrepreneurship as a Phenomenon of the Modern Market Economy

"Market failures" are the cornerstone of a modern market economy. With the adoption of sustainable development goals, the world economy has entered a new age, and economic development has received a new dimension. Traditional economic values, such as the acceleration of the growth rate of economic systems and positions in the international rankings in terms of general macroeconomic indicators (e.g., GDP volume, share in world markets, export volume), have been rethought and supplemented with new values corresponding to the goals of sustainable development.

Socio-economic values received global support, according to which economic systems strive to improve the level and quality of life of the population, and economic growth acts as a source of achieving these goals. Internal interests came out on top, and the results of the economic systems' development turned out to be rated from the standpoint of not general, but private benefits for each member of society through a system of indicators such as GDP per capita, real disposable income of the population, social inequality, income differentiation, and many others.

The choice between a "clean" market and a social market economy is a relic of the past and a global "institutional trap". A notable example of a "pure" market economy (as close as possible to the ideal model) is the US economic system. Business entities in the American economy are driven by the "invisible hand of the market"—competition and the desire to maximize marginal utility (benefit, profit).

Public goods and socially significant goods and services are the least attractive to private investors. A number of them are provided by the state for certain categories of the population, for example, basic school education. Some of the public goods are transferred to the category of economic goods. This is typical for infrastructure projects, in which private investors are attracted using the mechanism of public-private partnerships, for example, for the construction of private highways. At the same time, the rest of socially significant goods and services are provided on commercial terms and are not available to the general public. Moreover, these are even services of higher education and emergency medical care, which are free in most countries of the world.

A typical example of a social market economy can be called the economic system of Russia, formed from the "pure" social Soviet economy. Here, on the contrary, the widespread state paternalism is obvious. Public goods, including infrastructure services, are provided by the government and are free for everyone. Socially significant goods and services are also provided by the state, in particular, full coverage of the population with compulsory health insurance has been achieved, and most of the services of higher education are provided on the basis of state order, that is, they are free for the population.

A critical look at both the "clean" market and the social market economy demonstrates their obvious weak points: in the first case, it is insufficient sociality and a shortage of social services, and in the second case, it is imposed sociality and an excessive load on the state budget. None of the existing models of a market economy meets the goals of sustainable development. An alternative model that can be applied to any economic system is the model for the provision of public goods and the provision of socially significant goods and services by social entrepreneurship.

Social entrepreneurship is an amazing phenomenon of the modern market economy, which contradicts its foundations, but despite this, it is developing steadily around the world. There are three forms of social entrepreneurship manifestation. The first form is altruism. In this case, public goods and socially significant goods are provided free of charge and unselfishly on the terms of sponsorship, donations, and volunteering as a gesture of goodwill. This form is available and implemented in all economic systems.

The second form is non-profit entrepreneurship. In this case, the enterprise chooses a social orientation for itself and provides public goods with socially significant goods as its main goal but to maintain normal operation, it seeks to reimburse the incurred costs, often through government grants and special private funds. This form is the most typical of social market economies.

The third form is corporate social responsibility. It is available to any enterprise that provides public goods of socially significant goods voluntarily as an addition to their main activity in expectation of marketing benefits in the form of strengthening their business reputation: as an employer, user of resources and supplier of goods and services in the economy. Typically, strengthening the brand of a responsible enterprise ensures that the best workers are attracted, government support is increased, and sales are stimulated. This form is the most typical for "clean" market economies.

Social entrepreneurship is a progressive form of the entrepreneurial activity that fully meets the interests of sustainable development. However, on the way of its formation and development, there are many obstacles, ranging from insufficient awareness of modern business structures about the opportunities and benefits of social entrepreneurship to the lack of scientific theory and methodology for conducting social entrepreneurship and institutional barriers. Despite its high relevance, social entrepreneurship remains poorly understood.

This book is intended to fill the indicated gap and to highlight the economic issues of the social entrepreneurship functioning in a consistent manner. The book includes four semantic sections. The first section is devoted to the project activities, planning, and business management as prerequisites for the formation of social entrepreneurship. It examines the features of the transformation of business processes in the digital economy, creating favorable conditions for the formation and development of social entrepreneurship. The prospects for the integration of business entities and business risk management, which are also important for the launching of social enterprises, are also considered.

The second section examines state support and legal foundations for the functioning of social entrepreneurship. The issues of legal support of the information society, necessary for the popularization of social entrepreneurship, and the provision of environmental services as a special aspect of the activities of social enterprises in the interests of sustainable development, are disclosed. Special attention is paid to the support of small- and medium-sized businesses in the context of the COVID-19 pandemic, which complicates the conditions for managing social entrepreneurship.

The third section reveals modern international experience and prospects for the development of social entrepreneurship. The issues of business ethics transformation in the context of a pandemic, manifestations of corporate social responsibility, and the provision of social services, commercial changes in the efficiency of social entrepreneurship in a market economy have been investigated. There are also case studies of social entrepreneurship in Russia.

The fourth section examines the contribution of education and personnel management to the development of social entrepreneurship. The digital competencies of personnel necessary for conducting social entrepreneurship in the digital economy are considered. The issues of social transformations and safety culture in the age of intellectual machines as a manifestation of social entrepreneurship are studied. The fundamentals of personnel training in the age of intellectual machines, which are fundamentally important for social entrepreneurship, are reflected.

CONTENTS

Project Activities, Planning, and Business Management as Prerequisites for the Formation of Social Entrepreneurship

Methodology for the Management of Project Activities of an Enterprise   3
Victor P. Kuznetsov, Elena P. Kozlova, Ekaterina P. Garina, Elena V. Romanovskaya, and Natalia S. Andryashina

The Role of the Digital Economy in the Management System of Service Organizations   15
Zhanna V. Smirnova, Olga V. Golubeva, Zhanna V. Chaykina, Mariia V. Mukhina, and Svetlana N. Kaznacheeva

Planning and Production Management System Development in the Era of Intelligent Machines   25
Natalia S. Andryashina, Elena V. Romanovskaya, Elena P. Kozlova, Victor P. Kuznetsov, and Sergey D. Tsymbalov

Methods of Assessing the Potential Impact of Digital Technologies on Business Processes of the Company   37
Alexander N. Vizgunov, Yuri V. Trifonov, Vasily Yu. Trifonov, Artem V. Dorozhkin, and Oleg V. Yasenev

ix

Complexity Assessment Eliminating the Risk of Transmission of Digital Information in Enterprise Networks 47
Lyudmila M. Gruzdeva, Nadezhda V. Kapustina, Nana A. Kobiashvili, Igor A. Lebedev, and Konstantin A. Bogonosov

Communication Platform for Finding and Attracting Industrial Cooperation Partners 61
Svetlana N. Kuznetsova, Elena V. Romanovskaya, Victor P. Kuznetsov, Lakshitha Withanachchi, and Dmitry N. Lapaev

Mechanism for Responding to Risks of Economic Activity in Enterprises 69
Yaroslav S. Potashnik, Svetlana N. Kuznetsova, Ekaterina P. Garina, Elena P. Kozlova, and Natalia S. Andryashina

Evaluation of Management Effectiveness of the System Based on the Use of Management Indicators 77
Marat R. Usmanov, Ekaterina P. Garina, Elena V. Romanovskaya, Natalia S. Andryashina, and Dmitrii P. Vatletsov

Innovative Approaches to Business in the Digital Environment 87
Natalia M. Fomenko, Tatyana O. Tolstykh, Victoria Yu. Garnova, Ekaterina N. Yalunina, and Boris I. Kheyfits

The Weighted Average Cost of Capital for the Analysis of Innovative Projects Integrated into the Company 103
Sergey N. Yashin, Egor V. Koshelev, Natalya A. Yagunova, Victor P. Kuznetsov, and Elena V. Romanovskaya

Forecasting Potential for Project Activities as a Tool for Institutional Modernization of the Higher Education System: Domestic and Foreign Experience 113
Alexander G. Oganyan

CONTENTS xi

**Small Business and Innovation Processes in Russian
Regions: Prospects for Further Development** 125
Yuri I. Treshchevsky, Tatyana Yu. Solodimova,
and Larisa S. Korobeynikova

**State Support and Legal Basis for the Functioning of
Social Entrepreneurship**

**Current Issues of State Support for Small
and Medium-Sized Businesses in the Context
of the COVID-19 Pandemic** 137
Zhanna A. Zakharova, Pavel N. Zakharov,
and Vitaly V. Kislinsky

**Mechanisms of Financial Support for the Development
of Innovative Entrepreneurship in the Digital Economy** 151
Natalia G. Varaksa, Maria S. Alimova, Sergey A. Alimov,
Elena S. Rozhdestvenskaia, and Victor A. Konstantinov

**Corporate Legal Relations in the Digital Age: Current
Challenges and Trends in Legal Regulation** 161
Aleksandr A. Biryukov, Nazima Shafievna Ibragimova,
and Gennady V. Shevchenko

**Managing the Process of International Cooperation
and Integration of Small and Medium-Sized Businesses
Based on Infrastructure Modernization** 173
Tatyana Yu. Anopchenko and Vladislav I. Ostrovskiy

**Ethical Standards: Traditions and Innovations in Law
Enforcement in the Context of the Fourth Technological
Revolution** 185
Olga V. Akhrameeva, Denis V. Zakalyapin,
Dmitry V. Derkunsky, Pavel V. Slydnev,
and Vitaly V. Kovyazin

Problems Related to Codification of Russian Social Security Legislation 195
Svetlana A. Lukinova, Igor E. Nelgovsky, and Tatyana F. Vysheslavova

Consumer Rights Protection in a Digital Space: Problems and Ways of Their Solution 205
Marina A. Bychko, Elena N. Barkova, Elena N. Volodkova, Vladimir V. Cherevko, and Beslan B. Argunov

Role of the Internet Network in the Process of Forming Legal Culture of Entrepreneurs 217
Kirill A. Dolgopolov, Ludmila V. Kiryukhina, and Igor V. Przhilenskiy

Modern Trends in the Development of Environmental Emergencies Legislation: Theoretical and Legal Aspects 227
Eleonora S. Navasardova, Natalya G. Zhavoronkova, and Vyacheslav B. Agafonov

Special Aspects of Formation of Legal Awareness in an Information Society: The Role of Mindset 235
Alexandr A. Volkov, Tatyana F. Maslova, Valeriy V. Meleshkin, Andrey M. Salny, and Galina V. Stroi

The Use of Digital Technologies in Civil Proceedings 245
Galina O. Belanova, Svetlana I. Mukhametova, Alexey P. Chizhik, and Vera P. Kutina

Legal and Regulatory Framework for the Creative Industries in a Digital Age 257
Ivan A. Bliznets, Viktoriia S. Savina, and Ilia A. Gribkov

Modern International Experience and Prospects for the Development of Social Entrepreneurship

Reformation of the Social Support System for a Family, Mother/Fatherhood and Childhood as a Factor of Social and Economic Welfare of the Russian Society 269
Elena S. Vologdina and Olga A. Kuzmina

Methodological Foundations of an Expanded
Understanding of the Economic Mechanism of the Modern
Socio-Economic System of Russia   281
Elena E. Nikolaeva and Vadim V. Soldatov

Transforming Business Ethics in the Coronavirus Pandemic   289
Liudmila P. Sidorova and Timur M. Khusyainov

The System of Compliance Management of Corporate
Social Responsibility   299
Pavel A. Kanapuhin, Larisa M. Nikitina,
and Dmitry V. Borzakov

Legal Regulation of Modern Forms of Social Services
in the Russian Federation   313
Nataliya A. Baieva, Valentina I. Mineeva,
and Igor E. Nelgovsky

Social Entrepreneurship as a Subject of the Market
Economy and Consumer Society: Essence, Specifics
and Tendencies of Development   323
Aleksei V. Bogoviz

Corporate Social Responsibility as a Criterion of Assigning
Commercial Business to Social Entrepreneurship
in the Market Economy   331
Svetlana V. Lobova, Aleksei V. Bogoviz,
and Alexander N. Alekseev

Non-commercial Organizations as Subjects of Social
Entrepreneurship in the Market Economy   343
Vladimir S. Osipov, Elena L. Pozharskaya, Aleksei V. Bogoviz,
and Alexander N. Alekseev

Systemic Scientific Vision of Social Entrepreneurship
in the Unity of Its Manifestations: As Non-commercial
and Socially Responsible Business   355
Vladimir S. Osipov, Veronika V. Yankovskaya,
Elena N. Akimova, and Svetlana V. Lobova

Contribution of Education and Personnel Management to the Development of Social Entrepreneurship

Project Activities as One of the Tools Unlocking
the Students' Potential 369
Anna Storozheva and Elena Dadayan

Socio-Economic Aspects of Digital Maturity Management
of HR-System in Transport Company 381
Tatiana V. Aleksashina, Victoria I. Smagina,
and Karina V. Fionova

Digital Economy Influence on the Formation of Staff
Competencies 395
Anna E. Belolipetskaya, Tatyana A. Golovina,
Irina L. Avdeeva, and Andrey V. Polyanin

Electronic Services as Components of the Future Education 405
Tatiana E. Lebedeva, Maria P. Prokhorova,
Tatyana V. Krylova, Svetlana A. Vinogradova,
and Marina V. Lebedeva

Theoretical and Methodological Foundations
of the Research Modernization Processes in Traditional
Societies as an Integral Part of Ensuring National Security 415
Andrey I. Gorelikov

Additional Vocational Teacher Education in the Field
of the Formation of a Safety Culture in Transport
in the Era of Intelligent Machines 425
Galina S. Kamerilova, Marina A. Kartavykh, Elena L. Ageeva,
Marina A. Veryaskina, and Irina A. Gordeeva

The Methodology for Calculating the Productivity
of Office Personnel at the Stage of Intelligent Machines
Implementation 435
Vladimir A. Polyakov, Irina V. Fomicheva,
Natalia E. Efremova, Svetlana V. Nefedova,
and Tatyana V. Medvedeva

CONTENTS xv

Philosophical and Methodological Aspects of Labor Quality Management in the Era of Intelligent Machines 445
Sofya S. Stukanova, Irina P. Stukanova, Alexander V. Agafonov, and Igor A. Murog

Contemporary Information Society and Higher Legal Education: Formation of a Professional and a Personality of Prospective Lawyer 457
Alexandra M. Drozdova, Tatyana V. Vorotilina, and Igor V. Zhuzhgov

Problems of the Formation of Legal Awareness of Youth in the Process of Digitalization in Russian Education 469
Rustam Z. Abdulgaziev, Magomed R. Alsultanov, Albert S. Arshinov, Viktor N. Mamichev, and Dmitry I. Sostin

Conclusion 481

Index 483

Notes on Contributors

Rustam Z. Abdulgaziev, Ph.D. in Law, Associate Professor, Head of the Department of Criminal Law Disciplines of the Stavropol branch of "MIREA-Russian Technological University", Stavropol, Russia. His research interests cover the general theory of crime, issues of criminalization, and qualification of certain types of crimes. He is an active participant in scientific and practical events, the author of monographs, textbooks, and teaching guides. He has more than 130 published educational publications and scientific papers.

Alexander V. Agafonov, Ph.D. in Biology, Director of Cheboksary Institute (Branch) of the Moscow Polytechnic University (Cheboksary, Russia). His scientific interests include management in education. Alexander V. Agafonov participates in Scientific Conferences, and he has published about 30 works in peer-reviewed scientific journals.

Vyacheslav B. Agafonov Doctor of Law, Professor of the Department of Environmental and Natural Resource Law, Moscow State Law University (MSAL). He is the author of 3 textbooks (co-authored) on land and environmental law, 5 monographs (3 of which are co-authored), and more than 100 scientific and educational works on legal problems of environmental protection and nature management.

Elena L. Ageeva, Ph.D. in Biology, Associate Professor at the Department of Physiology and Human Life Safety, Minin Nizhny Novgorod State Pedagogical University. The sphere of scientific interests includes the physiology of sensory systems, professional and pedagogical education in the field of life safety. She has published more than 100 works, including articles in peer-reviewed Russian and foreign journals, textbooks.

Olga V. Akhrameeva, Ph.D. in Law, Senior Lecturer. In 2005 she graduated with honors from the Faculty of Law of the Stavropol State University, qualification—"Lawyer", specialty—"Jurisprudence". She was awarded with a Certificate of Honor of the Ministry of Justice of the Russian Federation.

Elena N. Akimova Doctor of Economics, Professor at the Department of Economic Theory. She is author of over 50 publications in Russian and foreign editions.

Tatiana V. Aleksashina, Ph.D. in Economics, Associate Professor of the Department of Labor Economics and Human Resource Management of the Russian University of Transport (Moscow). The range of scientific interests: studying the state of human resources, intellectual capital, HR systems at micro-, meso-, and macro-levels in the digital economy and Industry 4.0 to activate them in the interests of developing proactive workers and increasing the competitiveness of both an individual enterprise and the country's economy as a whole. More than 70 scientific papers have been published.

Alexander N. Alekseev Doctor of Economics, Professor at the Department of Organizational and Managerial Innovations, Plekhanov Russian University of Economics (Moscow, Russia). Sphere of scientific interests: digital economy, creative economy, and innovative personnel management. He has more than 250 publications in Russian and foreign peer-reviewed journals and books.

Sergey A. Alimov, Ph.D. in Economics, Associate Professor at the Department of Economics, Finance and Accounting, Orel State University named after I.S. Turgenev (Orel, Russia). His research interests are in the field of greening the economy, innovative development, financial and credit relations, accounting, the interaction between the economy and the environment. Sergey A. Alimov is the organizer of All-Russian and International Scientific and Practical Conferences, the author of collective monographs, textbooks, and study guides on topical issues of accounting, taxation, and audit. He has published over 200 papers in Russian and foreign peer-reviewed scientific journals and books.

NOTES ON CONTRIBUTORS   xix

Maria S. Alimova, Ph.D. in Economics, Associate Professor of the Department of Economics, Finance and Accounting, Orel State University named after I.S. Turgenev (Orel, Russia). Sphere of her scientific interests: topical issues of accounting and audit in the context of the application of international standards, theoretical and applied aspects of determining, evaluating, recording, analyzing, and monitoring value indicators, the added value of products (works, services), problems of convergence of Russian and international information accounting and tax space, and innovative regional development. Maria S. Alimova is the organizer of All-Russian and International Scientific and Practical Conferences, the author of textbooks and manuals on topical issues in the field of taxation, accounting, and control. She has published over 150 papers in Russian and foreign peer-reviewed scientific journals and books.

Magomed R. Alsultanov Senior Lecturer of the Department of Criminal Law Disciplines of the Stavropol branch of Russian Technological University (MIREA), (Stavropol, Russia). His scientific interests cover the problems of the formation of evidence in criminal proceedings, methodological features of the investigation of certain types of crimes. He is an active participant in scientific and practical events, the author of textbooks, and scientific articles. He has more than 30 published educational publications and scientific papers.

Natalia S. Andryashina, Ph.D. in Economics, Associate Professor at the Department of Enterprise Economics, Minin Nizhny Novgorod State Pedagogical University. Her research interests include creating a new product in the industry, lean manufacturing technologies, process optimization, and enterprise development. She is the author of over 120 publications. She has over 60 publications in foreign journals indexed by Scopus and Web of Science.

Tatyana Yu. Anopchenko Doctor of Economics, Professor. She is the Dean of the Faculty of Economics of Smolensk State University (Smolensk, Russia). She conducts lectures and supervises the work of postgraduates at Smolensk State University (Smolensk, Russia), Plekhanov Russian University of Economics (Moscow, Russia), and Southern Federal University (Rostov-on-Don, Russia). She is a visiting Professor at the Urgench State University (Uzbekistan). Her research interests are devoted to digital Industry 4.0, environmental management and ecological-economic risk management, territory marketing, economic development of emerging markets, and project management of the foreign economic activity. Tatyana Yu. Anopchenko conducts research sponsored by grants of the Russian Foundation for Basic Research (RFBR), organizes Scientific and Practical Conferences at the national and international levels, acts as a moderator and speaker of business and training events. She conducts fruitful research work, and she is the author of more than 220 publications in Russian and foreign peer-reviewed scientific journals and books, including more than 17 scientific papers published in publications indexed in the international databases WoS and Scopus. More than 20 graduate students have completed research under her supervision. Tatyana Yu. Anopchenko is an Honoured Worker of Higher Education of the Russian Federation, a member of the Expert Council on Higher Education under the State Duma Committee on Education and Science.

Beslan B. Argunov, Ph.D. in Law, Senior Lecturer of the Department of Administrative and Financial Law of the Stavropol Institute of Cooperation, Branch of the Autonomous Non-profit Organization of Higher Education the "Belgorod University of Cooperation, Economics, and Law" (Stavropol, Russia). Scientific interests in the development of public relations of Russian legal thought in the second half of the nineteenth and early twentieth centuries with modern significance and scientific validity of the theoretical foundations and features of the legal concept of P.G. Vinogradov, performed in the context of a sociological approach to law in Russian jurisprudence in the second half of the nineteenth and early twentieth centuries. He has published 17 articles in Russian peer-reviewed scientific journals and publications.

Albert S. Arshinov Senior Lecturer of the Department of Criminal Law Disciplines of the Stavropol branch of Russian Technological University (MIREA), (Stavropol, Russia). His scientific interests cover issues of exemption from criminal liability and punishment, problems of applying other measures of a criminal-legal nature. He is an active participant in scientific and practical events, the author of textbooks and scientific articles. He has more than 20 published educational publications and scientific papers.

Irina L. Avdeeva, Ph.D. in Economics, Associate Professor of the Department of Management and Public Administration of the Central Russian Institute of Management, the Branch of the Russian Presidential Academy of National Economy and Public Administration (Oryol,

Russia). Her research interests are change management, personnel management, digital economy, and management of integrated economic systems. Irina L. Avdeeva is the organizer of All-Russian and International Scientific and Practical Conferences, editor, and author of collective monographs. She has published over 150 papers in Russian and foreign peer-reviewed scientific journals and books.

Nataliya A. Baieva, Ph.D. in Law, Associate Professor. Her research interests include the welfare state, practical implementation of the idea of a welfare state, and problems of legal guarantees of the welfare state. She worked as a legal adviser in commercial organizations, the Head of the Department of Social and Legal Guarantees in the District Administration of Stavropol. For the last 20 years, she has been teaching at the North Caucasus Federal University at the Faculty of Law. For her fruitful work on the development and improvement of the educational process and contribution to the training of highly qualified specialists, she was awarded Diplomas of the Governor of the Stavropol Territory and the Ministry of Education of the Russian Federation.

Elena N. Barkova Senior Lecturer of the Department of Civil Law and Procedure of the Law Institute of the North Caucasus Federal University (Stavropol, Russia). She graduated from the Lomonosov Moscow State University, Law Institute and engaged in teaching and legal practice. Her research interests include civil regulation of the activities of legal entities and entrepreneurs. She has published about 20 papers in Russian and foreign peer-reviewed scientific journals and books.

Galina O. Belanova, Ph.D. in Law, Associate Professor of the Department of Civil Law and Procedure of the Law Institute of the North Caucasus Federal University (Stavropol, Russia). Her research interests include civil procedural law, the arbitration process, and notarial law. She has published over 100 papers in Russian and foreign peer-reviewed scientific journals.

Anna E. Belolipetskaya Junior Researcher of the Department of Management and Public Administration of the Central Russian Institute of Management, the Branch of the Russian Presidential Academy of National Economy and Public Administration (Oryol, Russia). Her research interests include personnel management, competency-based approach, and digital economy. Anna E. Belolipetskaya is a participant in All-Russian and International Scientific and Practical Conferences, the author of collective monographs. She has published over 30 papers in Russian and foreign peer-reviewed scientific journals and books.

Aleksandr A. Biryukov, Ph.D. in Law, Associate Professor of the Department of Civil Law and Procedure, North Caucasus Federal University (Stavropol, Russia). The area of his scientific interests is topical issues of property, corporate law, and intellectual property law. He takes an active part in scientific events at regional, national, and international levels. Aleksandr A. Biryukov is the author and co-author of more than 70 scientific works, including a monograph, textbooks, articles published in leading Russian peer-reviewed journals, as well as in foreign scientific periodicals.

Ivan A. Bliznets Doctor of Science (Law), the Academic Director of Scientific and Educational Center for Intellectual Property and Digital Economy (Digital IP) (Moscow, Russia) and Professor of the Moscow State Institute of Kutafin Moscow State Law University (MSAL) (Moscow, Russia). His scientific interests include intellectual property law, copyright, and related rights law. Ivan A. Bliznets organizes international scientific and practical conferences and is the editor and author of several scientific journals magazines and collective monographs. He has published more than 400 works in Russian and foreign peer-reviewed scientific journals and books.

Konstantin A. Bogonosov, Ph.D. in Technical Sciences, Associate Professor at the Department of Higher Mathematics and Physics, K.G. Razumovsky Moscow State University of Technology. His research interests are in the field of condensed matter physics, photonics, nanotechnology, information, and economic security. Konstantin A. Bogonosov is the author of publications in Russian and international journals. He has published over 30 articles in Russian and foreign peer-reviewed scientific journals and books.

Aleksei V. Bogoviz Doctor of Economics, Independent Researcher. He is one of the leading Russian economists, an expert in the field of agricultural economics, food security, sustainable economic development, advanced digital technologies, Industry 4.0, comprehensive studies on energy economics, and energy security. He has more than 200 publications in foreign peer-reviewed journals and books.

Dmitry V. Borzakov Ph.D. in Economics, Associate Professor of the Department of Economics and Management of Organizations, Voronezh

State University (Voronezh, Russia). His research interests include corporate social responsibility, compliance management, non-financial and integrated reporting, and stakeholder management. He has published 40 papers, including Russian peer-reviewed scientific journals.

Marina A. Bychko, Ph.D. in Law, Associate Professor, Associate Professor of the Department of Civil Law and Procedure, Head of the Basic Department of Legal Support for Business at the Law Institute of the North Caucasus Federal University (Stavropol, Russia). Her research interests include topical issues of civil law, consumer protection, business law. Marina A. Bychko is a member of the working group under the Ministry of Finance of the Stavropol Territory for the preparation and implementation of measures aimed at increasing the level of financial literacy of the population of the Stavropol Territory; member of the all-Russian public organization "Association of Russian Lawyers"; provides scientific support and legal assistance to the department for coordination of the consumer market and protection of consumer rights of the Committee for Economic Development and Trade of the Administration of Stavropol; actively interacts with the Office of the Federal Service for Supervision of Consumer Rights Protection and Human Welfare in the Stavropol Territory and public organizations for the protection of consumer rights. She has published over 100 papers in Russian and foreign peer-reviewed scientific journals and books.

Zhanna V. Chaykina, Ph.D. in Pedagogics, Associate Professor of the Department of Service Technologies and Technological Education, Minin Nizhny Novgorod Pedagogical University. Her research interests include knowledge of economics teaching methodology. Zhanna V. Chaykina is the author of publications in international scientific journals. She has published over 150 papers in Russian and foreign peer-reviewed scientific journals and books.

Vladimir V. Cherevko, Ph.D. in Law, Associate Professor, the Head of the Department of Forensic Expertise and Professor of the Department of Constitutional and Administrative Law of the Institute of Management and Integrated Security of the SBS EMERCOM of Russia (Moscow, Russia).

His research interests include customs law, organization of customs control of goods, law enforcement activities of customs authorities, foreign trade activities, business law, commercial law, financial law, administrative law, administrative process, forensic examination, globalization, and digitalization.

Vladimir V. Cherevko is the organizer of All-Russian and International Scientific and Practical Conferences and the author of collective monographs. He has published more than 200 scientific papers, including peer-reviewed scientific journals.

Alexey P. Chizhik, Ph.D. in Law, the Deputy Head of the Department "State Legal Disciplines".

Elena Dadayan, Ph.D. in Law, Associate Professor at the Department, Associate Professor of the Higher Attestation Commission. Courses taught: Civil Law, Private International Law. She was awarded a Certificate of Honor (Governor of the Krasnoyarsk Territory), 2017. Work experience: Total work experience—24 years, including scientific and pedagogical work—23 years.

Dmitry V. Derkunsky Senior Lecturer of the Department of State and Legal Disciplines of the MIREA—Stavropol branch of the Russian Technological University.

Kirill A. Dolgopolov, Ph.D. in Law, Associate Professor, the Head of the Department of Criminal Law and Procedure of the Law Institute of the North Caucasus Federal University. His research interests include features of criminal responsibility and sentencing to minors.

Data on publication activity in the Russian Science Citation Index (RSCI):

- Number of publications—192
- Number of citations—940
- Hirsch index—23

Artem V. Dorozhkin, Ph.D. in Economics, Associate Professor at the Department of Information Technologies and Instrumental Methods in Economics, Lobachevsky State University of Nizhny Novgorod. His research interests include business security, information security, antiraider attacks, anti-money laundering, information technology, and information law. Artem V. Dorozhkin has published over 20 papers in peer-reviewed scientific journals and books.

Alexandra M. Drozdova Doctor of Law, Professor at the Department of Legal Culture and Protection of Human Rights. At the same time, she is a member of the Qualification Collegium of Judges of the Stavropol Territory of the Russian Federation, an expert on the correspondence of the content and quality of training of students and graduates of higher professional education of the Federal Agency for Accountability of the Russian Federation. She was awarded with the badge "Honorary Worker of Higher Professional Education of the Russian Federation" (2005). Under the supervision of Professor Drozdova seven Ph.Ds. in Law were prepared. Currently, one Ph.D. student and two applicants are preparing dissertation research. Alexandra M. Drozdova is a scientist working in the field of state studies, comparative studies, jurisprudence, theory of international human rights law; the sphere of her scientific interests is the problems of the general theory of state and law, state law, as well as the implementation and protection of human rights. She made the most significant contribution to the development of problems of studying the regional features of the formation, development, and functioning of state authorities of the constituent entities of the Russian Federation in the North Caucasus and the process of formation of a new institution of executive power—the Southern and North Caucasus Federal Districts. She carried out a classification of the functions of the federal structure of the state, analyzed various approaches to defining the principles of federalism in general and in Russia in particular, studied the constitutional foundations of the system of state authorities of the constituent entities of the Russian Federation, and also analyzed the relationship between the state authorities of the constituent entities of the Federation.

Natalia E. Efremova, Ph.D. in Technical Sciences, Associate Professor at the Department of Economics and Management of the Tula branch of the Financial University. Her research interests include management theory and practice. Natalia E. Efremova is the author of publications in international scientific journals. She has published over 100 papers in Russian and foreign peer-reviewed scientific journals, textbooks, and monographs.

Karina V. Fionova Senior Lecturer. The sphere of scientific interests includes research of modern requirements and approaches to management by human resources; socio-economic development of the nation-state, including the transport industry; corporate social responsibility. She is the author of over 15 scientific articles and monographs.

Natalia M. Fomenko Doctor of Economics, Professor at the Department of Management Theory and Business Technologies of the Plekhanov Russian University of Economics (Moscow, Russia). She has many publications devoted to innovation assessment, innovation and communication technologies, digital economy, virtual enterprises, knowledge management, evaluation of the organization's partner selection, risk management, etc. Natalia M. Fomenko is the author of publications in international scientific journals. She has published 130 papers in Russian and foreign peer-reviewed scientific journals and books.

Irina V. Fomicheva, Ph.D. in Economics, Associate Professor at the Department of Economics and Management of the Tula branch of the Financial University. Her research interests include issues and problems of economics and management of enterprises, industries, and complexes. She is the author of publications in domestic and foreign publishing houses. She has published over 100 papers, including scientific monographs, articles in peer-reviewed journals, textbooks, and teaching aids.

Ekaterina P. Garina, Ph.D. in Economics, Associate Professor at the Department of Enterprise Economics, Minin Nizhny Novgorod State Pedagogical University. Her research interests are design and production practices for product development in mechanical engineering, engineering of corporate systems, the formation of knowledge, and tools and methods of change at enterprises. She is the author of over 120 publications. She has over 60 publications in foreign journals indexed by Scopus and Web of Science.

Victoria Yu. Garnova, Ph.D. in Economics, Associate Professor at the Department of Management Theory and Business Technologies of the Plekhanov Russian University of Economics (Moscow, Russia). Her scientific interests include the theory of economic growth, sustainable development, globalization, waste and secondary resources management, digital economy, and Industry 4.0. She organizes International Scientific and Practical Conferences. She is the deputy editor-in-chief of the Russian peer-reviewed scientific and practical journal "Scientific research and development. Economics of the firm". The journal is included in the American database of the periodic and continuing editions of Ulrich's. She has published 69 papers in Russian and foreign peer-reviewed scientific journals and books.

NOTES ON CONTRIBUTORS   xxvii

Tatyana A. Golovina Doctor of Economics, Professor, Head of the Department of Management and Public Administration of the Central Russian Institute of Management, the Branch of the Russian Presidential Academy of National Economy and Public Administration (Oryol, Russia). Her research interests include economics and national economy management, personnel management, and digital economy. Tatyana A. Golovina is the organizer of All-Russian and International Scientific and Practical Conferences, editor, and author of collective monographs; invited editor of international scientific journals. She has published over 200 papers in Russian and foreign peer-reviewed scientific journals and books.

Olga V. Golubeva, Ph.D. in Pedagogics, Assistant Professor of the Department of Service Technologies and Technological Education in Minin Nizhny Novgorod State Pedagogical University. The research interests include teaching methodics knowledge. Olga V. Golubeva is an author in international scientific journals and has published more than 130 works in Russian and foreign peer-reviewed scientific journals and books.

Irina A. Gordeeva, Ph.D. in Biology, Associate Professor at the Department of Physiology and Human Life Safety, Minin Nizhny Novgorod State Pedagogical University. Her research interests include the study of spatial hearing, psychophysiology, sensory systems, professional and pedagogical education in the field of life safety. Irina A. Gordeeva is the author of publications in international scientific journals. She has published over 75 papers in Russian and foreign peer-reviewed scientific journals and books.

Andrey I. Gorelikov, Ph.D. in History, Associate Professor at the Department of Public and Private Law of Komsomolsk-na-Amure State University (Komsomolsk-on-Amur, Russia). His research interests include modernization theory, state national policy, and its implementation on the example of the indigenous peoples of the Russian Far East. Andrey I. Gorelikov is an author of monographs, and a participant in scientific grants. He has published about 100 works in Russian and foreign peer-reviewed scientific journals.

Ilia A. Gribkov the Head of the Department of the Caucasus, Central Asia, and Eastern Europe of World Intellectual Property Organization

(RSAIP) (Geneva, Switzerland). His scientific interests include international law, comparative law, intellectual property law, copyright, and related rights law. Ilia A. Gribkov has wide practical experience in the sphere of intellectual property and comparative legal analysis.

Lyudmila M. Gruzdeva, Ph.D. in Technical Sciences, Associate Professor at the Department of Information Technologies in Legal Activity and Documentation Support of Management of the Russian University of Transport. Her research interests include issues of economic and information security, mathematical modeling, and information technology. Lyudmila M. Gruzdeva is the author of publications in international scientific journals. She has published over 100 papers in Russian and foreign peer-reviewed scientific journals and books.

Nazima Shafievna Ibragimova, Ph.D. in Law, Associate Professor of the Department of Civil Law and Procedure of the North Caucasus Federal University (Stavropol, Russia). Her research interests are in the field of private law, civil and arbitration proceedings. Nazima Shafievna Ibragimova is an active participant in scientific events at various levels; she is author and co-author of more than 90 scientific works, including a textbook, study guides, articles published in leading Russian peer-reviewed journals, as well as in foreign scientific periodicals.

Galina S. Kamerilova Doctor of Pedagogy, Professor at the Department of Physiology and Human Life Safety, Minin Nizhny Novgorod State Pedagogical University. Her research interests include urban ecology; environmental education; ecodesign; professional and pedagogical education in the field of life safety. Galina S. Kamerilova is the author of publications in international scientific journals. She has published more than 200 works in Russian and foreign peer-reviewed scientific journals, author of textbooks, teaching aids, and monographs.

Pavel A. Kanapuhin Doctor of Economics, Dean, Head of the Department of Economics, Marketing and Commerce, Faculty of Economics, Voronezh State University (Voronezh, Russia). The research interests include methodological and philosophical problems of economics, economic analysis of law, strategic and neuro-marketing. Pavel A. Kanapuhin is the organizer of All-Russian and International Scientific and Practical Conferences, editor, and author of collective monographs, textbooks, and teaching guides, a member of the editorial boards of many scientific

NOTES ON CONTRIBUTORS   xxix

journals. Pavel A. Kanapuhin has published about 200 works in Russian and foreign peer-reviewed scientific journals and books.

Nadezhda V. Kapustina Doctor of Economics, Professor at the Department of Economics of Transport Infrastructure and Management of Construction Business, Russian University of Transport. Her research interests include issues of economic security, risk management, project management, business valuation, and resource provision of management systems. Nadezhda V. Kapustina is the author of publications in international scientific journals. She has published over 170 papers in Russian and foreign peer-reviewed scientific journals and books.

Marina A. Kartavykh Doctor of Pedagogy, the Head of the Department of Physiology and Human Life Safety, Minin Nizhny Novgorod State Pedagogical University. The sphere of scientific interests includes environmental education, vocational and pedagogical education in the field of life safety. The concept of integrated clinical practice in vocational pedagogical education has been developed and published. More than 100 papers have been published in Russian and foreign peer-reviewed scientific journals, textbooks, teaching aids, and monographs.

Svetlana N. Kaznacheeva, Ph.D. in Pedagogics, Associate Professor of the Department of Management, Minin Nizhny Novgorod Pedagogical University. Her research interests are the organization of the management process and management. Svetlana N. Kaznacheeva is the author of publications in international scientific journals. She has published over 110 papers in Russian and foreign peer-reviewed scientific journals and books.

Boris I. Kheyfits Doctor of Economics, the Head of the R&D Department of ALFA-FEEDS LLC. His scientific interests include innovations in economic science and management, as well as new technologies in agriculture, feed/food processing, and implementation of new feed/food products on emerging markets.

Boris I. Kheyfits takes part in All-Russian and International Scientific and Practical Conferences and is the editor and author of collective monographs. He has published more than 50 works in Russian and foreign peer-reviewed scientific journals and books.

Timur M. Khusyainov Master of Social Work, Senior Lecturer at the Department of Social Sciences, Deputy Dean of the Faculty of Social

Sciences, National Research University Higher School of Economics (Nizhny Novgorod, Russia). The research interests include transformational processes of the labor market, socio-humanitarian aspects of digital technologies, philosophy of technology, and Virtual Reality. Timur M. Khusyainov is a co-author of several monographs, organizer of All-Russian and International Scientific and Practical Conferences, and author of more than 200 scientific papers in Russian and foreign publications.

Ludmila V. Kiryukhina Specialist of the partnership sector of the strategic development management, the Assistant of the Department of Legal Culture and Protection of Human Rights of the North Caucasus Federal University. She has more than 30 published scientific articles on jurisprudence, including the Russian Science Citation Index (RSCI) the winner of the V. Potanin Foundation Scholarship Program, 2017-2018.

She is the winner of the regional stage of the competition for the Russian national award "Student of the Year—2018" in the nomination "Grand Prix".

She is scholarship holder of the Chamber of Notaries of the Stavropol Territory—2016.

She is event-manager of the program "Improving the financial literacy of the population of the Stavropol Territory".

She is the winner of the Competition for a scholarship of the Governor of the Stavropol Territory, 2018

She is the Assessor of the Center for the Assessment of Competencies "OkVector".

She is also federal trainer of the Association of Trainers of the Russian Union of Youth (since 2018).

Her research interests include legal culture of youth, protection of property, and personal non-property rights of spouses.

Vitaly V. Kislinsky, Ph.D. student at the Vladimir branch of the Russian Academy of National Economy and Public Administration under the President of the Russian Federation. The research interests include regional economy, state regulation of the economy, and public-private partnership.

Nana A. Kobiashvili, Ph.D. in Pedagogy, Associate Professor at the Department of Management, the Dean of the School of Engineering (Faculty) of the Moscow Polytechnic University. Her research interests include the design of management systems for business processes and organizations, project management, and quality management systems.

Nana A. Kobiashvili has published over 50 works in Russian and foreign peer-reviewed scientific journals and books.

Victor A. Konstantinov, Ph.D. in Economics, Associate Professor at the Department of Economics, Finance and Accounting of the Orel State University named after I. S. Turgenev (Orel, Russia). His research interests include the theory of forced spending, the sustainable development of the country, and the economic reserves of the rasta domestic economy, social entrepreneurship, the digital economy, and the management of imputed economic benefits. Victor A. Konstantinov is the organizer of All-Russian and International Scientific and Practical Conferences, an active expert of the Innovation Promotion Foundation, and the author of collective monographs. He has published more than 120 papers in Russian and foreign peer-reviewed scientific journals and books. The pioneering author's results in the field of forced spending are the foundation for many modern studies.

Larisa S. Korobeynikova, Ph.D. in Economics, Associate Professor, Head of the Department of Economic Analysis and Audit of the Faculty of Economics, Voronezh State University (Voronezh, Russia). Her research interests include interaction between public authorities and business structures, analysis of the economic activities of enterprises, financial management. She is the organizer and participant of All-Russian and International Scientific and Scientific and Practical Conferences. She is author of over 500 scientific works, including monographs and textbooks published in central publishing houses.

Egor V. Koshelev, Ph.D. in Economics, Associate Professor at the Department of Management and Public Administration of the Lobachevsky National Research Nizhny Novgorod State University. His field of research includes financial and innovation management, innovative development of an industrial region, investment and innovation projects. Egor V. Koshelev is the author of over 150 scientific publications in Russian and foreign peer-reviewed scientific journals and books in the field of higher mathematics, finance, and innovation.

Vitaly V. Kovyazin, Ph.D. in Law, Associate Professor at the Department of State and Legal Disciplines of the MIREA- Stavropol branch of the Russian Technological University.

Elena P. Kozlova, Ph.D. in Economics, Associate Professor of the Department of Enterprise Economics, Minin Nizhny Novgorod Pedagogical State University. Her research interests include sustainable development of the enterprise economy and development of the engineering industry. Research work is carried out in the direction "Formation of a Mechanism for Sustainable Development of an Enterprise based on Technological Transformation". More than 100 papers have been published in Russian and foreign peer-reviewed scientific journals and books.

Tatyana V. Krylova, Ph.D. in Pedagogy, Associate Professor at the Department of Innovative Management Technologies, Minin Nizhny Novgorod Pedagogical University. Her research interests include organization of the management process and management. Tatyana V. Krylova is the author of publications in international scientific journals. She has published over 105 papers in Russian and foreign peer-reviewed scientific journals and books.

Vera P. Kutina, Ph.D. in Law, Associate Professor at the Saint Petersburg Law Academy, Associate Professor of the Department of Civil Procedure. The Department carries out research activities according to the scientific direction "Legal regulation of socio-economic relations in the context of globalization" together with the Department of Civil Law (Saint Petersburg, Russia).

Her research interests include current trends in the development of legislation on the protection of labor rights, ways to protect the rights of citizens in court proceedings, and issues of digitalization in the field of labor.

Olga A. Kuzmina, Ph.D. in History, Associate Professor of the Department of Public and Private Law of the Komsomolsk-na-Amure State University (KnASU) (Komsomolsk-on-Amur, Russia). The research interests of the researcher include issues of providing social assistance and state support to the population of the Russian Far East from the middle of the nineteenth century to the present. Kuzmina O.A. is the author of about 30 papers in Russian and foreign peer-reviewed scientific journals, the head of programs of additional professional education.

Victor P. Kuznetsov Doctor of Economics, Professor, the Head of the Department of Enterprise Economics, Minin Nizhny Novgorod State Pedagogical University. The research interests include economic analysis, corporate governance, and industrial restructuring. He supervises the research work of the Department in the direction "Advanced Technologies of Management of Mechanical Engineering Enterprises". He actively conducts scientific work, participates in seminars, and round tables on topical problems of the socio-economic development of the economy of the country and the region. Victor P. Kuznetsov has published over 200 papers in Russian and foreign peer-reviewed scientific journals and books.

Svetlana N. Kuznetsova, Ph.D. in Economics, Associate Professor, Department of Enterprise Economics, Minin Nizhny Novgorod Pedagogical University. The research interests include organization of entrepreneurial activity, anti-crisis management, organization of R&D and design, the current state of the Russian economy, the world economy, and international economic relations. Research work is carried out in the direction "Development of the organizational and economic mechanism for managing industrial parks". More than 200 papers have been published in Russian and foreign peer-reviewed scientific journals and books.

Dmitry N. Lapaev Doctor of Economics, Professor, the Deputy Director for Research of the Institute of Economics and Management of the Federal State Budgetary Educational Institution of Higher Education "Nizhny Novgorod State Technical University named after R.E. Alekseev", the Member of the Board of the Free Economic Society of Russia, the Head of the Nizhny Novgorod Regional branch of the VEO of Russia, the Member of the Presidium of the Russian Academy of Natural Sciences. He is a member of the editorial board at the territorial body of the Federal State Statistics Service for the Nizhny Novgorod Region for the release of the official statistical yearbook "Nizhny Novgorod Region". His research interests include multicriteria decision making in economics in the study of problems of stability, security, innovation, competitiveness, and efficiency of economic systems.

He supervises the research work of the institute. He actively conducts scientific work, participates in seminars, and round tables on topical problems of the economy. Dmitry N. Lapaev has published over 400 papers in Russian and foreign scientific journals.

Igor A. Lebedev, Ph.D. in Economics, the Director of the Department of Economic Security and Risk Management of the Financial University under the Government of the Russian Federation. His research interests include economic security, risk management, combating corporate fraud and corruption, financial investigations, and compliance control. He has published over 60 papers in Russian and foreign peer-reviewed scientific journals and books.

Marina V. Lebedeva, Ph.D. in Pedagogy, Associate Professor, the Head of the Department of English Language at the Higher School of Translation, Nizhny Novgorod State Linguistic University named after N.A. Dobrolyubov. Her research interests include methods of teaching English. Marina V. Lebedeva is the author of publications in international scientific journals. She has published over 14 papers in Russian and foreign peer-reviewed scientific journals and books.

Tatiana E. Lebedeva, Ph.D. in Pedagogy, Associate Professor at the Department of Innovative Management Technologies, Minin Nizhny Novgorod Pedagogical University. Her research interests include innovative technologies for the formation of educational space at the university, professional education in the field of tourism and marketing. Tatiana E. Lebedeva is the author of publications in Russian and international scientific journals. She has published more than 400 papers in Russian and foreign peer-reviewed scientific journals and books.

Svetlana V. Lobova Doctor of Economics, Professor at the Altai State University (Barnaul, Russia). Her research interests are labor market and employment, entrepreneurship, education economics, digital economy, labor efficiency, integration, and cooperation. Svetlana V. Lobova is the author of more than 300 scientific papers, including those published in highly rated peer-reviewed journals.

Svetlana A. Lukinova, Ph.D. in Law, Associate Professor. She graduated from the law faculty of Rostov State University on a full-time basis. She worked as a legal adviser. In 2000 she defended her thesis on the problems of regional labor law. Currently, she is Associate Professor at the Department of Environmental, Land, and Labor Law, and lecturer in social branches of law at the Law Institute of the North Caucasus Federal University (Stavropol, Russia).

Viktor N. Mamichev, Ph.D. in Law, Associate Professor of the Department of Criminal Law Disciplines of the Stavropol branch of Russian Technological University (MIREA), (Stavropol, Russia). His research interests cover topical problems of the theory of state and law. He is an active participant in scientific and practical events, the author of textbooks and scientific articles. He has more than 50 published educational publications and scientific papers.

Tatyana F. Maslova Doctor of Sociology, Associate Professor, Professor at the Department. Rewards:

She has received Honorary Diploma of the Ministry of Education and Science of the Russian Federation; Certificate of Honor of the Government of the Stavropol Territory; Letter of Gratitude from the Institute of Education and Social Sciences of North Caucasus Federal University for the role in founding the first department of sociology in the region; Diploma-recipient of the VII International educational and methodological competition of educational and scientific literature, published in 2017 and 2018. "Golden Coryphaeus" 06.12.2018 in the nomination "Pedagogical Sciences", registration number 319-12 textbook (team of authors) "Professional standard: regional aspects of training and retraining of teaching staff".

She was the winner of the International competition for research and educational projects, "Interclover 2020".

Her research interests include sociology of education, social relationships and interactions, sociocultural integration, sociology of migration, and sociology of local communities.

Tatyana V. Medvedeva, Ph.D. in Economics, Associate Professor at the Department of Economics and Management of the Tula branch of the Financial University. Her research interests are regional economics, state and municipal administration, and finance. Tatyana V. Medvedeva has published over 80 papers in Russian and foreign peer-reviewed scientific journals and books.

Valeriy V. Meleshkin, Ph.D. in Philosophy, Associate Professor of the Department of Legal Culture and Protection of Human Rights. He has 25 years of teaching experience in higher education. 70 scientific and 19 educational-methodical works were published.

His research interests include the problems of the formation of historical and legal consciousness, and questions of the methodology of history and law.

Valentina I. Mineeva, Ph.D. in Law, Associate Professor at the Department of Civil Law Disciplines. She has been working in educational institutions for more than 20 years. The main areas of research are labor law and environmental protection. She is the author of four monographs in the areas studied. She has published more than 50 works in Russian and foreign peer-reviewed scientific journals.

Svetlana I. Mukhametova Senior Lecturer at the Department of Civil Law and Procedure. Her research interests include civil process, civil law, family law, housing law, land law, and urban planning legislation.

She is the author and co-author of more than 60 published scientific papers, 4 monographs, a textbook, and textbooks on labor law, civil law, and civil procedure. 50 articles have been published in Russian and foreign peer-reviewed scientific journals. Annually takes an active part in the Saint Petersburg International Forum Intellectual Property and the Saint Petersburg International Labor Forum, in International, All-Russian, Interregional Scientific and Practical Conferences with reports and scientific reports.

Mariia V. Mukhina, Ph.D. in Pedagogics, Associate Professor of the Department of Service Technologies and Technological Education, Minin Nizhny Novgorod Pedagogical University. Her research interests are the organization of service activities and material cutting. Mariia V. Mukhina is the author of publications in international scientific journals. She has published over 140 papers in Russian and foreign peer-reviewed scientific journals and books.

Igor A. Murog Doctor of Technical Science, Director of Ryazan Institute (Branch) of the Moscow Polytechnic University (Ryazan, Russia). Igor A. Murog is an academic of the International Academy of Ecology and Life Security.

Eleonora S. Navasardova Doctor of Law, Professor, the Head of the Department of Ecological, Land, and Labour Law at North Caucasus Federal University (Stavropol, Russia). Her scientific interests are ecological law, natural resources law, environmental protection, rational nature management, EEU country-members environmental safety, and compliance. She conducts public work in the sphere of ecological education. Being a member of the editorial boards of scientific journals, she takes part in organizing international, All-Russia as well as regional Scientific and Practical Conferences. She is the author of more than 150 published scientific works.

Svetlana V. Nefedova, Ph.D. in Economics, Associate Professor at the Department of Economics and Management, Tula branch of the Financial University. Her research interests are the development of an accounting and analytical system in the context of globalization of economic processes. Svetlana V. Nefedova has published over 75 papers in Russian peer-reviewed scientific journals.

Igor E. Nelgovsky Doctor of Law, Professor of the Department of Civil Procedure Law of the North-West Branch of the Russian State University of Justice (St. Petersburg, Russia). His research interests include problems of civil, business, labor, and administrative law. He is author of over 100 scientific and educational works, including 5 monographs, participant of international scientific and practical conferences in the field of civil and business law.

Larisa M. Nikitina Doctor of Economics, Professor, Professor of the Department of Economics and Organization Management of the Faculty of Economics, Voronezh State University (Voronezh, Russia). Her research interests include corporate governance, corporate social responsibility, and social responsibility of business. She is author of over 200 scientific and educational works, including monographs and textbooks published in the central publishing houses of the country. She is Member of the editorial boards of 3 Russian scientific journals.

Elena E. Nikolaeva Doctor of Economics, Associate Professor, the Head of the Department of Economic Theory, Economics and Entrepreneurship. As of 09.01.2020, she has 299 publications, including 245 scientific works. Among them, there are three individual and 27 collective monographs, chapters in collective monographs (of which four are foreign, including one indexed in Scopus), and 43 articles in journals included in the VAK list (Bulletin of Tver State University).

Her research interests include methodology of economic research, theory of social reproduction, regional economics, distribution relations and their deformations, theoretical and practical problems of income and wages, the standard of living, world economy, history of economics, and history of economic studies.

Alexander G. Oganyan, Ph.D. in Economics, Associate Professor at the Department of Management of Spatial and Economic Systems Development. Scientific and teaching experience—5 years. *Taught disciplines*: Finance, Finance of Organizations (Enterprises), Long-term Financial

Policy, Foreign Investment, Investment Strategy, Financial Management of Small Business, World Economy, Financial Environment of Entrepreneurship and Entrepreneurial Risks, State Regulation of the Economy, and Banking. Directions of scientific research are state regulation of the reproduction of fixed assets of commercial enterprises (organizations); state economic regulation of the processes of development of small- and medium-sized businesses; management of the modernization of higher professional education in the region (socio-economic aspect). According to the research results, 26 publications have been published, including two monographs and four educational—methodological complexes.

Vladimir S. Osipov Doctor in Economics, Professor of Asset Management Department at MGIMO University (Russia), and also invited Professor of School of Economics and Management at Beijing Jiaotong University (China). He is a Member of the American Law and Economics Association, Editorial Boards Member of several scientific Journals. He has published over 200 articles in professional journals and sixteen books as author, co-author, editor, and co-editor. His primary research expertise embraces institutional policy and public administration. He is a Vice-Head of the Dissertation Council of Lomonosov Moscow State University.

Vladislav I. Ostrovskiy Junior Researcher at the Faculty of Management of the Southern Federal University (Rostov-on-Don, Russia). His research interests include international management and marketing, business economics, and project management. More than 17 scientific papers have been published based on the materials of his scientific research. Vladislav I. Ostrovskiy regularly participates in Scientific and Practical Conferences of various levels, where he reports and discusses the obtained scientific results in the course of scientific discourse. For two years, he has been carrying out research work with the financial support of the Russian Foundation for Basic Research in the framework of the scientific project No. 19-310-90078 "Optimization of management of processes of international cooperation and integration of small and medium-sized businesses".

Andrey V. Polyanin Doctor of Economics, Professor of the Department "Management and State Administration" in Central Russian Institute of Management, Branch of RANEPA, Orel, Russia. The research interests include economy and national economy management, personnel management, and digital economy. Andrey V. Polyanin is the organizer of Russian and International Scientific and Practical Conferences, edited and authored the collective monographies and is an honored editor of international scientific journals. He has published more than 250 works in Russian and foreign peer-reviewed scientific journals and books.

Vladimir A. Polyakov Doctor of Economics, the Head of the Department of Economics and Management, Tula branch of the Financial University. His research interests include marketing and advertising theory and practice. Vladimir A. Polyakov is the author of publications in international scientific journals. He has published over 200 papers in Russian and foreign peer-reviewed scientific journals, textbooks, teaching aids, and monographs.

Elena G. Popkova Doctor of Science (Economics), the founder and president of the Institute of Scientific Communications (Russia) and Leading researcher of the Center for applied research of the chair "Economic policy and public-private partnership" of Moscow State Institute of International Relations (MGIMO) (Moscow, Russia). Her scientific interests include the theory of economic growth, sustainable development, globalization, humanization of economic growth, emerging markets, social entrepreneurship, and the digital economy and Industry 4.0. Elena G. Popkova organizes Russian and international scientific and practical conferences and is the editor and author of collective monographs, and serves as a guest editor of international scientific journals. She has published more than 300 works in Russian and foreign peer-reviewed scientific journals and books.

Yaroslav S. Potashnik, Ph.D. in Economics, Associate Professor at the Department of Enterprise Economics, Minin Nizhny Novgorod Pedagogical University. Her research interests include economic security and innovative activity of economic systems. She is a regular participant in International and All-Russian Scientific Conferences. Yaroslav S. Potashnik has published over 40 works in Russian and foreign peer-reviewed scientific journals and books.

Elena L. Pozharskaya, Ph.D. in Economics, Associate Professor at the Department of Psychology of the Plekhanov Russian University of

Economics (Moscow, Russia). Her research interests include management psychology, economic psychology, business psychology, organizational consulting, training, and coaching. Elena L. Pozharskaya is a co-organizer of Russian and International Scientific and Practical Conferences. She is the executive editor and author of collective monographs. She has more than 80 publications in Russian and foreign peer-reviewed journals and books.

Maria P. Prokhorova, Ph.D. in Pedagogy, Associate Professor at the Department of Innovative Technologies of Management, Minin Nizhny Novgorod Pedagogical University. Her research interests include innovative development of vocational education, preparation of students for projects, and innovative activities. Maria P. Prokhorova is the author of publications in Russian and international scientific journals. She has published over 280 papers in Russian and foreign peer-reviewed scientific journals and books.

Igor V. Przhilenskiy, Ph.D. in Sociology, Associate Professor at the Department of Criminal Law and Procedure. In addition to basic training and work, he took part in international training programs: 2006—internship in Great Britain, London; 2007—a trip with a delegation of university workers to Poland, participation in a program of seminars on the topic "Functioning of local self-government and public service"; 2011—participation in the program of legal seminars at the European Court of Human Rights on the topic "Protection of human rights in the ECHR" (Strasbourg, France).

Research interests: appellate proceedings in criminal proceedings; grounds for canceling and changing the sentence on appeal; criminal law protection of private life, secrets of correspondence and other negotiations; realization of personal human rights and the European Convention for the Protection of Human Rights and Fundamental Freedoms.

Elena V. Romanovskaya, Ph.D. in Economics, Associate Professor at the Department of Enterprise Economics, Minin Nizhny Novgorod State Pedagogical University. Her research interests include processes of restructuring of industrial enterprises, reengineering of business processes, lean manufacturing technologies, and optimization of business processes. She is the author of over 120 publications. She has over 60 publications in foreign journals indexed by Scopus and Web of Science.

NOTES ON CONTRIBUTORS xli

Elena S. Rozhdestvenskaia, Ph.D. in Economics, Associate Professor at the Department of Economics, Finance and Accounting, a Member of the Academy of Military Sciences of the Russian Federation, a Member of the Orel regional branch of the public organization VEO of Russia. Her scientific interests are related to the study of problems of public finance, taxation, and the tax administration system; sustainable development problems and management of socio-economic processes; macroeconomic problems of the development of the Russian economy during the period of digitalization; problems of development of the tourism industry in the context of global market changes; accounting, tax, and management accounting systems. Elena S. Rozhdestvenskaia is the organizer of All-Russian and International Scientific and Practical Conferences. She is also the author of collective monographs, textbooks, and teaching aids.

She has published over 135 papers in Russian and foreign peer-reviewed scientific journals and books.

Andrey M. Salny, Ph.D. in History, Associate Professor of the Department of Legal Culture and Protection of Human Rights of the North Caucasus Federal University (Stavropol, Russia). The sphere of scientific interests includes issues of legal culture and legal education of youth. He has repeatedly participated in international conferences. I have more than 20 publications in Russian and international scientific journals.

Viktoriia S. Savina Doctor of Law, Professor of Russian State Academy of Intellectual Property (RSAIP) (Moscow, Russia). Her scientific interests include international private law, comparative law, intellectual property law, copyright, and related rights law. Viktoriia S. Savina organizes international scientific and practical conferences and is the editor and author of several scientific journals magazines and collective monographs. She has published more than 200 works in Russian and foreign peer-reviewed scientific journals and books.

Bruno S. Sergi is an instructor at Harvard University, where he is also a faculty affiliate at the Center for International Development and an Associate at the Harvard Davis Center for Russian and Eurasian Studies and the Harvard Ukrainian Research Institute. He is a full Professor at the University of Messina, Italy. His research and teaching interests tie to the broader topic of the economics of emerging markets. In addition, he is the co-director of the Lab for Entrepreneurship and Development (LEAD), a research lab based in Cambridge (USA) that aims to generate and share knowledge about entrepreneurship, development, and sustainability.

Gennady V. Shevchenko, Ph.D. in Law, Associate Professor (jurisprudence), Associate Professor of the Department of Legal and Special Disciplines of the Stavropol Branch of the Russian Academy of National Economy and Public Administration under the President of the Russian Federation (Stavropol, Russia).

His research interests extend to the field of private law and civil procedure. Special attention is paid to modern problems of legal regulation of obligations and relations in the field of human and civil rights and freedoms protection. Gennady V. Shevchenko participates as an organizer of Scientific and Practical Conferences at various levels and is the author and co-author of more than 150 scientific papers in peer-reviewed journals, collections, and books.

Liudmila P. Sidorova, Ph.D. in Philosophy, Head of the Department of Social Sciences, National Research University "Higher School of Economics" (Nizhny Novgorod, Russia). Her research interests include business ethics, social entrepreneurship, career management, management philosophy, theory of rationality, and Russian philosophy. Liudmila P. Sidorova is an editor and author of collective monographs, as well as a guest editor of leading Russian journals.

Pavel V. Slydnev, Ph.D. in Sociology, Associate Professor of the Department of State and Legal Disciplines of the MIREA- Stavropol branch of the Russian Technological University.

Victoria I. Smagina, Ph.D. in Economics. Her research interests include socio-economic development of the nation-state, including from the point of view of institutional theory; study of business processes that contribute to the creation of self-learning organizations; research of modern requirements and approaches to human resource management. She is the author of over 40 scientific articles and monographs in Russian and foreign peer-reviewed scientific journals.

Zhanna V. Smirnova, Ph.D. in Pedagogics, Associate Professor of the Department of Service Technologies and Technological Education at the Minin Nizhny Novgorod Pedagogical University. Her research interests include the theory of organizing the process of service activities of enterprises, social entrepreneurship, professional training of specialists.

Zhanna V. Smirnova is the author of publications in international scientific journals. She has published over 300 papers in Russian and foreign peer-reviewed scientific journals and books.

Vadim V. Soldatov, Ph.D. in Economics. During his work at the Department of Economic Theory, the main theoretical course "Economics (Economic Theory)" and six special courses have been developed and taught. During his work at the Department of Economic Theory, 83 works were published.

Tatyana Yu. Solodimova, Senior Lecturer at the Privolzhsky Institute for Advanced Studies of the Federal Tax Service (Nizhny Novgorod, Russia), a post-graduate student at Voronezh State University (Voronezh, Russia). Her research interests are tax regulation of the activities of business entities and state regulation of small business. She is participant of Scientific, and Scientific and Practical Conferences of various levels, author of 12 scientific works.

Dmitry I. Sostin, Ph.D. in History, Associate Professor of the Department of Criminal Law Disciplines of the Stavropol branch of Russian Technological University (MIREA), (Stavropol, Russia). His research interests cover the problems of modernization and the state and legal structure of Russia. He is an active participant in scientific and practical events, the author of monographs, teaching aids, and textbooks. He has more than 50 published educational publications and scientific papers.

Anna Storozheva, Ph.D. in Law, Associate Professor, the Head of the Department, Associate Professor of the Higher Attestation Commission. Courses taught: civil law and legal regulation of property insurance. Total experience—20 years, including scientific and pedagogical work—19 years.

Galina V. Stroi, Ph.D. in Psychology, Associate Professor at the Department of Psychophysiology and Life Safety.

Her research interests include problems of the quality of education; means and methods for measuring the quality of education; problems of measuring the level of competence formation among graduates of pedagogical universities; anthropological and psychological-pedagogical support of the process of ensuring the quality of training of the future teacher.

Sofya S. Stukanova Doctor of Economics, Professor at the Economics, Management and Finance Department of the National Research University of Electronic Technology (MIET), Moscow, Russia. Her scientific interests include human resources quality, the standard of living, labor resources quality, and development. Sofya S. Stukanova has published more than 100 works in Russian and foreign peer-reviewed scientific journals and books.

Irina P. Stukanova Doctor of Economics, Professor at the Management and Economics Department of the Cheboksary Institute (Branch) of the Moscow Polytechnic University (Cheboksary, Russia). Her scientific interests include regional markets development and methodology of managing socio-economic systems development. Irina P. Stukanova has published more than 150 works in Russian and foreign peer-reviewed scientific journals and books.

Tatyana O. Tolstykh Doctor of Economics, Professor at the Economy and Management Department of Industrial Management, National University of Science and Technology "MISIS" (Moscow, Russia). Her scientific interests include system analysis, strategy, innovation, projects, forecasting, industry, and digitalization. She has published more than 300 works in Russian and foreign peer-reviewed scientific journals and books. She is Member of dissertation councils at the Southwest State University, National University of Science and Technology "MISIS". The participant of RFBR grants "Fundamentals of developing mechanisms for effective digital service-oriented interaction of participants in socio-economic systems and networks", and "Methodology for the formation of a new economy of industrial systems based on the principles of ecosystem and circularity".

Yuri I. Treshchevsky Doctor of Economics, Professor, the Head of the Department of Economics and Organization Management of the Faculty of Economics, Voronezh State University (Voronezh, Russia). His research interests include management of enterprises and organizations, innovation management, regional economics, and territorial administration. He is participant and organizer of International and All-Russian Scientific and Scientific-Practical Conferences. He is the author of more than 700 scientific and educational-methodical works, including more than 40 monographs, teaching aids, and textbooks in central Russian publishing houses. He is Member of editorial boards of 7 Russian journals.

Yuri V. Trifonov Doctor of Economics, Professor, the Head of the Department of Information Technologies and Instrumental Methods in Economics, Lobachevsky State University of Nizhny Novgorod. His research interests include theory and knowledge of artificial intelligence techniques in economics. Yuri V. Trifonov is the author of publications in international scientific journals. He has published over 300 papers in Russian and foreign peer-reviewed scientific journals and books.

Vasily Yu. Trifonov, Ph.D. in Economic Sciences, Leading Engineer of the Strategic Development Department of the Joint Stock Company "Experimental Design Bureau of Mechanical Engineering named after I.I. Afrikantov" (part of the subsidiaries of JSC Atomenergomash—the machine-building holding of the State Corporation "Rosatom"). His research interests are economics and enterprise management, risk management, and business planning. Vasily Yu. Trifonov is the author of publications in international scientific journals. He has published over 20 papers in Russian and foreign peer-reviewed scientific journals and books.

Sergey D. Tsymbalov Doctor of Technical Sciences, Professor at the Department of Enterprise Economics, Minin Nizhny Novgorod State Pedagogical University, Project Manager (Ecology) of LLC SMiKom Group. His research interests lie in the field of environmental and economic aspects of the development of society, improvement of equipment and technologies in mechanical engineering, non-ferrous metallurgy, and the construction industry. He is the author of over 100 scientific papers.

Marat R. Usmanov, Ph.D. in Technical Sciences. He completed MBA training. His research interests include innovative development, Lean & Six Sigma methodology, process optimization, technology development for oil refineries, decarbonization, green energy, machine learning technologies and artificial intelligence, 3D modeling, and digital information models. Marat R. Usmanov is the author/co-author of several registered industrial patents, two monographs, and many scientific articles in Russian and foreign publications.

Natalia G. Varaksa Doctor of Economics, Associate Professor, and Professor at the Department of Economics, Finance and Accounting, Orel State University named after I.S. Turgenev (Orel, Russia), the Head of the ARFG Financial Literacy Competence Center, the Member of the Orel regional branch of the public organization VEO of Russia. Her scientific interests are related to the study of problems of public finance, the system of tax administration, problems of development of small- and medium-sized businesses, tourism industry, agriculture, accounting systems, analysis, and audit. Natalia G. Varaksa is the organizer of All-Russian and International Scientific and Practical Conferences, the author of collective monographs, study guides, and textbooks. She is the deputy editor-in-chief of the scientific and practical journal "Economic and Humanitarian Sciences". She has published over 250 papers in Russian and foreign peer-reviewed scientific journals and books.

Dmitrii P. Vatletsov, Ph.D. student at the Department of History and Archeology of the Russian Presidential Academy of National Economy and Public Administration. He graduated from Razumovsky Moscow State University of Technologies and Management. He is a private investor, developer. From time to time he advises and takes part in solving complex issues in the field of urban planning with representatives of the Administration and the Government of the Nizhny Novgorod region.

Marina A. Veryaskina, Ph.D. in Pedagogy, Associate Professor at the Department of Physiology and Human Life Safety, Minin Nizhny Novgorod State Pedagogical University. The sphere of scientific interests includes environmental education, vocational and pedagogical education in the field of life safety. Marina A. Veryaskina has published more than 50 works in Russian and foreign peer-reviewed scientific journals and textbooks.

Svetlana A. Vinogradova Candidate of Pedagogical Sciences, the Dean of the Faculty of Management of the Russian Academy of National Economy and Public Administration under the President of the Russian Federation, Nizhny Novgorod Institute of Management. Her research interests include improving the system of strategic and project management in government bodies and business structures. Svetlana A. Vinogradova is the author of publications in international scientific journals. She has published over 15 papers in Russian and foreign peer-reviewed scientific journals and books.

Alexander N. Vizgunov, Ph.D. in Economics, Associate Professor of the Department of Information Systems and Technologies, Faculty of Informatics, Mathematics and Computer Science of the National Research University "Higher School of Economics". His research interests include business process management and cost analysis. Alexander N. Vizgunov

NOTES ON CONTRIBUTORS xlvii

is the author of publications in international scientific journals. He has published over 100 papers in Russian and foreign peer-reviewed scientific journals and books.

Alexandr A. Volkov Professor at the Department of Legal Culture and Protection of Human Rights.

Data on publication activity in the Russian Science Citation Index (RSCI): Number of publications—120, Number of citations—687, Hirsch Index—16.

His research interests lie in the field of problems of building a legal democratic social state and problems of building an information society.

Elena N. Volodkova, Ph.D. in History, Associate Professor of the Department of Theory and Methodology of History and Social Studies of the State Budgetary Educational Institution of Higher Education "Stavropol State Pedagogical Institute", Dean of the Faculty of Correspondence and Distance Education (Stavropol, Russia). Her research interests include the protection of consumer rights, children's rights, the realization of the right to education, social history. Elena N. Volodkova is the author of collective monographs. She has published more than 50 papers in Russian and foreign peer-reviewed scientific journals and books.

Elena S. Vologdina, Ph.D. Senior Lecturer of the Department of Public and Private Law of the Komsomolsk-on-Amur State University (KnAGU) (Komsomolsk-on-Amur, Russia). Her research interests include state social policy and its implementation in the Russian Far East in historical retrospect and at the present stage. Vologdina E.S. published about 30 works in Russian and foreign peer-reviewed scientific journals, the head of programs of additional professional education.

Tatyana V. Vorotilina, Ph.D. in Law, Associate Professor at the Plekhanov Russian University of Economics.

Tatyana F. Vysheslavova, Ph.D. in Law, Associate Professor of the Department of Environmental, Land and Labor Law, North Caucasus Federal University (Stavropol, Russia). Her research interests include issues of the flexibility of labor law in the field of employment, as an element of the social state, problems of labor law, problems of social security law, and sustainable development of social legal relations. Tatyana F. Vysheslavova is a participant in a wide range of International Scientific and Practical Conferences. She has published over 100 scientific papers in Russian and foreign publications.

Lakshitha Withanachchi, Ph.D. student at the Department of Enterprise Economics, Minin Nizhny Novgorod Pedagogical University. Her research interests include economic analysis, corporate governance in industrial enterprises, and the tea industry in Sri Lanka.

Natalya A. Yagunova, Ph.D. in Economics, Associate Professor, Director, the Head of the Department of Economics and Law of the Pavlovsk branch of the Lobachevsky Nizhny Novgorod State University. Her research interests include economic activity, strategic planning and development of enterprises, modernization of production processes in industries, and personnel management. She is the author of over 135 publications.

Ekaterina N. Yalunina Doctor of Economics, Professor, Director of the Institute of Continuous and Distance Education of the Ural State Economic University. Her scientific interests are related to the study of issues of economics and enterprise management, improving the efficiency of management of business entities. Ekaterina N. Yalunina is the author of publications in international scientific journals. She has published over 100 papers in Russian and foreign peer-reviewed scientific journals and books.

Veronika V. Yankovskaya, Ph.D. in Economics, Associate Professor at the Department of Psychology, Plekhanov Russian University of Economics (PRUE). She received Ph.D. in Economics, Associate Professor at Department of Industrial Management of the State University of Management (GUU). She is the editorial expert of the portal Seychass.ru news stories from the field of economics and management since 2017. She has the professional experience of a consultant: Specialist of the Strategic Analysis Department of Volga-Dnepr Airlines; Expert, Consulting Department, Union; Analyst, Department of Federal and Regional Programs, Compulink. Her research interests include reforming the systems and structures of enterprise management; development and implementation of the strategy; problems of theory and practice of management, and management development model; humanization of labor of teaching staff (effectiveness and efficiency of teaching staff); information security. She has more than 150 publications in Russian and foreign peer-reviewed journals and books.

Oleg V. Yasenev the Head of the Laboratory for Customs Affairs, Associate Professor at the Department of World Economy and Customs, Lobachevsky Nizhny Novgorod State University. His research interests include foreign economic activity, customs, and information technology. Oleg V. Yasenev has published over 20 papers in peer-reviewed scientific journals and books.

Sergey N. Yashin Doctor of Economics, Professor, The Head of the Department of Management and Public Administration, Lobachevsky Nizhny Novgorod State University. The sphere of scientific activity includes management of innovation, innovative development, investment and innovation projects, the effectiveness of innovation, assessment of the effectiveness of investment, and innovation projects. Sergey N. Yashin is the author of publications in international scientific journals. He has published over 500 papers in Russian and foreign peer-reviewed scientific journals and books.

Denis V. Zakalyapin, Ph.D. in Law, Associate Professor, the Head of the Department of State and Legal Disciplines of the MIREA—Stavropol branch of the Russian Technological University.

Pavel N. Zakharov Doctor of Economics, Professor, the Director of the Institute of Economics and Management, Vladimir State University. He is Full Member of the Russian Academy of Natural Sciences, the Member of the dissertation council D 999.239.03. He has published over 200 scientific and educational-methodical works. He prepared three Ph.Ds in Economic. He is the editor-in-chief of the electronic scientific journal "Bulletin of the Vladimir State University. Series: Economic Sciences".

He was the organizer and member of the Organizing Committee of International Scientific and Practical Conferences.

His research interests include regional economics, innovation management, and strategic management.

Zhanna A. Zakharova, Ph.D. in Economics, Associate Professor at the Department of State and Municipal Administration of the Vladimir branch of the Russian Academy of National Economy and Public Administration under the President of the Russian Federation. She has published over 150 scientific and educational works. Her research interests include regional economics, innovation management, state regulation of the economy, and public-private partnership.

l   NOTES ON CONTRIBUTORS

Natalya G. Zhavoronkova Doctor of Law, Head of the Department of Environmental and Natural Resource Law of the Moscow State Law University (MSAL), Professor, Honored Lawyer of the Russian Federation.

Expert, member of working groups of several committees of the State Duma of the Russian Federation, consultant, and expert of the Ministry of Natural Resources, Ministry of Economic Development, Expert Council under the Government of the Russian Federation, Expert Council of the State Duma Committee of the Federal Assembly of the Russian Federation, member of the Scientific Advisory Council under the Supreme Court of the Russian Federation. She was Chairman of the Dissertation Council D212. 123. 03, established at the Moscow State Law University (MSAL). She is author of more than 100 scientific papers, 12 monographs, and responsible editor of more than 10 textbooks with the stamp of the Ministry of Science and Higher Education of the Russian Federation in the field of land, environmental, and energy law. For her contribution to science and higher education in 2018, she was awarded the diploma of the competition winner of university teachers "Golden Names of Higher Education", as well as the Certificate of Honor of the Ministry of Education and Science of the Russian Federation.

Igor V. Zhuzhgov, Ph.D. in Law, Associate Professor at the Department of Legal Culture and Protection of Human Rights. He holds Ph.D. in Law thesis (2001)—"Theory of law and state; history of law and state; history of political and legal doctrines". The topic of the dissertation for the degree of Ph.D. in Law is "Monitoring the legal space of the Russian Federation" (Dissertation Council of Stavropol State University, January 14, 2006).

He has more than 20 scientific and educational publications.

His research interest is in methodology of law.

LIST OF FIGURES

Methodology for the Management of Project Activities of an Enterprise

Fig. 1   Projects integration sustainable methods   8
Fig. 2   Automatic grinding system Koyama Series 400 TT S   10

The Role of the Digital Economy in the Management System of Service Organizations

Fig. 1   The level of staff satisfaction due to the use of the digital economy in restaurant business organizations   19
Fig. 2   The main innovative directions used in the restaurant business   20

Complexity Assessment Eliminating the Risk of Transmission of Digital Information in Enterprise Networks

Fig. 1   Categories of victims affected by information attacks in the third quarter of 2019ю   50
Fig. 2   Information attack methods   51
Fig. 3   Types of malicious software   52

Mechanism for Responding to Risks of Economic Activity in Enterprises

Fig. 1   Risk response options   71

lii LIST OF FIGURES

Fig. 2   Risk response options   73

Evaluation of Management Effectiveness of the System Based on the Use of Management Indicators

Fig. 1   The main stages of efficiency improvement systems in the "Processing" business sector of a separate business unit of the fuel and energy complex of the Russian Federation (Usmanov et al., 2019)   79

Innovative Approaches to Business in the Digital Environment

Fig. 1   Factors of the electronic network environment   89
Fig. 2   Organizations that have a website   90
Fig. 3   The main categories of activities in a network environment   92
Fig. 4   Option for classifying the types of effects of using digital platforms   93

The Weighted Average Cost of Capital for the Analysis of Innovative Projects Integrated into the Company

Fig. 1   The basic principles of WACC assessment of the company   105

Forecasting Potential for Project Activities as a Tool for Institutional Modernization of the Higher Education System: Domestic and Foreign Experience

Fig. 1   Project management model of an innovation-oriented university complex   119

Small Business and Innovation Processes in Russian Regions: Prospects for Further Development

Fig. 1   Clusters of small business development in Russian regions in 2013–2016 (*Source* Calculated and compiled by the authors according to the data from: Russian Statistical Yearbook [2013, 2014] http://www.gks.ru/wps/wcm/connect/rosstat_main/rosstat/ru/statistics/public ations/catalog/doc_1135087342078; Small and medium entrepreneurship in Russia [2015, 2016] http://www.gks.ru/wps/wcm/connect/rosstat_main/rosstat/ru/statistics/publications/catalog/doc_1139841601359)   127

LIST OF FIGURES   liii

Mechanisms of Financial Support for the Development of Innovative Entrepreneurship in the Digital Economy

Fig. 1   The main forms of financial support for innovative
         entrepreneurship in world practice (*Source* Compiled
         by the authors)   153
Fig. 2   Structural analysis of technological innovation costs
         by funding sources in 2018 as part of assessing the role
         of government financial support for innovative business
         (*Source* Compiled by the authors based on official statistical
         information. Science and Innovation section https://www.
         gks.ru/folder/14477)   154
Fig. 3   Analysis of existing forms of support for innovative
         entrepreneurship in the Russian Federation (*Source* Compiled
         by the authors, taking into account the data of the Strategy
         for innovative development of the Russian Federation
         for the period until 2020. By the order of the Government
         of the Russian Federation of December 8, 2011 No. 2227-r
         https://ac.gov.ru/files/attachment/4843.pdf)   156

Managing the Process of International Cooperation and Integration of Small and Medium-Sized Businesses Based on Infrastructure Modernization

Fig. 1   Algorithm for managing the process of international
         integration of small and medium-sized businesses based
         on the modernization of infrastructure (*Source* Developed
         and compiled by the authors)   176

Social Entrepreneurship as a Subject of the Market Economy and Consumer Society: Essence, Specifics and Tendencies of Development

Fig. 1   Regression curves of the dependence of social
         entrepreneurship's development on extent of market
         dominance and buyer sophistication in developed countries
         in 2020 (*Source* Calculated and built by the authors)   327
Fig. 2   Regression curves of the dependence of social
         entrepreneurship's development on extent of market
         dominance and buyer sophistication in developing countries
         in 2020 (*Source* Calculated and built by the authors)   327

liv   LIST OF FIGURES

Corporate Social Responsibility as a Criterion of Assigning Commercial Business to Social Entrepreneurship in the Market Economy

Fig. 1   Global Entrepreneurship Index (2019) in the selected countries, points 1–100 (*Source* Built by the authors based on GEDI [2020])   334

Fig. 2   Correlation between the manifestations of corporate social responsibility, which are accessible to commercial business, and the advantages of social entrepreneurship in developed countries in 2020, % (*Source* Calculated and built by the authors)   337

Fig. 3   Correlation between the manifestations of corporate social responsibility, which are accessible to commercial business, and the advantages of social entrepreneurship in developing countries in 2020, % (*Source* Calculated and built by the authors)   338

Fig. 4   Generalized correlation between the manifestations of corporate social responsibility and the advantages of social entrepreneurship in developed and developing countries in 2020, % (*Source* Calculated and built by the authors)   339

Non-commercial Organizations as Subjects of Social Entrepreneurship in the Market Economy

Fig. 1   Cross correlation between the indicators of non-commercial organizations and the indicators of their potential social and economic contribution in the countries of G7 in 2020, % (*Source* Calculated and built by the authors)   348

Fig. 2   Cross correlation between the indicators of non-commercial organizations and the indicators of their potential social and economic contribution in the countries of BRICS in 2020, % (*Source* Calculated and built by the authors)   349

Fig. 3   Generalized cross correlation between the indicators of non-commercial organizations and the indicators of their potential social and economic contribution in the countries of G7 and BRICS in 2020, % (*Source* Calculated and built by the authors)   350

Systemic Scientific Vision of Social Entrepreneurship in the Unity of Its Manifestations: As Non-commercial and Socially Responsible Business

Fig. 1   Index of economic freedom for groups of countries in 2020, points 1–100 (*Source* Built by the authors based on The Heritage Foundation, [2020])   359

Fig. 2   Correlation between business initiatives and the indicators of social market economy in free and mostly free countries, % (*Source* Calculated and built by the authors)   361

Fig. 3   Correlation between business initiatives and the indicators of social market economy in moderately free countries, % (*Source* Calculated and built by the authors)   361

Fig. 4   Correlation between business initiatives and the indicators of social market economy in mostly unfree countries, % (*Source* Calculated and built by the authors)   362

Fig. 5   Correlation between business initiatives and the indicators of social market economy in countries with different levels of economic freedom, % (*Source* Calculated and built by the authors)   362

Project Activities as One of the Tools Unlocking the Students' Potential

Fig. 1   Analysis of the quality of performed projects by the subgroups of students   376

Socio-Economic Aspects of Digital Maturity Management of HR-System in Transport Company

Fig. 1   Characterization of the personnel business processes of the Company (*Source* Author's compilation)   387

Digital Economy Influence on the Formation of Staff Competencies

Fig. 1   Digital economy as part of the global economy   398

Fig. 2   Levels of the digital economy   399

Fig. 3   The basic principles of the formation of a competency model in digital economy   401

Electronic Services as Components of the Future Education

Fig. 1   Demand for electronic services for a month by students of the University of Minin   411

LIST OF TABLES

Methodology for the Management of Project Activities of an Enterprise

Table 1	Type of methodology	5
Table 2	Strengths and shortcomings of the most important project management methodologies	7
Table 3	Analysis of identified issues	9

Planning and Production Management System Development in the Era of Intelligent Machines

Table 1	Production plan	28
Table 2	Budget capital costs on the investment project	29
Table 3	Product retrospective analysis of data	30
Table 4	Forecast financial model of the project	32

Methods of Assessing the Potential Impact of Digital Technologies on Business Processes of the Company

Table 1	Assessment of the need for the introduction of digital technologies depending on their impact on business processes and the level of risk	42
Table 2	An example of an assessment the feasibility of implementing digital technology	44

lvii

Evaluation of Management Effectiveness of the System Based on the Use of Management Indicators

| Table 1 | Key performance indicators for improvements (Usmanov et al., 2019) | 82 |

Innovative Approaches to Business in the Digital Environment

Table 1	Enterprises using information and communication technologies in Russia (% of the total) [Federal State Statistics Service. (2019)]	90
Table 2	Main characteristics of the development and application of business models in the digital environment (based on researches of authors)	94
Table 3	Expert points	97

The Weighted Average Cost of Capital for the Analysis of Innovative Projects Integrated into the Company

| Table 1 | Equity and paid liabilities of JSC "NPE Polet" | 108 |

Forecasting Potential for Project Activities as a Tool for Institutional Modernization of the Higher Education System: Domestic and Foreign Experience

| Table 1 | Assessment of efficiency of implementation of the project management system | 120 |

Current Issues of State Support for Small and Medium-Sized Businesses in the Context of the COVID-19 Pandemic

Table 1	Main indicators of activity of small and medium-sized businesses for the period from 2016 to 2018 in the Russian Federation	140
Table 2	Key performance indicators of individual entrepreneurs for the period from 2016 to 2018 in the Russian Federation	141
Table 3	National project targets	142
Table 4	Comparison of the volume of state support to the economy	143
Table 5	Comparison of measures of state support for business in the context of a pandemic in market economies and in Russia	147

Mechanisms of Financial Support for the Development of Innovative Entrepreneurship in the Digital Economy

Table 1 Implementation of the proposed mechanism for financial support of innovative entrepreneurship, optimization of tax costs   158

Reformation of the Social Support System for a Family, Mother/Fatherhood and Childhood as a Factor of Social and Economic Welfare of the Russian Society

Table 1 Federal benefits and compensatory allowances for families with children   271

The System of Compliance Management of Corporate Social Responsibility

Table 1 Compliance management functions and their content   303

Social Entrepreneurship as a Subject of the Market Economy and Consumer Society: Essence, Specifics and Tendencies of Development

Table 1 Statistics of social entrepreneurship in developed and developing countries, where it is most developed, and the factors of the market economy and consumer society in 2020, points 1–100   326

Corporate Social Responsibility as a Criterion of Assigning Commercial Business to Social Entrepreneurship in the Market Economy

Table 1 Manifestations of corporate social responsibility, which are accessible to commercial business, and advantages of social entrepreneurship in developed and developing countries in 2020   335

Non-commercial Organizations as Subjects of Social Entrepreneurship in the Market Economy

Table 1 Statistics of non-commercial organizations and their potential social and economic contribution in the countries of G7 and BRICS in 2020   347

lx LIST OF TABLES

Systemic Scientific Vision of Social Entrepreneurship in the Unity of Its Manifestations: As Non-commercial and Socially Responsible Business

Table 1	Classification of subjects of entrepreneurship by the criterion of their contribution to formation of the social market economy	357
Table 2	Statistics of social entrepreneurship and the social market economy in countries with different levels of economic freedom	360

Project Activities as One of the Tools Unlocking the Students' Potential

Table 1	Student questionnaire results	372
Table 2	Graduate survey results	377

Socio-Economic Aspects of Digital Maturity Management of HR-System in Transport Company

Table 1	The stages of the digital transformation of personnel management within the enterprise	385
Table 2	The main characteristics of the sample	386
Table 3	Understanding the goals of digitalization and ownership of digital competencies by employee category	387
Table 4	Characteristics of "digital" overload by employee category	388
Table 5	Factors associated with digitalization and the frequency of its occurrence in the workplace	389
Table 6	The choice of digital personnel services by frequency of demand	392

Electronic Services as Components of the Future Education

Table 1	Main directions in educational organizations	409
Table 2	Factors constraining the use of the Internet in Education	412

Philosophical and Methodological Aspects of Labor Quality Management in the Era of Intelligent Machines

Table 1	Managers' satisfaction with the level of knowledge of their subordinates, belonging to different age groups, % (Zhuk. S., 2015b)	448

Table 2	Labour productivity in selected countries, dollars/hour (Ilyina & Starostina, 2019)	449
Table 3	The population incidence by certain classes of diseases (with a diagnosis established for the first time in life), thousand (Malkov et al., 2019)	451
Table 4	Forecasted values of selected indicators of labor resources structure in Russia (Denisenko, 2010)	452
Table 5	Human Development Index for selected countries, 2018 (Conseysao et al., 2019)	452

Project Activities, Planning, and Business Management as Prerequisites for the Formation of Social Entrepreneurship

Methodology for the Management of Project Activities of an Enterprise

Victor P. Kuznetsov, Elena P. Kozlova, Ekaterina P. Garina, Elena V. Romanovskaya, and Natalia S. Andryashina

1 INTRODUCTION

Project management should play the leading role in the company, and managers should improve their skills in such areas as management philosophy, commitment to project success, improvement of processes and infrastructure on site, efficient accountability, project methodology and documentation development methodology, employee training, continuous communication of project information, and regular control.

V. P. Kuznetsov (✉) · E. P. Kozlova · E. P. Garina · E. V. Romanovskaya · N. S. Andryashina
Minin Nizhny Novgorod State Pedagogical University, Nizhny Novgorod, Russia

E. P. Kozlova
e-mail: elka-a89@mail.ru

E. V. Romanovskaya
e-mail: alenarom@list.ru

N. S. Andryashina
e-mail: natali_andr@bk.ru

© The Author(s), under exclusive license to Springer Nature Switzerland AG 2021
E. G. Popkova and B. S. Sergi (eds.), *Economic Issues of Social Entrepreneurship*,
https://doi.org/10.1007/978-3-030-77291-8_1

Jason Charvat believes that: "The adoption of a wrong methodology or the absence of project frames can very easily affect:

- project schedule and costs;
- lack of understanding in a team;
- loss of time for the execution of administrative tasks that make no sense;
- burnout project management etc."

The wrong choice of the methodology for a particular project may have irreversible effect. Jason Charvat in his research paper points to the need for classification of projects according to their size and complexity. These positions have an impact on the type of methodology to be chosen. Table 1 presents the matrix of choice which reveals these parameters (Charvat, 2003).

The attitude of modern enterprises changes, the process of application of methodologies accelerates: new technologies replace old ones, management systems are being transformed. While in 2014–2018 companies most commonly used the Project Management Body of Knowledge (PMBOK), today their interests have shifted toward flexible approaches.

According to statistical data provided for the 4th quarter of 2019 by Proektnye Servisy (Proektnye Servisy, 2019), one of the most common project management methodologies at this stage are as follows:

- Modern organization (Business Agility, portfolio management);
- Flexible management methods and Business Agility in product development (Agile, Kanban, Design Thinking, Product Management);
- Classic project management (based on PMBOK, ISO 21,500, PRINCE2).

These methodologies have been analyzed and compared for their major characteristics (Yashin et al., 2019). A study of these approaches has revealed their positive and negative characteristics, as well as key indicators reflecting the activity of industrial enterprises (Table 2).

Sustainability is the key criterion of success for industrial enterprises. It is necessary to develop a competitive project management ideology for big projects which primarily focus on reduction of energy consumption, waste

METHODOLOGY FOR THE MANAGEMENT OF PROJECT ... 5

Table 1 Type of methodology

Type of methodology	Project size	Comments
Project management frameworks methodologies		
Rational unified process	Medium or Large	Arguably an IT/software development methodology, i.e. belongs under Technology Management
PRINCE2	Medium or Large	High management ceremony
System Development Life Cycle (SDLC)	Small, Medium or Large	Arguably an IT/software development methodology, i.e. belongs under Technology Management
Solutions-based project	Small, Medium	Anmably an IT/software development
Methodology		methodology, i.e. belongs under Technology Managemen High management ceremony; Low management ceremony
TenStep	Small, Medium	Low mana < Yementceremony
Technology development management methodologies		
The "A < Yile"Group:		
Extreme Programming (XP)	Small, Medium	Low management ceremony
Sl:rum	Small, Meuium	Luw manaverm:ull:eremuny
Kanban	Small, Medium	Low management ceremony
Crystal	Small, Medium	Low management ceremony; Not suited to virtual teams
DynamicSys. Development (DSDM)	Small, Medium	Low management ceremony
Rapid Applications Development (RAD)	Medium or Large	Low management ceremony
Unicycle	Small, Medium or Large	High management ceremony

(continued)

Table 1 (continued)

Type of methodology	Project size	Comments
Code-and-fix Approach	Small	Not suited to virtual teams
V-methodology	Medium or Lar < Ye	Hi < Yh mana < Yementceremony
Waterfall	Medium or Large	High management ceremony
Open Source	Small, Medium	Low mana < Yementceremony
Spiral	Medium or Large	High management ceremony
Synchronize and stabilize	Medium or Large	
Reverse engineering development	Medium or Large projects	High management ceremony
General publication methodology	Medium	High management ceremony
Structured system analysis & design	Medium or Large	High management ceremony
Pramis	Medium or Lar < Ye	Hi < Yh mana < Yementceremony
Offshore development	Large	High management ceremony
General drug development	Large	High management ceremony
Classic building construction	Medium or Large	High management ceremony

disposal, and environmental impact mitigation. PRiSM (Projects integration Sustainable Methods) is one of such methodologies. This is a project management methodology that has been developed by Green Project Management (GPM) Global. It takes into account the entire life cycle of the project after its completion in order to improve its sustainability (Chelnokova, Kuznetsova, & Nabiev, 2017).

2 Materials and Method

Objectives and activities within the scope of the PRiSM model have been organized in a similar manner shown in Fig. 1.

METHODOLOGY FOR THE MANAGEMENT OF PROJECT ... 7

Table 2 Strengths and shortcomings of the most important project management methodologies

	Modern organization	*Flexible management methods and product development*	*Classic project management*
Strengths	makes it possible to adapt to changes faster, obtain a large number of breakthrough ideas and innovations, reduce costs (especially compared to competitors) and maintain prominent positions in the ever-changing markets	adapts to diverse requirements and processes of the company. This characteristic determines its relevance and a large number of systems from various fields created on the basis of it	Its use implies the definition of specific requirements to the result as early as at the first stage of the project by senior executive of the company. This position allows introducing a certain stability early in the project implementation. Early planning affords an opportunity to harmonize the project implementation
Shortcomings	requires a large number of company management practices and approaches	unlike PRINCE2 and PMBOK, this methodology is not standardized. Each team needs to develop its own management system based on the underlying principles	Intolerance to changes is a key area in classic project management

PRiSM has been developed based on the classic risk management process which includes the following four stages presented in the PMBOK guidance (Project Management Institute, 2017):

1. Identification
2. Analysis
3. Monitoring
4. Control.

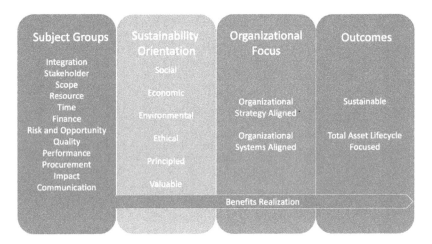

Fig. 1 Projects integration sustainable methods

2.1 Identification

It is best to approve the project management methodology after the practical approval of processes and templates during pilot projects; as a result, the application of this methodology by PJSC "GAZ" (hereinafter referred to as the business unit) has been tested and approved on the reference site of the company. The project methodology "Technological modification of the metallurgical production workflow in casting shop No. 7" has been put forward (Kuznetsov et al., 2018).

At the stage of identification, senior executives of the project answered several questions that were adapted to this type of project (about 40 questions: to identify threats (20 questions) and opportunities (20 questions). The parties concerned were involved in the preparation of this question list (Garina et al., 2017).

The analysis stage involves a qualitative risk analysis. This process is subjective, since the value which is assigned to each question is based on individual prejudices and useful values (Sergi et al., 2019). Domestic and foreign experience has been used as a basis for the suggestion of a quantitative assessment of questions using the 1 to 10-point scale of values.

The third stage requires the implementation of coordinated risk response plans as well as the identification of new risks throughout the

METHODOLOGY FOR THE MANAGEMENT OF PROJECT ... 9

project. Development of the right risk response measures will help project managers and the team to control project success (Smirnova et al., 2017). An important last stage is to assess the response to risks and the entire process of the project in order to turn it to advantage for future projects. Therefore, the Prism model creates a database which is mainly presented in graphical format. Thus, it is easy for managers to understand previous projects and obtain information about assumptions and constraints that significantly improve future projects (Auchey & Auchey, 2003).

3 Results

The production activities of casting shop No. 7 have been analyzed within the scope of suggested methodology drawing on the existing mechanism of sustainable development of an enterprise, and the following issues have been identified (Table 3) (Kozlova et al., 2020a).

In accordance with the identified issues, the following objectives have been set:

1. Improving the level of safety at work.
2. Conclusion of new contracts with international companies.
3. Reducing the number of employees required for grinding of castings.

Table 3 Analysis of identified issues

Economic	- *Formation of new requirements when receiving contracts from customers of automotive components in line with the international quality standards of the automotive industry—Valeo, Ford, Renault, GM*
	- *Large number of employees for manual processing of castings*
Environmental	- High percentage of waste product
Social	- High probability of accidents, as well as "white finger" syndrome due to constant vibration
	- Risk of eye and finger injury
	- High level of noise
Technological	- Inadequate deseaming
	- Loss of time due to routine breaks, absence and rotation of staff

4. Reduction in the number of defective articles during grinding, reduction of the thickness of the layer to be ground on all main journals and pin journals from the top of the joint line to 1 mm.

Proceeding from identified issues, a decision was made to purchase the automatic cutting and grinding system Koyama 400 S/400 TT S (Fig. 2) (Kozlova et al., 2020b).
This system offers the following advantages:

- Reduction of the number of employees. Only 2 operators are able to replace up to 10 workers involved in manual grinding.
- Short manipulator lever: manipulator lever length is about 400 mm, which compared to the average size of robot's lever of 1200 mm significantly reduces loads and increases the useful lifetime several times. In addition, long lever reduces the processing accuracy. And the length of Koyama lever guarantees regular consistent quality to a precision of 0.1 mm.
- Compact design: the area required for installation is 4–5 times smaller than the area required for a manual grinding compartment.
- Low operating expenditures: simple and reliable design does not require annual costs associated with replacement of expensive parts and assemblies. Simple settings do not require highly qualified and

Fig. 2 Automatic grinding system Koyama Series 400 TT S

METHODOLOGY FOR THE MANAGEMENT OF PROJECT ... 11

expensive personnel for configuration and reconfiguration. Operating expenditures are at least 10 times less than those associated with the CNC equipment.

- Cheap auxiliaries that are easy to manufacture: auxiliaries (fixtures) do not require high accuracy and are easy to manufacture. The cost of such auxiliaries is 7–8 times lower than that of high-precision auxiliaries for the CNC equipment.
- Patented technology of 115° angle of inclination: on the grinding disc and the grinding head. It allows grinding up to 90% of surface of castings per cycle.
- Diamond disk technology: the utilized technology of diamond coating on grinding discs and grinding heads allows leaving behind regular adjustments of the program for the compensation of wear and relevant deviations from the grinding edges when using the stone disk.
- System operator does not need to be highly skilled: no expert programmer is required for programming like with the use of the CNC equipment; new castings can be programmed and production program can be changed by the operator without any professional help (Kolmykova et al., 2018).
- The workers are no longer exposed to vibration. There is no risk of eye and finger injury, since it is eliminated due to the isolation of the grinding process in the closed chamber. There is low to no dust emission. The noise level is low. General working conditions have become much more decent for the personnel.

4 CONCLUSION

Following the work performed, it was concluded that efficient project management requires seamless integration of flexible methodologies and highly regulated provisions. The implementation of suggested project management methodology has made it possible to improve the level of sustainable development of an organization through:

1. cutting the costs of production, i.e. improving the economic sustainability of an enterprise;
2. changing the working conditions for personnel (improving the level of safety at work), i.e. increasing the degree of social sustainability;

3. cutting the energy costs resulting in the increase in the level of environmental sustainability;
4. transforming the workflow and introducing new advanced equipment conforming to international standards in automotive industry, resulting in the increase in the level of technological sustainability.

REFERENCES

Auchey, F. L., & Auchey, G. J. (2003). The use of the PRiSM model for improving the economic feasibility of the project. A document that was presented at PMI® Global Congress 2003–EMEA, the Hague, South Holland, the Netherlands. Newtown Square, Pennsylvania: Project Management Institute.

Charvat, J. (2003). *Project management methodologies: Selection, implementation and support of project methodologies and processes.* John Wiley & Sons.

Chelnokova, E. A., Kuznetsova, S. N., & Nabiev, R. D. (2017). Possibilities of using information and communication technologies in teaching economic disciplines in the university. *Vestnik of the Minin University, 3*(20), 8.

Garina, E. P., Kuznetsova, S. N., Romanovskaya, E. V., Garin, A. P., Kozlova, E. P., & Suchodoev, D. V. (2017). Forming of conditions for development of innovative activity of enterprises in high-tech industries of economy: A case of industrial parks. *International Journal of Entrepreneurship., 21*(3), 6.

Kolmykova, T. S., Merzlyakova, E. A., Bredikhin, V. V., Tolstykh, T. O., & Ovchinnikova, O. P. (2018). Problems of formation of perspective growth points of high-tech production. *Advances in Intelligent Systems and Computing, 622,* 469–475.

Kozlova, E. P., Potashnik, Y. S., Artemieva, M. V., Romanovskaya, E. V., & Andriashina, N. S. (2020a). Formation of an efficient mechanism for the sustainable development of industrial enterprises. From: Popkova, E. (editor) The Growth Poles of the World Economy: Origin, Changes and Future Prospects. *Notes of Lectures on Networks and Systems, 73,* 545–556.

Kozlova, E.P., Kuznetsov, V.P., Garina, E.P., Romanovskaya, E.V., Andriashina, N.S. (2020b). Methodological framework for assessing sustainable development of industrial enterprises (a technological approach). From: Popkova, E., Sergi, B. (editor) XXI Century from the Perspective of Modern Science: Intellectual, Digital and Innovative Aspects. ISC 2019. *Notes of Lectures on Networks and Systems, 91,* 670–679.

Kuznetsov, V. P., Garina, E. P., Romanovskaya, E. V., Kuznetsova, S. N., & Andryashina, N. S. (2018). Organizational design and rationalization of

METHODOLOGY FOR THE MANAGEMENT OF PROJECT ... 13

production systems of a machine-building enterprise (by the example of the contract assembly workshop). *Espacios., 39*(1), 25.

Popov, Y. (2008). Addressing the project management issues that arise as the organization grows up. *Upravlenie Proektami Magazine*, No. 4.

Project Management Institute. (2017). *Guidance on project management body of knowledge (Guidance on PMBOK)*.

Proektnye Servisy. (2019). This is the leading Russian company which is a professional provider of project management services: https://www.pmservices.ru/company-news/proektnye-servisy-v-cifrax-agile-pobezhdaet-waterfall/.

Sergi, B. S., Popkova, E. G., Bogoviz, A. V., & Ragulina J. V. (2019). *Entrepreneurship and economic growth: The experience of developed and developing countries. Entrepreneurship and development in the 21st century* (pp. 3–32). Emerald publishing.

Smirnova, Zh. V., Gruzdeva, M. L., & Krasikova, O. G. (2017). Open Electronic Courses in the Educational Activity of the University. *Vestnik of Minin University, 4*(21), 3.

Yashin, S. N., Koshelev, E. V., Ivanov, A. A., Garin, A. P., & Kozlova, E. P. (2019). Anti-crisis cluster-based innovative risk management strategy using the real put option. In E. Popkova (Ed.), *The Future of the World Financial System: Decline or Harmony. ISC 2018. Notes of lectures on networks and systems* (pp. 987–1001).

The Role of the Digital Economy in the Management System of Service Organizations

Zhanna V. Smirnova, Olga V. Golubeva,
Zhanna V. Chaykina, Mariia V. Mukhina,
and Svetlana N. Kaznacheeva

1 INTRODUCTION

The main development trends of the modern world are globalization and the digital economy. The digitalization of the economy affects all aspects of the organization and society as a whole, including the recruitment process.

The company cannot do without a retrieval system, recruitment, selection and employee engagement, as one of the prime objectives of the company is to develop a professional and competent team. The effective problem solving increases its human capital asset, which is the main factor of the company's competitive ability (Ageev, 2019).

The economic effect and efficiency of this company also depends on competency and efficiency of the personnel.

Z. V. Smirnova (✉) · O. V. Golubeva · Z. V. Chaykina · M. V. Mukhina ·
S. N. Kaznacheeva
Minin Nizhny Novgorod State Pedagogical University, Nizhny Novgorod,
Russia
e-mail: z.v.smirnova@mininuniver.ru

© The Author(s), under exclusive license to Springer Nature
Switzerland AG 2021
E. G. Popkova and B. S. Sergi (eds.), *Economic Issues of Social Entrepreneurship*,
https://doi.org/10.1007/978-3-030-77291-8_2

Human resource management is one of the most important segments of the company's life, which can significantly improve the efficiency of this enterprise.

In today's highly competitive environment, any company has to adapt to market conditions. However, market conditions are constantly changing, putting forward new requirements for business processes (Alekseenko, 2018).

At the present stage of restaurant development in Russia, an effective incentive program and well-developed motivation tools for staff are becoming increasingly important. The proper use of labour force in any organization ensures the activation of the human factor and the best production results (Sedykh, 2019).

The purpose of this study is to assess the current level of information management in the restaurant business and to study staff motivation activities and develop measures to improve it.

The introduction of modern information technologies in the restaurant business attracts modern specialists (Ilyashenko et al., 2019).

Nowadays the restaurant business is characterized by a high competitive level in the service market. Based on this, there is an increasing demand for new methods of servicing and working with clients, and search for new innovative technologies in service management.

2   Methodology

This study is based on the use of the basic concepts of staff motivation in restaurant business. To assess the role of the digital economy in the motivation management system in service organizations, an analysis of the existing employee engagement system in the Russian business of some companies in Nizhny Novgorod was carried out.

In the course of the survey of restaurants, the systems of staff incentives and motivation with the interconnection of information technologies were studied (Kuznetsov et al., 2019).

An incentive and an experienced manager perform two important tasks:

- firstly, the motivation of the team helps to determine the success of the organization;
- secondly, all people and firms are interconnected, and, consequently, all cities are in close correlation, thus motivation mainly determines an increase of the economy in the country.

We consider one of the methods of higher-performance incentives more specifically—the method of organized motivation:

– improving the quality of staff working life
– advanced training programs;
– total amount of work summarization;
– intellectualization of labour functions;
– proficient staff development;
– better working conditions.

These used qualities are not possible without the applying of information technologies, i.e. without the digital economydigital economy (Smirnova et al., 2019).

This study is based on the analysis and evaluation of the survey results to determine the development level and conditions for applying the digital economy to get the staff more motivated.

3 Analysis of Research Results

The restaurant industry is the sphere that applies a large amount of knowledge in the field of digital economy.

The way to understand the relationship between employee engagement and incentive work is performed through the individual characteristics and needs of each employee, which can be met with the maximum benefit— both for the employee and for the organization.

It is highly important to remember that an employee will work well if his/her needs are met. The higher the employee engagement is, the better results they show—this is an axiom. If a person gets what he wants from work, he/she will perform the duties well. If the important needs of the employee are not met, eventually there will be performance degradation (Myalkina et al., 2018). Inexperienced managers often create demotivators for their subordinates by their own actions, instead of building an efficient employee incentive programme. In fact, the formula for motivating employees is very simple, here are its components:

1. Understanding of the fact that the better the staff works, the higher the profit is.

2. Understanding of the fact that the better the needs of each employee are met, the higher the quality of performance.
3. Finding out the needs of subordinates, the motives that drive them in the work.
4. Partial satisfaction of these needs, and having an aim of total satisfaction—planning, management and control of the employee incentive programme (Burkhanova et al., 2020).

As for the last point—it is impossible to meet the needs fully, they are constantly growing, and that is why the employee incentive programme should grow with them.

In this regard, performance motivation is the highest form of employee incentives. It performs well when the working conditions are regulated with the help of various benefits, the individual needs of the staff are taken into account, the employees are interested in appropriate and effective work, according to the predetermined result (Garina et al., 2020a, b, c).

The system of performance motivation and stimulation of employees' work is the basis for managing results and increases their labour efficiency. It contributes to improving their skills, mastering modern methods and techniques, and using information technologies to improve the labour efficiency of all employees. In addition, it serves as an economic base for high production efficiency of the entire society (Kapustin, 2018).

The use of information technologies in the restaurant business is considered a new way for improving employee performance (Gruzdeva et al. 2019a, b). The restaurant business in Nizhny Novgorod focuses on software solutions for automating office work processes:

- order receiving and processing, applications for waiters, as well as electronic menus for customers;
- menu control;
- payment acceptance and cash services;
- managing loyalty programs;
- planning, accounting and management of expenses, performance monitoring, report generation;
- integration of a warehouse, accounting and management systems.

As a part of the study, a survey was conducted among restaurant employees in Nizhny Novgorod. The following questions were asked:

1. Are you satisfied with your workplace?
2. Do you think that the introduction of information technologies will have a positive impact on your work?
3. Do you think that the introduction of information technologies will increase labor efficiency?
4. Does the work with software motivate you?
5. Are you satisfied with the fact that the manager improves your work using the digital economy?

The study results are presented in Fig. 1.

The obtained survey data showed that **67%** of respondents are satisfied with their workplace. **89%** believe that the use of information technologies has a positive impact on the employee's work. **76%** of respondents believe that information technologies increase employee's efficiency and **82%** make the employee more motivated, **79%** of employees are satisfied with the management team that improves the employees' work using information technologies (Smirnova et al., 2020).

Based on this survey, we can make a general conclusion that the employee engagement in the restaurant business depends on the

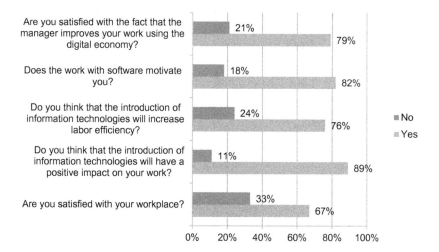

Fig. 1 The level of staff satisfaction due to the use of the digital economy in restaurant business organizations

personnel management system, the organization of the employee's workplace using aspects of the digital economy, which in turn increases labor efficiency and satisfaction (Egorov et al., 2019).

Having considered the motivation level of employees, we should note the directions of information technologies that are used in the restaurant business (Lvov et al., 2019). The main areas of information technology include:

- robot-based applications in a restaurant 75%;
- expanding mobile payment features 65%;
- radio-frequency identification technologies 78%.

Most restaurants in Nizhny Novgorod are ready to include the specification of such technologies in their work (Garina et al., 2019).

The readiness state to introduce innovative technologies is reflected in the employee survey in Fig. 2.

Thus, the digital economy is aimed at socio-economic development and involves not only the development of information technologies in the restaurant business, but also changes in the activities of the enterprise.

The restaurant business today is not a high-tech industry (Kazakova, 2011). The development of digital technology gives an opportunity to motivate employees to perform highly efficient work, expanding the quality and range of provided services.

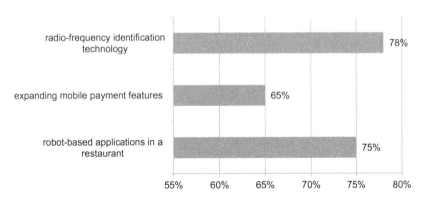

Fig. 2 The main innovative directions used in the restaurant business

4 Conclusions

The development of the digital economy provides an opportunity for communication, exchange of ideas and experience. Online platforms enable to join efforts together to create a business, invest and search for employees, partners, resources, and sales markets.

Digital technologies can also play a key role in employee trainings, sharing knowledge, and implementing innovative ideas, including the social sphere.

The development of digital technology is significant in the management system of service enterprises, in particular in the restaurant business.

Digital management and delivery services are seen as a means of reducing costs increasingly frequently, providing more efficient services to businesses, as well as being part of the manager's efforts to retain human resources.

Thus, the nature of the changes that have come to the restaurant business management system with its digitalization determine the fundamental changes in the management procedures and schemes at the level of the entire management paradigm.

In the "restaurant of the future", the client is considered as the core of the priority system. Understanding the forces that create changes in customer behavior, both inside and outside the restaurant industry, is of paramount importance for building a positive customer experience.

The study confirmed the influence of the digital economy in the management system of service organizations.

Further development of the system for managing organizations' service activities will significantly improve the use of the digital economy in order to form a quality process for the restaurant business.

References

Ageev, A. I. (2019). Methods of digital economy in terms of management and control activities in the real sector of the economy. In A. I. Ageev & V. A. Radina (Eds.), *Economic strategies* (Vol. 21, No. 3, pp. 44–56). '

Alekseenko, O. A. (2018). Digitalization of the world and the role of the state in the digital economy. In O. A. Alekseenko & I. V. Ilyin (Eds.), *Information society* (№ 2, pp. 25–28).

Burkhanova, I. Y., Vaganova, O. I., Kutepov, M. M., Smirnova, Z. V., & Chelnokova, E. A. (2020) Possibilities of social design in formation of competence of graduates of higher education. *Lecture Notes in Networks and Systems, 73,* 1057–1063.

Egorov, E. E., Semakhin, E. A., Romanovskaya, E. V., Smirnova, Z. V., Andryashina, N. S., Semenov, S. V., & Provalenova, N. V. (2019). Ensuring the accessibility of hospitality services and public catering for persons with disabilities of health International. *Journal of Innovative Technology and Exploring Engineering, 8*(12), 1746–1750.

Garina, E. P., Garin, A. P., Tsymbalov, S. D., Romanovskaya, E. V., & Andryashina, N. S. (2019). Modelling of approaches of product development and production processes: existing problems and proposed solutions ubiquitous computing and internet things: Prerequisites for the development of ICT. Book series: studies in computational intelligence (Vol. 826, pp: 1115–1127) https://doi.org/10.1007/978-3-030-13397-9_114.

Garina, E. P., Andryashina, N. S., Kuznetsov, V. P., Romanovskaya, E. V., & Muzayev, M. Z. (2020a). Formation of the determinants of socio-economic development of territories. *Lecture Notes in Networks and Systems, 91,* 170–178.

Garina, E. P., Kuznetsov, V. P., Romanovskaya, E. V., Andryashina, N. S., & Trifonova E. Y. (2020b). Increase of the efficiency of the industrial enterprise management system by the example of separate projects of contract production. *Lecture Notes in Networks and Systems, 73,* 453–462.

Garina, E. P., Romanovskaya, E. V., Andryashina, N. S., Kuznetsov, V. P., & Shpilevskaya, E. V. (2020c). Organizational and economic foundations of the management of the investment programs at the stage of their implementation. *Lecture Notes in Networks and Systems, 91,* 163–169.

Gruzdeva, M. L, Smirnova, Z. V, Chaikina, Z. V, Golubeva, O. V., & Cherney, O. T. (2019a). Using internet services in teaching methodology. *Lecture Notes in Networks and Systems, 57,* 1193–1199. https://doi.org/10.1007/978-3-030-00102-5_125.

Gruzdeva, M. L., Smirnova, Z. V., Chaikina, Z. V., Golubeva, O. V., & Cherney, O. T. (2019b). Using internet services in teaching methodology. *Lecture Notes in Networks and Systems, 57,* 1193–1199.

Ilyashenko, L. K., Markova, S. M., Mironov, A. G., Vaganova, O. I., & Smirnova, Z. V. (2019). Educational environment as a development resource for the learning process. *Amazonia Investiga, 8*(18), 303–312.

Kapustin, S. N. (2018) Digitalization of the exhibition industry: Achievements, prospects, challenges. In S. N. Kapustin & K. V. Simonov (Eds.), *Innovations* (№ 9, pp. 74–85).

Kazakova, K. S. (2011). Educational environment: Basic research approaches. *Proceedings of the Kola scientific center of the Russian Academy of Sciences.* No. 6. pp. 65–71.

Kuznetsov, V. P., Kuznetsova, S. N., Romanovskaya, E. V. Andryashina, N. S., & Garina, E. P. (2019). Technological renewal of industrial sectors through creation of high-tech industrial eco-clusters ubiquitous computing and the Internet things: Prerequisites for the development of ICT, book series: studies in computational intelligence (Vol. 826, pp. 1089–1095). https://doi.org/10.1007/978-3-030-13397-9_112.

Lvov, V. V., Smirnova, Z. V., Artemova, E. I., Averianova, T. A., Aleksiuk, I. O., & Tonkikh, A. P. (2019). State of university–Employer interaction models in Russia. *Journal of Entrepreneurship Education, 22*(4).

Myalkina, E. V., Sedykh, E. P., Zhitkova, V. A., Vaskina, A. V., & Isaykov, O. I. (2018). University resource center as an element of social development of the region. *Vestnik of Minin University, 6*(3) (24), 1.

Sedykh, E. P. (2019). Normative legal support system of project management in education. *Vestnik of Minin University, 7*(1) (26), 1.

Smirnova, Z. V., Kamenez, N. V., Vaganova, O. I., Kutepova, L. I., & Vezetiu, E. V. (2019). The experience of using the webinar in engineering specialists' training. *Amazonia Investiga, 8*(18), 279–287.

Smirnova, Z. V., Kuznetsova, E. A., Koldina, M. I., Dyudyakova, S. V., & Smirnov, A. B. (2020). Organization of an inclusive educational environment in a professional educational institution. *Lecture Notes in Networks and Systems, 73*, 1065–1072.

Planning and Production Management System Development in the Era of Intelligent Machines

Natalia S. Andryashina, Elena V. Romanovskaya, Elena P. Kozlova, Victor P. Kuznetsov, and Sergey D. Tsymbalov

1 Introduction

Production planning at the enterprise is the basis for the management of all other subsystems of the enterprise. At the same time, for Russian enterprises production planning is very relevant at present, as there is a very great competition with foreign manufacturers (Kuznetsova et al., 2017).

For mistakes in planning the enterprise pays a high price. The planned volume of production is determined on the basis of contracts with customers and own needs, as well as taking into account a strategic development of the enterprise (Potashnik et al., 2020), (Sedykh, 2019). In the enterprise's business plan, an article on production forecast based on

---

N. S. Andryashina (✉) · E. V. Romanovskaya · E. P. Kozlova ·
V. P. Kuznetsov · S. D. Tsymbalov
Minin Nizhny Novgorod State Pedagogical University, Nizhny Novgorod,
Russia
e-mail: natali_andr@bk.ru

E. V. Romanovskaya
e-mail: alenarom@list.ru

© The Author(s), under exclusive license to Springer Nature
Switzerland AG 2021
E. G. Popkova and B. S. Sergi (eds.), *Economic Issues of Social Entrepreneurship*,
https://doi.org/10.1007/978-3-030-77291-8_3

marketing analysis of the market is necessarily developed. It shall specify the number and range of the expected release nomenclature, as well as the means to achieve the goal: the equipment, the need for materials, and human resources (Garina et al, 2017.). In order to invest in the project, companys must carefully plan the production.

2 MATERIALS AND METHOD

At different times and in different countries, leading economists devoted much time to researching product planning at the enterprise. A huge contribution to the development of theory and methodology in terms of the study of production planning at the enterprise was made by such foreign and domestic researchers as: Alekseeva, M. M., Afitov, E. A., Babich, T. N., Bukhalkov, M. I., Volkov, V. P., Gorelick, O. M., Gruzinov, V. P., Drapkina, G. S., Zideleva, V. V., Zozulya, D. M., Ilyin, A. I., Kiselev, A. A., Lebedev, B. A., Melnikov, R. M., Plotnikov, S. L., Putyatina, L. M., Rodionov, V. B., Sklyarenko, V. K., Fatkhutdinov, R. A., Hanger, J. D., Tsarev, V. V., Chase, R. B., Chumakova, M. V., Shelekhova, L. V. But, at the same time, they all approach the economic meaning and indicators of planning with varying degrees of detail.

3 RESULTS

In order to improve the planning and production management at GAZvtorresurs LLC, we will consider the description of the production and technological processes for processing cast iron shavings of type 24A on the existing automatic hot briquetting line (LGB) and after its modernization by cold pressing (LHB) (Andryashina et al., 2020), (Kuznetsov et al., 2018).

Let us analyze the description of the existing technology at the enterprise (Romanovskaya et al., 2020).

At present, metal waste of type 24A is received by road from the subdivisions of GAZ PJSC to GAZvtorresurs LLC. Received iron shavings (24A) is processed into the metal waste of type 23A with the following technologies: on preliminary cold briquetting press, and heating the briquettes in a conveyor furnace to 800 C temperature, removing water and mineral oil from the pellets, hot (final) briquetting on press.

Let's highlight the shortcomings of this technological process:

- Horizontal hydraulic briquetting press B-6238 and a vertical mechanical press AC-5109 are outdated. They have great physical wear, which leads to frequent repairs as a consequence of equipment downtime.
- The furnace has expensive equipment made of heat-resistant steel.
- The line of hot briquetting is an object of high power consumption. Used energy such as natural gas, compressed air, water and electricity.
- The line of hot briquetting is a hazardous production facility (gas facility) and shall be registered in the public register of the HPF. This activity must be licensed, and is subject to special control Rostekhnadzor in the Volga Federal District.
- The briquetting line has a negative impact on the environment in the form of emissions of pollutants into the atmosphere. HPF LLC's emissions fee is 90% of the total amount of air pollution payments.

The obtained cast iron briquettes of type 23A are sold in the MP PJSC "GAZ" and third party consumers.

Consider the proposed changes in the framework of the project for the introduction of the briquetting line of cast-iron shavings by cold pressing method into production.

According to the project, it is planned to purchase a hydraulic press RUF90/3900/120 with a system of loading briquettes into big bags and modernization of transport systems of automatic line.

The line of metal shavings will include the following new and upgraded equipment:

- Briquetting press complete with vibration sieve—1 unit.
- Briquette loading system in big bags—1 pcs.
- Transportation systems—3 units.
- Rail trolley—1 unit.

Following equipment will be withdrawn from the existing automatic line:

- Furnace—1 unit.;
- Hydraulic Press B-6238—1 pcs.
- Mechanical press AC-5109—1 unit.

The advantages of cold briqueting technology are:

- Low specific energy consumption;
- High quality and density of briquettes;
- High performance with relatively small amounts;
- Coolant pressure during briquetting to the minimum possible values;
- Round-the-clock operation;
- High performance of lines 3500–3900 kg/hour (depending on the material).
- Serviced with minimum number of operating personnel 1–2 people.
- No negative impact on the environment.

The production plan is presented in Table 1.

Budget of capital expenditures for investment project "Modernization of automatic briquetting line cast iron shavings with a transition to the technology of cold pressing on the RUF90/3900/120 presses" is presented in Table 2.

Analysis of product data (type 23A) presented in Table 3 allows us to conclude the losses received by the company in 2018 and 2019 during the production of this product.

The forecast financial model of the equipment modernization project is presented in Table 4.

The following risks can be identified from this project (Chelnokova et al., 2017), (Yashina et al., 2020).

1. The risk of increase of total costs—production and organizational risk associated with incomplete and inaccurate data (minor consequences for the project).

Table 1 Production plan

Production plan with a capacity of 1,000 tons per month and the average selling price of 16,000 rubles/t		
2021	*2022*	*2023*
Volume/income (thousand rubles)	*Volume/income (thousand rubles)*	*Volume/income (thousand rubles)*
9,000/144,000	11,000/176,000	11,000/176,000

Table 2 Budget capital costs on the investment project

No. p.p	Name of investment projects	Amount, thousand rubles (without VAT)									Total investment cost plan for 2020, thousand rubles (without VAT)	Balance to project financing in 2021, thousand rubles (without VAT)	The volume of investments under the project (TOTAL), thousand rubles (without VAT)
		April	May	June	July	August	September	October	November	December			
1	Modernization automatic line briquetting iron shavings to technology by cold pressing in presses type RUF90 / 3900/120	300.00	500.00	1 400,00	0.00	4 250,00	500.00	1 200,00	5 600,00	27 550,00	41,300.00	900.00	42,200.00

Retrospective analysis data for product (waste 23A) is shown in Table 3

Table 3 Product retrospective analysis of data

Indicator	2016		2017		2018		2019	
	Total	per 1 ton	Total	per 1 ton	Total	per 1 ton	Total	per 1 ton
Volume, tons	8 264		8 256		7 220		7 849,99	
Revenue, RUB	74,130,782	8,970	93,693,051	11,348	95,954,106	13,290	108,830,779.33	13,863.81
variable costs, RUB	40,557,584	4,908	65,791,372	7,969	76,434,201	10,586	91,786,770.00	11,692.60
Materials	32,377,122	3,918	56,559,131	6,851	66,497,146	9,210	81,543,123.50	10,387.67
payroll	4,668,140	565	5,358,590	649	5,670,414	785	5,707,176.00	727.03
allocations to social needs	1,437,787	174	1,650,446	200	1,644,375	228	1,757,810.50	223.93
natural gas	1,797,731	218	1,998,957	242	2,410,486	334	2,536,578.00	323.13
transportation	276,804	33	224,248	27	211,780	29	242,082.00	30.84
margin profit, RUB	33,573,198	4,063	27,901,679	3,380	19,519,905	2,704	17,044,009,33	2,171.21
fixed costs, RUB	20,152,707	2,439	18,218,261	2,207	19,917,890	2,759	20,540,634.50	2,616.64
payroll fund (management apparatus)	489,062	59	537.523	65	530,395	73	588,124.00	74.92
allocations to social needs	150,631	18	165.557	20	143,192	20	183,286.50	23.35
electric power	1,987,277	240	2,887,849	350	4,295,522	595	4,745,585.50	604.53
compressed air	133,903	16	174,447	21	169.365	23	177,184.00	22.57
reconstruction funds (maintenance, repair, spare parts, accessories)	9,841,917	1,191	5,255,702	637	9,469,311	1,312	9,567,997.50	1,218.85
rent	2,016,051	244	2,016,051	244	2,016,051	279	2,016,060.00	256.82

Indicator	2016		2017		2018		2019	
	Total	per 1 ton	Total	per 1 ton	Total	per 1 ton	Total	per 1 ton
transportation costs for purchase m/o	5,463,152	661	6,799,799	824	2,910,766	403	2,881,064.00	367.01
other (fire protection)	70,714	9	381.333	46	383.288	53	381,333.00	48.58
Total cost, RUB	**60,710,291**	**7,346**	**84,009,633**	**10,176**	**96,352,091**	**13,345**	**112,327,404.50**	**14,309.24**
administrative, selling and distribution expenses (CDF 9%)	5,463,926	661	7,560,867	916	8,671,688	1,201	10,109,466.41	1,287.83
net profit, RUB	**7,956,565**	**963**	**2,122,551**	**257**	-9,069,673	-1,256	-13,606,091.57	-1,733.26

Table 4 Forecast financial model of the project

Indicators	2020	2021	2022	2023	2024	2025	2026	2027	Total
Profit and loss account (with inflation)									
The economic effect of reducing the cost of production (thousand rubles)	-	15,206	19,952	20,750	21,580	22,443	23,341	24,275	**147,547**
Additional income from the sale of 200 tons of briquettes (thousand rubles)		1,544	1,927	2,004	2,084	2,167	2,254	2,344	**14,323**
The increase in cost as a result of increased depreciation (thousand rubles)	-	(3,517)	(4,220)	(4,220)	(4,220)	(4,220)	(4,220)	(4,220)	**(28 837)**
Gross profit (thousand rubles)	-	**13,233**	**17,659**	**18,534**	**19,444**	**20,390**	**21,375**	**22,399**	**133,033**
Taxable income (thousand rubles)		**13,233**	**17,659**	**18,534**	**19,444**	**20,390**	**21,375**	**22,399**	**133,033**
Income tax (thousand rubles)	-	(2,647)	(3,532)	(3,707)	(3,889)	(4,078)	(4,275)	(4,480)	**(26,607)**
Net profit (thousand rubles)	-	**10,586**	**14,127**	**14,827**	**15,555**	**16,312**	**17,100**	**17,919**	**106,426**
Cash flow statement									
Net profit (thousand rubles)	-	10,586	14,127	14,827	15,555	16,312	17,100	17 919	**106,426**
Depreciation (thousand rubles)	-	3,517	4,220	4,220	4,220	4,220	4,220	4,220	**28 837**

Indicators	2020	2021	2022	2023	2024	2025	2026	2027	Total
Cash flow from operations (thousand rubles)	-	**14,103**	**18,347**	**19,047**	**19,775**	**20,532**	**21,320**	**22,139**	**135,263**
Investments (thousand rubles)	(41,300)	(900)	-	-	-	-	-	-	**(42,200)**
Cash flow for the period (thousand rubles)	**(41,300)**	**13,203**	**18,347**	**19,047**	**19,775**	**20,532**	**21,320**	**22,139**	**93,063**
Cash balance at the end of the period (thousand rubles)	(41,300)	(28,097)	(9,750)	9,297	29,072	49,604	70,924	93,063	
Discounted cash flow for the period (DCF) (RUB thousands)	(41,300)	11,541	14,019	12,722	11,546	10,479	9,511	8,633	**37,150**
Discounted cash balance at the end of the period (DCCF) (thousand rubles)	(41,300)	(29,759)	(15,740)	(3,019)	8,527	19,006	28,517	37,150	
Discount rate (%)	14.40%								
NPV (thousand rubles)	37,150								
IRR (%)	38.1%								
Payback period (years)	3.26	from March 2021		payback SOP		2.35			
Discounted payback period (years)	4.24		check						
PI	1.88		1.88						
Investments (thousand rubles)	(41,300)	(900)	-	-	-	-	-	-	

(continued)

Table 4 (continued)

Indicators	2020	2021	2022	2023	2024	2025	2026	2027	Total
Cash flow without investments (thousand rubles)	-	14,103	18,347	19,047	19,775	20,532	21,320	22,139	

2. The risk of a rise in prices for equipment, services and construction activities—the investment risk associated with an increase in the cost of the project or from failure to comply with the timing of the preparatory stages of work. Risk controlled (tendering suppliers, contractual penalties).
3. The risk of increasing inflation is the external economic risk associated with macroeconomic changes (the risk is accepted since it is impossible to influence it).
4. Risk of disruption of delivery terms—investment risk, and this is controlled risk (tendering of suppliers, contractual penalties).
5. The risk of rising prices for similar products in a third-party organization is an external risk associated with the demand for this type of product on the market. Risk controlled (purchase of equipment, manufacture of products by their own forces).
6. Risk of project abandonment—complete abandonment of the project may lead to an increase in the time frame for major repairs to existing equipment. Risk controlled (purchase of equipment according to the plan).

4 Conclusion

In order to develop a planning and production system at the enterprise, the authors developed a project to modernize an automatic cast iron briquetting line with a transition to cold pressing briquetting technology. The risks that are possible during the implementation of this project are considered. Those risks taken into account when drawing up the draft financial forecasting model until 2027. Discounted payback period of the project on modernization of briquetting iron shavings automatic line with the transition to cold pressing on presses of type RUF90/3900/120 will be 4.24 years at a discount rate of 14.4%. Net profit for the project at the end of 2027 will amount to almost 18 million rubles.

References

Andryashina, N. S., Romanovskaya, E. V., Garina, E. P., Kuznetsov, V. P., & Kuznetsova, S. N. (2019, April). Modernization of production under the conditions of modern technologies (by the Example of Metallurgical Production of PJSC "GAZ"). *Lecture Notes in Networks and Systems, 87*, 532–540.

Chelnokova, E. A., Kuznetsova, S. N., & Nabiev, R. D. (2017). Possibilities of using information and communication technologies in teaching economic disciplines in the university. *Vestnik of Minin University, 3*(20), 8.

Garina, E. P., Kuznetsova, S. N., Romanovskaya, E. V., Garin, A. P., Kozlova, E. P., & Suchodoev, D. V. (2017). Forming of conditions for development of innovative activity of enterprises in high-tech industries of economy: A case of industrial parks. *International Journal of Entrepreneurship, 21*(3), 6.

Kuznetsov, V. P., Garina, E. P., Romanovskaya, E. V., Kuznetsova, S. N., & Andryashina, N. S. (2018). Organizational design and rationalization of production systems of a machine-building enterprise (by the example of the contract assembly workshop). *Espacios., 39*(1), 25.

Kuznetsova, S. N., Garina, E. P., Kuznetsov, V. P., Romanovskaya, E. V., & Andryashina, N. S. (2017). Industrial parks formation as a tool for development of long-range manufacturing sectors. *Journal of Applied Economic Sciences, 12*, 2(48), 391–401.

Potashnik, Y. S., Artemyeva, M. V., Kuznetsova, S. N., Garin, A. P., & Letyagina, E. N. (2020). The status and trends in innovative activity of industrial enterprises of Nizhny Novgorod Region. *Lecture Notes in Networks and Systems, 73*, 525–534.

Romanovskaya, E. V., Garina, E. P., Andryashina, N. S., Kuznetsov, V. P., Tsymbalov, S. D. (2020). Improvement of the quality system of manufactured products at the enterprise of Mechanical Engineering. *Lecture Notes in Networks and Systems, 73*, 785–794.

Sedykh, E. P. (2019). A system of regulatory support for project management in education. *Vestnik of Minin University, 7*, No. 1(26), 1.

Yashina, N. I., Makarova, S. D., Kashina, O. I., Kuznetsov, V. P., & Romanovskaya, E. V. (2020). Methical approaches to analysis of performance of budgetary obligations on the basis of the risk-oriented approach. *Lecture Notes in Networks and Systems, 87*, 662–669.

Methods of Assessing the Potential Impact of Digital Technologies on Business Processes of the Company

Alexander N. Vizgunov, *Yuri V. Trifonov*,
Vasily Yu. Trifonov, *Artem V. Dorozhkin,*
and Oleg V. Yasenev

1 INTRODUCTION

In the framework of modern concepts of process management, where the introduction of information technology is considered as the main tool for improving business processes. Thus, T. Davenport, considering the differences between the concepts of gradual improvement of processes

---

A. N. Vizgunov (✉)
National Research University Higher School of Economics, Moscow, Russia

Y. V. Trifonov · A. V. Dorozhkin · O. V. Yasenev
Lobachevsky State University of Nizhny Novgorod, Nizhny Novgorod, Russia
e-mail: itime@iee.unn.ru

O. V. Yasenev
e-mail: ov.yasenev@iee.unn.ru

V. Yu. Trifonov
Afrikantov OKBM JSC, Nizhny Novgorod, Russia
e-mail: vutrifonov@okbm.nnov.ru

© The Author(s), under exclusive license to Springer Nature
Switzerland AG 2021
E. G. Popkova and B. S. Sergi (eds.), *Economic Issues of Social Entrepreneurship,*
https://doi.org/10.1007/978-3-030-77291-8_4

(such as Total Quality Management) and the reengineering of business processes. He indicates that, as part of gradual improvement, the methods of statistical process control are the main tool for implementing transformations, while as part of reengineering, information technology (Davenport, 1993). Numerous examples of the use of information technology as the basis for process reengineering are given by M. Hammer and J. Champy (1993). Thus, the advent of operational planning systems has dramatically reduced the time spent on preparing and updating plans. As a result, the use of teamwork systems provided the possibility of parallel processing of information in various units. So, the use of expert systems made it possible to ensure the performance of work requiring special knowledge by employees who are not experts.

As noted in (Chen, 2001), the key problem that impedes the efficient use of information technology in process transformation is the problem of the inconsistency of traditional approaches in order to design information systems (based on a waterfall or iterative development model) with modern business conditions. Traditional approaches suggest that the requirements for information systems can be uniquely determined by users at the very beginning of the project, and during the implementation of the system, these requirements should not change significantly. In the conditions of dynamic changes in the economic and technological environment, it is far from always possible to ensure the uniqueness and stability of requirements. Therefore, the solution to this problem was the emergence of systems that implement a subject-oriented approach to managing business processes (Fleischmann, 2010). These systems provide employees with the opportunity to independently carry out work on the design and improvement of processes, which is achieved due to the maximum simplicity of building business process models, the availability of effective analysis and control tools for created process models, and the automation of transition from a process model to an executable application.

In modern conditions of digitalization of the economy, where the role of digital technologies in the transformation of processes is becoming even more significant. Projects for the implementation of digital transformation are currently being implemented by many companies, which is typical in particular for Russia. Thus, according to the research "Digital Transformation in Russia" conducted by KMDA (KMDA, 2018), 9.4% of the surveyed companies already have a strategy of digital transformation. So, 25% companies are in the process of developing such a strategy, and 26.6% of companies plan to create such a strategy. However, as noted in the KPMG research "Digital Technologies in Russian Companies" (KPMG, 2019), few companies are achieving meaningful efficiency gains, who are implementing digital transformation projects. This is due to the fact that many companies do not conduct a preliminary assessment of the impact of implemented technologies on business tasks. These companies decide on the mass implementation of technologies based on the analysis of individual pilot projects, and the results of which often inspire unjustified optimism in the management. In order to eliminate this situation, when deciding on the introduction of new technologies, an assessment should be made of how these technologies will affect business processes, taking into account possible risks. This article is devoted to the development of a methodology for such kind of an assessment.

2 Materials and Method

When analyzing the impact of digital technology on business processes, various aspects of process execution must be considered. In accordance with (Leong et al., 1990), the following groups of indicators are defined that reflect various characteristics of the performance of business processes: indicators of lead time, reliability, quality, costs and flexibility. Digital technologies can influence the performance of each of the groups considered. For example, the implementation of Sibur companies of predictive analytics based on BigData ensured a fivefold reduction in equipment emergency stops (Lisovsky, 2018). This example shows the impact of digital technology on reliability indicators. The introduction of KAMAZ PJSC technology for creating digital counterpart of products and production is aimed at reducing the time for launching new products and the cost of production (KAMAZ, 2017). This example illustrates the impact of digital technology on time and cost metrics. Note that for an accurate assessment of the costs associated with the implementation of business processes, the company should implement a technology for process accounting of costs. For example, based on the ABC (Activity Based Costing) methodology—in detail, the problems of cost accounting associated with the implementation of business processes are considered by us in our work (Trifonov & Vizgunov, 2019). In our opinion, when assessing the impact of technology on business processes, it is also advisable to take into account the characteristics associated with the compliance of business processes with legal requirements. For example, the requirements of the Central Bank of Russia will determine the need to identify payments that have signs of fraud - that is, created without the consent of the client. In order to identify such payments, it is advisable to introduce fraud monitoring systems built on the basis of artificial intelligence.

As noted above, when assessing the feasibility of introducing digital technologies, in addition to analyzing their impact on the business processes of the company. It is necessary to conduct an analysis of the possible risks. The results of the KPMG research (KPMG, 2019) determine that the main obstacles faced by Russian companies in introducing innovative digital technologies include insufficient maturity of processes and a low level of automation (64% of respondents chose this answer option), lack of necessary competencies (58%), low IT literacy of employees (35%), lack of necessary infrastructure (35%), lack of sufficient funding (32%). These obstacles determine the main risks that should be analyzed in assessing the feasibility of implementing digital technologies. Also, when determining the risks associated with the introduction of digital technologies, the risks of information security, as well as the risks of deterioration of process control, should be taken into account.

Thus, the analysis of the feasibility of implementing digital technologies should, in our opinion, include the following analytical procedures:

1. Determining the significance of each characteristic (lead time, reliability, quality, costs, flexibility, compliance with legal requirements) in relation to the analyzed business process. For example, for those business processes that result in typical products that have stable demand in the long term (for example, gasoline production), the characteristic of flexibility will not be significant. Another example is for those processes, the implementation of which is strictly regulated by law (which is characteristic, in particular, for the banking sector), a characteristic of compliance with the requirements of the law will have a high level of significance.
2. The selection of those performance characteristics of business processes that will be affected by the implemented solution. The selection is made from the same characteristics that were indicated in the previous paragraph.
3. Definition for each selected characteristic of indicators reflecting the results of the introduction of new technologies. For example, when evaluating the time taken to complete business processes,

an indicator of the effectiveness of the operational cycle can be considered, which is the ratio of the total time taken to complete all the operations of the process to the total duration of the process (Kaplan & Norton, 1996).

4. Determining the forecast values of the selected indicators, which should be achieved as a result of the introduction of new technologies. The forecast of changes in the values of indicators can be based on an analysis of the experience of suppliers with implemented solutions, consultations with other companies that have implemented similar solutions.

5. Definition (based on the predicted change in the values of the selected indicators) of qualitative assessments of the impact of technology on various characteristics of processes by expert estimates method. The following scale can be used to determine qualitative assessments:

   0—technology does not affect the performance of the business process;

   1—the technology does not significantly improve the performance of the business process;

   2—technology significantly improves the performance of the business process.

6. The calculation of the final indicator of the impact of new technology on the performance characteristics of the process. For the calculation, the following formula is used:

$$D = \sum_{i=1}^{n} p_i * K_i$$

where D is a complex indicator of assessing the impact of new technologies on the performance characteristics of a business process,

K_i, where $i = 1, ..., n$ is the assessment of the impact of technology on the i-th characteristic of the business process, defined in step 5,

p_i, where $i = 1, ..., n$ is the significance of the i-th characteristic ($\sum_{i=1}^{n} p_i = 1$), determined in step 1,

n is the number of characteristics ($n = 6$).

7. Identification of risks associated with the introduction of new technologies. Risks should be determined taking into account

the specifics of the activities of a particular company. However, in determining risks, it is necessary to focus on those obstacles that arise when introducing digital technologies that were described above (lack of employee competencies, insufficient project financing, etc.).

8. Determining the impact of risk on project results. When determining the impact of risk on a project, the following scale can be used:

0—the risk is insignificant for the project;

1—moderate risk level;

2—high level of risk.

9. Determination of the aggregate level of risk that can be calculated using the formula:

$$R = \sum_{j=1}^{m} T_j$$

where R is a comprehensive measure of risk level assessment,

Tj, where j = 1, ..., m is the estimate of the level of the j-th risk, determined at step 5,

m is the number of assessed risks.

10. Final assessment of the need to implement digital technologies, depending on their impact on business processes and risk level. The four options of the final assessment presented in Table 1 can

Table 1 Assessment of the need for the introduction of digital technologies depending on their impact on business processes and the level of risk

Influence at processes (D) Level of risk (R)	High	Low
High	The introduction of digital technologies is advisable, but requires the implementation of additional measures aimed at reducing risks	The introduction of digital technology is impractical
Low	High priority for digital technology	Low priority for digital technology

(*Source* compiled by the authors)

be compared to possible combinations of business process impact assessment and risk level assessment.

3 RESULTS

Let us consider the application of the proposed methodology by the example of evaluating a number of digital technologies introduced by one of the Russian regional banks. It should be noted that in terms of introduction of digital technologies the banking sector is one of the leading branches of the Russian economy (KMDA, 2018). Thus, organizations of the banking sector are characterized by the constant introduction of innovative technologies, which determines the relevance of their use of the proposed methodology.

An assessment of the feasibility of introducing 3 types of digital technologies is presented in Table 2. We are talking about artificial intelligence-based systems for analyzing the correctness of filling out customer payment documents and identifying fraudulent transactions, as well as corporate chatbot. Corporate chatbot is used to automate internal administrative processes associated with organizing meetings (tasks of booking meeting rooms, and informing participants are automated), arranging vacations (the chatbot checks for available vacation days, agrees on the possibility of vacation with the management, sends the necessary documents to fill out), and other.

As can be seen from the table, the characteristics of business processes that are affected by the technologies in question are quite diverse. The system for analyzing the correctness of filling out payment documents ensures a reduction in the time required to control documents, which is achieved by replacing the visual control with an automatic one. It is also reducing costs due to the fact that the costs associated with the implementation and support of the system is slightly lower than the costs of the staff responsible for performing visual control. The main advantages of introducing a system for detecting fraudulent payments are associated with both a reduction in the verification time and ensuring compliance with legal requirements. The introduction of chatbot allows reducing the time of execution of operations, as well as improving the quality characteristics of the performed processes associated with increasing the accuracy and timeliness of delivery the necessary information.

As a result, the introduction of technologies under consideration does not involve any significant risks. At the same time, it should be borne in

44 A. N. VIZGUNOV ET AL.

Table 2 An example of an assessment the feasibility of implementing digital technology

Digital technology Assessment options	The system of filling out payment documents based on artificial intelligence	System of detection of fraudulent payments based on artificial intelligence	Corporate chat bot
Buisness process	Estimated customer service	Suspicious transaction monitoring	Internal administrative processes
Process characteristics affected by technology	1. Time 2. Costs	1. Time 2. Compliance with legal requirements	1. Time 2. Quality
Indicators reflecting the impact of (technology) on individual process characteristics	1. Time control document correctness 2. Cost of document control	1. The time to verify the document 2. Compliance of the verification procedure with the requirements of the Central Bank	1. Time for coordination 2. Quality of information provided
Impact on individual process characteristics	1. Significantly 2. Inconsequential	1. Significantly 2. Significantly	1. Significantly 2. Significantly
Cumulative impact on the process	High	High	High
Identified risks	Risk of deterioration in process control (low risk)	-	Inadequate IT literacy risk for employees (low risk)
Cumulative risk level	Low	Low	Low
Technology feasibility assessment	Appropriate	Appropriate	Appropriate

(*Source* compiled by the authors)

mind that the introduction of a system for analyzing the correctness of filling out payment documents can lead to a deterioration in the process control. At the first stage of the transition to automated control, a situation is possible when the system, due to an insufficiently representative statistical database, tracks not all erroneously executed documents. As for the corporate chatbot, here certain risks are associated with insufficient IT literacy of employees—not all company employees will be able to deal with the features of interaction with the chatbot.

4 CONCLUSION

The presented example illustrates the following advantages of the proposed methodology, which make it possible to use it effectively when making decisions related to evaluating the feasibility of introducing innovative digital technologies:

- a comprehensive assessment of the various characteristics of business processes that may be affected by implemented technologies;
- a comprehensive assessment of the risks specific to projects for the implementation of digital technologies;
- transparency of the analysis algorithm and the possibility of a visual representation of its results (as illustrated in Table 2);
- the possibility of conducting an evaluation in an online mode, which is especially relevant for companies, massively introducing digital technologies. This is typical, for example, for organizations of the banking sector and the sphere of insurance.

REFERENCES

Chen, Y. (2001). *Empirical modelling for participative business process reengineering*. University of Warwick.

Davenport, T. (1993). *Process innovation: Reengineering work through information technology* (p. 337). Harvard Business School Press.

Fleischmann, A. (2010). *What Is S-BPM? S-BPM ONE—Setting the stage for subject-oriented business process management* (pp. 85–106). Springer-Verlag.

Hammer, M., & Champy, J. (1993). *Reengineering the corporation. A manifesto for business revolution* (p. 212). Harper Business.

Kaplan, R., & Norton, D. (1996). *The balanced scorecard: Translating strategy into action* (p. 336). Harvard Business Review Press.

KMDA. (2018). Digital transformation in Russia. Analytical report. 2018. KMDA. https://komanda-a.pro/blog/dtr_2018. Accessed January 30, 2020.

KPMG. (2019). Digital technologies in Russian companies. 2019. KPMG. https://home.kpmg/ru/ru/home/insights/2019/01/digital-technologies-in-russian-companies-survey.html. Accessed January 30, 2020.

KAMAZ and Siemens AG signed a cooperation agreement. (2017). KAMAZ. https://kamaz.ru/press/releases/kamaz_i_kompaniya_simens_ag_podpisali_soglashenie_o_sotrudnichestve/. Accessed January 30, 2020.

Leong, K., Snyder, D. L., & Ward, P. T. (1990). Research in the process and content manufacturing strategy. *OMEGA International Journal of Management Science, 18*(2), 109–122.

Lisovsky, A. L. (2018). Optimization of business processes for the transition to sustainable development in the conditions of the fourth industrial revolution. *Strategic Decisions and Risk Management* (4), 10–19. https://doi.org/10.17747/2078-8886-2018-4-10-19.

Trifonov, Y. V., & Vizgunov, A. N. (2019). Key factors of effectiveness of developing an activity based cost accounting and analysis system at an enterprise. *Accounting. Analysis. Auditing, 6*(4), 24–31. (In Russ.) https://doi.org/10.26794/2408-9303-2019-6-4-24-31.

Complexity Assessment Eliminating the Risk of Transmission of Digital Information in Enterprise Networks

Lyudmila M. Gruzdeva, Nadezhda V. Kapustina, Nana A. Kobiashvili, Igor A. Lebedev, and Konstantin A. Bogonosov

1 INTRODUCTION

The problem of protecting digital information from malware, such as trojans and spyware, computer viruses, network worms, blackmail programs, is defined as the most relevant and significant in the modern

---

L. M. Gruzdeva (✉) · N. V. Kapustina
Russian University of Transport, Moscow, Russian Federation

N. A. Kobiashvili
Moscow Polytechnic University, Moscow, Russian Federation

I. A. Lebedev
Financial University under the Government of the Russian Federation, Moscow, Russian Federation
e-mail: ILebedev@fa.ru

K. A. Bogonosov
K.G. Razumovsky Moscow State University of Technologies and Management (the First Cossack University), Moscow, Russian Federation

© The Author(s), under exclusive license to Springer Nature Switzerland AG 2021
E. G. Popkov and B. S. Sergi (eds.), *Economic Issues of Social Entrepreneurship*,
https://doi.org/10.1007/978-3-030-77291-8_5

world (Paramonova et al., 2012; Shangin, 2014) despite the fact that the pioneer among the known viruses is a virus written in 1981.

Highly efficient operation of digital systems of information security of corporate data systems, their modernization, and design are impossible without a quantitative performance evaluation process to identify malicious attacks, the process of restoring affected nodes of information systems, and planning the preventive activities of infection.

By malicious influence we mean the spread of malicious attacks in the corporate digital data network, any of their actions that can lead to disruption of the operation in individual node elements of systems and the entire information network as a whole.

The risk of harmful influences is defined as the possibility of occurrence of such events, which results in the spread of malware in a corporate data network, resulting in a reduction or complete loss of system functionality.

As a result, there is a need to develop a mathematical model of the process to eliminate harmful influences. The application of the developed model makes it possible to assess the qualitative characteristics of the information security system and the operation of the corporate digital data network at different time periods, depending on the initial number of malicious attacks and anti-detection tools.

2 Materials and Method

Questions of development of the theory and practice of ensuring information security in telecommunication networks in order to reduce the risk of harmful influences of digital data transmission in corporate networks are devoted to the work of authors such as A. A. Grusho et al. (2019), V. F. Shangin (2014), A. I. Krapchatov (2009), L. Kleinrock (2013), V. M. Vishnevsky (2003), S. P. Rastorgouev (2014), A. A. Malyuk (2012), P. D. Zegzdha et al. (2017), A. B. Los et al. (2018).

The aim of the study is to develop a model for assessing the characteristics of the process of eliminating harmful influences, as well as the process of spreading malware in the network.

The following research methods were used in the framework of the research: economic-mathematical, calculation-analytical, simulation, statistical and quantitative methods.

The study was carried out in the following stages:

1. The categories of victims affected by information attacks in the III quarter of 2019 are identified
2. The structure of information attack methods is revealed
3. Types of malware investigated
4. A mathematical model has been developed to evaluate the characteristics of the process of eliminating harmful influences in a computer data network
5. Analysis of the proposed model and clarification of the most important characteristics in the process of eliminating the risks of malicious attacks in the mode of limited and unlimited time and other types of resources
6. Testing the developed model on the example of a computer data network as a mass service network

The hypothesis of the study is that the proposed mathematical model will predict the rate of spread of harmful influences, as well as the time of infection of digital data in the network.

As a result of the study, a mathematical model was developed based on the theory of mass service networks. Based on the presented mathematical model of the process of minimizing the malicious influences in the nodes of computer networks it is possible to identify certain characteristics of the malware distribution process.

3 Results

According to the company Positive Technologies, attackers are actively trying to attack the corporate information systems of public institutions, industrial companies, the financial sector, as well as educational and research institutes (Fig. 1).

According to preliminary data InfoWatch analysts, in 2019 the global number of registered data leaks from government organizations and commercial companies increased by about 10% compared with 2018 Klochko et al. (2016). As a result, 14 billion records were compromised, which is 50% more than in 2018. In turn, in 2018, 2263 cases of confidential information leakage were registered in the world, which is 6.2% more than in 2017 and 182.5% in 2011.

In Russia the number of leaks per year increased by more than 40%, the number of compromised records has increased about 6 times and amounted to about 170 million Klochko et al. (2016).

According to Positive Technologies Los et al. (2018), the most common attack method is considered to be the use of malicious information software. Information security violators often combine this method with social engineering and/or exploitation of web vulnerabilities (Fig. 2).

Since 2018, espionage software Los et al. (2018) has become the most popular. Using these programs, attackers accumulate confidential information for both private and legal entities. They are fixed in the system if the attacks are targeted (Fig. 3).

The mathematical modeling of the software setup process was the basis for modeling the process of eliminating malicious attacks in the nodes of a corporate information transfer network. The model under consideration was proposed by a number of scientists (Mamikonov et al., 1986) and then received subsequent development (Krapchatov, 2009).

Suppose that a corporate digital data network includes many computer systems or nodes (KS—S). In each of these nodes there is a Markov process (Dynkin, 1963; Kleinrock, 2013) aimed at eliminating harmful effects or programs. Thus, the system S may be one of the discrete states: $S_0, S_1, \ldots S_N$ Under N means the number of malicious actions. N as a special case in a network node can equal the number of malicious

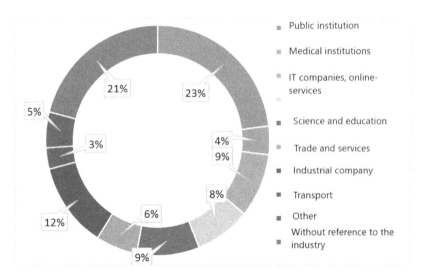

Fig. 1 Categories of victims affected by information attacks in the third quarter of 2019ю

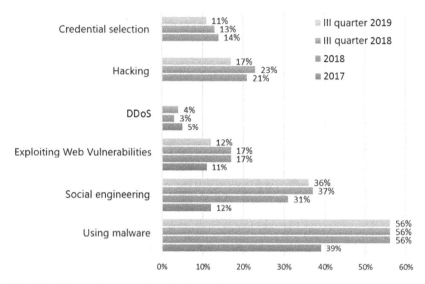

Fig. 2 Information attack methods

programs, and s_0 is an absorbing state, which means that all malicious programs are eliminated, and the scanning process of the node is completed.

The process of eliminating a malicious program or malicious attack in a computer network node is understood as its detection and instant recovery of a computer network. We take the elimination intensity of malicious attacks in proportion to their number.

Scanning performance of S system is determined by p_{ij}, which shows the probability that as a result of scanning a corporate system that contains i ($i = \overline{0, N}$) malicious attacks. As a result, may remain undetected j (j < i or $j \geq i$),($j = \overline{0, N}$). N indicates the number of malicious attacks before the scan process begins. Next, in the form of a matrix, we define

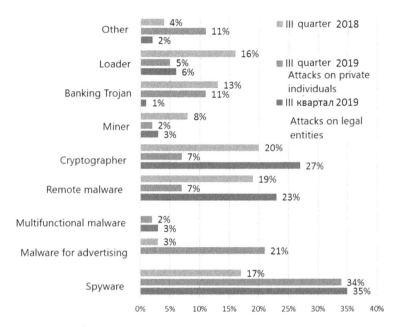

Fig. 3 Types of malicious software

the distribution p_{ij}:

$$P = \begin{pmatrix} 1 & 0 & 0 & \cdots & 0 & \cdots & 0 \\ \begin{pmatrix} p_{N,0} \\ p_{N-1,0} \\ \cdots \\ p_{i,0} \\ \cdots \\ p_{1,0} \end{pmatrix} & \begin{pmatrix} p_{N,N} & p_{N,N-1} & \cdots & p_{N,j} & \cdots & p_{N,1} \\ p_{N-1,N} & p_{N-1,N-1} & \cdots & p_{N-1,j} & \cdots & p_{N-1,1} \\ \cdots & \cdots & \cdots & \cdots & \cdots & \cdots \\ p_{i,N} & p_{i,N-1} & \cdots & p_{i,j} & \cdots & p_{i,1} \\ \cdots & \cdots & \cdots & \cdots & \cdots & \cdots \\ p_{1,N} & p_{1,N-1} & \cdots & p_{1,j} & \cdots & p_{1,1} \end{pmatrix} \\ \underbrace{}_{R} & \underbrace{}_{Q} \end{pmatrix} \quad (1)$$

The proposed model is based on the assumption that as a result of the elimination of a malicious program or an attack on a network node that this program can no longer appear. Thus, the computer system develops immunity to this effect. However, an information system can also be characterized by several absorbing states. System status data may indicate that the scanning process has stopped, but not all malicious attacks and programs have been eliminated.

An analysis of the developed model allows us to conclude that the most basic properties characterizing the process of eliminating malicious attacks in conditions of limited time and other types of resources are (Krapchatov, 2009; Mamikonov et al., 1986):

1. Mathematical expectation of time to eliminate j malicious attacks (j < i or $j \geq i$),($i, j = \overline{0, \ N}$),:

$$N(n) = 1 + Q + Q^2 + \dots + Q^n;$$

   where n is the number of cycles of malicious attacks;
2. The mathematical expectation of the time to eliminate all malicious programs in the computer information network:

$$t(n) = N(n)\varepsilon,$$

   where ε—a single column vector;
3. The probability of eliminating all attacking malicious programs in the computer information network:

$$B(n) = R + QR + \dots + Q^{n-1}R;$$

4. The mathematical expectation of a time parameter during which a constant number of malicious attacks are located in the computer information network:

$$M_i[r_i(n)] = \frac{1 - p_{ii}^{n+1}}{1 - p_{ii}};$$

5. The probability that there are j malicious attacks in the computer information network:

$$h_{ij}(n) = 1 - \prod_{\mu=1}^{n} \left(1 - p_{ij}^{\mu}\right),$$

where $h_{ij}(n)$ are the elements of the matrix $H(n)$.

In the process of sequential elimination of malware or attacks in unlimited time in the nodes of a computer information system, we can determine the main characteristics of the complexity in this process (Krapchatov, 2009; Mamikonov et al., 1986):

1. Mathematical wait time for elimination of all malicious attacks in the computer information network:

$$t = \begin{pmatrix} \sum_{i=1}^{N} \frac{1}{p_{i,i-1}} \\ \sum_{i=1}^{N-1} \frac{1}{p_{i,i-1}} \\ \cdots \\ \sum_{i=1}^{1} \frac{1}{p_{i,i-1}} \end{pmatrix},$$

where $p_{i,i-1}$ is the probability characterizing the fact that as a result of one scan in the computer system there will be i-1 malicious attacks;

2. Variance of the time period of elimination for all malware in the computer information network:

$$t_D = \begin{pmatrix} \left(\frac{2}{p_{N,N-1}} - 1\right)\left(\sum_{i=1}^{N} \frac{1}{p_{i,i-1}}\right) + \cdots + \left(\frac{2\cdot1}{p_{1,0}p_{1,0}} - 1\right) - \left(\sum_{i=1}^{N} \frac{1}{p_{i,i-1}}\right)^2 \\ \left(\frac{2}{p_{N-1,N-2}} - 1\right)\left(\sum_{i=1}^{N-1} \frac{1}{p_{i,i-1}}\right) + \cdots + \left(\frac{2\cdot1}{p_{1,0}p_{1,0}} - 1\right) - \left(\sum_{i=1}^{N-1} \frac{1}{p_{i,i-1}}\right) \\ \cdots\cdots\cdots\cdots\cdots\cdots\cdots\cdots\cdots\cdots\cdots\cdots \\ \left(\frac{2\cdot1}{p_{1,0}} - 1\right)\left(\frac{1}{p_{1,0}}\right) - \left(\frac{1}{p_{1,0}}\right)^2 \end{pmatrix};$$

3. Probability of elimination of all malicious attacks in computer information network tends to one: $B = \varepsilon$(vector size $N \times 1$);
4. Mathematical expectation of time parameters during which a constant number of malware is present in the computer information network:

$$\{M_i[r_i]\} = \begin{pmatrix} \frac{1}{p_{N,N-1}} \\ \frac{1}{p_{N-1,N-2}} \\ \cdots \\ \frac{1}{p_{1,0}} \end{pmatrix};$$

5. Variance of time parameters, during which a constant number of malicious attacks is present in the computer information network:

$$\{D_i[r_i]\} = \begin{pmatrix} \frac{1-p_{N,N-1}}{p_{N,N-1}} \\ \frac{1-p_{N-1,N-2}}{p_{N-1,N-2}} \\ \dots \\ \frac{1-p_{1,0}}{p_{1,0}} \end{pmatrix};$$

6. The probability that in a computer information network is present j malicious attacks:

$$H = \begin{pmatrix} 1 - p_{N,N-1} & 1 & \dots & 1 \\ 0 & 1 - p_{N-1,N-2} & \dots & 1 \\ \dots & \dots & \dots & \dots \\ 0 & 0 & \dots & 1 - p_{1,0} \end{pmatrix}.$$

Relying on the presented mathematical model of the process of eliminating malicious attacks in the nodes of a computer information system, it is possible to calculate certain characteristics of the process of the spread of malicious attacks.

Next, we study the computer information system for transmitting data as a mass service network (Vishnevsky, 2003). In this network packets circulate appropriate routing matrix $P = \|p_{ij}\|$, where p_{ij}—defined as the probability of sending the packet i-th to j-th unit, where $\forall\, p_{ij} \geq 0\ (i, j = \overline{1,\ M})$ and $\sum_{j=0}^{M} p_{ij} = 1\ \forall i = \overline{1, M}$.

Suppose that a malicious program enters as a packet in a computer information transfer network, then a random process of malware penetration will occur in the information system. The corporate system can be in one of the discrete states: $s_1, s_2, \dots, s_M$, where it $s_i\ (i = \overline{1,\ M})$ means that malicious programs are present in the i-th node.

On the example of a computer network, consider the proposed model. The network in question consists of five nodes. Packets in the studied network are forwarded in accordance with the considered matrix:

$$P = \begin{pmatrix} 1 & 0 & 0 & 0 & 0 \\ p_{21} & p_{22} & p_{23} & p_{24} & p_{25} \\ 0 & 0 & 1 & 0 & 0 \\ p_{41} & p_{42} & p_{43} & p_{44} & p_{45} \\ p_{51} & p_{52} & p_{53} & p_{54} & p_{55} \end{pmatrix} \qquad (2)$$

Using transformations, we represent the matrix (1) in block form:

$$P = \begin{pmatrix} 1 & 0 & |0 & 0 & 0 \\ 0 & 1 & |0 & 0 & 0 \\ \overline{p_{31}} & \overline{p_{32}} & |\overline{p_{33}} & \overline{p_{34}} & \overline{p_{35}} \\ p_{41} & p_{42} & |p_{43} & p_{44} & p_{45} \\ p_{51} & p_{52} & |p_{53} & p_{54} & p_{55} \end{pmatrix} \qquad (3)$$

Relying on (3), we obtain a matrix called fundamental:

$$M = (I - Q)^{-1}, \qquad (4)$$

where Q—square submatrix transitions;
I—unit matrix.

$$Q = \begin{pmatrix} p_{33} & p_{34} & p_{35} \\ p_{43} & p_{44} & p_{45} \\ p_{53} & p_{54} & p_{55} \end{pmatrix}.$$

Each of the elements in the studied matrix (4) corresponds to the average numerical indicator of the computer system getting into any state before the end of the process of the spread attacks. Multiplication of the unit vector ε, by the matrix M on the right side. This procedure will provide an average total number of times computer network falling into one or the other state before absorption:

$$M' = M \cdot \varepsilon.$$

By determining the time of the information system's stay in each state, it is possible to calculate the total time before the absorption period T':

$$T' = \tau \cdot M',$$

where the vector T is the time of finding the information system in each of the temporary states.

Matrix (2) gives a description of network junctions, which has two absorbing states. We define through b_{ij} the probability that a certain process will end in a certain absorbing state s_j provided that initially there was a state s_i $(i, j = \overline{1, M})$. Probabilities b_{ij} make up the matrix B. The columns of the matrix correspond to all-absorbing state, and the rows in turn temporary state, and:

$$B = M \cdot R, \qquad (5)$$

where $R = \begin{pmatrix} p_{31} & p_{32} \\ p_{41} & p_{42} \\ p_{51} & p_{52} \end{pmatrix}$.

Using matrix (5), we compare and evaluate the probabilistic characteristics of infection of the most sensitive nodes in the information network, and in the process of building protection to make the most vulnerable elements safe.

For clarity, we perform calculations for a system in which the transitions are defined by the following matrix:

$$P = \begin{pmatrix} 1 & 0 & 0 & 0 & 0 \\ 0,2 & 0,12 & 0,1 & 0,08 & 0,5 \\ 0 & 0 & 1 & 0 & 0 \\ 0,06 & 0,2 & 0,24 & 0,4 & 0,1 \\ 0,27 & 0,2 & 0,1 & 0,23 & 0,2 \end{pmatrix}.$$

According to the formula (5) we obtain the matrix:

$$B = \begin{pmatrix} 0,608 & 0,392 \\ 0,404 & 0,596 \\ 0,606 & 0,394 \end{pmatrix}.$$

Thus, if the process of spreading malicious attacks began, for example, from a computer network node at number three, then the probability of infection of a node at number one will be 0.608, and with number two it will be 0.392.

4 Conclusion

The introduction of malicious attacks by which attackers carry out their threats and attacks on the digital data of computer systems should be defined as malicious influence. With the help of malicious attacks, attackers can obtain the commercial secret of organizations, and personal data of users, user data from various systems and services. The results of these attacks will help to carry out cyber-attacks on the internal infrastructure of computer network. The main reason for successfully implemented attacks on digital resources is determined by the ineffective organization of protective barriers of corporate digital data transmission networks, which is not able to provide an appropriate level of opposition and elimination of malicious attacks.

The study proposed a mathematical model for identifying the most important characteristics of the process of eliminating malicious attacks. The model is able to determine the mathematical expectation of the time to eliminate the effects, the mathematical expectation of time to search for a given number of malicious attacks, the variance of the calculated values, under the condition of limited time resources, as well as in the process of sequentially eliminating malicious attacks in unlimited time resources mode. Practical application of the developed mathematical model makes it possible not only to evaluate the complexity of eliminating malicious attacks at the nodes of the information network but also to evaluate the qualitative characteristics of the corporate digital system at different time periods depending on the initial number of malicious attacks.

References

Analyst information security industry [electronic resource]//infowatch.ru: website. https://www.infowatch.ru/resources/analytics. Data Accessed 20 January 2020.

Analytics [Electronic resource]//Positive Technologies: website. https://www.ptsecurity.com/ru-ru/research/analytics/. Data Accessed 22 February 2020.

Dynkin, E. B. (1963). *Markov processes*. Fizmatlit.

Grusho, A. A., Grusho, N. A., Zabezhailo, M. I., & Timonina, E. E. (2019). Methods for assessing the security of computer systems for information support of the digital economy. *International Journal of Open Information Technologies*, 61–66.

Krapchatov, A. I. (2009). Models and methods of planning the development and debugging of software for automated information management

COMPLEXITY ASSESSMENT ELIMINATING THE RISK ... 59

systems. dissertation PHD (05.25.05). Russian State Humanitarian University. Moscow.

Kleinrock, L. (2013). *Queuing theory.* book on demand.

Klochko, E., Fomenko, N., & Nekrasova V. (2016). Modelling of network mechanisms of management in the conditions of organizational development. *Mediterranean Journal of Social Sciences, 1*(6), 101–105.

Los, A. B., Migalin, S. S., & Kovrizhnykh, M. A. (2018). Development of methods for automatic analysis of social networks to ensure the security of the organization. *High Availability Systems, 14*(4), 28–31.

Malyuk, A. A. (2012). *Information security theory.* Hotline: Telecom.

Mamikonov, A. G., Kulba, V. V., & Shelkov, A. B. (1986). *Reliability, protection and reservation of information in ACS.* Energoatomizdat.

Paramonova, P. P., et al. (2012). *Methods and models for assessing the infrastructure of the information protection system in corporate networks of industrial enterprises: Monograph* (p. 115). Publishing House LLC Studio NP-Print.

Rastorgouev, S. P. (2014). *Mathematical model information confrontation.* TsSOiP.

Shangin, V. F. (2014). *Information security and information protection.* DMC.

Vishnevsky, V. M. (2003). *Theoretical foundations of computer network design.* In V. M. Vishnevsky. Technosphere.

Zegzhda, P. D., Poltavtseva, M. A., & Lavrova, D. S. (2017). Systematization of cyber-physical systems and assessment of their safety. Information security problems. Computer systems. pp. 127–138.

Communication Platform for Finding and Attracting Industrial Cooperation Partners

Svetlana N. Kuznetsova, *Elena V. Romanovskaya*, *Victor P. Kuznetsov*, *Lakshitha Withanachchi, and Dmitry N. Lapaev*

1 INTRODUCTION

The main structure of the community, which is implementing a new paradigm of socio-economic development in the era of intelligent machines includes:

S. N. Kuznetsova (✉) · E. V. Romanovskaya · V. P. Kuznetsov · L. Withanachchi · D. N. Lapaev
Minin Nizhny Novgorod State Pedagogical University, Nizhny Novgorod, Russia
e-mail: dens@52.ru

E. V. Romanovskaya
e-mail: alenarom@list.ru

D. N. Lapaev
Nizhny Novgorod State Technical University n.a. R.E. Alekseev, Nizhny Novgorod, Russia

© The Author(s), under exclusive license to Springer Nature Switzerland AG 2021
E. G. Popkova and B. S. Sergi (eds.), *Economic Issues of Social Entrepreneurship*,
https://doi.org/10.1007/978-3-030-77291-8_6

- Russian and international production companies interested in investing and establishing production projects in Russia together with partners (Bezrukova et al., 2019);
- manufacturers with free capacity and interest in embedding their services and products in production chains—a consolidated offer (database) with contact details of manufacturers and suppliers—conditional association of interests without membership to promote their services or products as part of industrial cooperation (Kuznetsova & Kuznetsov, 2018).
- industrial parks and special economic zones, service companies, corporations for the development of subjects of Russia—investment development agencies of the regions of the Russian Federation (Bodrunov, 2018);
- Ministry of Industry and Trade of the Russian Federation, Industrial Development Fund, AEB, AHK, ITA, Confindustria, ROTOBO, KITA, industrial unions (Kuznetsova et al., 2018).

Consolidated proposal by community members for the target audience:

- contract manufacturing—implementation of standard technological operations according to requirements and technology of the customer;
- supply of components and other means of production according to customer technological requirements;
- creation of joint ventures for the production of industrial products;
- engineering prepared sites—industrial parks and special economic zones;
- services—engineering surveys, design, consulting, construction and operation of industrial facilities, and real estate management.

2 RESEARCH RESULTS

Industrial parks and special economic zones have begun introducing complex services in digitalization and cooperation.

The article considers the investment attractiveness rating of Russian industrial parks and special economic zones, in which only large objects are analyzed, since industrial sites are focused on foreign investors, which ensures an economic effect (Vikulov & Butrin, 2019).

By 2019, industrial parks and special economic zones are one of the most effective tools for the development of territories. Sites are increasingly being measured by the volume of attracted investments and tax deductions, the number of jobs created and the revenue of residents (Goremykin & Sokolov, 2019).

In 2019, there are several special economic zones of an industrial-production type that are focused on industry specifics. This approach allows gaining an advantage over sites with preferential business regimes.

But today, this model, when the PPT zone is only a platform for accommodating a limited number of residents, reduces its relevance, therefore, the study proposes to implement a complex mechanism for combining industrial, and technical-innovative activities (Mizikovsky et al., 2020).

It is proposed to interact with research institutes. Thus, the interaction between developers of new technologies and potential consumers is formed. Also, the generation of innovative projects is stimulated, and a system for training the necessary industry personnel and improving their skills is being built (Donichev, 2019).

A significant factor is the formation of a communication platform for searching and attracting partners for industrial cooperation, which will be the basis for the transfer of modern technologies, as well as cooperation (Ignatiev, 2019).

In addition to centers of competence, due to the combination of industrial, and technical-innovative activities in special economic zones. Other business development formats are being organized: industrial parks, business incubators, and small-sized production facilities intended for small enterprises (Knyaginin & Shchedrovitsky, 2018).

For residents, the strategy of integrating the two types of special economic zones and industrial parks means development of skills, technological independence, but most importantly, confidence in the future thanks to contract manufacturing and cooperation with world giants.

Measurement of the indicator of investment and information attractiveness is carried out according to 2 groups of parameters—the scale of activity (contribution of the site to the regional economy is calculated by 4 indicators) and efficiency (labor productivity, the ratio of resident's investments and the number of jobs). The results were normalized in the range from 0 to 1 (Konishchev, 2019).

The specific weight of industrial parks and special economic zones in the total number of employees does not exceed 0.5%, in investments—1%, and in shipment of the region—3%. Industrial parks and special economic zones are long-term projects, therefore they are relatively attractive, but give relatively low economic results (Mansurova, 2018).

For example, in «Maryino» investments of residents exceed investments in infrastructure 9 times, in «Rosva»—11 times, «Vorsino»—24. At KIP Master, the total revenue of residents per employee at the end of 2018 amounted to 11 million rubles, and at Preobrazhenka—21 million rubles (Salikov et al., 2018).

Park «Razvitie» for 1 million rubles of investments in infrastructure organized 1.5 places, «Khimgrad»—3, and «M8»—11 (Kuznetsova et al., 2020).

As a result of the creation and implementation of the communication platform, the following is carried out: customer focus, and transition to the side of small manufacturing companies (Kharchenko, 2018). A clear example is the Maryino park, which reduced the minimum size of the site to 0.4 hectares. And also analyzes the possibility of building an industrial center where small businesses use the new format—light industrial (Andryashina et al., 2020a, 2020b), as well as digitalization as industrial park, and the technological processes of residents.

The site's digitalization center, as a rule, is a geographic information system, which contains data on infrastructure facilities (Yanovsky, 2017). Next, services are introduced, the users of which are the back office, municipal authorities and investors (navigation within the park, emergency response procedures, logistics), cooperation, as a result of which industrial sites reduce transaction costs.

Geographically located companies enrich each other's expertise, negotiate faster, build production chains. All this gives rise to a synergistic effect (Potashnik et al., 2020).

3 Conclusion

Industrial parks and special zones are tools for regional development. The effectiveness of which depends on conditions of their use.

If the region does not have a created project support system, including assistance in obtaining financing, the possibility of cooperation between small and large businesses, improving the regulatory framework, creating a communication platform, then this process will not be effective (Romanovskaya et al., 2020a, 2020b, 2020c).

For example, the industry of the Nizhny Novgorod region represents a small but stable growth in the range of 6–7% and provides half of the tax deductions.

The most important obstacles for the development of industry are the policies of the Central Bank, which maintains a significant rate and inconsistency of the enterprises with the new structure of new economy (Andryashina et al., 2020a, 2020b).

A significant problem is the lack of cooperation between enterprises. Nizhny Novgorod companies purchase products worth 100 billion rubles outside the region, while competent actions in this direction have already saved more than 1 billion rubles.

The interaction of small and medium-sized businesses with government and interregional cooperation has special potential.

There are three main areas of activity to improve the situation of enterprises:

- development of diversification;
- interaction with all interested associations in order to lower the Central Bank rate;
- comprehensive development of cooperation.

Three industrial technoparks will be created in the Nizhny Novgorod Region: on the basis of the GAZ Group, CJSC Drobmash and the Sarov technopark in Satis, Diveevo District. More than 1 billion rubles will be raised from the federal budget during the construction period (2019–2021), and the total cost of projects will be about 1.7 billion rubles.

As a result of project implementation, by 2024, 43 small and medium-sized businesses will become residents of industrial technology parks, more than 1,000 jobs will be organized, and tax deductions to budgets of all levels in the amount of more than 1,500 million rubles will be attracted.

The regional fund provides 30% of the loan to co-financing programs. Fund is implementing a loan program from 3 to 5 million rubles for residents of industrial parks in the scientific, technical and innovative sphere. Reducing the minimum loan amount to 20 million rubles, which can significantly expand the range of potential participants in the program (Romanovskaya et al., 2020a, 2020b, 2020c).

Particular attention should be paid to the communication platform, designed for effective information interaction of stakeholders in the industry.

In particular, the role of the system in the implementation of the roadmap «Improving the competitiveness of industry in the Nizhny Novgorod region» will be important. The platform is used to execute such items as:

- placing the procurement plan of executive authorities on a communication platform;
- filling the industry platform;
- filling the catalog with products of enterprises;
- translation of the document flow of executive authorities with legal entities.

Particular attention is paid to cooperation with JSC Russian Export Center, and the possibilities of subsidizing and advising (Romanovskaya et al., 2020a, 2020b, 2020c).

The Center for the Development of Export Potential of the Nizhny Novgorod Region focuses mainly on helping small and medium-sized businesses.

An important area of the Center's activities is the selection of foreign counterparties for Nizhny Novgorod enterprises. In particular, the platform hosts information on requests from foreign companies to search for Russian products.

References

Andryashina, N. S., Romanovskaya, E. V., Garina, E. P., Kuznetsov, V. P., & Kuznetsova, S. N. (2020a). Modernization of production under the conditions of modern technologies (by the Example of Metallurgical Production of PJSC «GAZ»). *Lecture Notes in Networks and Systems, 87*, 532–540.

Andryashina, N. S., Romanovskaya, E. V., Kuznetsov, V. P., Kuznetsova, S. N., & Kozlova, E. P. (2020b). Development of the production system of the enterprise on the example of workshop of the PJSC «GAZ». *Lecture Notes in Networks and Systems, 73*, 747–758.

Bezrukova, T. L., Morkovina, S. S., & Jiang, S. (2019). The development of territorial-industrial clusters: Methodological foundations of management,

COMMUNICATION PLATFORM FOR FINDING AND ATTRACTING ...   67

formation factors, support vectors (monograph). In T. L. Bezrukova & S. S. Morkovina (Eds.), Sui Jiang M.: KnoRus.

Bodrunov, S. D. (2018). The Russian economic system: The future of high-tech material production. *Economic Revival of Russia, 2*(40), 5–16.

Donichev, O. A. (2019). Economic integration as a factor in reducing differentiation in the development of regions. *Bulletin of Vladimir State University named after Alexander Grigoryevich and Nikolay Grigoryevich Stoletov*. Series: Economic Sciences. No. 1, 4–14.

Goremykin, V. A., & Sokolov, S. V. (2019). Forms of enterprise integration. *Questions of the Regional Economy*, 87–96.

Ignatiev, M. N. (2019). On the concept of economic integration in business entities. *Economic Journal, 27*(3), 99–104.

Knyaginin, V. N., & Shchedrovitsky, P. G. (2018). The industrial policy of Russia: Who will pay the costs of globalization. Series «Ideologies» M.: Europe, p. 160.

Kharchenko, S. V. (2018). Modern information models of accounting support management and profit formation. In S.V. Kharchenko (Ed.), *Young scientist* (No. 12. pp. 377–382).

Konishchev, A. S. (2019). Integration of the process of operational logistics planning at the enterprise. Logistic systems in the global economy (No. 4, pp. 142–146).

Kuznetsova, S. N., & Kuznetsov, V. P. (2018). An effective tool for solving conversion tasks. *Economics and Management: Problems, Solutions, 1*(10), 113–116.

Kuznetsova, S. N., Kuznetsov, V. P., & Egorova A. O. (2018). Modern logistics systems of industrial sites. Storage and processing of agricultural raw materials (No. 1, pp. 71–74).

Kuznetsova, S. N., Kuznetsov, V. P., Kozlova, E. P., Potashnik, Y. S., & Tsymbalov, S. D. (2020). Transformational period of Russian development in the digital economy. *Lecture Notes in Networks and Systems, 91*, 663–669.

Mansurova, A. F. (2018). Integration as a category of economic science/Economics. *Innovation Quality control, 4*(9), 165.

Mizikovsky, I. E., Kozlova, E. P., Garina, E. P., Garin, A. P., & Kuznetsova, S. N. (2020). Improvement of cost allocation processes for maintenance and operation of industrial enterprise equipment. *Lecture Notes in Networks and Systems, 73*, 775–784.

Potashnik, Y. S., Artemyeva, M. V., Kuznetsova, S. N., Garin, A. P., & Letyagina, E. N. (2020). The status and trends in innovative activity of industrial enterprises of Nizhny Novgorod region. *Lecture Notes in Networks and Systems, 73*, 525–534.

Romanovskaya, E. V., Kuznetsov, V. P., Andryashina, N. S., Garina, E. P., & Garin, A. P. (2020a). Development of the system of operational and production planning in the conditions of complex industrial production. *Lecture Notes in Networks and Systems, 87*, 572–583.

Romanovskaya, E. V., Garina, E. P., Andryashina, N. S., Kuznetsov, V. P., & Tsymbalov, S. D. (2020b). Improvement of the quality system of manufactured products at the enterprise of mechanical engineering. *Lecture Notes in Networks and Systems, 73*, 785–794.

Romanovskaya, E. V., Garina, E. P., Andryashina, N. S., Kuznetsova, S. N., & Artemyeva, M. V. (2020c). Studying the experience of reengineering business processes in the practice of domestic enterprises: Problems and prospects of application. *Lecture Notes in Networks and Systems, 73*, 517–524.

Salikov Yu.A., Barzenkova A.S., Zenin A.A. (2018). A conceptual approach to the implementation of multi-purpose regional and sectoral integration based on cluster policy. *Technologies of the food and processing industry of the agro-industrial complex—Healthy food products* (No. 3. pp. 76–81).

Vikulov, V. A., & Butrin, A. G. (2019). Algorithm for the formation and management of an industrial enterprise interactions with suppliers of material resources and consumers of finished products. *Basic Research, 8* (part 5), 1141–1145.

Yanovsky, V. V. (2017). Methodological aspects of the impact of investments on business value/V.V. Yanovsky, S.V. Proskurnikov. *Bulletin of the Belgorod University of Cooperation, Economics and Law, 4–2*, 165–169.

Mechanism for Responding to Risks of Economic Activity in Enterprises

Yaroslav S. Potashnik, *Svetlana N. Kuznetsova*, *Ekaterina P. Garina*, *Elena P. Kozlova*, *and Natalia S. Andryashina*

1 INTRODUCTION

Active introduction of enterprises in various aspects of business intelligent machines contributes to the competitiveness of companies and the degree of competition in a variety of industry markets. As a consequence, significantly increases the importance of the effectiveness of implemented business management processes. In conditions of the uncertainty inherent in economic processes, one of the key areas of enterprise management is risk management, which is designed to identify possible risks, as well as strengthen their positive and neutralize the negative impact on achieving goals. The work of many specialists, including V.A., is devoted to the study of various aspects of risk management. Akimova, A.G. Badalova, K. V. Baldin, T, Barton, S.V. Valditsev, M.B. Gracheva, G.B. Kleiner, N. Taleb, M.G. Laposta, F.H. Nayta, V.L. Tambovtseva, T. Flynn, B.

Y. S. Potashnik (✉) · S. N. Kuznetsova · E. P. Garina · E. P. Kozlova · N. S. Andryashina
Minin Nizhny Novgorod State Pedagogical University, Nizhny Novgorod, Russia

N. S. Andryashina
e-mail: natali_andr@bk.ru

© The Author(s), under exclusive license to Springer Nature Switzerland AG 2021
E. G. Popkova and B. S. Sergi (eds.), *Economic Issues of Social Entrepreneurship*,
https://doi.org/10.1007/978-3-030-77291-8_7

69

Hedges, J. Hubbard et al. However, until now there are, in our view, some methodological issues that are not fully reflected in publications. In particular, it requires clarification mechanism to respond to the risks of economic activities of enterprises, including the sequence of implementation and maintenance of appropriate action, which the subject of this study.

2 Materials and Method

As part of the study, risks are defined as internal or external to the enterprise events (i.e., the occurrence or change of one or more circumstances) that may affect the achievement of enterprise goals (Kuznetsov et al., 2018). Impact of risk may be both negative and positive (3, 2012). For example, typical risks with negative consequences for enterprises are higher prices for used resources, breach of obligations by partners, departure of key employees, deterioration of macroeconomic conditions, theft, fires, etc. As examples of risks with a positive influence on business operations can be reduced admission to participation in tenders for public procurement, withdrawal from the market of a key competitor, or a favorable change in tax legislation (Knight, 2003).

Basic processes implemented in the framework of risk management, are the identification, analysis, and response (Garina et al., 2018). Identification involves the risk detection, determining the causes and effects, and description of other essential characteristics (Egorova et al., 2016). Risk analysis is carried out in order to diagnose their levels, acceptability of the levels (corresponding to the minimum acceptable level for risks with a negative impact and the target level for risks with a positive impact) and to rank the risks in terms of priority in responding to them. The level of risk, in general, is defined as the combination of the probability of occurrence and consequences. The probability of risk is understood as the degree of probability of its occurrence. Risk consequences mean the effect (negative or positive) of risk on the values of economic performance targets: content, quality, timing, cost, and profitability. For example, quitting of a key specialist from an enterprise can lead to an increase in the time required to bring an innovation to the market by 10%, and a decrease in inflation by 3%—to a comparable increase in profitability (Taleb, 2016).

For each risk, the initial (LFR initial, before response) and acceptable (LFR acceptable) levels are determined. Based on a comparison of the initial LFR and the acceptable LFR, conclusions are drawn about the priority of the risk in terms of the implementation of modifying effects in relation to it. The greater the discrepancy between the initial LFR and acceptable LFR, the higher the priority (Smirnova et al., 2019).

Risk response consists in selecting, detailing and implementing response options. A plan containing a list of identified risks, their initial and acceptable levels, basic and standby response options, start points and total duration of their implementation, the target residual level of risk (i.e. after response), the necessary resources, and those who are responsible for the implementation of the plan.

The following methods were used during the study: system approach, logical analysis and synthesis, abstraction, sociological survey, expert assessment method.

3 Results

The study found that the main purpose of responding to the risks of economic activity in enterprises is to ensure that their levels meet acceptable (desired) values. Six key risk response options have been identified (Fig. 1).

Promotion involves the implementation of actions that increase the risk and (or) the consequences of risk. It can be implemented in relation to risks with positive or negative consequences. For example, timely collection of information about government plans regarding industry

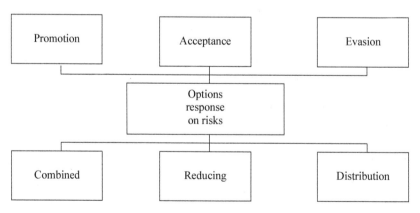

Fig. 1 Risk response options

regulation may allow the company to take advantage of opportunities that open up. Or decreases to a certain level of expenses for advertising a new product, may increase the risk of failure to achieve the target sales. However, if the residual level of risk does not exceed the acceptable, the company will save money.

Acceptance does not imply any impact on the likelihood and consequences of the risk. It is implemented both in relation to risks with positive and negative consequences. Acceptance is carried out in two main ways: active, when a reserve is created to take advantage of the emerging opportunity or to compensate for possible losses (redundancy), and passive, when measures are taken are only undertaken in the event of a positive or negative event.

Evasion involves the abandonment of activities leading to the occurrence of the risk in question. Implemented to risks with negative consequences. For example, refusal to develop unstable markets, relations with partners who systematically violate contractual obligations, use borrowed capital on unfavorable conditions, etc.

Redistribution involves the implementation of actions to transfer or otherwise distribute consequences of the occurrence of risk. It is implemented both in relation to risks with positive and negative consequences. For example, the implementation of multidirectional actions by an enterprise (projects, including in unrelated markets, cooperation with different partners, etc.) can help to use the available additional opportunities, gain experience, achieve synergy, and reduce negative consequences occurrence of problems in one of the directions.

Reduction involves the implementation of enterprise actions to reduce the likelihood and (or) the consequences of risk. Implemented to risks with negative consequences. An example of actions to reduce the likelihood of risk is a careful study of the concept and individual stages of the implementation of an innovative project, the formation of a qualified team of managers and executors, which reduces the likelihood of a project failure. An example of reducing the effects of formation and development of a company action plans in various emergency situations (e.g., under conditions of significant adverse changes in the external and internal environment, natural disasters, etc.).

Combined option involves the implementation of several previously described approaches simultaneously. For example, in order to reduce the risk of non-compliance with the timing of a new product, an enterprise may improve the quality of internal processes ("reduction" option) and at the same time attract collective work of third party partners ("distribution" option).

The risk response process, according to the authors, should include four main stages.

At the first stage the risks are divided into two categories: regulated and unregulated. Regulated risks should include those the level of which the enterprise is able to adjust in the direction that it desires for itself, and unregulated—risks, the level of which the enterprise cannot significantly affect. For example, the value of risks such as the erroneous assessment of the market potential of a new product or accidents at work can usually be adjusted by activities carried out by the enterprise. The values of the risk levels as a change in the government approach to industry regulation or a decrease in the purchasing power of targeted buyers, the company usually cannot change.

At the second stage, depending on the adjustability and the relationship between the values of the initial and acceptable levels, one or more response options are selected for each risk. In this case, enterprises can take advantage of the recommendations proposed by the authors, presented in Fig. 2.

The response option "Promotion" is recommended to be applied in relation to regulated risks, when the value of their initial level is lower than acceptable, and raising the level is economically feasible.

The response option "acceptance" can be applied to both regulated and non-regulated risks when the value of their initial level is less than or equal to the value of an acceptable level. Also, this option is recommended if the initial level of risk value slightly exceeds the acceptable value, but the use of other response is either impossible or impractical. Simultaneously, an acceptable level value must be increased to a value of the initial level of risk.

The "Evasion" response option can be applied to both regulated and non-regulated risks if the value of their initial level is critical, significantly

	Risks with a level value not exceeding an acceptable value	Risks from the level value exceeding the acceptable value
Regulated risks	Promotion, acceptance	Acceptance, evasion, redistribution, reduction
Unregulated risks	Acceptance	Acceptance, evasion

Fig. 2 Risk response options

exceeding the value of an acceptable level and there are no alternative effective ways of responding.

The "redistribution" and "reduction" response options can be applied to regulated risks if the value of their initial level exceeds the value of an acceptable level of risk.

At the third phase - to develop specific measures to respond to risks. If for some risks the response measures are mandatory, established by the government, regulators, or standards (for example, the creation of a mandatory reserve, the implementation of required insurance, etc.), then they are necessarily included in the risk plan. If alternatives are possible among these measures, it is chosen to achieve an acceptable level of risk at a minimum cost. If there are no strict requirements, the company develops measures based on the principles of expediency and efficiency.

Response measures must correspond to risk levels and the enterprise should have sufficient resources for implementation. For example, if the risk of not achieving the profitability targets for the project is low, the company should probably not use the "evasion" option. Or if the company does not have enough free cash resources to form cash reserves, it might be better to use not the "acceptance" option, but the "redistribution" option with a request to the insurance company.

Measures should allow not only to bring the values of risk levels to acceptable values but also to achieve the goals of the enterprise in terms of profitability and competitiveness. In the event that alternative responses can potentially be applied to risks, the most attractive in terms of cost–benefit ratio is selected as the main one. In this case, the plan must take into account direct and opportunity costs; possible additional costs associated with responding to secondary risks (which may arise as a result of the implementation of a response measure); impact on costs associated with responding to other risks; the degree of influence on the level of risk and economic efficiency of the economic activity of the enterprise as a whole. Other responses may be considered as a backup.

To ensure the timely response to unidentified risks, it is recommended to create a reserve of resources (for example, in the amount of 5–10% of the total cost associated with exposure to risks). In the subsequent identification of these risks, the procedure described above may be applied to identify the measures of impact.

At the fourth stage, the risk response plan is implemented. At the same time, monitoring is carried out, which involves periodic risks review of economic activity in order to adjust their estimates, identify new risks, and diagnose the status of response measures. Persons responsible for the implementation of the risk response plan must report periodically to the appropriate manager, characterizing the effectiveness of the plan implementation. He also should inform about unforeseen implications and adjustments that are required.

Presented by the author response mechanism for risks of economic activities in enterprises and recommendations have been tested on a number of industrial enterprises of Nizhniy Novgorod. In the course of a sociological survey conducted among the heads of departments responsible for the development and implementation of risk management measures, it was found that the implementation of the mechanism and recommendations made it possible to increase the efficiency of the risk response process by an average of 5 -10%.

4 Conclusion

When planning a response to business risks, it is necessary to take into account the manageability of the enterprise, i.e. the ability of the enterprise significantly influence the probability and consequences of risks. Also, for each risk it is required to identify the initial and acceptable levels. Depending on the controllability and relations between the initial values and acceptable levels of risk for each necessary to select one or several options for response, also develop measures to ensure consistency between the initial and acceptable levels of risk.

References

Egorova, A. O., Kuznetsov, V. P., & Zokirova, N. K. (2016). Features of the influence of risk factors on the activity of mechanical engineering enterprises. *Vestnik of Minin University* (1), 5.

Garina, E. P., Garin, A. P., Kuznetsov, V. P., Popkova, E. G., & Potashnik, Y. S. (2018). Comparison of approaches to development of industrial production in the context of the development of a complex product. *Advances in Intelligent Systems and Computing, 622,* 422–431. https://doi.org/10.1007/978-3-319-75383-6_54.

GOST R ISO 31000:2010. (2010). *Risk management. Principles and guidance* (p. 19).

Knight, F. H. (2003). *Risk, uncertainty and profit.* Translated from English (p. 360). Delo.

Kuznetsov, V. P., Romanovskaya, E. V., Egorova, A. O., Andryashina, N. S., & Kozlova, E. P. (2018). Approaches to developing a new product in the car building industry. *Advances in Intelligent Systems and Computing, 622*, 494–501. https://doi.org/10.1007/978-3-319-75383-6_63.

Mescon, M., Albert, M., & Hedowrie, F. (2006). *Fundamentals of management* (p. 672). Williams.

Risk management standards. (2008). *Federation of European association of risk-managers* (p. 16).

Risk Management Organizations. (2014). *Integrated model—Committee of Sponsorship Organizations of the Treadway Commission* (COSO) (p. 111).

Smirnova, Zh. V., & Kochnova, K. A. (2019). Training of employees of service enterprises using information technology. *Vestnik of Minin University, 7*(1), 5.

The international standard ISO 31000–2018. (2012). *Risk management—Guide* (p. 18). Standardinform.

Taleb, N. (2016). *Black Swan. Under the sign of unpredictability* (p. 736). Kolibri.

Evaluation of Management Effectiveness of the System Based on the Use of Management Indicators

Marat R. Usmanov, Ekaterina P. Garina◉,
Elena V. Romanovskaya◉, Natalia S. Andryashina◉,
and Dmitrii P. Vatletsov

1 INTRODUCTION

Manufacturers of high-tech industries, faced with the crisis of high costs and competitiveness. They do understand that the principles of

---

M. R. Usmanov (✉)
LUKOIL-Nizhegorodniinefteproekt LLC, Nizhny Novgorod, Russia
e-mail: Marat.Usmanov@lukoil.com

E. P. Garina · E. V. Romanovskaya · N. S. Andryashina
Minin Nizhny Novgorod State Pedagogical University, Nizhny Novgorod, Russia
e-mail: alenarom@list.ru

N. S. Andryashina
e-mail: natali_andr@bk.ru

D. P. Vatletsov
Nizhny Novgorod Institute of Management, Branch of RANEPA, Nizhny Novgorod, Russia
e-mail: saha9103861931@yandex.ru

© The Author(s), under exclusive license to Springer Nature Switzerland AG 2021
E. G. Popkova and B. S. Sergi (eds.), *Economic Issues of Social Entrepreneurship*,
https://doi.org/10.1007/978-3-030-77291-8_8

77

lean thinking should be introduced into production—the practice of continuous review and improvement of products, processes, standards, with a focus on increasing the efficiency of these indicators through the implementation of initiatives to change them and system improvement of production. Where a system of continuous improvement (it is also a system of uninterrupted improvements, a system of efficiency, continuance improvement, lean production, kaizen) is a set of practices and procedures that focus on continuous improvement of processes and systems, including through the re-equipment of production facilities, changes schemes of the enterprise, its management system, etc., All those systems are aimed at resolving the priority conflict of participants: changing patterns of work as a result of ongoing improvements of systems on the background of its preservation due to limited capital investment in manufacturing (Kuznetsov et al., 2019). At the same time, a specific set of measures is laid at the heart of the improvements, which allows providing an increase in productivity (changing the scheme, breaking up bottlenecks, revising standards by searching for reserves, etc.) (Garina, 2017).

The purpose of the study is to systematize and generalize the experience of continuous improvements at refineries in the business sector "Processing" of the fuel and energy complex in the Russian Federation, as well as a detailed presentation of the methodology and tools for assessing the effectiveness of continuous improvements in order to strengthen control over business parameters.

The management practices of continuous improvements and evaluating the effectiveness of the formed systems in the production and design complexes of the Russian Federation are summarized on the example of the technological support center of a separate business unit "Processing" in the sector of the Russian fuel and energy complex in order to consolidate the accumulated research experience with its subsequent implementation in design and production activities (Usmanov et al., 2018).

2   Materials and Method

The categorical apparatus on the research topic is considered (Bredillet, 2010; Browning et al., 2006; Davis et al., 1996; Ren & Yeo, 2006), as well as the relevant practices of continuous improvement in the company, the potential of using scientific analysis and monitoring the implementation of strategic development goals on the example of highlighted business sector.

3 Results

To date, the research project complex a range of tools used system of continuous improvement, such as: forming a flow (Continuous Flow); place of value creation (Gemba); value stream mapping (Value Stream Mapping); constant improvement (Kaizen) and others. The level of output on the implementation of continuous improvements is determined through benchmarking, roadmaps for improving efficiency, key performance indicators for improvements (KPI—indicators of the attainability of strategic goals)—a metric system designed to analyze critical areas of the organization's activities (Usmanov et al., 2019).

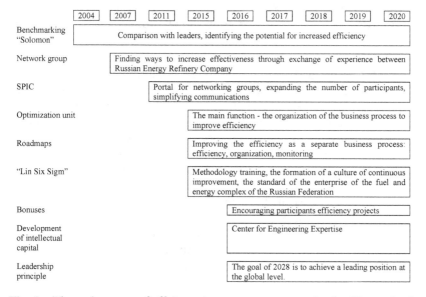

Fig. 1 The main stages of efficiency improvement systems in the "Processing" business sector of a separate business unit of the fuel and energy complex of the Russian Federation (Usmanov et al., 2019)

Figure 1 shows the main stages of systems development to improve efficiency in the selected business sectors.

Focus on efficiency in terms of productivity, cost, technical and instrumental equipment, the reliability and safety of the equipment, designed initially as a program to bridge the gap (PLRO). As a result later transformed into a road map to improve efficiency, where potential actions and ideas are justified in the early stages of study, such as: differentiation on the scale and type of production, size and direction of improvements, including the confirmation of resources and a preliminary assessment of the effects and costs of implementation in a time period of up to three years. With a view to updating provided quarterly reports, the purpose of which—taking into account the current prices, adaptation projects schedules, costs, and actually obtained effects. For the reporting period, the management of a separate business unit of the fuel and energy complex of the Russian Federation develops and sets normative + target indicators of KPI.

Assessment of the KPI implementation practice in the "Processing" business sector of the business entity under study at this stage showed that:

1. During the first years of the system's implementation, the initially established tasks were repeatedly exceeded, which increases the magnitude of the effects of implemented improvements;
2. The use of the cash equivalent in the form of the economic effect of each event is considered appropriate for the organization of work;
3. The roadmap activities are considered as extra-budgetary tasks (ambition plan) to be evaluated by KPI (provided by the incentive system). In this case, empirically derived rule when about $2/3$ of expected effects of the roadmap included in the budget, and $1/3$ is optional and, in particular, is a source of compensation for loss of profits in case of force majeure (Potashnik et al., 2017). For comparison, an approach can be observed with a border in which the performance of tasks to be evaluated by KPI is laid only with the achieved result corresponding to normative indicators.

Determining the potential of continuous improvement system and the practice of technological development of a separate business unit of the fuel and energy complex of the Russian Federation, we establish that the economic effect of implementing improvement measures over the past three years is largely determined by the developed system of continuous improvements (Tolstykh et al., 2020):

a. An organizational resource of successful investments with an expected payback period of less than one year;
b. A factor in increasing operational efficiency management practices;
c. A tool for motivating company personnel, it is increasing the involvement of enterprise groups in the improvement system.

Key performance indicators introduced in the evaluated business unit of the enterprise in the "Processing" sector of the fuel and energy complex of the Russian Federation since 2015 to emphasize the company management on individual focus areas and identify areas of potential improvement in the future (Table 1). They are implemented through a percentage in the variable part salaries of employees for certain categories and correlate with the percentage of planned and qualitative indicators in the research complex.

The results of the implementation of the continuous improvement system in evaluated business unit for the period from 2016 to 2018 as part of the continuous improvement system, more than 700 events were carried out covering ten enterprises with a relative increase in indicators of total revenue and operating income, the volume of processing of raw materials, and the percentage of bonus employees. At the stage of the 2019-2020th time period, the task of bringing all production capacities to a new level of manufacturability through the modernization of corporate systems becomes urgent (Parshina et al., 2019).

4 Conclusion

Generalization and systematization of experience in implementation of management practices in a separate business unit "Processing" of the enterprise of the fuel and energy complex of the Russian Federation it is possible to determine the following:

1. For employees of the company are provided:

a. Possibility to exchange information, for dialogue with external stakeholders;

82 M. R. USMANOV ET AL.

Table 1 Key performance indicators for improvements (Usmanov et al., 2019)

Business functions	KPI	Business functions	KPI
Production	The percentage of refusals/complaints Output, units Speed Production capacity, load percentage Productivity Operational efficiency of productive assets	Commercialization, sales	Product availability Loading time Order Execution Time (NOTIF)
Procurement, warehousing	Canceled Purchase Requests The percentage of completion of purchase orders Order Cycle Time Frequency of "emergency" purchases The number of rejected shipments Unloading Time Inventory level	Finance, Accounting	Net profit margin Cost of goods sold Operating income Unit cost Working capital Accounts receivable turnover Inventory turnover ratio Return on Investment (ROI) The difference in the budget Capital expenditures (CAPEX)
Commercialization, sales	Order Processing Time Time to work with consumer claims The accuracy of sales forecasts Market share growth Marketing expenses	Lean	Extra time Cycle times Operation time Order processing cycle time Efficiency of the production process Muda

b. Potential permanent employee training (promoting learning in practice);

c. Focus on indicators of effectiveness, the efficiency of changes when creating new options for solutions, and their implementation. At the same time, key performance indicators for the implementation of the continuous improvement system in a separate business unit of the Processing sector of the Russian energy sector are realized through a percentage in the variable part of the salary of employees in certain categories. But it indirectly reflected in the remuneration of all categories of company employees (in the form of one-time bonuses from the average percent of proven economic effect). The main reason for this is that most events exceed the established limit of payments in terms of their effects. We believe that all key specialists and employees, regardless of activity type, should also be involved in the development of an improvement system, including applying key performance indicators for them.

2. Management of the "Environment of change" is carried out through:

a. Formation of measured strategic development goals;
b. Development of detailed tactical plans with the possibility of adjusting them. Moreover, in the organizational and methodological plans, include the development of organizational structures based on specific dates for proposed changes. But it does not include the development of an open organizational system coupled with the balanced system of indicators.

3. Key performance indicators for improvements introduced by the business unit (Table 1) partially contain metrics that are not achievable for implementation by ordinary employees of the company, and various management systems based on indicators (MTP, KPI, operational controlling indicators) are presented collectively, while as a distinctive feature of this tool is its targeting and linking to a specific economic gain, in contrast to the general incentive system for energy companies, which is focused on the implementation of factory-wide KPIs.

The experience of the practical application of control systems based on indicators on the example of a center for technological support of a business unit indicates the need for their gradation:

– A system of indicators of investment activity within the framework of the strategic development of the company (Balanced Scorecard methodology, in the Russian-language version of the BSC) and a system designed to manage process changes. And since the strategy is development priorities, this determines the limited number of indicators;

- A system of operational performance indicators (a system of operational controlling) that evaluates the activities of a business unit in various functional areas (production, finance, logistics, sales, etc.), and a system designed to control deviations of existing processes, i.e. feedback formation in enterprise. The number of operational performance indicators is not limited;
- Key performance indicators in the form of personalized targets set for specific groups of employees in the achievement of strategic and operational objectives of the company, providing:

a. The motivation of employees to continuous improvement;
b. The possibility of an objective assessment of the activities of employees;
c. The possibility of correlating the size of employee remuneration with the results of their activities.

Moreover, as experts note (Kochnev, 2020), when creating the KPI system, it is necessary to rely on previously designed systems of strategic indicators (MTP) and operational controlling, only then subsequently form a system of key indicators. In fact, in the study of business unit is only part of the indicators used to assess the effectiveness of strategic objectives, and only a few—to correlate with the development strategy of medium-term goals. Key performance indicators in the form of personalized targets are not set for individual groups of employees.

References

Bredillet, C. N. (2010). Blowing hot and cold on project management. *Project Management Journal, 41*(3), 4–20.

Browning, T. R., Fricke, E., & Negele, H. (2006). Key concepts in modeling product development processes. Published online in Wiley InterScience (www.interscience.wiley.com). https://doi.org/10.1002/sys.20047.

Davis, F. D., & Venkatesh, V. (1996). A critical assessment of potential measurement biases in the technology acceptance model: Three experiments. *International Journal of Human-Computer Studies, 45*(1), 19–45.

Garina, E. P. (2017). Design of conditions for efficient organization of technological process for productive maintenance of equipment at industry enterprises. *Bulletin of NGIEI, 1*(68), 91–101.

Kochnev, A. F. (2020). BSC, KPI. http://www.kpilib.ru/article.php?page=635. Accessed 12 April 2020.

Kuznetsov, V., Garina, E., Bardakov, A., Kornilov, D., & Lapaev, D. (2019). Re-engineering the business process of sales in view of life cycle stage and the company organisational structure. *International Journal of Trade and Global Markets, 12*(3–4), 412–423.

Parshina, A. A., Levchuk, V. V., Shpilevskaya, E. V., Garina, E. P., & Garin, A. P. (2018, April). The study of modern approaches to development of economic systems through managing their complexity. In *International conference project "the future of the global financial system: Downfall of harmony"* (pp. 726–733). Springer.

Potashnik, Y. S., Garina, E. P., Romanovskaya, E. V., Garin, A. P., & Tsymbalov, S. D. (2017, July). Determining the value of own investment capital of industrial enterprises. In *Advances in Intelligent Systems and Computing* (pp. 170–178). Springer.

Ren, Y., & Yeo, K. T. (2006). Research challenges on complex product systems innovation. *Journal of the Chinese Institute of Industrial Engineers, 23*, 519–529.

Tolstykh, T. O., Shkarupeta, E. V., Malkova, T. B., Alpeeva, E. A., & Garina, E. P. (2020). Algorithm for assessing the efficiency of innovational technologies of industrial enterprises. In *Growth poles of the global economy: Emergence, changes and future perspectives* (pp. 463–471). Springer.

Usmanov, M. R., Podvintsev, I. B., & Gimaletdinov, R. R. (2018). Improving productivity and operating efficiency of production assets. Technological support of oil refining, petrochemical and gas processing (p. 304). Peter.

Usmanov, M. R., Only, I. S., Gimaletdinov, R. R., & Firsov, A. V. (2019). Increased productivity and operational efficiency of production assets. Implementation of a system of continuous improvements at manufacturing enterprises and in research and design complexes (Vol. 2, p. 224). Quartz.

Innovative Approaches to Business in the Digital Environment

Natalia M. Fomenko, Tatyana O. Tolstykh, Victoria Yu. Garnova, Ekaterina N. Yalunina, and Boris I. Kheyfits

1 INTRODUCTION

The twenty-first century is characterized by rapid changes affecting all areas of activity. Globalization of the main processes and their integration into the economic activities of enterprises are the main realities of the ongoing transformations in society, while the technological revolution leads to the large-scale use of digital technologies. Artificial intelligence, robotics, intelligent machines, virtual reality and other innovations have a significant impact on the activities of modern organizations. In such

---

N. M. Fomenko (✉) · V. Yu. Garnova
Plekhanov Russian University of Economics, Moscow, Russia

T. O. Tolstykh
National University of Science & Technology (MISIS), Moscow, Russia

E. N. Yalunina
Ural State University of Economics, Ekaterinburg, Russia

B. I. Kheyfits
K.G. Razumovsky Moscow State University of Technologies and Management (the First Cossack University), Moscow, Russia

© The Author(s), under exclusive license to Springer Nature Switzerland AG 2021
E. G. Popkova and B. S. Sergi (eds.), *Economic Issues of Social Entrepreneurship*,
https://doi.org/10.1007/978-3-030-77291-8_9

conditions, the competitiveness of organizations is defined as the basic component of enterprise success.

A modern organization is a complex system that must meet high requirements and have a complex level of management activity (Kolmykova et al., 2018). Management functions are multifaceted and include all aspects of the functioning of the enterprise, including the collection, processing, and analysis of information for decision-making. An efficiently functioning organized information system can increase the level of competitiveness and the ability to adapt in a timely manner to rapidly changing conditions.

The production resource of the information society in the digital age, at the same time as other production factors, becomes not so much information as knowledge. The application of knowledge and its generation are crucial in the development of a modern organization and serve as one of the factors for increasing competitiveness. With full confidence, it can be argued that during the formation of a new technological structure, a new global electronic environment appeared, which was called the digital economy. Among the main characteristics of the electronic environment are the factors presented in Fig. 1.

The development of the digital economy is characterized by a transformation of the industrial economy through the creation of a flexible network of new forms of the organization's production and business activities. The effectiveness of such an economy is confirmed by the creation of communication interactions between members of temporarily organized associations. Such an economy is characterized by processes:

- Galloping development and implementation of *Internet* technologies;
- The availability of economic facilities and infrastructure to ensure their livelihoods, which leads to an increase in the volume of social and economic activities;
- Application of global communications;
- Reorganization of traditional forms into digital;
- Modernization of infrastructure through the digitalization of public and commercial activities.

The basic component of the development and formation of innovative forms of the digital economy is the development of the global *Internet*

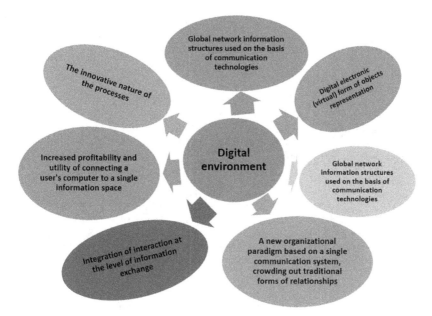

Fig. 1 Factors of the electronic network environment

network. Statistical studies of Rosstat in 2019 on the dissemination of the application of information and network technologies are presented in Table 1.

According to 2018 data, slightly more than 50% of the surveyed organizations of this representative sample have a website, which in modern realities is quite archaic (Fig. 2). At the same time, the largest share (according to Rosstat) is made up of organizations engaged in educational activities in higher educational institutions. And among organizations conducting purchases in an electronic environment—energy organizations and telecommunications enterprises.

According to the research, it is clearly seen that despite the rapid growth of information and communication technologies in the conditions of Russian enterprises, there are large reserves.

Table 1 Enterprises using information and communication technologies in Russia (% of the total) [Federal State Statistics Service. (2019)]

	2010	2011	2012	2013	2014	2015	2016	2017	2018
Enterprises applying:									
personal computers	93.8	94.1	94.0	94.0	93.8	92.3	92.4	92.1	94.0
servers [2]	18.2	19.7	18.9	19.7	26.6	47.7	50.8	50.6	53.4
local area networks	68.4	71.3	71.7	73.4	67.2	63.5	62.3	61.1	63.9
email	81.9	83.1	85.2	86.5	84.2	84.0	87.6	88.3	90.9
global information networks	83.4	85.6	87.5	88.7	89.8	89.0	89.6	89.7	92.0
of which:									
The Internet	82.4	84.8	86.9	88.1	89.0	88.1	88.7	88.9	91.1
including broadband	56.7	63.4	76.6	79.4	81.2	79.5	81.8	83.2	86.5
Intranet	13.1	16.1	14.7	16.7	16.8	19.2	21.6	26.2	31.3
Extranet	5.3	6.1	6.4	7.7	14.3	16.9	15.0	16.6	18.5
Organizations that have a website	28.5	33.0	37.8	41.3	40.3	42.6	45.9	47.4	50.9

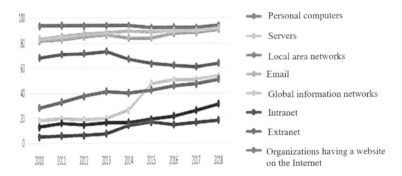

Fig. 2 Organizations that have a website

2 Materials and Method

A significant contribution to the formation of the digital electronic environment methodology was made by the work of domestic and foreign scientists: Bell D. (1973), Efimov E. and Fomenko (2009), Ivanova D. (2000), Castels M. (2000), Filimonova et al. (2018), Klochko et al. (2016), Tolstykh T. (2018a, b), Martin W. (1988), Masuda J. (1980), Timofeeva, A. (2016), Sidorova O. (2011), Shchepkina N. (2018), etc.

Among the distinctive features of digital forms of organization, one can note the use (with the goal of creating competitive products) of the collective assets of a group of companies that form the product value chain. At the same time, mutual cooperation and support, centralization, and decentralization of management, as well as the predominance of horizontal links between partners are displayed. In such circumstances, new forms of functioning and development of management systems of organizations are emerging.

The structure of economic organizations is undergoing changes. In such conditions, organizations function as virtual organizations, while changing the structure and form of labor organization.

The main feature of the digital electronic market is the heterogeneity of its structure. This is confirmed by many ways to organize a business in a digital environment. The basis of any project, including electronic, is a certain business model of enterprise management (Fomenko, 2016). Its choice is determined by the goals and objectives of the project implementation. Digitalization of economic processes leads to the expansion of information and economic space.

3 RESULTS

The main objectives of the implementation of Internet projects are the transformation of a traditional enterprise into an organization with automated current business processes and planning processes (Fomenko & Pavlyukova, 2016) Such organizations offer the buyer an innovative product while also providing additional information over the traditional business approach (Fig. 3). Thus, the flexibility and adaptive capacity of such enterprises is increasing. Collaboration of all elements will improve the level of decision-making and competitiveness of the organization in modern conditions.

The main feature of digital technology is that if an organization does not have the capacity or risk to participate fully in the digital environment, it has the ability to form virtual corporations (on the Internet market). Thus, it can be a participant of one real and several associations of virtual corporations, thus having its own information space and increasing the effect of its activities (Fig. 4).

To assess the possibility of organizations using virtual space, an expert assessment was carried out based on the ranking method of alternatives (solution alternatives) (Table 2). The application of this method is based

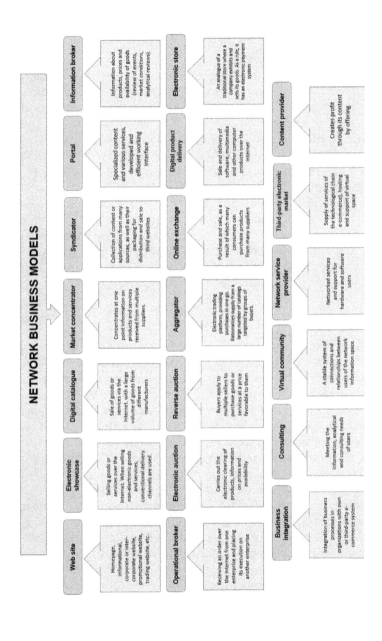

Fig. 3 The main categories of activities in a network environment

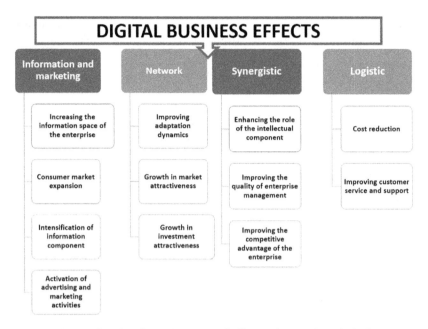

Fig. 4 Option for classifying the types of effects of using digital platforms

on the theory of fuzzy sets. This allows reducing the influence of subjective factors on the final result and leads to the consideration of alternatives parameters "advantages" and "disadvantages".

A fuzzy set is constructed for each alternative A_i.

Matrix A will look like this:

Table 2 Main characteristics of the development and application of business models in the digital environment (based on researches of authors)

Business models of business organization in a digital environment	Ease of implementation	Virtualization reality	Possibility of internet trade	Consulting services
Web site	5	2	4	5
Electronic showcase	5	1	4	2
Digital catalogue	5	1	1	3
Market concentrator	2	2	2	5
Syndicator	2	2	2	5
Portal	5	4	3	
Information broker	3	1	1	5
Operational broker	3	1	5	1
Electronic auction	2	2	5	3
Aggregator	2	2	5	3
Online exchange	2	2	5	2
Digital product delivery	3	1	5	3
Content provider	2	2	2	5
Electronic store	3	2	5	3
Business integration	1	5	3	3
Consulting	3	2	1	5
Virtual community	1	5	1	1
Network service provider	3	2	2	5
Third-party electronic market	2	3	2	5

$$A = \begin{vmatrix} 5\ 2\ 4\ 5 \\ 5\ 1\ 4\ 2 \\ 5\ 1\ 1\ 3 \\ 2\ 2\ 2\ 5 \\ 2\ 2\ 2\ 5 \\ 5\ 4\ 3\ 5 \\ 3\ 1\ 1\ 5 \\ 3\ 1\ 5\ 1 \\ 2\ 2\ 5\ 3 \\ 2\ 2\ 5\ 3 \\ 2\ 2\ 5\ 2 \\ 3\ 1\ 5\ 3 \\ 2\ 2\ 2\ 5 \\ 3\ 2\ 5\ 3 \\ 1\ 5\ 3\ 3 \\ 3\ 2\ 1\ 5 \\ 1\ 5\ 1\ 1 \\ 3\ 2\ 2\ 5 \end{vmatrix}$$

Function of the fuzzy set A_i, quantitatively characterizing the degree of correspondence of the ji-th criterion to the alternative:

$$\left| \mu_{A_i}\left(y_j \right) = \frac{u^i_j}{\max\limits_{j}\left(\left| u^i_j \right| \right)} \right.$$

A fuzzy set is constructed on the basis of the proposed expert estimates that take into account the importance of the criterion B. This data can have a characteristic "property - the degree of importance of the property" and a membership function $\mu_B(y_i)$ that allows to evaluate the degree of importance of the criterion. Point estimation of the property's importance is used. Vector $\vec{\omega} = \left(\omega(y_1), \omega(y_2), \ldots, \omega\left(y_p\right)\right)$—is a vector of expert opinion, the coordinates of which will be a score for the importance of each of the parameters by which alternatives are evaluated.

The values of the function are determined by the formula based on the values of which the matrix B is built:

$$\mu_B(y_j) = \frac{\omega(y_j)}{\sum\limits_{y_j \in U_1} \omega(y_j)}$$

$$B = \begin{vmatrix}
1 & 0.4 & 0.8 & 1 \\
1 & 0.2 & 0.8 & 0.4 \\
1 & 0.2 & 0.2 & 0.1 \\
0.4 & 0.4 & 0.4 & 1 \\
0.4 & 0.4 & 0.4 & 1 \\
1 & 0.8 & 0.1 & 1 \\
0.1 & 0.2 & 0.2 & 1 \\
0.1 & 0.2 & 1 & 0.2 \\
0.4 & 0.4 & 1 & 0.1 \\
0.4 & 0.4 & 1 & 0.1 \\
0.4 & 0.4 & 1 & 0.4 \\
0.1 & 0.2 & 1 & 0.1 \\
0.4 & 0.4 & 0.4 & 1 \\
0.1 & 0.4 & 1 & 0.1 \\
0.2 & 1 & 0.1 & 0.1 \\
0.1 & 0.4 & 0.2 & 1 \\
0.2 & 1 & 0.2 & 0.2 \\
0.1 & 0.4 & 0.4 & 1
\end{vmatrix}$$

As an expert group, specialists in the field of information technology and digitalization were selected consisting of two people and the head of the working group. Based on the assessments made by experts, we constructed Table 3.

Matrix C reflects the proportion of expert opinion in total points: Expert Qualification Weight (k_w): Expert 1—0.7; expert 2—0.3.

Taking into account certain weights of the expert group, an indicator is determined whose data are summarized in the matrix S:

$$a_j^0 = \frac{1}{m} \sum_{i=1}^{m} k_w * \mu_{b_i}^j, \text{ Where m—number of experts.}$$

Table 3 Expert points

Types of risks	Experts	
	1	2
Web site	10	9
Electronic showcase	3	7
Digital catalogue	2	2
Market concentrator	5	3
Syndicator	7	4
Portal	9	1
Information broker	3	4
Operational broker	5	6
Electronic auction	6	4
Aggregator	2	1
Online exchange	5	3
Digital product delivery	7	7
Content provider	8	6
Electronic store	5	4
Business integration	3	2
Consulting	7	10
Virtual community	10	10
Network service provider	4	5
Total	101	88

Elements of the degree of membership on the basis of which the preference of alternatives is determined is represented by the matrix W:

$$W = B \times S$$

$$C = \begin{vmatrix} 0.10 & 0.11 \\ 0.03 & 0.07 \\ 0.02 & 0.02 \\ 0.05 & 0.03 \\ 0.07 & 0.04 \\ 0.09 & 0.01 \\ 0.03 & 0.04 \\ 0.05 & 0.06 \\ 0.06 & 0.04 \\ 0.02 & 0.01 \\ 0.05 & 0.03 \\ 0.07 & 0.07 \\ 0.08 & 0.06 \\ 0.05 & 0.04 \\ 0.03 & 0.02 \\ 0.07 & 0.11 \\ 0.04 & 0.11 \end{vmatrix} \quad S = \begin{vmatrix} 0.103 \\ 0.042 \\ 0.02 \\ 0.103 \\ 0.042 \\ 0.02 \\ 0.103 \\ 0.042 \\ 0.02 \\ 0.103 \\ 0.042 \\ 0.02 \\ 0.103 \\ 0.042 \\ 0.02 \\ 0.103 \\ 0.042 \end{vmatrix} \quad W = \begin{vmatrix} 0.33 \\ 0.10 \\ 0.03 \\ 0.23 \\ 0.09 \\ 0.06 \\ 0.15 \\ 0.06 \\ 0.04 \\ 0.20 \\ 0.09 \\ 0.03 \\ 0.23 \\ 0.07 \\ 0.03 \\ 0.18 \\ 0.07 \end{vmatrix}$$

By conducting an expert assessment of business models in a digital environment, it was determined that the most suitable for the initial development of digital platforms, in terms of ease of implementation and providing the largest possible number of services at the initial stage, are the implementation of the Website and the Aggregator.

Due to the novelty of network technologies and the *Internet*, there is no single methodology for determining the effectiveness of *Internet* projects. In each case, a decision is made depending on the situation of the project implementation. In the course of the study, the authors identified possible internal (corporate) and external (global) effects of enterprise network business:

1. Improving the information and economic space of the enterprise (information and marketing effect). This is achieved by reducing restrictions on the territorial distribution of partners in joint activities. External and internal resources become available to the organization in an unlimited amount.

INNOVATIVE APPROACHES TO BUSINESS ... 99

2. Joint formation of resources (network effect). Employees of the enterprise get the opportunity to quickly influence the development of the situation, and suppliers or manufacturers form a single information space with the very ability to manage demand.
3. Effective coordination (synergistic effect). It entails improving the quality of work coordination with a large number of participants, changing the structure and its costs.
4. Saving operating expenses on logistic (logistic effect). It increases the interaction efficiency of customers by improving the image of the enterprise and reducing the cost of the internal information environment.

4 Conclusion

In summary, we would like to note that in today's circumstances there is still no clarity of evaluation of the digital form of management of the organization and the mechanisms available, which, in turn, does not allow highlighting advantages, new capabilities, and application efficiency correctly. On the one hand, the use of new information technologies and the digital environment contains a large number of opportunities and reserves. On the other hand, innovative business conditions are created in which business activities (from production to marketing of products) are transferred to a new digital environment, which has properties different from the traditional one and increases the organization's competitiveness by improving the level of decision-making.

Acknowledgements The study was performed as part of the RFBR grant No. 20-010-00470.

References

Bell, D. (1973). *The coming of post-industrial society.*
Castels, M. (2000). *The information age: Economics, society and culture.* Translated from English under scientific edition of O.I. SU-HSE.
Efimov, E. N., & Fomenko, N. M. (2009). Trends in the development of a networked electronic environment. *Management Systems and Information Technology, 2–1*(36), 122–126.

Federal State Statistics Service. (2019). *Regions of Russia: socio-economic indicators—2019.* https://www.gks.ru/folder/14478. Accessed Date 5 February 2020.

Filimonova, N. M., Kapustina, N. V., Bezdenezhnykh, V. V., & Kobiashvili, N. A. (2018). Trends in the sharing economy: Bibliometric analysis. Digital economy: Complexity and variety vs. rationality. *Lecture Notes in Networks and Systems, 87.* Elena G. Popkova • Bruno S. Sergi Editors http://www.spr inger.com/series/15179. Accessed Date 5 February 2020.

Fomenko, N. M. (2016, October 8–9). Enterprise integration in the network electronic market: choice of the internet-project implementation directions. Managing service, education and knowledge management in the knowledge economic era: proceedings of the 2016 international congress on management and technology in knowledge, service, tourism & hospitality (Serve 2016), Jakarta, Indonesia & Vladimir state university, Vladimir, Russia. EH Leiden, The Netherlands, pp. 37–40.

Fomenko, N. M., & Pavlyukova, A. V. (2016). Trends in the development of network management mechanisms in the electronic environment of the organization/News of higher educational institutions North Caucasus Region. *Social Sciences, 3*(191), 82–88.

Indicators of the Digital Economy. (2019). https://www.gks.ru/folder/14478. Accessed Date 14 January 2020.

Ivanov, D. V. (2000). Virtualization of society. SPb "St. Petersburg Oriental Studies".

Klochko, E. N., Fomenko, N. M., & Nekrasova, V. V. (2016). Modeling of network mechanisms of management in the conditions of organizational development. *International Review of Management and Marketing, 6*(S1), 101–106.

Kolmykova, T. S., Merzlyakova, E. A., Bredikhin, V. V., Tolstykh, T. O., & Ovchinnikova, O. P. (2018). Problems of formation of perspective growth points of high-tech production. *Advances in Intelligent Systems and Computing, 622,* 469–475.

Martin, W. (1988). *Information society.* Progress.

Masuda, Y. (1980). *The information society as post-industrial society.* Tokyo.

Schepkina, N. N. (2018). Electronic auctions in the context of digital transformation: Achievements and miscalculations. *Problems of Economics (Kharkov), 2*(36), 134–140.

Sidorova, O. V. (2011). E-commerce as a new form of organization of economic activity. *Creative Economy, 5*(9), 63–68.

Timofeeva, A. A., Bulganina, S. V., Khachaturova, M. S., Klochko E.N., Nekrasova, M. L., Zakharova, E. N., & Fomenko, N. M. (2016). Features of the implementation of integrated marketing communications: Resistance to change. *International Review of Management and Marketing, 6*(S1), 27–32.

Tolstykh, T. O., Kretova, N. N., Trushevskaya, A. A., Dedova, E. S., & Lutsenko, M. S. (2018a). Problems and prospects for implementing inter-dimensional and Inter-industry projects in digital economy. *Advances in Intelligent Systems and Computing, 622,* 485–493.

Tolstykh, T., Savon, D., Safronov, A., Shkarupeta, E., & Ivanochkina, T. (2018b). Economic transformations based on competence approach in the digital age. *Proceedings of the 32nd International Business Information Management Association Conference,* IBIMA 2018—Vision 2020: Sustainable economic development and application of innovation management from regional expansion to global growth, pp. 7723–7729.

The Weighted Average Cost of Capital for the Analysis of Innovative Projects Integrated into the Company

Sergey N. Yashin, Egor V. Koshelev, Natalya A. Yagunova, Victor P. Kuznetsov, and Elena V. Romanovskaya

1 Introduction

An innovative business needs to be evaluated more carefully than a company's usual investment activity. In this case, the features of the analysis of innovative projects are important that integrated into an existing enterprise, but are unusual for it (Limitovsky, 2015).

Currently, there are many approaches to assessing the cost of capital of projects and companies. Most often, the weighted average cost of capital (WACC) is taken as such. And here, both an understanding of the financial meaning of this indicator and the method of its calculation are important.

So, Fernandez (2004) believes that WACC is only the rate at which free cash flows (FCF) should be discounted to obtain the same result as the valuation using own cash flows. In the same work, he argues that

---

S. N. Yashin (✉) · E. V. Koshelev · N. A. Yagunova
Lobachevsky State University of Nizhny Novgorod, Nizhny Novgorod, Russia

V. P. Kuznetsov · E. V. Romanovskaya
Minin Nizhny Novgorod State Pedagogical University, Nizhny Novgorod, Russia

© The Author(s), under exclusive license to Springer Nature Switzerland AG 2021
E. G. Popkova and B. S. Sergi (eds.), *Economic Issues of Social Entrepreneurship*,
https://doi.org/10.1007/978-3-030-77291-8_10

103

the correct WACC calculation is based on the correct assessment of tax shields. The cost of tax shields depends on the debt policy of the company.

In another work, Fernandez (2007) proves the thesis that if a company targets its leverage in terms of market value, it has less value than if it targets it leverage in terms of book value. At the same time, three valuation methods (adjusted present value [APV], WACC and cash flows of equity) always give the same result. Fernandez (2007) also shows the relationship between the cost of equity, the value of unclaimed equity, the value of debt, and the weighted average cost of capital. It illustrates the equivalence of the three approaches to a solid assessment of the company's value in the form of eternal rent for companies growing at a constant rate of growth and, finally, for any company.

Thus, the principle of calculating WACC itself is quite complicated and must take into account various important aspects. For this purpose, various WACC calculation formulas are applied in practice, which, although based on different principles, nevertheless give approximately the same result.

First, the so-called "training" formula is often used, which is provided in many textbooks, monographs, and scientific articles (Brealey et al., 2011; Brigham & Gapenski, 1993; Brigham & Houston, 2009; Damodaran, 2002; Farber et al., 2006; Ogier et al., 2004; Kruschwitz & Lorenz, 2019; Limitovsky, 2015; Porras, 2011).

Secondly, a simplified Modigliani–Miller formula is also used (Limitovsky, 2015; Modigliani & Miller, 1963; Trifonov et al., 2014).

However, even the application of this or that principle of WACC calculation according to the appropriate formula does not allow to take into account the most important factors of the value formation of the company's business, including innovative development. Such factors include: adequate assessment of the debt tax shield (Arzac & Glosten, 2005; Cooper & Nyborg, 2006; Kemsley & Nissim, 2002), structural planning (Flannery & Rangan, 2006; Leary & Roberts, 2005) and the assessment of risky forms of financing for companies and projects (Ruback, 2002).

2   Materials and Method

In this article, we consider in detail innovative projects of a company that are integrated into an existing enterprise and at the same time are unusual. Evaluation of the estimated WACC of the enterprise in this case is the most difficult task that should be carried out in several stages. In addition, it is noteworthy that this assessment situation does not imply the creation of an economically isolated project in the form of creating a new company for the project, and this allows concentrating innovative resources in the hands of a large owner and thus increasing the size and value of the company's business.

Thus, we distinguish the following principles for calculating WACC in this case (Fig. 1). Unlike the point of view of Limitovsky (2015), this article proposes to evaluate not the estimated WACC of the project, but the estimated WACC of the company as a whole, since the cost of capital invested in an innovative project will be unreasonably high if the WACC project is used. The fact is that the project is integrated into the existing enterprise, therefore it is more logical to perceive not a separate project, as in the case of economically isolated projects, but the entire complex (portfolio) of company projects that are already being implemented and will be implemented in the near future. Such an approach will allow taking into account various systemic financial effects, for example, expressed in the fact that the cash flows of some projects partially finance the implementation of other projects. This is possible only in the case of projects integrated into an existing enterprise.

Using this principle, we can formulate the main stages of the assessment of the estimated WACC of the company.

1. The calculation of the shares of financial leverage:
   This stage is necessary because the company may have various borrowed sources of financing: existing long-term loans and short-term loans, as well as new loans that the company takes in addition to realize new investment or innovative opportunities. As a result, for each type of loan, its own financial leverage is obtained, which will be taken into account in further calculations.
2. Calculation of the specific weights of each type of capital:

Fig. 1 The basic principles of WACC assessment of the company

This data will be needed when calculating the WACC project. Moreover, the types of capital are naturally considered the same as in the case of calculating financial leverage.

3. Correction of the β coefficient for financial risk:

The business risk that the founders of the innovation project take is related to the industry sector of the project, therefore the risk β_U is taken not by the enterprise, but by the industry in which the project is implemented. However, after this it is necessary to take into account the effect of borrowed financing on the β coefficient. For this purpose, the Hamada formula (1972) can be used in the calculations:

$$\beta_L = \beta_U \left[1 + (1 - T)\frac{D}{S} \right], \tag{1}$$

where β_L is the coefficient of a β financially dependent company;

β_U—coefficient of β financially independent company;

T—income tax rate (%);

D—the amount of borrowed capital of the company (rubles);

S—the amount of equity capital of the company (rubles).

However, in this form, this formula is not suitable for solving our problem. It needs to be slightly modified for two reasons. Firstly, as mentioned earlier, various sources of debt financing are analyzed, which ultimately leads to the calculation of the individual components of financial leverage. Secondly, the peculiarities of the Russian tax legislation are such that not all interest on the obligations of the company can be attributed to the expenses of the organization. There is a certain limit according to Article 269 of the Tax Code of the Russian Federation. Thus, to calculate the β coefficient of a financially dependent company, we will use the formula

$$\beta_L = \beta_U \left[1 + \sum_{j=1}^{m} (1 - \lambda_j T)\frac{D_j}{S} \right], \tag{2}$$

where λ_j is the share of j-percent with a tax shield, that is, attributable to the expenses of the company;

D_j—the value of the j-th debt of the company (rub.).

4. Calculation of the cost of project equity:

It is produced for a financially dependent company according to the CAPM model (Sharpe, 1964):

$$k_{sL} = k_{RF} + MRP \cdot \beta_L, \tag{3}$$

where k_{sL} is the cost of equity of a financially dependent company (%);
k_{RF}—rate of risk-free capital investment (%);
MRP—premium for the risk of investing in the economy of a country (%).

5. Calculation of the WACC project:
In this case, this can be done according to the formula that Limitovsky (2015) uses in his book:

$$WACC_{project} = \sum\nolimits_{j=1}^{n} w_j(k_j - r_j T), \tag{4}$$

where w_j is the share of the j-th type of capital in the value of the total capital of the company;
k_j—"pre-tax" value of the j-th type of capital (%);
r_j—part of the cost of capital of the j-th type attributable to the expenses of the company (%).

6. Evaluation of the β project coefficient:
The CAPM model is also used for this. From the relation

$$WACC_{project} = k_{RF} + MRP \cdot \beta_{project} \tag{5}$$

can be expressed β as the project coefficient as

$$\beta_{project} = \frac{WACC_{project} - k_{RF}}{MRP}. \tag{6}$$

7. Evaluation of the weighted average β coefficient of company's assets:
This β coefficient is calculated as

$$\beta_a = \sum\nolimits_{i=1}^{n} w_i \beta_i, \tag{7}$$

where w_i is the share of the i-th asset in the portfolio of the company;

β_i—is the β coefficient of the i-th asset of the company's portfolio.

8. Calculation of WACC of the company:
As a result, the WACC of the company as a whole will be different from the WACC of a project, since the company also implements projects of a different industry. We can find the WACC of the entire enterprise using the CAPM model again, i.e.

$$WACC_{company} = k_{RF} + MRP \cdot \beta_a. \tag{8}$$

3   RESULTS

In order to illustrate the presented algorithm, let us consider the following example. The Federal Research and Production Center of JSC "Research and Production Enterprise 'Polet'" (formerly the Gorky Research Institute of Radio Communications) was established in 1964 and is one of the industry leaders in the field of aviation radio communications for military and civilian purposes. JSC "RPE 'Polet'" intends to implement an atypical project of development and production of a program complex designed for automation of works in mobilization subdivisions of the central executive bodies of state power (CIOGV) of the subject of the Russian Federation and local self-government bodies of municipalities. Data on the company's equity capital, its current paid obligations, as well as on the new credit line, which is opened for the company by the bank for a new innovative project, are presented in Table 1. Accounts payable in liabilities are not taken into account, since they are free of charge. The marginal rate of exemption from income tax in the last column of the

Table 1   Equity and paid liabilities of JSC "NPE Polet"

Type of capital	Capital valuation		Cost (%)	Tax exemption Rate (%)
	Thousand roubles	% to total		
Equity	2,499,222	52.55	–	–
Long term loans	469.602	9.87	11.32	$6.25 \cdot 1,25 = 7.8125$
Short-term loans	658.733	13.85	13	$6.25 \cdot 1.25 = 7.8125$
Credit line	1,128,335	23.72	14.16	$6.25 \cdot 1.25 = 7.8125$
Total	4,755,892	100	–	–

THE WEIGHTED AVERAGE COST OF CAPITAL FOR THE ANALYSIS ... 109

table is calculated on the basis of Article 269 of the Tax Code of the Russian Federation using a key rate as of December 16, 2019, equal to 6.25%.

Assessing sequentially calculated WACC of the company using the phases shown earlier, we finally obtain the formula (8), which

$$WACC_{company} = 5.5\% + 13.35\% \cdot 1.33 = 23.256\%.$$

It is noteworthy that this rate is expressed in US dollars. Then, for a final assessment of the effect of an innovative project, for example, using the criterion of net present value (NPV), the cash flows of the project should also be previously converted into US dollars.

Finally, we note that the company WACC, equal to 23.256%, is significantly lower than the WACC project, which is equal to 32.504%. Thus, if the cash flows of an innovative project integrated into an existing enterprise are discounted at an overestimated rate of the WACC project, then, firstly, it will reduce the NPV value of the project, and secondly, it will not allow taking into account various systemic financial effects, for example, in that the cash flows of some projects partially finance the implementation of other projects. That is, the new projects of the company are actually linked to the already operating through cash flows of the whole company as a large project complex.

As a result, this approach allows us to take into account the integration of a new innovation project into an existing enterprise both in the NPV numerator—through the systemic financial effects of project cash flows and in the NPV denominator—by discounting project cash flows not at the WACC rate of an individual project, but at the company's WACC rate.

4 Conclusion

In conclusion, we formulate the most important findings:

1. For the analysis of innovative projects integrated into the company, but unusual for it. It is proposed to evaluate not the estimated WACC of the project, but the estimated WACC of the company as a whole, since the cost of capital invested in the innovative project, if the WACC project is used, will be unreasonably high. Such an approach will allow taking into account various systemic financial

effects, for example, expressed in the fact that the cash flows of some projects partially finance the implementation of other projects. This is possible only in the case of projects integrated into an existing enterprise.

2. The assessment of the estimated WACC of the company in this case is a difficult task that should be carried out in several stages.

3. This approach allows taking into account the integration of a new innovative project into an existing enterprise, both in the NPV numerator—through the systemic financial effects of project cash flows and in the NPV denominator—by discounting project cash flows not at the WACC rate of an individual project, but at the company's WACC rate.

The results of this study may be useful to financial analysts of companies and their top managers for making adequate decisions regarding the effectiveness of innovative projects.

Acknowledgements The study was carried out with the financial support of RDIF within the framework of the scientific project No.19-010-00932 "Creation of the model of evolution of the innovative system of industrial regions in the modern conditions of socio-economic development".

References

Arzac, E. R., & Glosten, L. R. (2005). A reconsideration of tax shield valuation. *European Financial Management, 11*(4), 453–461.

Brealey, R.A., Myers, S. C., & Allen, F. (2011). *Principles of corporate finance* (10th ed.). McGraw-Hill.

Brigham, E. F., & Gapenski, L. C. (1993). *Intermediate financial management* (4th ed.). The Dryden Press.

Brigham, E. F., & Houston, J. F. (2009). *Fundamentals of financial management* (12th ed.). Cengage Learning.

Cooper, I. A., & Nyborg, K. G. (2006). The value of tax shields IS equal to the present value of tax shields. *Journal of Financial Economics, 81,* 215–225.

Damodaran, A. (2002). *Investment valuation: Tools and techniques for determining the value of any asset*. Wiley.

Farber, A., Gillet, R. L., & Szafarz, A. (2006). A general formula for the WACC. *International Journal of Business, 11*(2), 211–218.

Fernandez, P. (2004). The value of tax shields is NOT equal to the present value of tax shields. *Journal of Financial Economics, 73*(1), 145–165.

THE WEIGHTED AVERAGE COST OF CAPITAL FOR THE ANALYSIS ... 111

Fernandez, P. (2007, Fall/Winter). A more realistic valuation: APV and WACC with constant book leverage ratio. *Journal of Applied Finance, 17*(2), 13–20.

Flannery, M. J., & Rangan, K. P. (2006). Partial adjustment toward target capital structures. *Journal of Financial Economics, 79,* 469–506.

Hamada, R. S. (1972). The effect of the firm's capital structure on the systematic risk of common stocks. *The Journal of Finance, 27*(2), 435–452.

Kemsley, D., & Nissim, D. (2002). Valuation of the debt-tax shield. *Journal of Finance, 57*(5), 2045–2073.

Kruschwitz, L., & Lorenz, D. (2019). *Investitionsrechnung.* Verlag De Gruyter Oldenbourg.

Leary, M., & Roberts, M. R. (2005). Do firms rebalance their capital structures? *Journal of Finance, 60*(6), 2575–2619.

Limitovsky, M. A. (2015). *Investment projects and real options in emerging markets.* Yurait.

Modigliani, F., & Miller, M. (1963). Corporate income taxes and the cost of capital: A correction. *American Economic Review, 53,* 433–443.

Ogier, T., Rugman, J., & Spicer, L. (2004). *The real cost of capital: A business field guide to better financial decisions* (320 pp.). FT Prentice Hall.

Porras, E. V. (2011). *The cost of capital.* Palgrave Macmillan.

Ruback, R. (2002). Capital cash flows: A simple approach to valuing risky cash flows. *Financial Management, 31,* 85–103.

Sharpe, W. F. (1964, September). Capital asset prices: A theory of market equilibrium under conditions of risk. *Journal of Finance, 19,* 425–442.

Trifonov, Yu. V., Yashin, S. N., & Koshelev, E. V. (2014). Taking into account the impact of risk distribution between project participants on its investment attractiveness. *Financial Analytics: Problems and Solutions, 24*(210), 2–8.

Forecasting Potential for Project Activities as a Tool for Institutional Modernization of the Higher Education System: Domestic and Foreign Experience

Alexander G. Oganyan

1 Introduction

Under current conditions, it is apparent that a considerable part of actors in the institutional structure of the national higher education system identified best international practices as their development milestones; in addition, the public authorities, including the higher education system, distinguish the process-oriented project-based approach in the organization of the innovation management as the most preferred one. In comparison with foreign research and educational organizations, when assessing the ultimate effectiveness of innovations implemented in various forms, domestic projects are slightly inferior to foreign projects in a number of indicators, which, in turn, has a detrimental effect on the process of institutional modernization. However, even if success is guaranteed for innovation projects implemented by higher education institutions, there is a lack of the effect of replication of positive experience at the level

---

A. G. Oganyan (✉)
Southern Federal University, Rostov-on-Don, Russia

© The Author(s), under exclusive license to Springer Nature Switzerland AG 2021
E. G. Popkova and B. S. Sergi (eds.), *Economic Issues of Social Entrepreneurship*,
https://doi.org/10.1007/978-3-030-77291-8_11

113

of creation of innovation projects with high adaptivity to the needs of potential consumers, which is perceptible for the system as a whole.

Thus, qualitative changes, determined by the forecasting potential for project activities and identified as a tool for institutional modernization of the higher education system, must be concomitantly correlated with the restoration of the degree of efficiency of the management system, taking into account the possibility of the comprehensive use of the project-based approach. This innovation-oriented transformational conversion provides an opportunity to reduce the costs for the institutional modernization management process; in particular, it allows mitigating the risks of innovation activity of actors in the institutional structure of the higher education system, while supporting the generation of intellectual growth potential of the national higher education system and localizing in its format highly qualified experts who are able to ensure competitiveness of commercialized results of innovation activity. Thus, the need arises for more in-depth research on innovation management problems in the context of consideration of the forecasting potential for project activities as a tool for institutional modernization of the higher education system.

2   Materials and Method

The research has been carried out with the use of general scientific and specific scientific methods which represent specific features of innovative activities, including the methods of system analysis, process-based and project-based approaches in innovation management, design and modeling of basic and innovative processes of actors in the institutional structure of the higher domestic education system. Active development of innovative activities by actors in the institutional structure of the higher education system brings us to the conclusion that this is primarily due to the search for viable sources for improving the economic efficiency of performance results. The achievement of desired goal is greatly facilitated by the strengthening of adaptive characteristics of the ultimate outcome of innovative activities of actors in the institutional structure of the domestic higher education system, implemented in the form of innovative goods, technologies, etc. In this regard, in a broad sense, the innovative project of a higher education institution can be identified as a set of efficient integration of internal structural–functional elements with individual, innovation-oriented projects, localized according to the criterion of their type classification (organizational, technological, research type, etc.), however, having the same focus and making it possible to improve the operating efficiency of actors in the institutional structure of the domestic higher education system in one of the key areas defined by the system policy.

We can identify the main aspects which characterize the essence of the project-based approach during the process of management of innovative activities of an actor in the institutional structure of the higher education system:

- The project-based approach is identified in the system of management of innovative activities of actors in the institutional structure of the higher education system as an efficient instrument; hence, results obtained can be assessed in an integrated manner, taking into account the contribution of each implemented innovation-oriented project, which was localized, as we have already noted, according to the criterion of their type classification (organizational, technological, research type, etc.).
- The use of the project-based approach as a priority approach provides the opportunity for actors in the institutional structure of the higher education system to implement the process-oriented and project-oriented types of innovation management.
- The project-based approach serves as a certain internal driver which exercises the function of a tool for the promotion of processes of institutional modernization of the higher education system.

3 Results

Project-based management of innovative activities of actors in the institutional structure of the higher education system should be treated as an advanced method for improving various functional management processes in general and achieving the goals at various stages of innovative activities, which clearly distinguishes the special forecasting potential for project activities as a tool for institutional modernization of the higher education system (Milova, 2014). Active adaptation of actors in the Russian higher education system to the use of project management is an important means of achieving stability and long-term nature of development of processes of institutional modernization of the higher education system.

The key inductive criteria characterizing the features of the project innovation management of higher education institutions are as follows:

I. The associated representation of project management as an efficient instrument of implementation of the innovation project by the actor in the institutional higher education system is determined by the following: provision of conditions for focus on end-consumer and achievement of high adaptivity of the project to the needs of potential consumers (Jeppesen & Molin, 2003; Mokhnachev et al., 2012).

II. Modernization of the organization structure of higher education institutions, research institutes and other organizations as actors in the higher education system improves the efficiency of the implementation of innovation projects at the level of the following components: standardization and increase in the quality of implementation of certain processes of innovative activities (Dodgson, 2000); identification of specialized structural units endued with a special range of powers, mainly exercising coordination functions during the implementation of innovation projects (Swan et al., 1999); enhancing the efficiency of direct and feedback communication during the implementation of the innovation project.

III. Intellectual capacity development through training, improving the level of professional knowledge, and involving high-potential skilled professionals in the development of innovative activities.

IV. Introduction of modern information technologies to support the processes for the management of innovative activities of actors in the institutional structure of the higher education system (Galstian, 2001).

The results from the analysis of Russian and foreign experience in the use of project management obtained during the research revealed that it is necessary to comply with the important condition of the process management efficiency, which includes, in particular, optimization and organization of efficient feedback (Mindeli & Zavarukhin, 2001).

Therefore, taking into account the use of the project-based approach, the following priorities for improving innovative activities of actors in the institutional structure of the higher education system can be identified:

- Focus on final (ultimate) outcomes of activities of actors in the institutional structure of the higher education system, including innovative activities, shift away from the focus on intermediate stages of assessment from the perspective of achievement of functional outcomes.
- Identification of activities of actors in the institutional structure of the higher education system as a cumulative set of processes with the differentiation into functional and innovative in each of them.
- Increasing the adaptive management capabilities through the increased use of the project-based approach (Etzkowitz & Leydesdorff, 2000) with a view to increasing the innovative activities of actors in the institutional structure of the higher education system.

The possibilities of the use of the adaptive mechanism of institutional modernization of the higher education system can be fully translated into action through the use of special strategies for managing the process of institutional modernization, the principle fundamental in the development of scenarios of which (Kianto et al., 2010) consists of the feedback effect and the use of a balance score card.

However, in case of a more in-depth statement of the research problem and also consideration of it from the perspective of postulates of modern innovative management (Ilyenkova, 2008), the adaptive mechanism of institutional modernization of the higher education system is designed to form such conditions for actors in its institutional structure that would enable their effective operation in various markets (education, labor, innovative products etc.) and intensify the action of the mechanism of institutional modernization of the higher education system, which includes two function chains:

- chain of strategic management of the process of institutional modernization of the higher education system (choice of the vector of development of different actors in the institutional structure of the higher education system, change of the chosen vector, its instrumental support, etc.);
- chain of semistrategic management of the process of institutional modernization of the higher education system (analysis, assessment and subsequent monitoring of state of the educational market, labor market, innovative-product market, etc.) (Latukha, 2007).

In order to strengthen the adaptive capabilities of actors in the institutional structure of the higher education system, it will be reasonable to identify the so-called "project centers", organizationally concentrated in the format of consolidated elements of the management structure (the faculty can be such a consolidated element in case of a higher education institution). Symmetrical signals from the education market, labor market, innovative-product market etc. determine the behavior scenarios for actors in the institutional structure of the higher education system depending on the current situation and facilitate the effective adaptation to changes in staffing of the process of innovative transformation of Russian economy (Ovchinnikov & Oganyan, 2019).

In this regard, integration processes that are implemented within the framework of internal mergers of actors in the institutional structure of the higher education system, are based on the protection of national priority projects and selected national and regional programs, which necessitates the use of the tools of contemporary project management theory.

Figure 1 presents a formalized alternative model of innovation-oriented management for a key actor in the institutional structure of the higher education system—a university complex (serving as an advanced model for the optimal form of integration of science, education and innovation).

At the same time, in order to optimize the conditions for the implementation of integration processes at the level of the merger of the project management system in the system of management of an innovation-oriented university complex, we believe that it would be expedient if uniform project management standards were adopted by a higher education institution, which, in turn, would necessitate the creation of a brand new organizational unit—a resource center for strategic project management of a university complex, the key function of which should consist in control, coordination and regulation of the process of preparation and implementation of projects within the area of its competence (Grudzinsky, 2004; Makoveeva, 2012).

Further, we shall formalize the methods for the formation of the knowledge management structure in an innovation-oriented university complex.

In order to optimize the action of mechanisms for control over project implementation, we offer a proprietary methodology of monitoring its

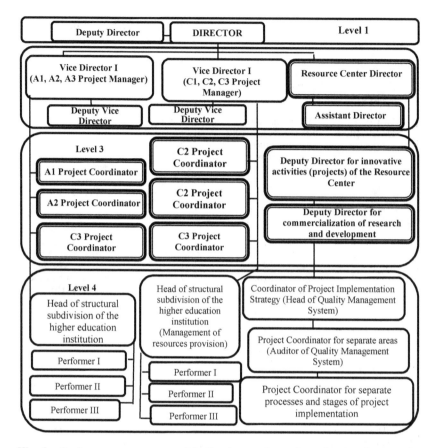

Fig. 1 Project management model of an innovation-oriented university complex

dynamics according to the degree of achievement of desired outcome and achievable effect, presented in Table 1.

The methodology makes it possible to solve several critical issues related to the use of the model of project management of such a complex organization structure as an innovation-oriented university complex.

De facto, the actual responsibility for project management is not delegated to the latter by the management system of a higher level (project managers), who do not act as direct project managers with the necessary range of competences (Oganyan, 2018).

Table 1 Assessment of efficiency of implementation of the project management system

Item no.	Criteria			
	System element	Expected result	Achievable effect	Formed potential
1	Project stage implementation management	– Allocation and division of responsibilities among project implementation actors – Development of a viable system for monitoring the project implementation results at each particular stage – Implementation and timely modernization of the automated system for project stage implementation management	– optimization of performance of responsibility centers – Formation of a flexible system for the adjustment of the project implementation process – Reduction of the time frame for management decisions	– Increasing the capabilities of ensuring efficient manageability of the project – Neutralizing "miscalculation" errors throughout all stages of project implementation – Saving resources from minimizing the risks associated with errors in the implementation of project stages

(continued)

Further, it is important to strike a balance between the degree of administration (including financial monitoring and control) of the project implementation process and real (actual) self-regulation and independence of an innovation-oriented university complex in the management of various resources.

4 Conclusion

The innovation-oriented transformational conversion provides an opportunity to reduce the costs for the institutional modernization management process; in particular, it allows mitigating the risks of innovation activity of actors in the institutional structure of the higher education system, while supporting the generation of intellectual growth potential of the

FORECASTING POTENTIAL FOR PROJECT ACTIVITIES AS A TOOL ... 121

Table 1 (continued)

Item no.	Criteria			
	System element	Expected result	Achievable effect	Formed potential
2	Partnership relations management	– Development of the best possible forms of integrative partnerships in key areas of interaction within the scope of project implementation – Introduction and timely modernization of the automated system for managing the contact relationship with partners within the scope of project implementation	– Optimization of performance in the framework of performance of contracts with project partners – Reduction of the time frame for management decisions, achieved due to the presence of common information space for the support of partnership relations	– Improving the efficiency of partnership relations management – Improving the efficiency of work in the system of contractual relationship with partners
3	Project cost management	– Expansion of formalization of all project cost management processes – Implementation and timely modernization of the automated system for project implementation cost management	– Actors in the management system of a higher education institution are given the opportunity to improve the accuracy of forecasting and planning of anticipated project implementation results	– Improving the efficiency of management of resource and financial expenses of the project

(continued)

national higher education system and localizing in its format highly qualified experts who are able to ensure competitiveness of commercialized results of innovation activity.

The innovation project of an actor in the institutional structure of the higher education system is identified as a set of efficient integration

Table 1 (continued)

Item no.	Criteria			
	System element	*Expected result*	*Achievable effect*	*Formed potential*
4	Budgeting process management (budget management of a university complex)	– Projection of the budgeting process on the project activities of a higher education institution – Implementation and timely modernization of the automated system for budgeting of project activities of a higher education institution	– Optimization of the integrative interaction of systems for budgeting the activities of a higher education institution and budgeting the project activities	– Improving the manageability of project activities due to the optimum integration with primary activities

of internal structural–functional elements with individual, innovation-oriented projects, localized according to the criterion of their type classification (organizational, technological, research type, etc.), yet having the same focus and making it possible to improve the operating efficiency of actors in the institutional structure of the domestic higher education system in one of the key areas defined by the system policy.

The forecasting potential for project activities as a tool for institutional modernization of the higher education system is characterized by a close interaction with integration processes that are implemented within the framework of internal mergers of actors in the institutional structure of the higher education system, based on the protection of national priority projects and selected national and local programs, which necessitates the use of the tools of contemporary project management theory.

REFERENCES

Dodgson, M. (2000). *The management of technological innovation: An international and strategic approach.* Oxford University Press.

Etzkowitz, H., & Leydesdorff, L. (2000). The dynamics of innovation: From National Systems and "Mode 2" to a Triple helix of university—Industry—Government relations. *Research Policy, 29,* 109–123.

Galstian, K. G. (2001). *Theoretical aspects of the formation of innovative processes: Preprint.* Publishing House of the Saint Petersburg State University of Economics and Finance.

Grudzinsky, A. O. (2004). *Project-oriented university. Professional business organization of a higher education institution.* Publishing House of the Lobachevsky State University of Nizhny Novgorod.

Ilyenkova, S. D. (2008). *Innovation management.* UNITY-DANA.

Jeppesen, L. B., & Molin, M. (2003). Consumers as co-developers: Learning and innovation outside the firm. *Technology Analysis & Strategic Management, 15*(3), 363–383.

Kianto, A., Hurmelinna-Laukkanen, P., & Ritala, P. (2010). Intellectual capital in service- and product-oriented companies. *Journal of Intellectual Capital, 11*(3), 305–325.

Latukha, O. A. (2007). *Integrated assessment of innovative activities of a higher education institution: Theoretical and methodological aspects: Synopsis of the thesis ... of the Candidate of Economic Sciences: 08.00.05.* Publishing House of the Vladivostok State University of Economics and Service, Novosibirsk.

Makoveeva, V. V. (2012). Modern approaches to managing integration processes in the higher professional education system. *Bulletin of the Tomsk State University, 2*(355), 115–119.

Milova, Y. Y. (2014). *Management of Innovation activities of a higher education institution.* Economics, Management, Finance: Proceedings of the III International Research Conference. Perm: Merkurii, pp. 25–27.

Mindeli, L., & Zavarukhin, V. (2001). International aspects of innovation policy. *World Economy and International Relations, 5,* 59–60.

Mokhnachev, S. A., Mokhnachev, K. S., & Shamaeva, N. P. (2012). Integration of education, science and business: Trends at the mesolevel. *Fundamental Studies, 3*(Part 3), 707–711.

Oganyan, A. G. (2018). Some aspects of theoretical and methodological approaches to the innovative transformation of the higher education system as an imperative of formation of the knowledge economy. *Theoretical and Methodological Journal "Vestnik Universiteta", 7,* 30–37.

Ovchinnikov, V. N., & Oganyan, A. G. (2019). Conceptual (structural-functional) model of the business mechanism of the institutional modernization of the higher education system as a driver of the innovative transformation of the Russian economic system. *Bulletin of the University, 6,* 115–123.

Swan, J., Newell, S., Scarbrough, H., & Hislop, D. (1999). Knowledge management and innovation: Networks and networking. *Journal of Knowledge Management, 3*(4), 262–275.

Small Business and Innovation Processes in Russian Regions: Prospects for Further Development

Yuri I. Treshchevsky, *Tatyana Yu. Solodimova, and Larisa S. Korobeynikova*

1 INTRODUCTION

Global practice demonstrates high level of innovation processes in the small business sector. In this regard, small business development in the current Russian context is presented in documents of regulatory and administrative authorities as one of the promising areas for improvement of socioeconomic systems at macro-, meso- and microlevels. There is an indemonstrable statement according to which it is small business that is most sensitive to innovation and advanced design and engineering solutions.

The modern age is often characterized as an "innovation race" in design and engineering field, supported by their creative use. In this regard, small enterprises are given a weighty part in perception and use of novel technologies, providing them with high level of competitiveness based on creatively different management decisions. This is noted, in

---

Y. I. Treshchevsky (✉) · T. Yu. Solodimova · L. S. Korobeynikova
Voronezh State University, Voronezh, Russia

L. S. Korobeynikova
e-mail: korobeinikova@vsu.ru

© The Author(s), under exclusive license to Springer Nature Switzerland AG 2021
E. G. Popkova and B. S. Sergi (eds.), *Economic Issues of Social Entrepreneurship*,
https://doi.org/10.1007/978-3-030-77291-8_12

125

particular, by Shnaider and Lapaev (2013), Orynbasarova and Baimurzina (2013). The positive aspects of small business which contribute to the diffusion of technological and organizational innovations, include their prompt response to changes in demands on the market, high rate of capital turnover, and the use of gaps in the market with low quantity demanded (Sazhin, 2015).

The problems of introducing novel engineering and technologies in small business in Russia usually include underfunding, as well as low level of technical and managerial literacy (Orynbasarova & Baimurzina, 2013; Sanzheeva, 2015). Many authors point out high level of risk in the implementation and promotion of design and engineering innovations, especially in small business due to a low level of human capacity, unstable funding, uncertain positions of authorities, high level of pessimism among representatives of small business sector with regard to the prospects of the economy as a whole (Altufyeva, 2019; Endovitsky et al., 2017; Kosobutskaya et al., 2020; Risin et al., 2017; Treshchevsky et al., 2018, 2019).

2 METHODOLOGY

In order to assess small business as a carrier of innovation, we proceeded from the following provisions: this sector is reflective of specific features of design and engineering development of regions and, in this regard, is severely differentiated; the crucial role in the creation and use of innovations is played by enterprises of the manufacturing and transport sector; construction and trade enterprises are more oriented towards the dissemination of new technology and technological solutions rather than creation of them; the composition of main parameters determining the dynamics of small business includes: the number of small enterprises per 1,000 population, the staff number per 1,000 population, turnovers (revenue) of small enterprises per 1,000 population. Reduction of absolute indicator values to specific values (per 1,000 population) is determined by the need to reduce the influence of size of Russian regions on calculation results.

The clustering method, proposed by a number of foreign scientists (Hartigan & Wong, 1979; Oldenderfer & Blashfield, 1989) was used to assess the state of small business in regions by the above parameters.

We have used clustering to identify the regions which differentiate in terms of a set of parameters of small business development presented in Fig. 1. Data for the analysis have been obtained from official statistical books (Russian Statistical Yearbook, 2013, 2014; Small and medium entrepreneurship in Russia, 2015, 2016). In order to bring the indicators to a comparable form, their standardized values were calculated and used as the basis for the comparison of parameters of small business development throughout the country.

The level of innovative development (innovativeness) of regions is specified based on the data from the studies of the Higher School of Economics (Abdrakhmanova et al., 2017). Only the most general data were accepted for the analysis—the affiliation of the regions with one of the groups, in proportion to a decrease in the level of innovativeness; Group I, Group II, Group III, Group IV.

Due to the limited amount of material presented in the paper, the levels of small business development were only compared in most general

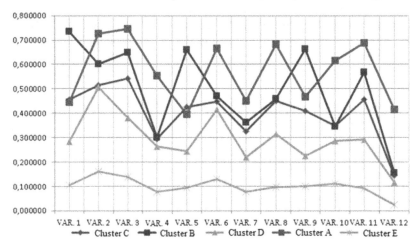

Fig. 1 Clusters of small business development in Russian regions in 2013–2016 (*Source* Calculated and compiled by the authors according to the data from: Russian Statistical Yearbook [2013, 2014] http://www.gks.ru/wps/wcm/connect/rosstat_main/rosstat/ru/statistics/publications/catalog/doc_1135087342078; Small and medium entrepreneurship in Russia [2015, 2016] http://www.gks.ru/wps/wcm/connect/rosstat_main/rosstat/ru/statistics/publications/catalog/doc_1139841601359)

128 Y. I. TRESHCHEVSKY ET AL.

terms, without detailing the features of each Cluster and Group of innovativeness.

3 RESULTS

As follows from the analysis, five groups of regions (Clusters) differing in terms of levels of small business development (Fig. 1) have been identified in Russia with a high level of confidence.

Cluster "A" contains 12 regions,[1] including two regions of Group 1 in the rating, five regions of Group 2; three regions of Group 3; and one region of Group 4. As we can see, the results of the rating and the cluster analysis are generally close (the representatives of the top-rated groups dominate in the Cluster). The Cluster is distinguished by the highest level of small business development. As for the indicator "Number of small enterprises" in construction, trade and transport, Cluster "A" is far ahead of other clusters. The relevant indicators are presented in Fig. 1. At the same time, the manufacturing sector is characterized by the weak position for this indicator.

The values of the indicator "Average staff number" are also higher than in other clusters in construction, trade, transport and communications. In the manufacturing sector, the values of this indicator are much lower than in other clusters.

The maximum value of the indicator "Turnovers (revenue) of small enterprises" has been recorded in the trade sector, which, in turn, corresponds to the maximum value of the indicator in terms of the number of small enterprises in this field with a fairly low value of average staff number compared to construction and transport.

The minimum indicator of turnovers of small enterprises corresponds to the transport and communications sector, although the indicator which describes the average staff number in this field is at its maximum.

Thus, Cluster "A" has combined the regions in which the construction and trade sectors of small business expansion are most developed.

---

[1] The regional composition of Cluster "A" (affiliation with the innovative development group is specified in-between parenthesis [Abdrakhmanova et al., 2017]): Belgorod Region (II), Voronezh Region (II), Kaliningrad Region (IV), Magadan Region (III), Novosibirsk Region (I), Samara Region (II), Sakhalin Region (III), Smolensk Region (III), Tyumen Region (II), Primorsky Krai (III) and Khabarovsk Krai (II), Republic of Tatarstan (I).

SMALL BUSINESS AND INNOVATION PROCESSES IN RUSSIAN ... 129

The regions of this group are substantially differentiated according to the rating of innovative development. Group 1 consists of only two regions, Group 2, which is fairly advanced in terms of innovation, is represented by five regions, and Group 4, being an outsider, is represented by one region only. In general, we can state that the regions of this group are characterized by the above-average level of innovative development, while the level of innovativeness in these regions is fairly high.

Cluster "B" also contains 12 regions,[2] including two regions of Group 1, one region of Group 2, eight regions of Group 3, and one region of Group 4. The distinctive feature of this Cluster is the high level of small business development in the manufacturing sector. Traditionally, the enterprises of this sector have been considered to have high design and engineering as well as innovative capacity. However, only three regions out of 12 regions are included in Group 1 and Group 2 in terms of the level of innovative development. One region is an outsider. Most regions are concentrated in the middle group—Group 3. Thus, the version about the substantial impact of small business, concentrated in the manufacturing sector, on innovativeness of regions, is not confirmed.

Cluster "B" occupies the medium position in terms of the level of small business development, falling behind Cluster "B" in the manufacturing sector the most. This Cluster consists of 25 regions,[3] mainly belonging to rating groups II and III. As we can see, Cluster "C" is average in terms of small business and innovative development. Nine regions are on the list of leading regions in terms of innovative development, while one region is on the list of outsiders. In other words, low level of small business development in general, and in the manufacturing sector in particular, did not lead to apparent lag in the field of innovative development.

---

[2] The regional composition of Cluster "B": Vladimir Region (III), Ivanovo Region (III), Kaluga Region (I), Kirov Region (III), Kostroma Region (IV), Nizhny Novgorod Region (I), Ryazan Region (III), Sverdlovsk Region (II), Tula Region (III), Yaroslavl Region (III), Kamchatka Krai (III), Mari El Republic (III).

[3] The regional composition of Cluster "C": Arkhangelsk Region (III), Bryansk Region (III), Vologda Region (III), Irkutsk Region (III), Leningrad Region (III), Lipetsk Region (II), Moscow Region (II), Murmansk Region (III), Novgorod Region (III), Omsk Region (III), Oryol Region (III), Penza Region (II), Pskov Region (IV), Rostov Region (III), Tver Region (III), Tomsk Region (I), Ulyanovsk Region (II), Chelyabinsk Region (II), Altai Krai (III), Krasnodar Krai (III), Krasnoyarsk Krai (I), Perm Krai (II), Republic of Karelia (III), Chuvash Republic (I), Udmurt Republic (III).

Cluster "D" contains 19 regions,[4] which generally include representatives of the rating group III.

The indicators of all analyzable parameters of small business development in Cluster "D" are quite low. The rating of innovative development in most regions is Level 3; four regions are part of the group of outsiders. Only four out of nineteen regions are part of the top-ranking groups. Thus, it may be concluded that a significant lag of regions in terms of small business expansion is usually accompanied by a low level of innovative development.

Cluster "E" contains 10 regions[5] falling almost entirely within rating group IV. This Cluster is characterized by extremely low values of small business development; in addition, the regions within it lag behind in terms of innovative development—nine out of ten constituent entities of the Russian Federation are included with Group 4.

4 Conclusion

The analysis has shown that Russian regions are significantly differentiated in terms of the level of small business development. In general, the regions are statistically significantly divided into five groups. The most advanced Cluster "A" with a relatively high level of small business development in construction and trade has quite a pronounced specialization. Despite the dominance of small business in "non-technological" sectors, the overall level of innovativeness of regions in Cluster "A" is high. At the same time, in one of the potentially most technology-intensive sectors—manufacturing sector, the expansion of small business is insufficient, which hinders its innovative development.

---

[4] The regional composition of Cluster "D": Amur Region (IV), Astrakhan Region (III), Volgograd Region (III), Kemerovsk Region (III), Kurgan Region (III), Kursk Region (III), Orenburg Region (III), Saratov Region (III), Tambov Region (II), Jewish Autonomous Region (IV); Stavropol Territory (II); Republic of Adygea (III), Republic of Altai (III), Republic of Bashkortostan (I), Republic of Komi (III), Republic of Mordovia (1), Republic of Yakutia (III), Republic of Khakassia (IV), Chukotka Autonomous Region (IV).

[5] The regional composition of Cluster "E": Zabaykalsky Krai (IV); Buryat Republic (III), Republic of Dagestan (IV), Republic of Ingushetia (IV), Republic of Kalmykia (IV), Republic of North Ossetia-Alania (IV), Republic of Tyva (IV); Kabardino-Balkar Republic (IV), Karachai-Circassian Republic (IV), Chechen Republic (IV).

Cluster "B" is slightly inferior to Cluster "A" in terms of the overall level of small business development, but leads in terms of its presence in the manufacturing sector. The level of innovative development is generally average. In other words, the manufacturing sector does not play the role of a driver of innovative development and involvement of sectors related to it—transport, construction, and trade—in small business. Just as Cluster "A", it is characterized by the fragmentary nature of small business development.

Cluster "C", which is average in terms of small business development, is also average in terms of the rating of innovative development. That is, the industry specialization of small business is not related to the level of innovativeness of regions in large systems with average level of development.

In general, we can observe a strong differentiation of regions by ratings of innovativeness across all three clusters with high and average levels of small business development.

Clusters "D" and especially "E" are characterized by a fairly low level of small business development. The innovation ratings of regions within them are equally low. It is fair to assume that both phenomena reflect the low level of socioeconomic activity of economic entities in these regions.

In general, one can claim with certainty that there are relationships between the levels of small business development and innovativeness of Russian regions. However, they can only be observed at the qualitative level. Quantitative relationships have not yet been conclusively established. In further theoretical research, attention should be paid to structural features of small business: industry-specific and sectoral features, involvement in activities of higher education institutions, research and development organizations, as well as large corporate entities.

On the practical level, it is necessary to differentiate the tools to support small business according to the involvement of enterprises in innovative development of regions and strategically important sectors of economy.

REFERENCES

Abdrakhmanova, G. I., et al. (2017). *Rating of innovative development of the constituent entities of the Russian Federation* (Issue 5, 260 pp.). Higher School of Economics, National Research University.

Altufyeva, N. V. (2019.) Strategic priorities for development of small and medium research and development enterprises in the Republic of Bashkortostan. *Regionalnaya Ekonomika. Yug Rossii, 7*(2), 60–66. https://doi.org/10.15688/re.volsu.2019.2.6.

Endovitsky, D. A., et al. (2017). Analysis of the economic optimism of the institutional groups and socio-economic systems. *Journal of Advanced Research in Law and Economics, VII*(6) (28), 1745–1752. https://doi.org/10.14505/jarle.

Hartigan, I. A., & Wong, M. A. (1979). Algoritm AS 136: A K-means clustering algorithm. *Journal of the Royal Statistical Society Series C, 28*(1), 100–108.

Kosobutskaya, A. Yu., et al. (2020). Advantages and opportunities for the development of small business E-commerce in the B2B sector. In *Digital economy: Complexity and variety vs. rationality* (Vol. 87, pp. 524–531). Springer Nature Switzerland AG.

Oldenderfer, M., & Blashfield, R. (1989). *Cluster analysis. Factorial, discriminated and cluster analysis* (215 pp.). Finansy i Statistika.

Orynbasarova, S. E., & Baimurzina, D. B. (2013). Innovations and small business strategy in the Republic of Kazakhstan. *Upravlenie Innovatsiyami: Teoriya, Metodologiya, Praktika* (5), 55–61.

Risin, I. E., et al. (2017). Public authorities and business on the possibilities of region's development. In *Overcoming uncertainty of institutional environment as a tool of global crisis management*. Contributions to Economics (pp. 55–62). Springer. https://doi.org/10.1007/978-3-319-60696-5_8.

Russian Statistical Yearbook. (2013, 2014). http://www.gks.ru/wps/wcm/connect/rosstat_main/rosstat/ru/statistics/publications/catalog/doc_113508 7342078.

Sanzheeva, D. D. (2015). Innovations in small business: Challenges and prospects. *Bulletin of Buryat State University* (2-2), 128–132.

Sazhin, Y. B. (2015). Relevance of innovations in small and medium business management practices. *Innovatsii v Menedzhmente* (4), 52–59.

Shnaider, O. V., & Lapaev, P. Y. (2013). On the relationship between innovations and small business at the current stage of development of economic relations. *Azimut Nauchnykh Issledovaniy: Ekonomika i Upravlenie* (4), 44–46.

Small and medium entrepreneurship in Russia. (2015, 2016). http://www.gks.ru/wps/wcm/connect/rosstat_main/rosstat/ru/statistics/publications/catalog/doc_1139841601359.

Treshchevsky, Y. I., et al. (2018). The system of state support for small and medium entrepreneurship and evaluation of its effectiveness. *Revista ESPACIOS, 39*(12), 12.

Treshchevsky, Y. I., et al. (2019). *Small business risks—Entrepreneurs' assessments* (Vol. 110). 5th International Conference on Economics, Management, Law and Education (EMLE 2019), Krasnodar, Russia. Atlantis Press. https://doi.org/10.2991/aebmr.k.191225.005.

State Support and Legal Basis
for the Functioning of Social Entrepreneurship

Current Issues of State Support for Small and Medium-Sized Businesses in the Context of the COVID-19 Pandemic

Zhanna A. Zakharova, Pavel N. Zakharov, and Vitaly V. Kislinsky

1 Introduction

2020 will go down in modern history under the sign of unprecedented restrictive and preventive measures in all countries of the world. Of course, quarantine measures have a huge negative impact on both the population and business structures. At the same time, it should be emphasized that there are significant prospects for a number of industries and economic activities (food industry, IT, production of personal protective equipment, etc.), but for most enterprises (tourism, restaurant business, consumer services, passenger transportation, etc.), the pandemic has brought huge economic losses and losses. Of course, the most vulnerable segment of the market economy in this case were small and medium-sized businesses.

Z. A. Zakharova (✉) · V. V. Kislinsky
Vladimir Branch of Russian Presidential Academy of National Economy and Public Administration, Vladimir, Russia

P. N. Zakharov
Vladimir State University, Vladimir, Russia

© The Author(s), under exclusive license to Springer Nature Switzerland AG 2021
E. G. Popkova and B. S. Sergi (eds.), *Economic Issues of Social Entrepreneurship*,
https://doi.org/10.1007/978-3-030-77291-8_13

137

In this regard, government measures to support both the population and business structures are being implemented in all countries of the world. At the same time, it should be noted that financial support of the population can be considered as an indirect measure of business support (maintaining effective demand in the market).

Based on the results of the review of the world's best practices, conclusions and proposals were formulated that are applicable for state support of small and medium-sized businesses in Russia in the context of the crisis situation.

2   Materials and Methods

Research made by Gachegov (2018), E. A. Mazilov and A. E. Kremin (2018), A. V. Vilensky et al. (2018), E. M. Bukhvald (2019a, b, 2020) shows the important role of small and medium-sized businesses in ensuring positive dynamics of socio-economic development of the national economy.

However, it is necessary to take into account the potential instability of small and medium-sized businesses, especially during economic crises.

In this regard, the authors summarized the experience of countries with developed market economies in terms of state support for small and medium-sized businesses during the pandemic, as well as the experience of Russia.

3   Results

As evidenced by foreign experience, small business plays a huge role in providing employment or rather self-employment of the population. Thus, in the United States, one small business accounts for 1 in every 12 people of the population, in Japan for every 18 people, and in Russia for every 60 people of the country's population. According to the Federal state statistics service, the share of the employed population in small businesses in 2018 in the whole country was 20%. When as in foreign countries, this figure varies: in Germany, France, Italy—65–80%; in the United States—60%; in Japan—80–88% (Gachegov, 2018).

In addition, the development of small, medium and individual entrepreneurship plays a significant role in the socio-economic development of the country and regions. Thus, in the studies of E. A. Mazilov and A. E. Kremin (2018), A. V. Vilensky et al. (2018) proves that

CURRENT ISSUES OF STATE SUPPORT FOR SMALL AND MEDIUM-SIZED ...   139

the development of small and medium-sized businesses creates prerequisites for: diversification of the structure of the economy, efficient use of available resources, increasing the degree of satisfaction of local market demand, involvement in the production of material and financial savings of the population, introduction and dissemination of innovative technologies (Mukoseev, 2012), etc.

The Decree of the President of the Russian Federation dated May 7, 2018 No 204 "On national goals and strategic objectives for the development of the Russian Federation for the period up to 2024" pays attention to the development of small and medium-sized businesses, as evidenced by the presence of a section on the creation of a priority national project "Small and medium-sized businesses and support for individual entrepreneurship".

The need for its development is caused by the fact that to date, unlike in foreign countries, the development of small business in Russia has not solved the problem of ensuring employment. In this regard, the main criterion of this project, the increase in the number of employed in small and medium enterprises (SMEs), including individual entrepreneurs, to 25 million. There is no doubt that this is a significant indicator, especially given that the number of people employed in the field of small and medium-sized businesses has decreased significantly over the past ten years (Vilensky et al., 2018).

At the same time, before the implementation of the National project "Small and medium-sized businesses and support for individual entrepreneurship", the main indicator of the development of small and medium-sized businesses was officially considered to be an increase in the number of SMEs and individual entrepreneurs. However, the growth rate of this indicator varied greatly across different regions. For example, over the period from 2008 to 2016, the number of small businesses (including microenterprises) in the Ural Federal district increased by 274.8%, especially in the Sverdlovsk region—by 275.5%, as well as in the Republic of Tatarstan—273.9%, and in the Central Federal district (CFD) in regions such as the Ivanovo and Kostroma regions by only 35.2%.

At the same time, since 2016, there has been a decrease in the number of small businesses in the Russian Federation as a whole and in almost all regions of the Russian Federation. And the number of people employed in the small business sector has especially decreased according to data for 2019, although the National project has been implemented for a year and this indicator should grow, not decrease (Table 1).

140 Z. A. ZAKHAROVA ET AL.

Table 1 Main indicators of activity of small and medium-sized businesses for the period from 2016 to 2018 in the Russian Federation

Indicator	2016	2017	2018	2019
Number of small businesses, including micro (units)	2,770,562	2,754,577	2,659,943	–
Number of employees in the field of small business (people)	11,040,056	11,986,265	11,819,790	10,371,772
Investments in fixed assets of small enterprises (thousand rubles)	801,623,255.15	998,497,452	1,057,403,576.6	–
Turnover of enterprises (thousand rubles)	38,877,026,922	48,459,178,116	53,314,226,876.6	52,963,904,465
Number of medium-sized enterprises (units)	13,230	13,309	13,682	–
Number of employees in medium-sized enterprises (people)	15,445,630	1,567,300	1,535,400	–

Thus, according to Table 1, the number of small businesses, including microenterprises, decreased by 4% between 2016 and 2018. The number of people employed in the small business sector increased by 7% during the study period, but in 2018 and 2019, compared to 2017, there is a decrease in this indicator. At the same time, in 2017, the number of employees at small enterprises managed to exceed the pre-crisis indicator of 2008 (11,412, thousand people). In 2019, compared to 2018, the number of employed people decreased significantly by almost 1.5 million people, or 12.25%. At the same time, with a decrease in the number of small businesses and a decrease in the number of self-employed, turnover

CURRENT ISSUES OF STATE SUPPORT FOR SMALL AND MEDIUM-SIZED ... 141

Table 2 Key performance indicators of individual entrepreneurs for the period from 2016 to 2018 in the Russian Federation

Indicator	2016	2017	2018
Number of individual entrepreneurs (units)	2,792,013	2,568,829	2,630,816
Number of employees in the field of individual entrepreneurship (people)	4,984,000	5,811,552	5,976,700
Revenue of individual entrepreneurs (billion rubles)	7,894.0	14,102.5	15,003.8

and investment in fixed assets in this sector of the economy increased. The number of medium-sized enterprises in the period from 2016 to 2018 increased by 452 units, but with a decrease in the number of employees in medium-sized enterprises, which is also a mixed trend.

An ambiguous picture has emerged in the development of individual entrepreneurship. The main performance indicators of individual entrepreneurs are presented in Table 2.

Thus, according to Table 2 for the period from 2016 to 2018, the number of individual entrepreneurs decreased, but at the same time, the number of employed in the field of individual entrepreneurship increased from 4984.0 to 5976.7 thousand people and the increase in revenue from sales of products (goods, works and services) almost doubled. However, the increase in the number of people employed in the field of individual entrepreneurship was also uneven across regions. The main growth is observed in the Sverdlovsk region. And, for example, in a region such as the city of Moscow, we should note a decrease in this indicator for the period under review.

But, despite some positive trends in the development of this sector and the significant role of small and medium enterprises in the socio-economic development of regions, small and medium business is faced with a significant circle of problems, which most researchers refer (Zakharova & Kislinsky, 2019):

- high level of uncertainty caused by the existing state economic policy (increasing taxes, fees, mandatory introduction of online products that require additional costs, etc.);
- insufficient development in many regions of Russia of large capital that provides orders for small businesses;

- there are no coordinating centers in the regions that provide small businesses with information about the types of economic activities that are in demand by the population of this territory or other regions;
- low availability of credit financing;
- etc.

In addition, one of the significant problems in the development of small business is a decrease in the motivation of economic entities in the implementation of any economic activity, which modern researchers associate with a lack of high-quality institutional environment for ensuring entrepreneurial activity, the lack of adequate dialogue between the government and business (Vilensky et al., 2018).

Separate problems of small and medium enterprises trying to solve the government of the Russian Federation in the framework of the national project "Small and medium entrepreneurship and support individual entrepreneurial initiatives," according to which support for this sector is supposed to allocate 481.5 billion rubles, of which: Federal budget funds—416.2 billion (86.4%); funds of subjects of the Russian Federation—11.4 billion rubles.

The term of implementation of the national project: from October, 2018 to 2024 (inclusive).

The national project targets by year of implementation are presented in Table 3.

Table 3 National project targets

Target indicator	Base value	Year					
		2019	2020	2021	2022	2023	2024
1. Number of people employed in the SME sector, including sole proprietors (millions)	19.2	19.6	20.5	21.6	22.9	24.0	25.0
2. Share of SMEs in GDP (%)	22.3	22.9	23.5	25.0	27.5	30.0	32.5
3. Share of exports of SMEs, including sole proprietors, in total non-commodity exports (%)	8.6	8.8	9.0	9.25	9.5	9.75	10.0

CURRENT ISSUES OF STATE SUPPORT FOR SMALL AND MEDIUM-SIZED ... 143

According to the national project implementation plan, by the end of 2024, the number of employed SMEs should increase to 25 million people (the average annual growth rate is planned to be 4.5%), and the share of SMEs in GDP should increase to 32.5% (the average annual growth rate is 6.5%). In addition, an ambitious goal has been set to increase SME exports to 10% of the total volume of the non-commodity sector (an average annual growth rate of 2.5%).

However, these plans will be difficult to achieve in the context of the outbreak of the coronovirus pandemic in the country, which has increased the already high degree of uncertainty in the market environment, causing significant damage to the economy of services, including intellectual and impression economy, reducing the business activity of small and medium-sized businesses, based on the state ban on doing business in many types of economic activities (hairdressing, leisure, household, etc. services), creating problems for agricultural workers, self-employed and migrant workers, who transfer a significant part of their wages to poor regions of the world (Kuzminov, 2020).

In this regard, the governments of many market economies behave like socialists, supporting the level of income of citizens, developing programs to support small and medium-sized businesses, etc.

Thus, according to Table 4, the level of support for people and businesses in market economy countries accounts for a significant share of GDP in their countries. For example, in The Netherlands, the level of support is about 40% of the country's GDP, while in Russia this figure

Table 4 Comparison of the volume of state support to the economy

Indicator	USA	Germany	France	The Netherlands	UK	Russia
Total support (\$ billion)	2,000	810	372.6	378	423.5	...
Volume of business support (\$ billion)	850	540	118.8	378	399.3	20
GDP (\$ billion)	21,349	3,964	2,762	955	2,829	1,610
The total amount of support (% of GDP)	9.37	20.43	13.49	39.58	14.97	...
The volume of business support (% of GDP)	3.98	13.62	4.30	39.58	14.11	1.24

was 1.24%, which is very insignificant compared to the world's leading economies.

At the same time, foreign countries apply a wide variety of measures to support small and medium-sized businesses and self-employed people.

So one of the support measures is to provide the amount of monthly and weekly allowances (USA) either for a small business unit (France, The Netherlands), or for one employed business employee whose activities had to be suspended during the pandemic (UK, USA, Russia). The main period for providing this type of support in Europe is three months, with a possible extension in the US of 39 weeks, that is, until the end of 2020. In Russia, this type of support is designed for 2 months. The amount of support also varies significantly, so if in the UK the total amount for three months for each employee of the affected business is 7.5 thousand pounds, in Russia for 2 months it is 271, 4 pounds.

A very interesting measure of support is the establishment of one-time grants and one-time payments for small businesses, either depending on the number of employees employed (Germany), or depending on the type of economic activity (UK). For example, in the UK, one-time support for retail, hotel and tourism businesses is 25 thousand pounds (2,250 thousand rubles) and farms from 3 to 10 thousand pounds (270–900 thousand rubles). In our country, lump-sum payments are not provided for the most affected economic activities in the context of the pandemic.

The next measure of business support envisaged in the context of the pandemic is tax exemption. There are differences in the types of taxes that businesses are exempt from paying, in the terms for which taxpayers are exempt from paying taxes, and in the types of economic activities that are given this measure of support. For example, in the United States, small businesses are granted tax exemption for 3 months, and for payroll tax—until 2021. In the UK, in addition to the three-month VAT exemption, retail, hotel and tourism businesses are granted an exemption for income tax and property value tax until 2021. In Russia, there is an exemption from paying taxes for the second quarter, that is, only for three months and only for the types of economic activities, according to the Government of the country, most affected by the pandemic.

And another measure of support that should be given attention is business lending programs that provide: either interest-free loans for short-term businesses that have been temporarily stopped (UK); or lending to businesses at a reduced rate to ensure uninterrupted payment of wages (USA, Russia); or loans to small businesses through the mechanism of state guarantees (Germany, France, The Netherlands). In some countries, loans already held by small and medium-sized businesses are deferred for six months (The Netherlands).

In addition to the above-mentioned support measures, market economy countries also use the exemption of businesses and the population from paying utility bills, rent, etc. for three months.

As the analysis of measures of state support for business in the context of the pandemic in market economies and in Russia has shown, in the latter they are much weaker and not sufficiently diverse. In addition, the level of support is often calculated based on the minimum wage.

However, setting a reduced credit rate and payments per employee in the small and medium-sized business segment in the amount of the minimum wage is not enough to maintain effective demand in the context of a pandemic. Thus, in most countries of the world, the minimum wage is set according to the recommendations of the ILO at least 50% of the average wage, and in the European Union—at least 60%. According to the Federal state statistics service in our country, the average monthly salary of employees at the beginning of 2020 was 47,257 rubles. If we follow the ILO methodology, we need to raise the minimum wage to 23,500 rubles, and accordingly, the amount of state support for maintaining wages in the small and medium-sized business sector should be set based on this amount.

A. G. Aganbegyan suggests that the minimum wage increase should be financed from the accumulated funds of private enterprises and joint-stock companies. So, in 2018, their net financial result (profit after loss) increased by 46.6%, in 2019-by another 17.5%, and only by 72%. At the same time, they increased their salaries by only 20%, and their investments by even less. The decrease in investment volume and not a significant increase in wages due to profit once again confirms the thesis that in the conditions of a liberal model of economy, business prefers short-term profit planning to long-term, and it is not socially oriented. At present, joint-stock companies and large private enterprises have accumulated a significant amount on the accounts of domestic banks-about 40 trillion rubles, and they have sent a lot of funds to offshore and foreign accounts, where they still have hundreds of billions of dollars. And raising the minimum wage would cost them just 5 trillion rubles (Aganbegyan, 2020).

Thus, the practice of state regulation of market economy development, especially in crisis situations, indicates the inapplicability of the liberal model, especially in relation to small and medium-sized businesses, which are inherently potentially unstable. Given the high role of small and medium enterprises in the national economy development and ensuring high levels of socio-economic welfare global trend is the widespread use of government methods direct support to small and medium businesses.

4 Conclusion

Taking into account the generalization of the experience of the most developed countries of the world, Russia needs to significantly expand state support measures for small and medium-sized businesses that find themselves in a difficult situation as a result of the COVID-19 pandemic. It is also necessary to provide one-time grants, increase the period and amount of monthly support for each employee of the affected business (non-food trade, hotels and restaurants, tourist business), reduce taxes (for example, personal income tax) and increase the period of tax exemption, especially for businesses whose activities have been suspended.

Undoubtedly, it is necessary to increase the amount of state support for maintaining wages in the small and medium-sized business sector, which is set based on half of the average monthly wage in the country's economy (23,500 rubles). In this case, if we consider the structure of employed in small and medium-sized businesses and individual entrepreneurs by type of economic activity, the share of businesses affected by the pandemic (non-food trade, construction, hotels and catering, travel agencies) will be 41.4%, or about 8 million people. Accordingly, about 5.6 trillion rubles should be allocated only for this measure of support, taking into account its increase to 3 months.

The source of funding for the above measures can be the redistribution of funding for the national project "Small and medium-sized businesses and support for individual business initiatives", as well as the creation of favorable conditions for the involvement in economic turnover of Bank deposits accumulated by legal entities (Table 5).

Table 5 Comparison of measures of state support for business in the context of a pandemic in market economies and in Russia

Indicator	USA	Germany	France	The Netherlands	UK	Russia
Amounts of monthly and weekly allowances	Unemployment benefit for up to 39 weeks until 2021, if the employee was left ill due to the pandemic ($1,200 per week)	-	Monthly allowances for small businesses and the self-employed, calculated for 3 months with a possible extension from 1 thousand euros to 3.5 thousand euros	From 1.5 thousand euros in the first month, up to 3.5 thousand euros for the next 3 months, and 4.0 thousand euros each for 3 months for the most affected companies (catering and tourism sector	Monthly benefits calculated for 3 months for employees of enterprises whose activities had to be stopped, for each employee 2.5 thousand pounds	Monthly allowance calculated for 2 months (April and May) for employees of the enterprise whose activities were suspended and the most affected, for each employee 12.1 thousand rubles
One-time grants, one-time payments for businesses	…	When applying for emergency assistance to a company with a staff of up to five people, up to 9 thousand euros, and up to ten people—up to 15 thousand euros	…	…	25 thousand pounds for retail, hotel and tourism businesses, from 3 to 10 thousand pounds—farms	-

(continued)

Table 5 (continued)

Indicator	USA	Germany	France	The Netherlands	UK	Russia
Deferred tax payments for businesses	Three-month tax deferral for small businesses Deferred payroll tax until 2021	Three-month tax deferral	Three-month deferred tax (corporate income tax, payroll tax and social contributions)	Three-month deferred payment of taxes (income tax, corporate tax, VAT refund and payroll tax)	A three-month delay for VAT payment and deferral of payment of income tax until 2021 Exemption from property value tax until 2021 for retail, hotel and tourism businesses	Deferred tax for small and medium-sized businesses for the second quarter of 2020
Business lending programs	Non-refundable loans to businesses that employ up to 500 people up to $10 million for uninterrupted payment of the wage "Coronavirus" loans at low rates—3.75% for small businesses and 2.75% for non-commercial organization. The loan repayment period will be up to 30 years	Lending to businesses by the state development Bank KfW, through the program of state guarantees (covering up to 90% of the loss)	Loans to small businesses through the state guarantee program (300 billion euro)	Lending to small and medium-sized businesses through the GO and BMKB programs with state guarantees Reducing the interest rate to 2% A six-month deferment of loan repayment	Interest-free loan up to 1 year	Lending to businesses at 2% per annum for uninterrupted payment of wage

CURRENT ISSUES OF STATE SUPPORT FOR SMALL AND MEDIUM-SIZED ...   149

REFERENCES

Aganbegyan, A. G. (2020). *Fighting coronovirus without destroying the economy* [Electronic resource]. https://www.ranepa.ru/sobytiya/novosti/akademik-aganbegyan-otsenil-ekonomicheskuyu-situatsiyu-rossii-v-krizise/ (accessed 22 April 2020).

Bukhvald E. M. (2019a). New project on small business: The problem of federal-regional interactions. *Audit and Financial Analysis* (5), 170–175.

Bukhvald, E. M. (2019b). The vicious duality of state support for small business. *World of Change* (2), 51–68.

Bukhvald E. M. (2020). Small business in Russia: What to expect in the near future? *Bulletin of the Vladimir State University Named After Alexander Grigoryevich and Nikolay Grigoryevich Stoletov. Series: Economic Sciences* (1) (23), 114–128.

Gachegov, M. A. (2018). Small and medium-sized businesses in Russia in 2017: The state of the sector, the system of state support. *Russian Entrepreneurship,* *19*(12), 3891.

Kuzminov, Ya. (2020). *The rich will remain rich, the poor will remain poor* [Electronic resource]. http://kapital-rus.ru/articles/article/bogatye_osta nutsya_bogatymi_bednye__bednymi_radi_chego_my_stradaem_rasskaza/ (accessed 22 April 2020).

Mazilov, F. A., & Kremin, A. E. (2018). The role of small business in the socio-economic development of Russian regions: Problems and trends. *Problems of Territory Development* (2) (94), 7–18.

Mukoseev, D. V. (2012). Economic essence and criteria for determining small business. *Modern Scientific Research and Innovation* (5), 22–32.

Vilensky, A. V., Domnina I. N., & Maevskaya L. I. (2018). *Impact of small entrepreneurship on the socio-economic development of regions of the Russian Federation* (scientific paper). Institute of Economics, RAS.

Zakharova, Zh. A., & Kislinsky V. V. (2019). Actual problems of small business development in the regions of the center of Russia. *Regional Economy and Management: Electronic Scientific Journal* (3) (69), 22.

Mechanisms of Financial Support for the Development of Innovative Entrepreneurship in the Digital Economy

Natalia G. Varaksa, *Maria S. Alimova*,
Sergey A. Alimov, *Elena S. Rozhdestvenskaia*,
and Victor A. Konstantinov

1 INTRODUCTION

Today, in the conditions of an unstable socio-economic situation in the country and on the world stage, risks of the functioning of the financial system of the Russian Federation are increasing, so is the pressure of external challenges on the totality of budgetary instruments of the state and regions. Issues of innovative development and digitalization of the economy come to the fore, which should affect all levels of the hierarchy of entrepreneurial activities: from consumers of innovative products to the largest innovative enterprises.

In 2019, the rating of Russia in the Global Innovation Index has not changed compared to 2018, our country ranks 46th among the countries of the world and lags behind the leading countries in the main indicators of the effectiveness of innovation activity (Global Innovation Index, 2019).

N. G. Varaksa (✉) · M. S. Alimova · S. A. Alimov · E. S. Rozhdestvenskaia ·
V. A. Konstantinov
Orel State University, Orel, Russia

© The Author(s), under exclusive license to Springer Nature   151
Switzerland AG 2021
E. G. Popkova and B. S. Sergi (eds.), *Economic Issues of Social Entrepreneurship*,
https://doi.org/10.1007/978-3-030-77291-8_14

In these conditions, special attention should be paid to increasing the innovative activity of business entities and the development of their innovative potential through the use of effective financial support mechanisms at all stages of the creation and implementation of an innovative product.

2 Materials and Method

Methodological tools for studying the mechanisms of financial support for innovative entrepreneurship include economic and statistical methods of analysis, comparison, analogy, graphical interpretation tools, as well as a systematic approach.

Considering the theoretical basis of the study, we note that many domestic and foreign scientists raise the issues of adaptation of innovative processes and the transformation of entrepreneurship to the digital economy, and evaluate the mechanisms of financial support for the innovation sector. Fang Zhao and Alan Collier (2016) emphasize the recognition of digital entrepreneurship as a new and growing field of research, which justifies the need to develop various financial support mechanisms to increase their effectiveness. A. Vdigitalization. Babkin and O. V. Chistyakova (2017), L. P. Dashkov and O. A. Repushevskaya (2019) and other scientists consider the of business entities as a tool for the growth of their innovative activity.

A. V. Zakharkina and O. A. Kuznetsova (2019) evaluate the existing tools for entrepreneurship development and conclude that, without taking into account regional characteristics, such tools lose their practical value.

S. G. Tyaglov and I. V. Takmasheva (2018) see the problems of low innovation activity in inter-territorial differences in the level of accessibility of digital and innovative technologies, in inter-regional gaps in the level of financing and in the inefficiency of government measures. I. V. Danilova et al. (2018), in the analysis of resources and results of innovative development highlight problems in the resource supply block of the innovation sector. V. V. Zabolotskaya (2015), A. Ya. Mortaza (2017) suggest transforming foreign models of financial support for innovative entrepreneurship to Russian reality, and S. A. Ilyina (2016) suggests improving tax tools to support innovative entrepreneurship.

Despite the available researches by scientists, the contribution of implemented support measures for the development of innovative entrepreneurship and activation of the innovation process is not adequately evaluated. For this reason this situation requires the development of new effective financial support mechanisms available for most business entities, covering all stages of the creation and commercialization of an innovative product.

3 Results

In world practice, various sources of financing and forms of financial support for innovative entrepreneurship are used (Fig. 1).

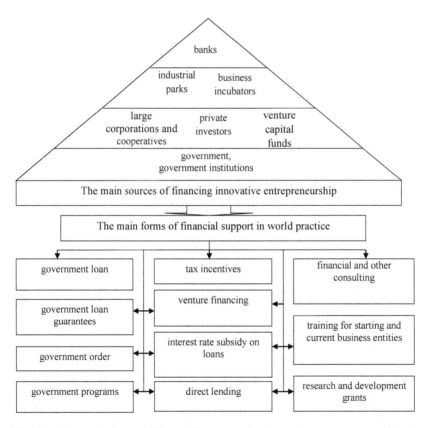

Fig. 1 The main forms of financial support for innovative entrepreneurship in world practice (*Source* Compiled by the authors)

Most of the identified forms of financial support for innovative entrepreneurship are actively implemented in Russia, however, a number of barriers arise that limit their availability and widespread use among business entities.

The main factors hindering the development of the innovative activity of business entities in Russia are insufficient financial support at all stages of the creation and implementation of an innovative product, low demand for innovations, high risks, and a lack of own sources of financing.

Investment of innovative entrepreneurship is the basic mechanism of financial support, which allows to remove a key barrier for the development of promising projects in the early stages, due to the lack of available funding.

For the purpose of assessing the significance of direct financing of innovative entrepreneurship by the federal, regional, and local budgets, we will analyze the cost structure of technological innovations by sources (Fig. 2).

Based on the data in Fig. 2, it can be concluded that today government support in the form of financing innovative entrepreneurship in the digital economy is insufficient, which is determined by the low share of budget funds in the costs of technological innovation. The total share of participation (federal, regional and local budgets) in the innovative costs of Russian enterprises in 2018 amounted to 30.35%, while a similar share

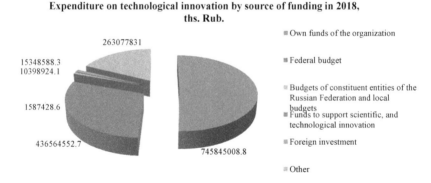

Fig. 2 Structural analysis of technological innovation costs by funding sources in 2018 as part of assessing the role of government financial support for innovative business (*Source* Compiled by the authors based on official statistical information. Science and Innovation section https://www.gks.ru/folder/14477)

of investments made at the expense of own funds amounted to 50.64%. In addition, according to the estimates of leading Russian and foreign scientist financiers, the share of government participation in the financial support of enterprises engaged in innovative activity in developed countries that have high positions in the ranking of innovative countries according to Bloomberg, such as the USA, Switzerland, Sweden, exceeds 40%.

In order to develop recommendations on improving measures of financial support for innovative entrepreneurship in the digital economy, it is necessary to analyze the current forms of its provision, stimulating the growth of production and commercialization of innovative products on the territory of the country (commercialization can be carried out outside the Russian Federation—export of innovations) (Fig. 3).

In order to increase the innovative activity of the business and accelerate the growth rate for creation and registration of new innovative companies of various sizes, it is necessary today to intensify the work of individual mechanisms for financial support of innovative entrepreneurship in the framework of achieving indicators of the digital economy. This requires the establishment of a balanced and sustainable development sector, as well as the necessary level of openness of the national innovation system and economy, as well as integration of Russia into the world processes of creation and use of innovative products and technologies created in all sectors of the national economy.

One of the important forms of direct financial support to entrepreneurship is direct subsidizing of expenses. However, the effectiveness of this measure is estimated below the average level due to its limited and difficult to obtain, as well as the uneven distribution among the subjects of the Russian Federation. For the most part, this type of support is concentrated in several regions. In this regard, we propose, when subsidizing, to take into account current and forecasted indicators of innovative potential, as well as industry and regional specifics, within the framework of priority directions for the government development.

We consider the provision of various tax benefits and preferences as one of the most effective and efficient mechanisms of indirect financial support in the digital economic conditions of innovative entrepreneurship.

However, the current tax advantages require a review of the effectiveness of stimulating innovation processes and should be differentiated for different business entities. Legislatively established tax incentives for

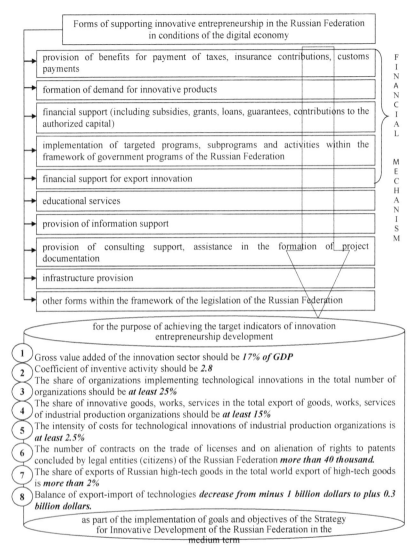

Fig. 3 Analysis of existing forms of support for innovative entrepreneurship in the Russian Federation (*Source* Compiled by the authors, taking into account the data of the Strategy for innovative development of the Russian Federation for the period until 2020. By the order of the Government of the Russian Federation of December 8, 2011 No. 2227-r https://ac.gov.ru/files/attachment/4843.pdf)

MECHANISMS OF FINANCIAL SUPPORT FOR THE DEVELOPMENT ... 157

the innovative development of specific territories, participants of innovation infrastructure, certain types of innovation activity or operations, the analysis of which indicates their limited application by different scale entities of innovative entrepreneurship, which requires an assessment of their effectiveness for the development of the innovation sector.

As part of the studies, the authors (Varaksa et al., 2020) revealed that at different stages of creating an innovative product, the main cost element in the structure of value added is wages and social payments. The share of the workers salary involved in scientific research in the enterprise sector in 2019 is 90.02%. The share of labor costs in the structure of domestic current costs (excluding depreciation) amounted to 42.07%. In order to stimulate innovation processes, we propose to amend Chapter 23 of the Tax Code of the Russian Federation and establish a lower rate for individuals with innovative income tax on the income of individuals with a share of employees engaged in various stages of innovation creation at least 90%. The proposed changes will reduce the absolute tax burden for business entities. The tax rate can be set at 10%, while the falling budget revenues will be compensated by the growth of indicators of innovative activity and obtaining not only economic but also social effects.

One of the promising measures of indirect financial support in terms of reducing tax costs is the tax rate reduction or complete removal from taxation of property tax for innovative enterprises that have expensive real estate on their balance sheets—laboratory buildings, research and development buildings, and their practical testing, innovative production, etc.

This financial support mechanism for innovative entrepreneurship can be implemented taking into account the provisions presented in Table 1.

Due to the fact that the property tax of organizations is regional taxes, we believe it is necessary to consider proposed changes in the regional tax policy.

4 Conclusions/Recommendations

Thus, the government as a key source of financing innovative activities and financial support for innovative entrepreneurship today applies various measures of direct and indirect impact, forms the infrastructure, implements special support programs. All these measures, on the one hand, can improve indicators of innovative activity, on the other parties—require a systematic analysis and assessment of the relevance and

Table 1 Implementation of the proposed mechanism for financial support of innovative entrepreneurship, optimization of tax costs

Implementation option	Conditions	Tax relief	Possible tax savings
Reducing rate on the property tax of organizations	The cost of real estate used for innovation is more than 150 million rubles or a share of the value of real estate used for innovation in a total value of more than 80%	Options for reducing the corporate property tax rate to: − 0.5%; − 1%; − 1.5%	If the tax rate is reduced to 0.5%, tax savings will amount to: 2,550,000 rubles (if the cost of real estate 150 million rubles)
Complete tax deduction of property	1. The share of personnel engaged in the production of innovative products and technologies in the total number of enterprises, more than 90% 2. The share of the value of real estate used for innovation in the total value of more than 80%	Withdrawal from the value of property tax for the value of real estate used for innovation or deduction of the value of property of organizations from the value of all property	In the case of taxation on property of organizations the value of immovable property used for innovation, and the savings will amount to RUB 2,640,000 (if the value of real estate 150 million rubles and 80% share). In the case of full tax deduction, the savings will amount to 3,300,000 rubles

Source Compiled by the authors

effectiveness of each implemented measure in relation to the innovation sphere and innovative entrepreneurship, which is the generator of innovations in the digital economy and technologies.

Functioning of innovative entrepreneurship should be accompanied not only by active financial support of federal and regional authorities but also by the formation of effective forms interaction and partnership of the government-science-business. And active promotion of the best regional practices in order to increase innovative activity.

The practical significance of proposed mechanisms for financial support of innovative entrepreneurship in the framework of direct subsidies and the provision of tax advantages on corporate property tax and personal income tax will increase their accessibility to businesses, reduce tax costs and the level of fiscal burden in order to maximize the socio-economic effect and faster development of innovative technologies.

REFERENCES

Babkin, A. V., & Chistyakova, O. V. (2017). The digital economy and its impact on the competitiveness of enterprise structures. *Russian Enterprise* (24), 4087–4102.

Danilova, I. V., Savelieva, I. P., & Kilina, I. P. (2018). Development of the region's innovative sector as the condition for formation of information economics in the economic space of the Russian Federation. *Bulletin of the South Ural State University. Ser. Economics and Management, 12*(2), 15–29. https://doi.org/10.14529/em180202 (in Russian).

Dashkov, L. P., & Repushevskaya, O. A. (2019). The impact of the digital transformation on entrepreneurship. *Bulletin of the Russian University of Cooperation* (4) (38), 40–45.

Global Innovation Index. (2019). https://www.globalinnovationindex.org/Home.

Ilyina, S. A. (2016). Tax incentives for innovative activities of small and medium enterprises in Russia. *Taxes and Taxation, 8*(146), 652–667. https://doi.org/10.7256/1812-8688.2016.9.20225.

Mortaza, A. Ya. (2017). The mechanisms of financial incentives and credit support of small business in the global economy. *MIR (Modernizatsiia. Innovatsii. Razvitie)/MIR (Modernization. Innovation. Research), 8*(1), 51–59. https://doi.org/10.18184/2079-4665.2017.8.1.51-59.

Official statistical information. Science and Innovation section. https://www.gks.ru/folder/14477.

Strategy of innovative development of the Russian Federation for the period until 2020, approved. By the order of the Government of the Russian Federation of December 8, 2011 No. 2227-p. https://ac.gov.ru/files/attachment/4843.pdf.

Tyaglov, S. G., & Takmasheva, I. V. (2018). An indicative assessment of the innovative potential of business entities in the digital economy. *Bulletin of the Rostov State Economic University (RINH)*, (4) (64), 123–135.

Varaksa, N. G., Alimov, S. A., Alimova, M. S., & Konstantinov, V. A. (2020). Structuring the added value of biomedicine products in the innovative economy. In E. Popkova & B. Sergi (Eds.), *The 21st century from the positions of modern science: Intellectual, digital and innovative aspects*. ISC 2019. Lecture Notes in Networks and Systems (Vol. 91, pp. 561–569). Springer. https://doi.org/10.1007/978-3-030-32015-7_63.

Zabolotskaya, V. V. (2015). Modern foreign models of financial support for innovative activities of small and medium enterprises. *Economics: Theory and Practice, 1*(37), 53–60.

Zakharkina, A. V., & Kuznetsova, O. A. (2019). Improving regional regulatory platform tools for the development of small and medium businesses. *Vestnik Omskogo universiteta. Seriya "Pravo"/Herald of Omsk University. Series "Law", 16*(4), 94–103. https://doi.org/10.24147/1990-5173.2019.16(4). 94-103 (in Russian).

Zhao, F., & Collier, A. (2016, September). *Digital entrepreneurship: Research and practice.* Conference: 9th Annual Conference of the EuroMed Academy of Business, Warsaw, Poland, pp. 2173–2182. https://www.researchgate.net/publication/309242001_Digital_Entrepreneurship_Research_and_Practice.

Corporate Legal Relations in the Digital Age: Current Challenges and Trends in Legal Regulation

Aleksandr A. Biryukov, *Nazima Shafievna Ibragimova*, *and Gennady V. Shevchenko*

1 Introduction

The twenty-first century, according to scientists, publicists, and politicians, has become the beginning of a new era—the era of high technologies, which is replacing the industrial way of the twentieth century, and high-tech developments in various sectors of economy and management are becoming the main vector of transformation of industrial society into a post-industrial one.

A significant role in the development of these processes is played by fundamentally new ways of creating, storing and transmitting information, which have received the generally accepted name of digital technologies, and the process of introducing such technologies into the daily life of modern society has become known as digitalization.

A. A. Biryukov (✉) · N. S. Ibragimova
North-Caucasus Federal University, Stavropol, Russia

G. V. Shevchenko
Stavropol Branch of the Russian Presidential Academy of National Economy and Public Administration, Stavropol, Russia

© The Author(s), under exclusive license to Springer Nature Switzerland AG 2021
E. G. Popkova and B. S. Sergi (eds.), *Economic Issues of Social Entrepreneurship*,
https://doi.org/10.1007/978-3-030-77291-8_15

161

According to Vaypan's (2017) fair observation: "… the development of digital platforms, technologies and the environment is likely to erode the traditional functioning of analog material-intensive markets and economic sectors and, in general, radically change the foundations of human life, which will entail significant changes in the legal regulation of economic relations".

Indeed, this process has also affected the legal sphere. Law as a regulator of public relations immediately responds to modern challenges, so we can observe the gradual emergence and justification in jurisprudence of such concepts as "information law", "Internet law", "cyber law", "digital law" and "digital rights", "digital jurisprudence" and, finally, "digitalization of law" (Khlebnikov, 2017; Smirnov et al., 2020; Vasilevich, 2019).

In the modern legal world, digitalization is not the main "trend" of financial or administrative law, although these industries are most adapted to the possibility of being regulated in a digital format. Today, digitalization is most affected by those industries: "… the effectiveness of which depends on the quality of information collection, storage and analysis: tax law, electoral law, information law, criminology, etc." (Saurin, 2019). In addition, the concepts of "digital justice" (digitalization of the judicial system), "digital notary", etc. have been actively discussed recently, and there are already some successes in this area.

In Russia, digitalization is gradually but slowly affecting private law. As part of the implementation of the priority national program related to the introduction of elements of the digital economy in Russia, it is planned to create a comprehensive legal regulation of relevant relations, including the introduction of civil turnover based on digital technologies.

Relatively recently, the Civil Code (Civil Code of the Russian Federation) has legally established digital rights as objects of civil rights, and creates regulatory conditions for regulating smart contracts and making transactions using electronic and technical means.

However, the analysis of the proposed concepts and legal innovations does not give a clear idea of how the regulation of corporate legal relations will continue to develop within the digital economy In this context, it should be borne in mind that corporate legal relations are a part of the market, including the global market, which is also subject to the rapid process of digital transformation, and this process began much earlier in the world than in Russia.

In the Strategy for the Development of the Information Society in the Russian Federation for 2017–2030, the federal project "Regulatory regulation of the digital environment" and other plans for information and technological modernization adopted in recent years, the term "corporation" is mentioned only in relation to state-owned companies and state corporations. These documents do not say anything clearly about how digitalization will affect corporate law, which subjects are organizations based on private capital, and what forecasts, goals and objectives there are on this issue.

According to experts, today "... the problem of developing the digital economy in the corporate business environment is not well developed not only in economics, but also in legal science" (Sitdikova & Starodumova, 2019). In this vein, scientists say that now the ground has been ripe for changes in legislation, taking into account the new legal relations that arise in connection with the creation of the so-called "digital ecosystems" (Gorodov & Egorova, 2018).

2   Materials and Method

In the process of studying the problems raised in this article, general scientific and private scientific methods of cognition were used, including: dialectical, analysis and synthesis, comparative law, formal law, etc. Using the dialectical method of cognition, the evolution of corporate legal relations in connection to the development of information technologies used in corporate governance and accounting of assets in the form of securities of corporate participants is considered.

The method of comparative law allowed us to study the main doctrinal and legislative approaches to the "digitalization" of corporate law in Europe, the United States, and Russia.

The use of the analysis and synthesis method, as well as the formal legal method, made it possible to formulate the main conclusions about trends and prospects related to the possibility of formally fixing special norms in corporate legislation that allow using modern digital platforms to regulate corporate decision-making processes and other significant corporate actions.

3 Results

What are the legal prerequisites for changes in the system of corporate relations before the so-called "The Fourth Industrial Revolution"? To begin with, over the past half-century, corporate law has finally taken shape as an integral part of private law.

Corporate legal relations received doctrinal background and legislative consolidation in the countries of Western European and Anglo-American law, and then in those countries that, as a result of changes in political regimes or state economic models, abandoned administrative and command methods of regulating the economy and shifted to the use of market mechanisms and management tools. These countries include the Russian Federation and the States formed in the post-Soviet space, the countries of the former socialist camp.

Corporations are mostly the main participants in civil turnover, and often certain segments of the economy moving to the digital space and its international markets depend on their activities (for example, civil aircraft construction, the energy market, etc.). This gives reason to speak not only about the active use of digital technologies by corporations, but also about the fact that in the very near future there will be a "digitalization" of legal acts regulating such activities.

Despite some differences in approaches to the subject of corporate law and the classification of corporations in the European and Anglo-American legal systems, the doctrine has now formed a uniform approach, according to which a corporation is an organization (association) based on the principles of membership, with a common goal. Moreover, such an organization can be either a commercial or non-commercial legal entity, and in some European legal systems—partially legal associations of persons (Sukhanov, 2014). Under Russian law, a corporation can only be a legal entity, i.e. institutions with legal personality.

In recent periodicals on business and corporate law, there is increasing recognition that in the near future, the legal regulation of corporate governance will inevitably face the need to digitalize a number of major corporate procedures. The time of adoption and practical implementation of the relevant innovations depends only on the successful interaction of lawyers and IT specialists.

Corporate governance is becoming one of the promising areas for digitalization of relevant processes and, first of all, it may soon affect the procedure for making corporate decisions by the will-forming bodies of corporations. The highest management body of a corporation is a meeting of its members, which can be held either in person or in absentia. The difference is that participants must be present together to discuss issues on the agenda and make decisions on issues put to the vote. The normative conditions for making decisions in the form of absentee voting are provided for in article 181.2 of the Civil Code of the Russian Federation, which allows the assembly to make a decision by absentee voting, including voting by electronic or other technical means.

At the same time, corporate legislation may prohibit making decisions on certain issues on the agenda in the form of absentee voting. The same restrictions and prohibitions may be prescribed in the charter of the corporation. The use of blockchain technologies (distributed registries) in the work of meetings has been discussed for a long time, and experts emphasize the exceptional efficiency and potential of using such technology for corporate governance (Sannikova, 2019).

Indeed, we can note the following advantages in using such platforms: security of information, transparency of the voting procedure, minimizing the possibility of abuse of voting rights, including in hostile takeovers, and excluding the possibility of other fraud, such as retroactive voting.

The use of the blockchain mode in organizing meetings can lead to the involvement of minority shareholders in the corporate management process, and finally, to reduce the costs associated with holding meetings and surveys. Among the possible advantages and prospects of switching the voting system to a blockchain basis, European scientists point out the rejection of the form of mandatory annual meetings, since shareholders can be informed and involved in voting at any time (Lafarre & Elst, 2018).

Also, according to experts, voting on the blockchain platform minimizes the opportunity to use a proxy vote, which will also eliminate unfair behavior in corporate voting (Yermack, 2017).

The problem of remote voting on substantive corporate matters using digital technologies and platforms is particularly relevant in the light of recent events related to the spread of the COVID-19 pandemic. Restrictions and prohibitions related to the introduction of quarantine, self-isolation and other protective measures have shown the ineffectiveness of traditional methods of holding face-to-face meetings of corporations, since such conditions cannot be provided in the current circumstances, but there is still an urgent need to hold such meetings and formalize decisions that cannot be taken in absentia. Moreover, the issue is not only about the difficulties that arise with holding meetings of shareholders or participants of limited liability companies, but also the work of the supervisory boards of companies.

Voting options on the blockchain platform are described in sufficient detail on the pages of special legal periodicals, so in this work we deliberately avoid technical and procedural issues related to the use of distributed registry technologies (Bazin et al., 2018).

According to experts, technically conducting the voting process using blockchain is most beneficial for companies with "millions" of shareholders, which allows them to have a deeper impact on corporate governance (Pileggi, 2018).

Is Russian corporate law ready for such changes? Even a cursory analysis of part one of the Civil Code of the Russian Federation and special laws on corporate legal entities, regarding the regulation of meetings, suggests that there are no direct obstacles to the use of this method of voting. First, there is a direct permission to conduct voting in absentia, and secondly, the Civil Code, as mentioned above, allows the use of electronic or other technical tools when voting.

If we interpret the terminology "electronic or other technical means" broadly, then the blockchain, even with some degree of conditionality, can be classified as a type of such means. The absence of legal obstacles to the use of the above-mentioned technology in corporate practice is also confirmed by the authoritative legal expert community (Laptev, 2018; Novoselova & Medvedeva, 2017).

Meanwhile, the absence of actual legislative obstacles does not mean that the introduction of blockchain technology is a matter of the next few days and the next annual meetings of corporations will be held everywhere on this platform. In our opinion, the slowdown in this process today is due to a number of factors.

To begin with, the main problem is the gaps in the legislation on the use of digital technologies, or simply put, the lack of clearly defined norms that would give an idea of what a blockchain is. In this regard, domestic legislation is only taking the first steps.

Several countries, including the United States (Vermont, Wyoming, Delaware, Arizona), Estonia, Sweden, France, and others, can "boast" of a legal mechanism for using blockchain technologies. However, even in those countries where such legislation is being formed, the priority is to develop and adopt rules on the use of blockchain in such areas as public registers, transactions, and cybersecurity. Corporate legal relations, with the exception of maintaining the register of shareholders and conducting transactions with shares, still play a secondary role.

It can be assumed that a balanced approach on the part of the legislator to the regulatory consolidation of blockchain technologies is quite justified taking into account that it is extremely difficult to describe the essence and principles of normative regulation of this model in the language of jurisprudence, and it is also difficult to do this in by-laws. Otherwise, you can achieve a situation in which such a law becomes clear only to a narrow circle of specialists.

In this regard, the following questions immediately arise: whether such legal innovations can pass the test of practice; whether the judicial system is ready to effectively resolve corporate disputes, the subject of which will be the use of complex digital technologies; how many decisions of corporate meetings will be challenged on this basis, etc. Even in those countries where blockchain technologies have already been reflected in national legislation, judicial practice in such cases is either lacking or extremely poor.

Another crucial point concerns the mandatory procedure for confirming decisions of general meetings of business entities by notaries or registrars as defined in article 67.1, paragraph 3 of the Civil Code of the Russian Federation. To date, this confirmation applies only to physical meetings.

However, as noted above, modern realities may dictate their own conditions that exclude the possibility of holding a physical meeting, as required by law, in a situation where it is also impossible to postpone a decision on a particular issue. For example, many companies, both in Russia and abroad, have faced this situation when it has become impossible to meet in person due to the coronavirus pandemic.

As possible solutions to this problem, we can suggest excluding from corporate legislation provisions that require mandatory meetings with voting in person on certain matters on the agenda. In this case, the possibility of considering these issues and making decisions in absentia will allow using digital technologies for such purposes.

The corresponding amendments will also be required in article 67.1 of the Civil Code of the Russian Federation regarding either the elimination of certification procedures, their implementation at corporate meetings in absentia using the capabilities of a digital notary. Since corporations (especially joint-stock companies) transfer a significant share of authority to supervisory boards, over time, the voting model using blockchain technologies can be regulated for decision-making at this level of corporate governance.

As part of the global innovation changes, the process of digitalization of registers of corporate securities holders is developing more intensively in comparison with corporate governance. The transition from certificated securities to dematerialized has become a generally recognized global practice in recent decades, which has led to the need to create special registers, as well as to the emergence of a special entity on the financial market—the register holder. The turnover of equities, shares in the authorized capital mediates corporate relations, as well as allows the securities market to function.

According to article 8 of the Federal Law "on the securities market", the register of securities owners is a system of records formed at a certain point in time about persons who have opened personal accounts, records about securities accounted for in these accounts, records about encumbered securities and other records in accordance with the legislation of the Russian Federation. Maintaining the register is connected with the system of accounting of documents related to maintaining the register, as well as documents associated with accounting and transfer of rights to securities, organized by the registry holder.

Maintaining securities registers is a global practice and the rules for maintaining such registers are approximately the same in those states where the turnover of financial assets of corporations is an integral part of the internal and external stock market. The registers reflect information about the securities themselves, their owners, as well as transactions that are made with such securities.

At the time, the refusal to maintain the register exclusively on paper was due to several reasons, the main of which are the transition from certificated securities to dematerialized (in the form of records in the register), the increase in the volume of transactions with securities, etc. The electronic register that replaced the paper-based register, with all its advantages, has also become the object of criticism in recent years, primarily on grounds of unreliability, namely the possibility of data loss or distortion.

It is not surprising that registries have become the focus of prospects for the use of blockchain platforms. The state of Delaware (USA) has become a pioneer in the use of blockchain technology for maintaining corporate registers. Amendments made in 2017 to the Delaware General

Corporations Law (DGCL) allowed companies to use distributed ledger technology to maintain records in corporate securities registries.

In articles published in the American legal and business periodicals, the following advantages of the adopted initiatives were justified. First, the possibility of direct interaction between investors and issuers, provided that shares are registered on this platform. Second, transparency of data on the owners of securities. Third, automation of corporate actions such as distribution and payment of dividends, and splitting of shares. Fourth, better management of the so-called capitalization table (Wonnie, 2018).

The prospects for introducing blockchain platforms into the practice of Russian corporate registry holders are assessed rather cautiously, but mostly in a positive, optimistic way. Scientists have constructed various scenarios for the transition of Russian depositories to distributed registry platforms.

In general, in recent publications on this issue in the Russian legal periodicals, most experts agree that the existing Russian system of accounting for corporate securities is not ready for such innovations. The limiting factor here is the inability to adapt this accounting principle to Russian realities, since the "Delaware" model assumes direct participation of the corporation itself in maintaining the register. Taking into account the current Russian system of registrars: "...the registrars will pass on the costs of implementing the blockchain to their clients, who will also have to pay for the services of registrars themselves as intermediaries" (Sannikova, 2019).

Indeed, in this scenario, the very goal of the blockchain, which is so actively debated by adherents of this idea—the reduction of the institution of mediation—is called into question. There are other scenarios that provide for the gradual replacement of the registry holder with a digital program that will be controlled by artificial intelligence (Laptev, 2019).

Thus, the reform of the rules of the Civil Code in this direction, as well as the relevant provisions of company law and legislation governing the securities market, for the near future seems rather uncertain than a real prospect.

4 Conclusion

In countries with a developed system of corporate law in recent years, the general trend is the introduction of digital technologies in the process of regulating corporate legal relations, and the greatest interest in innovation is represented by such institutions as accounting and disposal of demateri-alized corporate securities, as well as the activities of higher management bodies.

Modernization of approaches in corporate governance, accounting of corporate assets in the form of securities and their turnover on the stock markets dictate the need to change corporate legislation in order to comply with modern initiatives, and above all, in the legal regulation of the use of new digital formats, including distributed ledger technologies.

The inevitability of impending changes in the legislative regulation of a number of corporate procedures today is dictated by the challenges facing civilization in the context of the COVID-19 pandemic, as well as the threat of a global crisis, the high probability of which is predicted as a result of the collapse of certain sectors of the economy.

A significant part of the participants in such markets are corporations. In this situation, it is corporations that are most interested in creating an effective, modern legal model for regulating corporate relations that reflects the needs of companies and their participants regarding:

- transparency of the actions of persons engaged in corporate gover-nance, including within the framework of the company's supervisory board;
- reliability of information about the owners of corporate securities included in the registers, as well as the relevance of data on the value of assets and transactions;
- the optimal form of holding meetings of participants that allows you to quickly make decisions, including on significant corporate actions.

Such processes cannot remain without the participation of supervi-sory authorities. Therefore, the development of amendments to corporate legislation will affect not only the interests of corporations, but also the regulator. We believe that the greatest balance of interests of all partici-pants in corporate legal relations, as well as the interests of public law, can be achieved if the digitalization of corporate law is discussed and becomes part of the national program (strategy) of the digital economy.

REFERENCES

Bazin, D., Markov, A., & Tsykalo, Yu. (2018). Blockchain in corporate governance: Can this technology be used for voting at general meetings right now? *Corporate Strategies, 43*(9759). https://www.eg-online.ru/product/ks/5906/ (data accessed: 20 May 2020).

Gorodov, O. A., & Egorova, M. A. (2018). The main directions of improving legal regulation in the digital economy in Russia. *Law and the Digital Economy, 1*, 4–5.

Khlebnikov, P. (2017). Digitalization of law as a consequence of digitalization of life. *Housing Law, 9*, 93–102.

Lafarre, A., & Elst, C. (2018). *Blockchain technology for corporate governance and shareholder activism* (Law Working Paper, 390/2018; Tilburg Law School Research Paper, 2018-7). European Corporate Governance Institute (ECGI). https://ssrn.com/abstract=3135209 (data accessed: 20 May 2020).

Laptev, V. A. (2018). Blockchain technology in the corporate compliance system. *Law and Digital Economy, 2*, 31–33.

Laptev, V. A. (2019). Prospects for the use of blockchain technology in the field of corporate registers for business in Russia. *Business Law, 3*, 23–28.

Novoselova, L., & Medvedeva, T. (2017). Blockchain for voting of shareholders. *Economy and Law, 10*, 10–21.

Pileggi, F. G. X. (2018). *Blockchain technology and Delaware corporate law.* https://www.delawarelitigation.com/2018/04/articles/commentary/blockchain-and-delaware-corporate-law (data accessed: 20 May 2020).

Sannikova, L. V. (2019). Blockchain in corporate governance: Problems and prospects. *Law and Economics, 4*, 27–36.

Saurin, A. A. (2019). Digitization as a factor of transformation of law. *Constitutional and Municipal Law, 8*, 26–31.

Sitdikova, L. B., & Starodumova, SYu. (2019). Information component in corporate relations in the digital economy. *Russian Justice, 11*, 9–10.

Smirnov, D. A., Tereshchenko, E. A., Botasheva, L. E., Trofimov, M. S., Melnikova, V. A., & Dolgopolov, K. A. (2020). Digital jurisprudence. *Revista Inclusions, 7*(1), 273–283.

Sukhanov, E. A. (2014). *Comparative corporate law.* Statute.

Vasilevich, G. A. (2019). Digitalization of law as a means of increasing its effectiveness. *Constitutional and Municipal Law, 8*, 32–35.

Vaypan, V. A. (2017). Fundamentals of legal regulation of the digital economy. *Law and Economics, 11*, 5–18.

Wonnie, S. (2018). *Bullish on blockchain: Examining Delaware's approach to distributed ledger technology in corporate governance law and beyond.* https://www.hblr.org/2018/01/bullish-on-blockchain-examining-delawares-approach-to-distributed-ledger-technology-in-corporate-governance-law-and-beyond/ (data accessed: 20 May 2020).

Yermack, D. (2017). *Corporate governance and blockchains.* https://papers.ssrn.com/sol3/papers.cfm?abstract_id=2700475 (data accessed: 20 May 2020).

Managing the Process of International Cooperation and Integration of Small and Medium-Sized Businesses Based on Infrastructure Modernization

Tatyana Yu. Anopchenko and *Vladislav I. Ostrovskiy*

1 Introduction

One of the key success factors in the development of international cooperation and integration processes, as well as the most important object of public administration, is infrastructure provision. The resource endowments of entrepreneurship depend on infrastructure provision, which determines the prospects for its international cooperation and integration. At the same time, the creation and development of infrastructure places a heavy burden on the state budget. In times of crisis, as a rule, there is a deficit of state budgets at all levels of the budget system. In the current crisis conditions of 2020 opportunities to replenish the regional budget are limited due to the decline in business activity and business losses, as well as increased budget expenditures related to the implementation of social support measures for the population.

T. Yu. Anopchenko (✉)
Smolensk State University, Smolensk, Russia

T. Yu. Anopchenko · V. I. Ostrovskiy
Southern Federal University, Rostov-on-Don, Russia

© The Author(s), under exclusive license to Springer Nature Switzerland AG 2021
E. G. Popkova and B. S. Sergi (eds.), *Economic Issues of Social Entrepreneurship*,
https://doi.org/10.1007/978-3-030-77291-8_16

173

In this regard, financing the infrastructure of international cooperation and integration should be a reasonable anti-crisis measure aimed at launching a mechanism for support of small and medium-sized businesses in Russia. For this purpose, the need for infrastructure must have an objective justification in order to prevent overspending of targeted funds and the development of unnecessary infrastructure while maintaining a shortage of necessary infrastructure.

2 MATERIALS AND METHOD

The state policy in the field of supporting small and medium-sized businesses in the format of international cooperation and integration is aimed at modernizing the infrastructure support for this process, which includes financial, social, innovative, institutional, telecommunications, transport and information elements. The advantages of managing the process of international cooperation and integration of small and medium-sized businesses based on the modernization of infrastructure support are:

- high availability, namely reliance on electronic communications, provides an opportunity for mass use of support measures by small and medium-sized businesses;
- high efficiency, including the use of electronic communications that reduce transaction and marketing costs, while expanding the target audience and maximizing results;
- the minimum level of risk is minimal, since small and medium-sized businesses with high international and innovative activity are characterized by global competitiveness, which increases the potential for their successful international integration and cooperation. (Anopchenko, 2018).

Infrastructure support for international cooperation and business integration should be provided on a commercial basis, that is, it should be an economic (and not a public) good. At the same time, it is necessary to provide measures to ensure the availability of services for the use of this infrastructure for small and medium-sized businesses on preferential terms, that is, the implementation of services for the use of infrastructure should be flexible (Ostrovskaya et al., 2017; Saliy, 2016).

At the same time, it is necessary to consider international cooperation and integration as an alternative mechanism for crisis management in competition with other available mechanisms, including import substitution and internally oriented business development. Therefore, international cooperation and integration should provide both commercial advantages for the subjects involved in these processes, and social advantages for the region—acceleration of economic growth, increase in tax revenues to the regional budget, etc.

3 Results

Infrastructure support contributes to the development of international cooperation and business integration processes only if it is complete and integrated, and not fragmented. It is also important to take into account the specifics of priority sectors of the economy for the region that have the greatest opportunities for developing international cooperation and integration (Ostrovskiy, 2019a). To meet the full range of conditions for managing the process of international integration of small and medium-sized businesses based on infrastructure modernization, the authors developed the following promising algorithm (Fig. 1).

At the first stage of management, the intensity of international cooperation and integration processes in the region is measured using the following indicators:

- the number of residents of special economic zones when distinguishing regional and foreign enterprises;
- the number of residents of technoparks when distinguishing regional and foreign enterprises;
- the number of subjects of mergers and acquisitions when distinguishing regional and foreign enterprises;
- the share of enterprises engaged in transnational electronic cooperation in the form of exchange of resources with foreign enterprises, development of export activities, access to imported materials and components.

The second stage is associated with a multi-criteria assessment of the success of international cooperation and integration projects both in relation to an individual SME entity and the region as a whole.

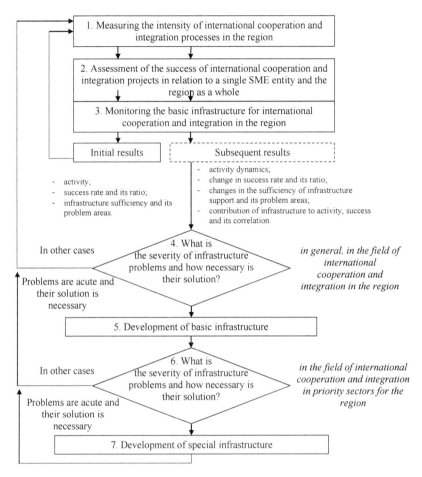

Fig. 1 Algorithm for managing the process of international integration of small and medium-sized businesses based on the modernization of infrastructure (*Source* Developed and compiled by the authors)

It is proposed to evaluate the success of an individual SME enterprise taking into account the peculiarities of the functioning of small and medium-sized businesses at the present stage (Lui et al., 2019) by following criteria:

MANAGING THE PROCESS OF INTERNATIONAL COOPERATION ... 177

- additional profit obtained through international cooperation and integration (financial criterion);
- reduced costs and increased profitability achieved through international cooperation and integration (financial criterion);
- additional market share (sales volume) gained through participation in international cooperation and integration projects (marketing criterion);
- increase in the loyalty of stakeholders (employees, consumers, contractors) achieved through participation in international cooperation and integration projects (marketing criterion).

It is recommended to evaluate the success of the regional socioeconomic system as a whole using the following criteria:

- increase in tax revenues of the regional budget achieved through the involvement of enterprises in the processes of international cooperation and integration (financial criterion);
- additional income (improving the standard of living of the population) received by employees of enterprises due to their participation in the processes of international cooperation and integration (financial criterion);
- additional employment (jobs) provided in the region through international cooperation and integration (corporate responsibility criterion);
- reduction of environmental costs achieved by transferring harmful production facilities to other countries through international cooperation and integration (corporate responsibility criterion);
- increase in the quality and availability of goods and services achieved through the involvement of enterprises in the processes of international cooperation and integration (corporate responsibility criterion);
- innovations developed (in the process of transnational R&D) and implemented through the involvement of enterprises in the processes of international cooperation and integration (criterion of innovative development);
- import substitution achieved in the region due to the involvement of enterprises in the processes of international cooperation and integration (criterion of innovative development);

- crowding out foreign enterprises from the regional market due to the involvement of enterprises in the processes of international cooperation and integration (criterion of innovative development);
- increase in the competitiveness of the regional economy, achieved through the involvement of enterprises in the processes of international cooperation and integration (criterion of innovative development).

The third stage is monitoring the basic infrastructure for international cooperation and integration in the region. Basic infrastructure support for entrepreneurship includes financial, social, innovation, institutional, telecommunications, transport and information elements (Ostrovskiy, 2019b). Financial infrastructure is the provision of enterprises with financial resources—both their own and borrowed. Social infrastructure is determined by the quantity, availability, and quality of human resources. Innovative infrastructure determines the conditions for innovative development of entrepreneurship, which largely determines its global competitiveness and, consequently, opportunities for international cooperation and integration. The institutional infrastructure determines the availability of public services and state support for subjects of international cooperation and integration. Telecommunications infrastructure provides enterprises with access to modern information and communication technologies, the main ones being the computer and the Internet. The transport infrastructure determines the conditions of delivery (transportation), storage and logistics of exported products. Information infrastructure defines information support for international cooperation and integration.

It is recommended to monitor the basic infrastructure support in the context of the following components of the business infrastructure:

- financial infrastructure, evaluated by the criterion of availability of borrowed financial resources, the possibility of obtaining and profitability of tax credit conditions;
- social infrastructure, evaluated by the criterion of sufficiency of highly qualified personnel necessary for the organization of international cooperation and integration processes, availability, quality and convenience of educational and training programs for entrepreneurs on international cooperation and integration;

MANAGING THE PROCESS OF INTERNATIONAL COOPERATION ... 179

- innovative infrastructure evaluated by the criterion of sufficiency of innovative technologies for participation of regional enterprises in the processes of international cooperation and integration;
- institutional infrastructure evaluated by the criteria of completeness, availability and quality of electronic public services in the field of expertise and transaction support, activity and effectiveness of meetings with foreign delegations, organization of foreign business missions and exhibition and fair activities;
- telecommunications infrastructure evaluated by the criterion of availability and quality of information and communication technologies;
- transport infrastructure evaluated by the criterion of availability and quality of transport and logistics services;
- information infrastructure, evaluated by the criterion of awareness of regional enterprises about the possibilities of international cooperation and integration, availability and quality of consulting services, as well as the results of state-conducted marketing research on foreign markets (Morozova et al., 2019; Popkova & Gulzat, 2020).

The initial results obtained as a result of monitoring allow characterizing the activity of international cooperation and integration in the region, the success of these processes and the ratio of success of a single SME entity and the regional socio-economic system as a whole, as well as the sufficiency of infrastructure support and its problem areas. The proposed algorithm assumes that the described monitoring will be repeated in the next time period, for example, in a year.

Subsequent results make it possible to characterize the dynamics of international cooperation and integration activity in the region, changes in success and its ratio, changes in the sufficiency of infrastructure support and its problem areas, as well as the contribution of infrastructure to activity, success and its ratio.

At the fourth stage, the results of monitoring are analyzed in general in the field of international cooperation and integration in the region, that is, without reference to specific sectors of the economy. The analysis is aimed at identifying the severity of infrastructure problems and the need to solve them. Problems are recognized as acute, and their solution is necessary if:

- the changes in the activity of international cooperation and integration are largely due to infrastructure support (the correlation of the corresponding indicators should be more than 50%);
- the success of international cooperation and integration is largely due to infrastructure support (the correlation of the corresponding indicators should be more than 50%);
- there is an acute shortage of infrastructure for international cooperation and integration;
- according to expert estimates, there is a high probability that due to the development of infrastructure support, there will be a significant increase in the activity and success of international cooperation and integration.

If all these conditions are met, the fifth stage of the proposed algorithm involves the development of basic infrastructure. Modernization of infrastructure will create a high-quality regulatory environment for small and medium-sized businesses in modern Russia and will allow businesses to mobilize internal potential reserves.

Attracting private investment plays an important role in this process. Modern Russia has accumulated experience in implementing public–private partnership projects in the infrastructure sector, which should be used to develop infrastructure support for international cooperation and integration of entrepreneurship in the regions. Private investments can be attracted only if there is a high probability of their return (payback), as well as a profit on the invested capital (Dorina et al., 2019; Lopatina et al., 2014).

There is a risk of non-allocation or limited allocation of state financial support for exports due to the deterioration of the macroeconomic environment or due to the emergence of other priorities. In this regard, the model provided for risk prevention measures:

1. formation of public–private partnership mechanisms can help attract non-government resources (loans, guarantees);
2. maintaining a constant dialogue with the responsible executive authorities and the Export Support Center on updating the state policy of export support (Business Support Fund in the Stavropol territory, 2020);

MANAGING THE PROCESS OF INTERNATIONAL COOPERATION ... 181

3. forming a significant request for the use of non-financial mechanisms to support exports by businesses.

At the sixth stage, we analyze the severity of infrastructure problems in the field of international cooperation and integration, as well as the need to solve them in priority sectors for the region.

When infrastructure problems are acute and need to be solved, special infrastructure support is developed at the seventh stage.

The development of the institutional environment to support non-oil exports according to the Passport of a priority project "Systemic development of international cooperation and exports" (Website of the Russian Government, 2016) will meet the needs of small and medium-sized exporters in the measures of financial and non-financial support.

The developed algorithm for managing the process of international integration of small and medium-sized businesses based on the modernization of infrastructure provides certain advantages:

1. step-by-step development of infrastructure for international cooperation and business integration, which takes into account the indicators of the regional state budget and allows for tranche funding of management activities, first of basic infrastructure, then of special industry infrastructure, which is especially important in times of crisis;
2. development of only targeted infrastructure, which ensures high accuracy of infrastructure projects developed in the region through regular and detailed monitoring;
3. consideration of the industry specifics of the region, which helps to distinguish between basic and special infrastructure, that is, to create and develop exactly the infrastructure that is most in demand in the region, meets the strategic guidelines for its development, and also achieve high efficiency;
4. attracting private investment in the development of infrastructure provision on the terms of public–private partnership, which contributes to the redistribution of financial and risk burden between the state and private-corporate budgets.

Taken together, these advantages provide budget savings and maximize the effectiveness of managing the development of infrastructure support for international cooperation and integration processes and encourage the involvement of small and medium-sized businesses in these processes.

4 Conclusion

The authors prove that infrastructure provides the basis for the development of international cooperation and integration processes. It is obvious that the most important object of public administration is infrastructure support, but its contribution can be achieved only if it is complete and comprehensive, and if the specifics of priority sectors of the economy for the region that have the greatest opportunities for developing international cooperation and integration are taken into account.

The authors have developed a promising algorithm for managing the process of international cooperation and integration of small and medium-sized businesses, which helps to achieve savings and improve the efficiency of budget spending, as well as improve the quality of the regulatory environment for small and medium-sized businesses in modern Russia.

Acknowledgements The reported study was funded by RFBR, project number 19-310-90078.

References

Anopchenko, T. Y., & Ostrovskiy, V. I. (2018). Possibilities of the international cooperation of subjects of small and medium-sized business under the conditions of financial crisis. In E. G. Popkova (Ed.), *The future of the global financial system: Downfall or harmony* (pp. 414–420). Springer Nature AG.

Dorina, E., Meshcheryakova, O., Boris, O., Momotova, O., & Vorontsova, G. (2019). *Public-private partnership as a mechanism to stimulate innovation in Belarus Republic. Modern tools for sustainable development of territories*. Special Topic: Project Management in the Regions of Russia. Future Academy, 245–252. https://doi.org/10.15405/epsbs.2019.12.05.29.

Lopatina, E. U., Tselih, C. N., Chugunova, E. V., & Ostrovskaya, V. N. (2014). Managing risks of venture entrepreneurship. *Asian Social Science, 10*(23), 191–198.

Lui, Kh., Khokhlova, G. I., Kretova, N. V., & Korshunova, E. I. (2019). Small and medium-sized businesses: Features of functioning at the present stage.

MANAGING THE PROCESS OF INTERNATIONAL COOPERATION ... 183

Russian Journal of Entrepreneurship, 20(4), 865–872. https://doi.org/10. 18334/rp.20.4.40594/.

Morozova, I. A., Moskovtsev, A. F., & Smetanina, A. I. (2019). Infrastructure support for entrepreneurship in the digital economy of Russia. *Creative Economy, 13*(4), 671–684.

Ostrovskaya, V. N., Tyurina, Y. G., Bogoviz, A. V., Przhedetskaya, N. V., & Lobova, S. V. (2017). Foreign economic activities of subjects of SME in the context of cooperation of Russia and Europe. In *Contributions to economics* (9783319606958, pp. 597–603). https://doi.org/10.1007/978-3-319-60696-5_75.

Ostrovskiy, V. I. (2019a). The role of international cooperation and integration of small and medium-sized businesses in the implementation of a new quality of socio-economic progress in Russia. *Humanities of the South of Russia, 8*(4), 257–268. https://doi.org/10.23683/2227-8656.2019.4.26.

Ostrovskiy, V. I. (2019b). Features of development of international cooperation and integration of small and medium-sized businesses. *Financial Economics, 4,* 1062–1066.

Popkova, E. G., & Gulzat, K. (2020). Technological revolution in the 21st century: Digital society vs artificial intelligence. In E. G. Popkova & B. S. Sergi (Eds.), *The 21st century from the positions of modern science: Intellectual, digital and innovative aspects.* Lecture Notes in Networks and Systems (Vol. 91, pp. 339–345). https://doi.org/10.1007/978-3-030-32015-7_38.

Saliy, V. V. (2016). The essence of small business support infrastructure and its development at the present stage. *Scientific Notes of the St. Petersburg Branch of the Russian Customs Academy Named After V. B. Bobkov, 2*(58), 46–52.

The Fund for Support of Entrepreneurship in the Stavropol Region. (2020). *Export Support Center.* https://fppsk26.ru/centr-podderzhki-eksporta (data accessed: 27 September 2020).

Website of the Russian Government. (2016). *Passport of the priority project "System measures for the development of international cooperation and export".* http://government.ru/projects/selection/650/25593/ (data accessed: 27 September 2020).

Ethical Standards: Traditions and Innovations in Law Enforcement in the Context of the Fourth Technological Revolution

Olga V. Akhrameeva⊙, Denis V. Zakalyapin⊙, Dmitry V. Derkunsky⊙, Pavel V. Slydnev⊙, and Vitaly V. Kovyazin⊙

1 Introduction

Digitalization entails the mechanization and algorithmization of the process of providing services and state functions, processes and procedures for ensuring and protecting the rights of citizens and legal entities, which transforms the legal regulation of the implementation of state functions. In turn, the algorithmization of law enforcement processes leads to changes in the regulation of the activities of law enforcement communities in both the public sector and related professions, for example, the bar, notaries (Smirnov et al., 2020).

On the one hand, these changes are aimed at ensuring access for a wide range of consumers of state functions and services (Kasevich et al., 2019). On the other hand, there are issues of regulating not only the technical aspect of providing services and/or state functions, but also regulating

---

O. V. Akhrameeva (✉) · D. V. Zakalyapin · D. V. Derkunsky · P. V. Slydnev · V. V. Kovyazin
Stavropol Branch of Russian Technological University (MIREA), Stavropol, Russia

© The Author(s), under exclusive license to Springer Nature Switzerland AG 2021
E. G. Popkova and B. S. Sergi (Eds.), *Economic Issues of Social Entrepreneurship*,
https://doi.org/10.1007/978-3-030-77291-8_17

the security of public and private life of the direct performers of these functions and services. In particular, these security issues relate not only to the mechanization of the process with its positive aspects such as reducing queues, deadlines for obtaining information and/or documents, reducing the volume of paper turnover, etc. However, these issues also have a negative side—pressure on performers from citizen-consumers using electronic recording tools (audio, video, etc.). Thus, despite the positive aspects of digitalization, it makes performers a kind of hostages of technological progress on the part of citizens-applicants, which is expressed in various charges: from unprofessional performance of their duties to charges of unethical behavior.

2 Materials and Method

In the course of this work, the following methods were used: universal systematic method of cognition, comparative legal and formal legal methods, as well as the method of logical analysis of normative legal acts.

The subject of the study is the normative regulators of internal relations of organizations and institutions authorized to implement state functions, taking into account the use of digital technologies.

Currently, there is a need to draft legislation and/or law enforcement regulations that are aimed at protecting the interests of all participants in this process in the conditions of mechanization (algorithmization) of procedures using technological innovations and the Internet environment. This normative task concerns not only the authorities, but also professional communities. The latter have an effective way to resolve some of the previously mentioned issues (in upholding the principles of professionalism, security, etc.), i.e. codes of corporate or professional ethics.

3 Results

Modern technological challenges are changing priorities in the process of providing legal assistance and protecting rights. Academician of the Russian Academy of Sciences Khabrieva (**2018, 2019**) noted that the practice is on the way to fill in the gaps in legal regulation in this area due to ethical standards formed by non-state professional communities of law enforcement lawyers. So, relatively recently, 25–30 years ago, the main burden of law enforcement agencies was associated with offences of a violent nature, and now more and more often crimes related to information technologies come to the fore. This has been true for in legal and notarial activities. If earlier the main areas of professional development and consulting were related to contractual relations, now they are issues of ensuring the rights of citizens and their legitimate interests through digital content and/or its fixation.

However, how is it possible to ensure the interests of professionals in the conditions of mechanization (algorithmization) of procedures? It seems that in addition to the common methods of protection provided for by procedural and criminal legislation, corporate and ethical standards can play a preventive role. The main feature of the latter is the focus on protecting the interests of corporate representatives, rapid response to changes in the requests of society and state policy in the formation of norms, and, accordingly, the rapid formation of corporate and ethical standards. In addition, an important feature is the ability to independently resolve the issue of whether the achievements of similar foreign corporations (The International Union of Notaries, the Code of Conduct for Lawyers of the member States of the European Community) or relevant acts of supranational entities (acts of the CIS) should be taken into account.

Traditionally, the purpose of these codes was to ensure the effective resolution of internal corporate disputes and regulate certain issues of professional activity that were not reflected in state legislation. Currently, due to frequent changes in federal legislation, professional law enforcement communities are faced with fragmented regulation of procedural or process-related issues of providing legal assistance, ensuring and protecting the rights of citizens and legal entities based on the new social relations of the Fourth Industrial Revolution. First of all, this concerns the issue of dissemination and protection of information, its exchange using new technological approaches, when it is necessary to distribute information to an unlimited number of people or an individual, while guaranteeing the preservation of professional secrecy and the image of the professional community. This also applies to information on personal websites, and the use of social pages, messengers, etc.

Thus, the issue of the volume of information distributed and the order of its distribution is primarily determined by the professional association.

Another issue is ensuring an appropriate level of professionalism and highly professional execution of tasks. After all, with the inevitable acceleration of the general pace of life in society, specialists who implement functions delegated by the state (Akhrameeva et al., 2019) are required to quickly perform their professional duties using the latest technologies. At the same time, the applicants (principals) themselves, who use modern technologies, do not take into account that the performance of functions assigned by the state is in conflict with federal legislation, which clearly defines the procedures for their implementation. As a result, there is a conflict that can be resolved by the corporation itself, which determines both the scope of possible use of the technology and the responsibility for their non-use.

However, the technological lifestyle of modern society also affects the private life of the entire population, including the issue of 24-hour surveillance, the use of video, audio, and photo recording tools, which is relevant to the activities of law enforcement agencies. Issues of protection of both the civilian population and the performers of state functions are directly related to state powers. However, the professional community that performs certain functions, such as the bar, notary, etc., is forced to solve security issues on its own. And first of all, with the help of corporate and ethical standards that oblige both to improve their skills, including in the field of technology application, and to exercise self-restraint in the information space, etc.

The main steps that ensure the uniform functioning of the relevant non-state law enforcement communities are disciplinary measures taken by the same community.

One of the problematic aspects of using the resources of the Internet environment (blog sphere, social sites, messengers, etc.) is the placement of information about professional activities for use by an unlimited number of people.

The Code of Professional Ethics of Notaries of the Russian Federation (Laws, Codes and Regulations of the Russian Federation, 2019) provides for a special Chapter 8 on the conditions for placing information about the activities of a particular notary. Paragraph 8.2 explicitly prohibits the publication of information that creates advantages of this notary over others. In case of violation of this norm in paragraph 9.2.27, a disciplinary penalty is applied.

Moreover, it should be remembered that information once posted on the Internet and subsequently deleted can still be used at any time. Therefore, in order to avoid complaints, notaries' web pages are often placed on the site of the notary chamber of the relevant region.

In addition to prohibitions, the Code of Professional Ethics of Notaries establishes a mandatory minimum that must contain information about the notary and his activities. In particular, it includes not only the list of notarial actions and their brief description, but also the amount of notary fees for these actions, the rates of fee for legal and technical services that accompany the registration of notarial documents (paragraph 8.3.4 of the Code), the procedure for obtaining benefits, as well as liability for violation of these requirements (paragraph 9.2.7 of the Code). Moreover, the obligation to inform citizens about the above aspects applies not only to the Internet sphere, but also to face-to-face communication between the notary and the applicant citizen.

This is certainly primarily aimed at informing citizens, but also at the unity of notarial practice, since paragraph 9.2.13 and paragraph 9.2.16 of the Code stipulate separate disciplinary penalties for violation of the requirements for providing the above information.

At the same time, paragraph 9.2.29 of the Code establishes an independent basis for disciplinary action for violation of restrictions, failure to perform or improper performance of duties related to informing the public about their activities. Thus, it is impossible to refuse to publish information about notary activities at all.

Also, professional duties include, as mentioned above, requirements for professional development, maintenance of the necessary level of knowledge and practical skills (paragraph 3.1.6 of the Code). Although this is not provided for in Chapter 3, which describes the general requirements for professional conduct of a notary, but in conjunction with paragraph 9.2.1, disciplinary responsibility is imposed for violation of the rules and procedure for performing notarial actions due to lack of relevant knowledge.

As previously mentioned, the regulation of the level of professionalism, its preliminary verification, certain conditions and the procedure for its improvement, traditionally refers to internal corporate regulation. However, detailed regulation of the conditions and procedure for professional development is associated with detailed regulation of disciplinary liability.

At the beginning of our article, we pointed out certain aspects of the professional activities of law enforcement agencies that provide services or perform certain government functions, as well as consumer claims. The latter includes the issues concerning the unethical behaviuor both in the process of providing services and non-working time.

With regard to non-working hours, the Code of Professional Ethics of Notaries also focuses on two aspects of notaries' ethical and professional conduct. Thus, notaries are prohibited from performing actions that directly harm the notary, the notary community, undermine the prestige and trust of notaries (paragraph 9.2.20 of the Code). These requirements apply to non-working time.

In addition to this prohibition, notaries are also prohibited from performing actions that may affect the professional honour and authority of other notaries, the notary chamber and its bodies (clause 9.2.25 of the Code). This prohibition applies to the conduct of a notary at any time: work and personal.

Regarding to the related non-governmental law enforcement community, the bar, we note that the corporate norms in the Code of Professional Ethics of Lawyers (2003) do not contain such detailed instructions concerning the issues we are considering. At the same time, unlike the notary community, the bar association uses the standards adopted by the international non-state legal institution. For example, the Federal Chamber of Lawyers has published on its website The International Principles of Conduct of Legal Professionals in Social Networks (Federal Chamber of Lawyers of the Russian Federation, 2014), which define the following general principle of using modern information technologies.

On the one hand, network information platforms are clearly not suitable for professional advocacy due to insecurity. On the other hand, it is assumed that they can be used, but only if confidential information is protected in accordance with professional, moral and legal obligations.

Also, the bar association (Chernyavskaya, 2019) decided on the permissible amount of information provided about the lawyer's activities, including on the Internet: "… the information that misleads potential clients about the characteristics of a lawyer and the legal assistance he/she provides is unacceptable. It is the issue of publishing false information on the Internet about the number of the lawyer's clients ho were acquitted, as well as the rate of successful cases" (Kluvgant, 2015).

With regard to the conduct of lawyers during off-duty hours, the Code of Professional Ethics for Advocates also does not contain detailed provisions on both the duties of lawyers and the grounds for disciplinary action. However, there is a general provision that stipulates "in any situation, including off-duty hours, … to maintain honour and dignity, to avoid anything that could damage the authority of the bar or undermine its credibility…" (article 9, paragraph 5, of the Code). It seems that this principle of behavior applies to all professions performing state functions to ensure and protect the rights of citizens and legal entities. This also applies to representatives of state structures (for example, law enforcement agencies).

Thus, the change in the content of the norms of corporate and ethical codes of professional law enforcement communities is aimed precisely at the safe use of the Internet sphere, modern technologies, and information platforms. In particular, with regard to the two legal communities we are considering, these are the changes in the norms of ethical regulation of the use of the Internet environment. Notaries use the Internet to exchange requests and documents with individual organizations and institutions through specially installed programs, while the blogosphere is not used (except for providing evidence). For the legal profession, it is possible to use the blogosphere for consulting, forming a client base, etc.

4 Conclusion

The impossibility of rapid legislative response to changes in the country's public life entails the need to use other regulators, in particular, corporate and ethical standards of individual communities. Such communities in the field of law enforcement are professional communities of lawyers and notaries.

The authors focused on the impossibility of ensuring security in the conditions of the Fourth Technological Revolution, when new ways of communication, collecting and processing information, including, and sometimes primarily, video and audio recording, have come to the fore. Technological challenges are not ignored by professional communities that directly protect the rights and interests of citizens and legal entities. The authors considered the ethical and corporate standards of corporations of lawyers and notaries that ensure safety in the process of professional activity.

It is important to focus on the differences in the use of information technologies in professional activities and private life: security requirements relate to both sides of life, while they are implied in ethical standards, but not so unambiguous. The most categorical rules are provided for the dissemination of information, conduct during official and off-duty hours in the Code of Professional Ethics of Notaries, up to the application of disciplinary penalties. the Code of Professional Ethics for Advocates provides only a general rule for maintaining ethical behavior:

"in all circumstances [must] maintain the honour and dignity inherent in ... the profession" (article 4, paragraph 1, of the Code of Professional Ethics for Advocates). As for the use of Internet technologies in professional activities, of Professional Ethics for Advocates does not provide for any rules, but refers to other rules of the international legal community that provide for the possibility of using the blogosphere in legal activities, if the security of confidential information is ensured.

Thus, digitalization provides great opportunities for collecting information and promoting business, but it reveals a negative side in the form of the inability to ensure the security of both professional activities and personal life, its confidentiality. Moreover, once posted information on the Internet remains in the network forever. And the only way to guarantee security is to follow the traditional rules for posting and using information, especially when the questions concern performing professional duties. The same applies to security in personal and professional life.

Acknowledgements The article was prepared with the financial support of the RFBR grant No. 19-011-00820 (a) "Legal policy of the Russian state, its priorities and principles in the digital economy and digital technological order: conceptual, methodological, and industry-specific aspects of digitalization of law and legal regulation".

References

Akhrameeva, O., Dediukhina, I., Zhdanova, O., Maksimov, V., & Sagalaeva, E. (2019). *Ratio of unification and national legal traditions in the modern Russian law of succession.* https://www.futureacademy.org.uk/files/images/upload/SCTCMG2019FA008.pdf (data accessed: 15 May 2020).

Chernyavskaya, E. (2019). *The Russian Federal Bar Association (RFBA) of the Russian Federation: lawyers do not have the right to publish on the Internet the percentage of successful cases that does not correspond to reality.* http://www.gar ant.ru/news/1270150/#ixzz5m9WGYLBh (data accessed: 15 May 2020).

Code of Professional Ethics of Lawyers. (2003). *Bulletin of the Federal Chamber of Lawyers of the Russian Federation, 2–3.*

Federal Chamber of Lawyers of the Russian Federation. (2014). *The international principles of conduct of legal professionals in social networks.* https://fparf.ru/documents/international-acts/international-principles-of-conduct-of-legal-professionals-in-social-networks/?sphrase_id=42309 (data accessed: 15 May 2020).

Kasevich, E., Atayan, G., Amvrosova, O., Stankevich, G., & Kara-Kazaryan, T. (2019). *Perspectives on the use of new information and communication technology (ICT) in the modern economy* (pp. 439–445). Advances in Intelligent Systems and Computing. Springer.

Khabrieva, T. Y. (2018). Law before the challenges of digital reality. *Journal of Russian Law, 9*, 5–16.

Khabrieva, T. Y. (2019). *Law in the context of digitalization: A textbook.* Saint Petersburg University for the Humanities of Trade Unions.

Kluvgant, V. (2015). *Legal ethics on the Internet.* https://www.advgazeta.ru/mneniya/advokatskaya-etika-v-internete/ (data accessed: 15 May 2020).

Laws, Codes and Regulations of the Russian Federation. (2019). *Code of Professional Ethics for notaries in the Russian Federation (approved by the Ministry of justice of the Russian Federation 12.08.2019, 19.01.2016).* https://legalacts.ru/kodeks/kodeks-professionalnoi-etiki-notari usov-v-rossiiskoi-federatsii/ (data accessed: 15 May 2020).

Smirnov, D. A., Tereshchenko, E. A., Botasheva, L. E., Trofimov, M. S., Melnikova, V. A., & Dolgopolov, K. A. (2020). Digital jurisprudence. *Revista Inclusiones, 7*(1), 273–283.

Problems Related to Codification of Russian Social Security Legislation

Svetlana A. Lukinovaⓘ*, Igor E. Nelgovsky*ⓘ*, and Tatyana F. Vysheslavova*ⓘ

1 INTRODUCTION

The relevance of the research into the problems related to codification of sources of social security law in the Russian Federation is due to the fact that Russian legislation is characterized by explosive development of lawmaking in all spheres of social relations due to the transition to market relations in the post-Soviet period, which is manifested in codification main branches of legislation of—civil, criminal, administrative, labor, tax, family, land, procedural etc.

Jurisprudence has generally accepted that relevant codes regulate social relations that are the most important and significant for society and the State (Navasardova et al., 2018).

Article 7 of the Constitution of the Russian Federation of 1993 declared Russia a social state, so the question naturally arises: why our State has not yet codified social security legislation and has no specialized code, or is social security not a priority for Russian State policy?

S. A. Lukinova (✉) · T. F. Vysheslavova
North Caucasian Federal University, Stavropol, Russia

I. E. Nelgovsky
North-West Branch of the Russian State University of Justice, St. Petersburg, Russia

© The Author(s), under exclusive license to Springer Nature Switzerland AG 2021
E. G. Popkova and B. S. Sergi (eds.), *Economic Issues of Social Entrepreneurship*,
https://doi.org/10.1007/978-3-030-77291-8_18

That is not the case however, as confirmed by legislative acts in the framework of constitutional reform and improving the level of social security and protection of households with children, adopted in the Russian Federation since early 2020.

However, codification of social security legislation is outside the plans of the legislative branch of power, which, according to experts, has its adverse impact on the level of social protection of citizens.

Considering the fact that Article 72 of the Basic Law of the Russian Federation included social security legislation with the area of joint responsibility of the Russian Federation and its constituent entities, the idea of adopting a code in this field was implemented in a number of the constituent entities of the Russian Federation. Social codes were adopted in Germany and France as a consequence of the consolidation of legislation.

However, most countries are guided by international acts, in particular, legislative acts of the Council of Europe (for example, European Code of Social Security of April 16, 1964, European Social Charter of October 18, 1961, European Convention on Social Security of December 16, 1972 etc.) Azarova et al. (1998).

2 Materials and Method

The formation of the modern system of sources of social security law in the Russian Federation has started after the collapse of the Soviet Union, has continued extensively after the adoption of the Constitution of the Russian Federation in 1993, and is still in progress by now (Voronin & Przhilenskiy, 2019). It should also be stated that in 2018, our country implemented a pension reform that gave rise to social tension (Baieva et al., 2019). The lawmaking in the Russian Federation in the field of provision of pensions and benefits compared to western countries (Chappell, 2017) confirms the need for a balanced economic and science-based approach to rulemaking in this important field. Ignoring it leads to protests, legal nihilism, decline in efficiency of legal regulation, and violation of constitutional rights of citizens to social security services.

The research was carried out based on the analysis and synthesis of new statutory regulations on social security and practice in the application of these regulations (Gabrilyan et al., 2019). ·

The need to study the problems of sources of social security law in Russia is objectively determined by the need to adopt the principles of a law-bound and social State and to enforce the rights and freedoms of individuals and citizens, which often turns out to be very problematic in the real world (Grief, 1990).

3 RESULTS

The analysis of problems related to the codification of social security legislation has inference that it is almost impossible to solve them without a clear definition of the goal and principles of social protection of citizens. The thing is that the State is currently struggling with the rapid increase in poverty among its citizens, aggravated by the pandemic, in an effort to ensure their survival at a level of subsistence minimum that does not even meet their physiological needs. This demonstrates the incompatibility of our State with the criterion of a Social State, which should provide living conditions that would be worthy of an individual as a personality. International-legal experience in social field must be taken into account in the development of the Code (Smirnov et al., 2020). There is a long-standing objective need for the adoption of the Social Code, while its absence is indicative of a serious gap in social security legislation of our State. The adoption of the Social Security Code will not only contribute greatly to law-making and law-enforcement processes, but will also improve legal consciousness of citizens in terms of norms of social security law, having a positive impact on their legal awareness. The structure of the future code must meet the traditional requirement to divide industry norms into general and specific parts.

The general part will identify the goals and objectives of social security, its underlying principles, the hierarchy of sources of social security law, their effect in time and space, will define the actors in this sector, their rights and liabilities, as well as other key general aspects. The Social Security Code should formalize the rules on the range of rule-making entities and their competence, considering that at this stage, the rule-making competence is actually vested in state non-budgetary funds, non-state pension funds, and supreme judicial authorities, which is inconsistent with the general provisions of theory of law (Tuchkova, 2016). The special part of the codified act should be concerned with individual institutions of social security law: employed (pensionable) service, types of pensions, social allowances, and benefits, provision of various social services, etc. Each Chapter must present a social security system, determine its elements (subject matter, conditions, amount and duration of social security benefits). The Social Code (Social Security Code) must contain not only substantive but also procedural rules, regulating relations for the establishment of legal facts that give rise to the emergence of social assistance, relations related to the defense of violated rights to a certain type of social security, the process of providing social assistance to people in need (Kobylinskaya & Karsanova, 2014).

The post-Soviet period of development of the system of sources of social security law is characterized by the emergence of new sources which are strange to Soviet legislation. We are referring to the recognition of priority of international legal principles and norms by the Constitution of the Russian Federation of 1993, the assignment of Article 72 of the Law on Social Security to the joint competence of the Russian Federation and its constituent entities, endowment of local self-government authorities with rule making powers, enhancement of the role of social partnership agreements, collective labor agreements, local acts of organizations regulating social security issues. However, the vast majority of constituent entities of the Russian Federation cannot raise the level of guarantees of citizens' rights in the field of social security due to the lack of funds in the budget, which results in discrimination of citizens at their place of residence and a decrease in the level of state guarantees of social security.

Legal regulation of social security relations is traditionally characterized by the combination of unity with differentiation, intended to take into account the working conditions and psycho-physiological features of an actor in the definition of social security conditions. In this day and age, the lawmaker seeks to neutralize the differentiated approach in granting non-contributory pensions and to enshrine privileged conditions and a significantly higher level of social security of judges, procurators, enlisted personnel, and civil servants at various levels compared to the average level of social security of citizens covered by legislation on non-contributory pension (Dashkevich, 2011). The contracts represented by agreements and collective labor agreements (Baieva et al., 2018) also have a certain degree of importance in the source system of the sector. Generally speaking, the modern system of sources of social security law in Russia can be described as a multilevel sophisticated system which is difficult to perceive not only to citizens, but also to public and other authorities putting these rules to practice. The texts of legal acts on pensions and allowances contain a great number of reference rules, leading to multiple conflicts that make it difficult for citizens to exercise their rights. The legislation on non-contributory and contributory pensions is constantly changing, and an individual and the Constitution do not benefit from these changes. In addition, the lawmaker has not yet unified the basic definitions in this sector—"pension", "allowance", "benefit" etc.

Many serious shortcomings of current social security legislation in Russia identified above make individual authors to conclude that there is a need to abandon the idea of the adoption of a unified codified act, but to consistently opt for the so-called "stagewise" codification of sources of social security law.

In testimony of soundness of their ideas, they cite the legislator's attempts in recent years to partially codify the separate legal institutes of the sector—social insurance, social and health care, which is reflected in the adoption of the relevant framework legislation.

The fairness of presentation of regulated social relations in the source of law should be recognized as the main indicator of its quality. Hence, the requirement of Article 2 of the Constitution of the Russian Federation of 1993 on recognition of individuals and their rights as supreme value should be recognized as the criterion for assessing the degree of objectivity of the legal act on social security. Therefore, one cannot accept the adoption of legal acts that would diminish the rights of an individual to social security services or reduce their level (Abdulgaziyev, 2019). Derogation from this principle leads to social tension, violations, unlawful conduct, and legal nihilism (Zhuzhgov et al., 2019).

In order to make legal sources perfect and effective, significant improvements must be achieved in both law-making and law-enforcement. We are primarily referring to the problems of integrity and unity of Russian legal framework, correct understanding of the correlation of legal sources at the federal level and constituent entities of the Russian Federation, system nature of development of legal sources, their codification, use of objective differentiation criteria in legal regulation of tangible relations.

Unfortunately, the authors have not reached consensus on the issue of the adoption of the Social Code, so some scholars believe that the adoption of the code will not have any significant impact on the quality of social security in our country, because quality depends on the content of legal act rather than on the form or type of it (Telegin, 2015). Unfortunately, the level of social protection of an individual in modern Russian conditions depends on the place of his/her residence, the economic and budgetary potential of the region, and the desire of the State to transfer the solution of social security problems to constituent entities of the Russian Federation. This situation objectively necessitates the formalization of uniform minimum social standards in the codified law for all citizens with regard to levels, types, and conditions of social security. In equivalent to Article 6 of Labor Code of the Russian Federation in the Social Security Code, it is necessary to distinguish the powers of public authorities of the Russian Federation and its constituent entities, and enshrine in legal acts the principle of impermissibility for constituent entities of the Russian Federation to impair the legal position of citizens in the field of social security compared to established federal social security legislation. Furthermore, the law-making competence of constituent entities of the Russian Federation and local self-government authorities must not only be clearly defined by the Federation, but also supported by particular financial guarantees specified in legislation. Only then the actual discrimination of citizens on the basis of place of residence, which is prohibited by the Basic Law of the country, will be eliminated. One should recognize the opinion that legislative and executive authorities should be held responsible for the adoption of legal acts that are not conducive to the public good (Aparina et al., 2019) as a fair opinion. Special emphasis should be made on the fact that the adoption of the Social Security Code must be preceded by a solid piece of work to define and formalize the main guidelines and principles of State Policy in social security of citizens, based on the norms of the working Constitution of the Russian Federation and positive international-legal experience. Otherwise, the efficiency of codification will be purely legal-technical in nature and will not result in increased level of social security (Anderson, 1994).

The most serious shortcoming of the system of sources of social security law consists in the vast array of regulations of rule-making bodies at various levels. The problem resides in the fact that most directions, explanations and letters coming from executive authorities do not have any signs of regulatory acts, yet de facto they cover for laws.

In this regard, there is a point of view according to which it is expedient to carry out a stagewise systematization of sources by certain types of social security, examples of which already exist (laws on child benefits, health care, and social services), discussion on the Pension Code of the Russian Federation (Frolov & Trukhanovich, 2004). Considering the fact that Article 72 of the Basic Law of the Russian Federation included social security legislation with the area of joint responsibility of the Russian Federation and its constituent entities, the idea of adopting a code in this field was implemented in a number of the constituent entities of the Russian Federation. Thus, the Code on social protection of certain categories of citizens was adopted on July 4, 2008 in Omsk Region (Kasevich et al., 2019).

It should be emphasized that the question on the need to adopt the Social Code (Social Security Code) in Russia is controversial (Dashkevich, 2011). However, many researchers believe that the adopted code will not affect the level and quality of social security in Russia, since the content of the legal act is much more important than its form. Thus, many countries with advanced social security system—United Kingdom, Sweden, Italy, Belgium, etc. have no social security codes at all, but this level of social security is high.

Social codes were adopted in Germany and France as a consequence of the consolidation of legislation. Many countries are guided by international instruments such as legislative acts of the Council of Europe (Pavlenko, 2016).

The adoption of the Social Security Code must be preceded by the development of the concept of the State Policy of the Russian Federation in social protection of citizens, based on the best international experience in social sphere, and Article 7 of the Basic Law. When drawing up the draft Social Security Code, one should not only rely on the concept of social policy of the State, but also take into account the national positive experiences of law-making (Baieva et al., 2017).

The adoption of the Code must be preceded by a thorough revision of legal acts on social security to reveal those acts that have already ceased to be in force and cause numerous contradictions in law enforcement. This will make it possible to put in order the vast array of legal acts at various levels, to bring them to a common denominator, and to take into account the relationship not only with existing industry standards but also with other branches of law that are one way or another involved in relations in the field of social security—financial, labor, civil and other. The structure of the Code should take into account national standards of jurisprudence, i.e. to consist of a general part and a special part.

The general part will identify the goals and objectives of social security, its underlying principles, the hierarchy of sources of social security law, their effect in time and space, will define the actors in this sector, their rights and liabilities, as well as other key general aspects. The Social Security Code should formalize the rules on the range of rule-making entities and their competence, considering that at this stage, the rule-making competence is actually vested in state non-budgetary funds, non-state pension funds, and supreme judicial authorities, which is inconsistent with the general provisions of theory of law (Tuchkova, 2016). The special part of the codified act should be concerned with individual institutions of social security law: employed (pensionable) service, types of pensions, social allowances, and benefits, provision of various social services, etc. Each Chapter must present a social security system, determine its elements (subject matter, conditions, amount and duration of social security benefits). The Social Code (Social Security Code) must contain not only substantive but also procedural rules. One should establish the responsibility of legislative and executive authorities for the adoption of sources that fail to meet public interests.

4 Conclusion

The completed research leads us to the conclusion that currently there is a long-standing objective need for the adoption of the Social Code (Social Security Code) of the Russian Federation, and its absence is a serious gap in legislation, causing the problems related to enforcement and exercise of the constitutional right of citizens to social security services.

The adoption of the Code will not only contribute greatly to law-making and law-enforcement processes, but will also improve legal consciousness of citizens in terms of norms of social security law, will raise legal awareness and culture.

When the draft code is developed, it is important to clearly define the goal, objectives and principles of social security legislation of the Russian Federation, relying on international law acts, and Articles 2 and 7 of Constitution of the Russian Federation of 1993, competence of authorities of constituent entities of the Russian Federation and local self-government authorities in the field of social security, and to formalize financial guarantees to exercise the rights of abovementioned lawmakers.

The Social Code of the Russian Federation should formalize its priority in the system of sources of social security law, which will be a safeguard against the adoption of regulatory acts which are inconsistent with it, reduce the level of guarantees of social rights of citizens, and actually diminish the constitutional right of an individual to social security services in old age, in case of permanent disability, in case of loss of breadwinner, etc.

It appears important to formalize a uniform terminology and a transparent (clear) way of determining the amount of both State and insurance pensions in the Code.

The adoption of the Social Security Code should result in the elimination of discrimination of citizens in the field of social protection and in the actual increase in its level.

REFERENCES

Abdulgaziyev, R. Z. (2019). Legal consciousness as a factor in the formation of the rule of law. *Revista Dilemas Contemporáneos: Educación, Política y Valores, 7*, 37.

Anderson, J. (1994). *Public policymaking: An introduction.* Boston.

Aparina, O. U., Gabriyan, R. R., Klukovskaya I. N., & Semenov, V. E. (2019). Problems of definition and consolidation of the principles of anticorruption policy in the modern world. *Dilemas Contemporáneos: Educación, Política y Valores*, Year VII, No.1.

Arakcheev, V. S. (2011). On the necessity and feasibility of adopting the social code of the Russian Federation. *Bulletin of Tomsk State University, 1*, 13–19.

Azarova, E. G., Vinogradova, Z. D., & Polupanov, M. I. (1998). The concept of development of legislation on social security. *Concepts of development of Russian legislation*, pp. 165–166.

Baieva, N. A., Burkin, D. O., Vysheslavova, T. F., Lukinova, & S. A. (2018). Current problems faced by Russia in the state-legal policy in social partnership in the labor field (Scopus). *Journal of Advanced Research in Law and Economics, 5*(2), 1564–1570.

Baieva, N. A., Burkin, D. O., Vysheslavova, T. F., & Lukinova, S. A. (2017). The concept of the social state and its implementation in the Russian Federation. *Journal of Advanced Research in Law and Economics, 8*, 5 (27), 1446–1455.

Baieva, N. A., Vysheslavova, T. F., & Lukinova, S. A. (2019). Principle of equity in the law of social security. *Journal of Advanced Research in Dynamical & Control Systems, 11*(Special Issue-08), 2754–2759.

Chappell, R. (2017). *Social welfare in Canadian society.* Nelson.

Dashkevich, V. V. (2011). To the question of the need for codification of social legislation. *Bulletin of Kras GAUU, 8*, 255.

Frolov, O. P., & Trukhanovich, L. V. (2004). *Preparation of the social code of the Russian Federation—The next stage in the codification of Russian legislation.* http://www.kapr.ru/articles/2004/4/3492.html (data accessed: 29 May 2020).

Gabrilyan, R. R., Klukovskaya, I. N., Cardanova, A. K., & Serdyukov, A. A. (2019, Noviembre). *La democracia: el camino del razonamiento y la tradición patriarcal a la doctrina jurídica y la práctica estatal.* Dilemas Contemporáneos: Educación, Política y Valores, Edición Especial.

Grief, N. (1990). *Constitutional Laf and International Law.* United Kingdom Law in the Mid. s. Part.

Grosz, M. (2010). *Sustainable waste trade under WTO Law.* Law Faculty of the University of Zurich.

Kasevich, E. V., Atayan, G. Y., Amvrosova, O. N., Stankevich, G. V., & Kara-Kazaryan, T. V. (2019). *Perspectives on the use of new information and communication technology (ICT) in the modern economy* (pp. 439–445). Advances in Intelligent Systems and Computing. Springer.

Kobylinskaya, S. V., & Karsanova, Z.K. (2014). On the role of codification of the systematization of the Russian legislation on social security. In *Proceedings of the Kuban State Agrarian University* (Vol. 48) (pp. 195–198).

Kobzeva, S. I. (2014). *Sources of social security law.* M, pp. 26–39.

Navasardova, E. S., Nutrikhin, R. V., Zinovyeva, T. N., Shishkin, V. A., & Joludeva, J. V. (2018). Codification of the natural resource legislation in the Russian Empire. *Journal of Advanced Research in Law and Economics, 9*(1), 183–193.

Pavlenko, D. S. (2016). Problems of codification of social security law in Russia. *Young Scientist, 6*(6), 95–96. https://moluch.ru/archive/110/27486/ (data accessed: 29 May 2020).

Smirnov, D. A., Tereshchenko, E. A., Botasheva, L. E., Trofimov, M. S., Melnikova, V. A., & Dolgopolov, K. A. (2020). Digital jurisprudence. *Revista Inclusiones, 7*(1), 273–283.

Smirnov, D. A., Zhukov, A. P., Aparina, O. Y., Lauta, O. N., & Zakalyapin, D. V. (2019). Use of the transformational leadership model in police management. *Amazonia Investiga, 8*(20), 54–55.

Telegin, T. D. (2015). *The right to social security in questions and answers: TC Velby, Prospect,* pp. 77–78.

Tuchkova, E. G. (2016). *The right of social security of Russia.* M.: Prospect.

Voronin, M. V., & Przhilenskiy, I. V. (2019). Social and legal technologies in the system of legal policy. *Journal of Politics and Law, 12*(5), 48–52.

Weiss, C. H., & Bucuvala, M. J. (1980). *Social science research and decision – making.* Columbia University Press.

Zhuzhgov, I. V., Volkov, A. A., Salnyy, A. M., Kulikova, T. B., & Ryasnyanskaya, N. A. (2019). Legal space monitoring: Theoretical and legal aspects. *Opcion, 35*(20), 2337–2365.

Consumer Rights Protection in a Digital Space: Problems and Ways of Their Solution

Marina A. Bychko[ID], Elena N. Barkova[ID], Elena N. Volodkova[ID], Vladimir V. Cherevko[ID], and Beslan B. Argunov[ID]

1 INTRODUCTION

Penetration of digital technologies in all spheres of human life entail globalization of consumer markets, active changes in the economy, including those arising from the digitalization of sales channels, emergence of new digital products, smart electronics, and the transition to remote interaction with the consumer. E-trade in goods, works and services became predominant, especially during the coronavirus pandemic which affected the entire mankind. The issues of adequate protection of online consumers, adaptation of current legislation to modern digital realia have

---

M. A. Bychko (✉) · E. N. Barkova
North-Caucasus Federal University, Stavropol, Russia

E. N. Volodkova
Stavropol State Pedagogical Institute, Stavropol, Russia

V. V. Cherevko
Institute Of Management And Integrated Security, Moscow, Russia
e-mail: Cherevkovv@bk.ru

B. B. Argunov
Stavropol Institute of Cooperation, Stavropol, Russia

© The Author(s), under exclusive license to Springer Nature Switzerland AG 2021
E. G. Popkova and B. S. Sergi (eds.), *Economic Issues of Social Entrepreneurship*,
https://Doi.org/10.1007/978-3-030-77291-8_19

205

recently become aggravated. Regulation of consumer rights protection mechanisms using national legislation only is already obsolete. International legislation, containing general provisions regulating the relationship between consumers and their contracting parties in digital markets, must underlie legal regulation of e-commerce. The emerged a need to establish a transnational consumer's law in the field of digital reality. The first steps in this direction were made quite a while ago, in 1996, by the UN Commission, which developed the UNCITRAL Model Law concerning e-commerce, based on which more than 72 countries adopted their legislation. This law is a body of norms that was selected at the international level and regulated e-commerce.

Russian consumer protection legislation is currently on the threshold of codification. This was due to the positive experiences of Brazil, France, and Italy, where consumer protection legislation has long been codified, as well as suggestions of the need to systematize the existing disparate consumer protection norms in Russia, that have been emerging in the domestic doctrine in recent decades (Railian, 2017). The objectives and motives justifying the codification of consumer protection legislation include the need to develop the Fundamental Principles of consumer protection legislation that would correspond to the digital transformation of market relations; active use of online platforms, not only as direct sellers, but also as information intermediaries for online sales of goods, works, and services; increasing the importance of remote interaction with the consumer and other reasons.

2   Materials and Method

Dialectic-materialistic method, general scientific method and specific scientific method constitute the methodological basis for the study of issues of consumer rights protection in the context of the digital economy.

The possibility to identify the features of the position of consumers in the digital space, to show the relation between the level of consumer protection from the mode of acquisition of goods (services) emerged with the use of the dialectic-materialistic method.

Comparison, synthesis, and analysis methods enabled the comparative legal analysis of provisions of current Russian, foreign and international consumer protection legislation. The use of abovementioned general scientific methods and formal-legal method made it possible to define the priorities for improving Russian legislation and to introduce specific proposals concerning the possibility of implementation of best foreign practices.

3 RESULTS

The use of modern information technologies and communication systems brought consumers to a whole new level of living. At the same time, the problem of insufficient legal protection of rights and interests of online consumers became apparent. Current consumer protection legislation needs to be systematized and supplemented in terms of the regulation of position of consumers in digital markets. The legal community is looking for acceptable legal instruments to regulate the digital economy in general (Melnikova et al., 2019) and the consumer sector in particular.

Based on international and foreign practices, decision was made in Russia to codify legislation on consumer rights protection until 2023. The designated solution was included in the Plan of action for the implementation of the state policy strategy of the Russian Federation in the field of consumer rights protection until 2030, with the result that the Concept of codification of consumer protection legislation of the Russian Federation is already drawn up. During the discussion of this Concept at the Saint Petersburg International Legal Forum (May 14–18, 2019), the experts once again stressed the timeliness of the codification, the need for which arises from changes in the related economy to the digitalization of sales channels, emergence of smart electronics, and the Internet of Things. This is a weighty argument for the revision of not only fundamental, but also special provisions ensuring fundamental consumer rights. Domestic doctrine discusses the potential form of this codification already: it will be a Consumer Protection Code, like in France and Italy, or Fundamental Principles of consumer protection legislation, combining provisions of different branches of law and regulating consumer relations. As concerns Russia, the codification process has historically been difficult all the time. Many codification ideas, including the creation of the Code of Commerce, were never implemented, and some were not very consistent and not always effective. (Navasardova et al., 2018). We hope that modern consumer protection legislation will not suffer the same fate.

In our opinion, special attention should be paid to the opinion of Professor Railian who insists on greater expedience of adoption of fundamental principles of consumer protection legislation rather than Consumer Protection Code. His reasoning is primarily based on the layered architecture of legislation in the field of consumer rights protection. The fact that legislation on consumer rights protection is a complex branch of legislation has long been pointed out by legal scholars; in particular, this viewpoint was defended by one of the authors of this research, Bychko (2000). Professor Railian (2017) believes that codes are most appropriate for unitary states, and it would be more reasonable if Russia recalled the experience of Soviet legal regulation—"Basic Codes", which, according to him, would correspond to the federal structure of the State and the need to implement the framework legal regulation of joint competences of the Federal Center and the regions. This problem could be fully solved with the use of the fundamental principles of legislation having the status of Federal Law. We rally the above opinion. We believe that the form of codification is important, of course, but the most important thing is that consumer protection legislation will finally be systematized and brought to conformity with digital realia.

Another way to improve Russian consumer protection legislation must be the creation of an online service for the pre-trial management of consumer disputes. Such service has been functioning for more than 20 years and proved to be very efficient abroad. As of 2013, 32% of countries created services for the resolution of disputes in e-commerce (Koroliova, 2017) at that point in time. Existing dispute resolution (DR) mechanisms are extensively used and are gaining popularity among consumers. That said, the present ability of such regulation increases the level of trust to e-commerce, and this fact was pointed out by the researchers. In early 2016, the European Commission created a new DR platform which included 117 such organizations from 17 states (United Nations Guidelines on Consumer Protection, 2016). The operation principle comes down to the submission of a complaint via a platform that directs it to the seller.

The United States are leading in terms of online dispute resolution and management. According to information provided by the United Nations Conference on Trade and Development in "A guide on consumer rights protection"—the first comprehensive international reference guide published in 2018 by the UN, the platform is used to resolve 60 million disputes per year, compared to less than 300,000 disputes resolved within the framework of the judiciary system of the United States (United Nations Guidelines on Consumer Protection, 2016). There are recommendations for providers containing best practices of online dispute resolution, according to which the providers shall be obliged to inform the consumer of the procedure, place, and time frames for the submission of a complaint (Muratova, 2019). However, American law prioritizes protection of businesses over ordinary consumers in resolution of disputes (Winn & Webber, 2006), which compares it unfavorably with the law of the European Union. Professor Beloglavek at the Masaryk University in Brno emphasizes that the degree of consumer protection in the United States is lower than that in European countries which comply with the EU law (Beloglavek, 2012).

It is important to note that in all online transactions, including in online dispute resolution, special emphasis is made on the preservation of confidentiality of personal data of consumers and protection against cybercrimes. The relevance of this issue has been raised quite a while ago in foreign countries (Quirk & Rothchild, 2017). One way to ensure protection of information from cyber threats is to create and adopt special laws and regulations which would establish responsibility for unauthorized access to information, illegal copying, distortion and unauthorized use of information with a criminal and mercenary motive (Abdulgaziev et al., 2019).

Russia has already prepared a Draft Law to create a legal framework for the development of a system of alternative online dispute resolution mechanisms, but it is still being finalized at the instruction of the Government of the Russian Federation. We believe it necessary to make this mechanism free for consumers, by analogy with the best foreign counterparts. We do not share the opinion of the law drafters regarding the voluntary basis of the use of online dispute resolution platforms, which, according to their plan, will create a basis for the formation of a competitive environment in e-commerce. We believe that such an approach will become a basis for the emergence of "defunct standards", and will postpone the start of effective operation of a new online mechanism for long. Initially, all participants of e-commerce should be bound by obligation to use this platform. Only then, when it is widely recognized and its effectiveness is proven, will it be voluntarily used for the first time.

In order to fulfill the task of ensuring expedited introduction of digital technologies in the economy and social sphere set by the Government of the Russian Federation (Kasevich et al., 2019), the first steps in online consulting and provision of information to Russian consumers have already been made. In 2016, the Public Information Resource in the field of consumer rights protection (PIR CRP) was created. In 2018, decision was made to use it as a basis for the creation of a new digital platform and a mobile application for consumers to provide additional information services and new opportunities.

As to the administration of justice in cases arising from consumer disputes in offline commerce, digital technologies are widely used here as well, and an active process of implementing digital technologies in civil legal proceedings is currently under way (Smirnov et al., 2020). That said, hopefully the judges will not be replaced by robots, the so-called Artificial Intelligence, since the judiciary system in a number of cases implies a decision that is made not only on the basis of the principle of legality, which may be comprehensible by the robot, but also the principle of justice, which is only possible with the participation of a man (Baieva et al., 2019). The need to determine the amount of compensation for moral injury caused to the consumer could be the most striking example of it.

The completed research has shown that current Russian legislation guarantees different levels of protection of consumer of offline and online products. Purchasing products on online platforms is particularly dangerous. We are referring to specifics of participation in the so-called retail business—commerce using aggregators. The problems related to the operation of such platforms have been identified before and have been discussed at several European events as a consequence of major disputes (Ostanina, 2019). The discussion was focused upon two online platforms: call-a-taxi service Uber, where drivers were not considered employees of a taxi company and could work without any license, and the Airbnb accommodation booking service, which was owned by various individuals, and the accommodation did not meet the necessary requirements. The platforms positioned themselves as intermediaries aimed at bringing the contracting parties together. Pursuant to the judgment of the European Court of Justice, the call-a-taxi service is a transportation service rather than an information service. A similar judgment was made with regard to the accommodation booking service.

It should be pointed out that similar problems affected Russian consumers as well. Here, it would be relevant to point out the practice of the Supreme Court of the Russian Federation which made its judgment No. 5-KG17-220 of 09.01.2018 with regard to the call-a-taxi website, when a trip with the use of this service ended in death for a passenger due to a traffic violation by a driver whose driving license had been suspended before for the same reason. The owners of the call-a-taxi website tried to avoid taking on responsibility, claiming that their website only provides intermediary services. Nevertheless, the court brought them to responsibility, having applied provisions on agency relationship (Chapter 52 of the Civil Code of the Russian Federation).

As a result of the identified issue of bringing online platforms to responsibility, a draft EU Directive on online intermediary platforms was prepared in Europe in 2016, which is commonly referred to as the Academic Project (Cauffman, 2016). In our opinion, the most important things in this document are suggestions about establishing solidary responsibility of the online platform with an end supplier. However, there are few situations when it can be established. The online platform will be brought to solidary responsibility together with tier-one supplier only if it does not comply with the requirement to inform the consumer that he/she enters into a transaction with a particular supplier, rather than with an online platform. The second case of solidary responsibility will be a situation when "predominant influence" on the decision of the consumer to enter into a transaction is exerted by business reputation of the online platform rather than the image of the seller. As envisioned by the project, the fact of "predominant influence" must be assessed according to several criteria: the contracting parties concluded an agreement on the platform, the platform processed payments, the amount of which was determined by the platform operator, etc. While analyzing these criteria, the operation of any large website which won consumers' confidence and has good business reputation, e.g. Booking.com, comes to mind. At this point, it should be noted that amid the coronavirus pandemic, for the first time ever, the consumers of tourism services who had purchased tourist products beforehand to have a rest during public holidays and vacations, were faced with the problem of refunding money paid for booking of tours and hotels. Major online booking systems ceased to respond to the demand of consumers regarding the refund of money paid for cancelled bookings, and companies have started to aggressively position themselves as mere intermediaries between the lodging establishments and tourist consumers. Russian consumer who lodged a claim to the platform was given a recommendation to address the accommodation facility. It, in turn, suggested postponing the date of arrival or refunding money as soon as it resumes its activities suspended due to restrictive measures and bans on tourist services. Once again, the consumer turned out to be the most vulnerable party in the current situation. His/her money was transferred long before the scheduled tour as a prepayment for the booking, and all this while it was used for economic purposes of the accommodation facility and the online platform. Russian legislation, namely the Law of the Russian Federation "On consumer rights protection", despite amendments in it that took effect on January 1, 2019 and were given the tacit name "the Law on aggregators", cannot protect the consumer under the conditions described above. In our opinion, responsibility established by the legislator for the owner of the aggregator does not meet current needs. In our situation, the provision of Paragraph 2.2. of Article 12 of the Law of the Russian Federation "Consumer on rights protection" is non-effective as well. In the case under consideration, the term of contract has not yet become due. The contract for the provision of tourist services was terminated by consumers in advance due to their unwillingness to expose themselves to the danger of getting infected. In addition, the contract provided for the possibility of abandoning its performance by the consumer for any reason whatsoever without the application of penal sanctions on the part of the contractor.

We believe that in such cases the aggregator must bear at least joint responsibility with the contractor (seller) working on his/her platform, better yet solidary responsibility. We can see the following arguments: first, the consumer, despite any indications on the end seller (contractor) by the platform, gets oriented by the name, business reputation of the owner of the aggregator (online platform), as in the example with the online hotel booking system Booking.com. First, consumers who conclude contracts on such platforms show their level of trust to the contracting party. In this case, we can observe an analogy with the franchising agreement, pursuant to which the copyright holder shall bear either solidary or joint responsibility together with the user of exclusive rights before the consumer. Second, we fully agree with the opinion that was expressed in the print media, according to which it is unacceptable to grant privileges to some entrepreneurs over others, which violates "the principle of equality of entrepreneurs before the law" (Suvorov, 2019). We are referring to effective sanctions prescribed for sellers (contractors) in offline transactions with consumers, and exemption from responsibility in e-commerce. We should give a comparable example of hypermarkets, supermarkets, and the owners of the aggregator (online platform). The former bear the entire responsibility to the consumer pursuant to the Law of the Russian Federation "Consumer rights on protection". In addition, the consumer has the right to address not only to the seller but also to the manufacturer and importer of the goods for the satisfaction of his/her claims. So how come that the consumer does not have the right to choose a person to lodge his/her claims when making a transaction with the owner of the aggregator?! As a matter of fact, online consumers are even more vulnerable compared to their offline "fellows". We deem it necessary to put the owners of the aggregators (online platforms) on equal footing with similar business entities in offline commerce and hold them responsible for the violation of rights of online consumers.

4 Conclusion

E-commerce with the involvement of the consumer is developing very rapidly, but many issues related to the provision of protection of consumers' rights and interests are still unresolved. These issues are pressing for the entire world community. The convergence of Russian and foreign experiences of effective consumer rights protection will make it possible to create uniform legal regulation of consumer relations, to eliminate conflicts in law enforcement, to develop unified principles of cooperation and mutual assistance in order to preclude unfair cross-border practices, to improve not only international, but also national legislations in this field. Critical issues for all countries should be resolved: increasing the level of protection of rights of online consumers and their trust in e-commerce; determining the legal status and responsibility of operators of intermediary online platforms (retail trade websites), the owners of the aggregators with regard to the transactions made on them, etc.

The current state of Russian consumer protection legislation is distinguished by a large number of diverse laws and regulations and poorly conforms to digital realia. This is a weighty argument for its systematization in the form of codification and improvement towards the formalization of standards, ensuring effective protection of rights of online consumers.

Russia needs to create an online service for the pre-trial management of consumer disputes. It should be free for consumers and mandatory for all online sellers (contractors). Otherwise, the mechanism would not be in-demand and would become formal.

The consumer concluding a contract on the Internet must have the same level of protection as the consumer in offline commerce. To this end, it is necessary to give the consumer the right to choose the entity for submission of claims about the purchased goods (services) in the digital market. It is not only the immediate seller (contractor), but also

214   M. A. BYCHKO ET AL.

the owner of the aggregator through which the contract is concluded, that should be held responsible for non-performance or improper performance of the contract with the consumer. The owner of the aggregator must bear solidary or joint responsibility.

REFERENCES

Abdulgaziev, R. Z., Alsultanov, M. R., Mamichev, V. N., Sarukhanyan, A. R., Sostin, D. I., & Sukhorukova, A. N. (2019). Social causation of criminalization of cyber crime committed with the use of information technology. *International Journal of Advanced Trends in Computer Science and Engineering, 8*(5), 2459–2463.

Baieva, N. A., Vysheslavova, T. F., & Lukinova, S. A. (2019). The principle of justice in social security law. *Journal of Advanced Research in Dynamical & Control Systems, 11*(Special Issue-08), 2754–2759.

Beloglavek, A. (2012). *Consumer protection in arbitration.* http://www-arbitrationlaw.com/files/free_pdfs/01-cover_pagetoc.pdf/ (data accessed 12 May 2020).

Bychko, M. A. (2000). *Development of legislation on consumer rights protection in Russia: Historical and legal aspect* (Synopsis of the Ph.D. thesis in Legal Science). Stavropol.

Cauffman, K. (2016). *The commission's European agenda for the collaborative economy—(Too) platform and service provider friendly?* https://www.researchgate.net/publication/311582253_The_Commission's_European_Agenda_for_the_Collaborative_Economy_-_Too_Platform_and_Service_Provider_Friendly (data accessed 12 May 2020).

Kasevich, E. V., Atayan, G. Y., Amvrosova, O. N., Stankevich, G. V., & Kara-Kazaryan, T. V. (2019). *Perspectives on the use of new information and communication technology (ICT) in the modern economy* (pp. 439–445). Advances in Intelligent Systems and Computing. Springer.

Koroliova, A. N. (2017). Consumer rights protection in the context of formation of the digital commodity market. *Legal Bulletin of the Samara State University, 3.*

Melnikova, M. P., Bychko, M. A., Komarevceva, I. A., Melnichuk, M. A., & Dzhanbidaeva, Z. S. (2019). Legal education in the digital age: Problems and prospects. *JURIDICAS CUC, 301*–320.

Muratova, O. V. (2019). The concept of multinational consumer right these days. *Chastnoe Pravo, 7.*

Navasardova, E. S., Nutrikhin, R. V., Zinovyeva, T. N., Shishkin, V. A., & Joludeva, J. V. (2018). Codification of the natural resource legislation in the Russian Empire. *Journal of Advanced Research in Law and Economics, 9*(1), 183–193.

Ostanina, E. A. (2019). Standard form contract executed online, and protection of consumer rights. *Property Relations in the Russian Federation*, 8.

Quirk, P., & Rothchild, J. (2017). Consumer protection and the internet. In *Handbook of research on international consumer law*. https://www.research chgate.net/publication/289710022_Consumer_protection_and_the_internet (data accessed 12 May 2020).

Railian, A. A. (2017). Consumer Protection Code of the Russian Federation or Fundamental Principles of consumer protection legislation of the Russian Federation? *Zhurnal Rossiyskogo Prava*, 11.

Smirnov, D. A., Tereshchenko, E. A., Botasheva, L. E., Trofimov, M. S., Melnikova, V. A., & Dolgopolov, K. A. (2020). Digital jurisprudence. *Revista Inclusiones*, *7*(1), 273–283.

Suvorov, E. D. (2019). Particular issues of e-commerce: Revisiting the responsibility of the owners of the aggregators before consumers. *Bulletin of Economic Justice of the Russian Federation*, 9.

United Nations Guidelines on Consumer Protection. (2016). https://unctad.org/en/Pages/DITC/CompetitionLaw/UN-Guidelines-on-Consumer-Protection.aspx (data accessed 12 May 2020).

Winn, J., & Webber, M. (2006). *The impact of EU unfair contract terms law on US business-to-consumer Internet merchants*. https://www.researchgate.net/publication/254137525_The_Impact_of_EU_Unfair_Contract_Terms_Law_on_US_Business-to Consumer_Internet_Merchants (data accessed 12 May 2020).

Role of the Internet Network in the Process of Forming Legal Culture of Entrepreneurs

Kirill A. Dolgopolov, *Ludmila V. Kiryukhina*, *and Igor V. Przhilenskiy*

1 Introduction

In recent times, the Internet has been increasingly widely used by commercial entities in diverse areas of business activity in Russia and abroad. This is due to the fact that the use of the Internet significantly reduces the costs of doing business as well as time expenditures related to relevant business activities. In addition, today's online platforms are replete with diverse educational content for education and implementation of business activity.

The progress recorded in the formation and expansion of the digital economy is primarily determined by the continuous development and rapid proliferation of information and communication technologies as well as the sustained retreat in prices of their acquisition and use, which makes them more affordable. In addition, one should point out the massive transition of various formats of socioeconomic activity to online platforms and the rapid development of e-commerce.

K. A. Dolgopolov (✉) · L. V. Kiryukhina · I. V. Przhilenskiy
North-Caucasus Federal University, Stavropol, Russia

I. V. Przhilenskiy
e-mail: yesdreamer@yandex.ru

© The Author(s), under exclusive license to Springer Nature Switzerland AG 2021
E. G. Popkova and B. S. Sergi (eds.), *Economic Issues of Social Entrepreneurship*,
https://doi.org/10.1007/978-3-030-77291-8_20

217

2 Materials and Method

One should distinguish one of the basic methods—the comparative legal method, in the scope of which the sources of law reflecting the state of legal culture of e-commerce entities on the Internet were compared. Further, a general scientific method of deduction was used, which enabled the comprehensive assessment of legal issues in regulating business-to-business relations in Internet space.

The method of analyzing the state of legal regulation of commercial relations on the Internet, as well as legal culture as an independent phenomenon, including its structure, functions, and essence directly in connection with the Internet-space, and in the context of specific subjects of study, was made the fundamental method of research.

An axiological method was used for the writing of the paper, in terms of which legal culture on the Internet was examined as an emerging system of legal values, in particular, legal awareness, legislation related to the formation of legal culture on the Internet, and legal activity of entrepreneurs.

3 Results

Today, there is an active selection of mechanisms that will allow achieving the necessary balance in our society between legal culture within the framework of business and legal culture on the Internet, taking into account the specifics of culture of Russian society as a whole. We should point out that the process of free expression of personal views, ideas, and beliefs, which is directly enshrined in legislation of our country, can be generally limited by certain restrictions related to the activities in the Internet (Ivanova, 2018). As a rule, the law reflects the joint will, which is seen as the final agreement in the process of reaching a single compromise in society. Taking into consideration the fact that the conflicts may arise at various levels, in any society, we, nonetheless, believe that the use of efficient mechanisms for solving them appears to be expedient.

The progress in commercial use of the Internet has formed a specific list of issues related to legal regulation in this field (Belykh & Bolobonova, 2020). Today, there is a significant need to solve the problems related to legal culture of entrepreneurs through the adaptation of the existing and development of new legal acts regulating the business relations involving the use of the Internet.

The significance of the online platforms which have the form of an updated instrument for the management of communication of business entities, along with the function of discussing information, arises from substantial amounts of funding that are currently focused on the development of diverse formats of activity of the Internet resources. The number of advertisements in online media, within the framework of activity of multidimensional blogs and operation of other online resources is rapidly increasing. In addition, there is an ongoing work to create the up-to-date software which could be used in the Internet by all representatives of society, by e-commerce entities in particular.

At present, business entities have found themselves in an age of information technologies, in which the fundamental problem is seen as a significant growth and at the same time intelligence into the processes of provision of information from one entity to another. This procedure, of course, has its impact on legal culture: there is a correlation between the material and spiritual aspects of life, which is attributed, in one respect, to the existence of information elements subject to the above changes in legal culture, while in other respect, to the origin of the detailed distinction between emotional and informational aspects of legal culture.

Rapid development of information systems on the Internet directly from the perspective of a universal communication mechanism contributes to the fact that news information is instantly recognized as the property of a great number of users and has a significant impact on the formation of everyday awareness. We should note that the principle of accessibility, and at the same time distance of business entities with regard to information, serves to elimination of the boundary between traditional and Internet platforms. The impact of features under consideration on business activity leads to the transformation of legal culture of business representatives.

Results of analytical activity that focuses on the area of e-commerce (Gruntovskii, 2018) are to some extent reflective of the fact that legal culture, on a par with elements of legal awareness, plays a significant role in the process of internet space formation (Abdrakhmanov, 2018). Legal culture as such is generally regarded as a fundamental component from the perspective of the implementation of activities of e-commerce entities within the scope of relations on the Internet and the most important phenomenon of all socioeconomic and information life of society. We should also point out that it is aimed at developing an adequate perception of the multidimensional phenomena of law by-commerce representatives, reflection of the place of these phenomena in traditional environment and in virtual reality space. With such positions, legal culture of an entrepreneur on the Internet can be analyzed as a derivative of personal culture in general.

At present, legal awareness on the Internet can no longer be studied without taking into account the specifics of activities of e-commerce entities, their information and legal activity, progressive ideas and judgments about entrepreneurship, law, and the Internet. Legal culture is recognized as a socioeconomic and informational phenomenon.

In terms of the level of formedness of a person, entrepreneurial legal awareness from the perspective of virtual space can be represented in the framework of legal preparation of legal entities directly to the working process in virtual space, perception and use of advanced regulatory and legislative ideas and drives on the Internet. The level of this training is important in terms of the skills of using the provisions of international legislation, as well as the competence-based procedure for assessing the personalized knowledge of law and legal actions in the Internet environment. Within this position, actions of e-commerce entities can be characterized by the existence of corresponding orientations from the perspective of legal culture.

In our opinion, it is necessary to take into account the degree of development of legal culture of entrepreneurs within the framework of Internet relations, the depth of knowledge of specialized legislative acts regulating e-commerce, as well as other acts relating directly to the legal regulation of the Internet, the ability to knowledgeably master these regulatory acts. We assume it should be pointed out that within the scope of the assessment of legal culture on the online platforms, as well as during the analysis of common legal awareness, they distinguish between common, professional and general-theoretical levels (Rozhkova, 2018) of legal culture of entrepreneurs in Internet relations.

In our opinion, the usual degree of development of legal culture of entrepreneurs is limited to working within the limits of sporadic actions in the worldwide web, which involves, in addition to direct information and technical functions, implementation of the process of communication with legal provisions regulating commercial activities in virtual space. This kind of legal awareness is extremely superficial; in addition, e-commerce entities at the stage under discussion understand the precepts of law from the perspective of legal acts, and use them in their direct activity in virtual reality when bridging the current gaps in law.

It is important to establish that the level of professional knowledge of legal culture of commercial entities is developed in those entities that carry out their activity on the platform of Internet technologies in a professional manner and use necessary legal provisions in a digital environment. Such e-commerce representatives can most often be characterized by a significant degree of understanding and use of legal acts on the Internet (Gruntovskii, 2018).

We should point to the fact that the theoretic degree of the analyzed systematization is determined by the actions of researchers in the Internet space, including actions of legal and economic researchers, which, similar to the process of resolution of personal commercial problems on the Internet, directly handle the categories of law and e-commerce on virtual reality platforms at a scientific level.

In such a situation, the essential characteristic of legal awareness is developed within the framework of the application of a specific tool which requires the analysis of legal behavior of e-commerce representatives in the worldwide web. More specifically, the attitude of entrepreneurs towards those regulatory acts they have to use. In addition, the study of specific features, modes of action of entrepreneurs within the framework of virtual relation to good and bad behavior, as well as the consideration of the level of activity of assigned entities in virtual space and beyond it (Malko et al., 2018) becomes important.

While having a certain degree of legal culture, e-commerce entity within the scope of Internet relations is able to lawfully and with ease focus on the Internet; we should point out that it is obliged to act in compliance with laws and other acts regulating the Internet (Grigoriev, 2020). Today, this provision is critical, since the laws of different countries have been increasingly violated on the online platforms, and there have been other forms of crime as well. This fact stems from the fact that a legal culture in the area of interest must fulfil several useful preventive and important functions. In our opinion, it is expedient to distinguish the following functions:

- value-conscious and legal function, in the process of its execution by entrepreneurs, the provisions of law, the legal behavior of partners, as well as attitude towards them from the perspective of legal provisions are manifested in the quality of objects of valuation activities;
- transformational function, which is characterized within the worldwide web by legal and moral obligations of the businessmen in order

to gain the most detailed understanding of functioning of virtual space, its improvement and development;
- communicative function, which is analyzed by means of communication, connection, contacts of entrepreneurs within the framework of Internet relations with each other on online platforms.

It should be emphasized that a significant role is played directly by the communicative function of legal culture on the Internet, which is conditioned by the process of transfer of legal information with a view not only to notifying the public of current legal provisions, but also developing respect to them (Rozhkova, 2018).

Please note that multiple communication channels are available for the transfer of legal information. At the same time, for the most part, business entities acquire information about effective laws and regulations or newly-adopted laws from general sources of communication, such as social networks: Instagram, Facebook, Twitter, VK etc. Today, official Instagram accounts are kept by many public authorities, including the State Duma of the Russian Federation and the Investigation Committee. Professional accounts of legal practitioners who use this web platform to provide initial advice on drafting of legal documents, to provide initial consulting on legal issues, to give explanations for existing legislation, and to inform subscribers of changes in legislation free-of-charge (Shatilina, 2018). In addition, multidimensional communities of legal and economic experts are being created and maintained in social networks. It should be noted that these general sources of legal information largely impact the development of legal culture of entrepreneurs.

Hence, the formation and progress of online communities, social networks, and online platforms in contemporary world promoted the update of sources of legal information, creation of the cutting-edge forms of communication, and bringing legal culture in information networks to a new level (Naumov, 2018). Social networks are designed to assist in gaining and understanding legal information that is needed by entrepreneurs. Online platforms, while providing access to information characterized by different quality and levels, multidimensional cultural values and objectives, can contribute to both positive and negative changes in legal culture of e-commerce entities. The online community has the potential to express respect for the right and the law, to develop legal awareness, legal culture, and to promote active good behavior of entrepreneurs. At the same time, the presence of a massive layer of unreliable information contributes to contrary processes.

We believe that it should be pointed out that the essence of legal culture of entrepreneurs on the Internet is characterized by the following components:

- Legal awareness. As noted above, legal awareness is recognized as the fundamental part of legal culture of entrepreneurs. In particular, this category covers conventional views about a variety of legal phenomena that are predominant on the Internet, namely provisions, principles, system of law, and legal relations. At present, similar judgments are not recognized as consistent; they are more based on feelings rather than knowledge, since their sources are considered from the general perspective. Sources of information that have not been verified;
- Values. Legal culture is characterized not only by representations. It includes values and value systems of e-commerce entities. Legal policies of commercial entities are of paramount importance, since they assist in translating judgements and milestones into everyday life, or the practical orientation of business representatives into virtual space. The policy concerning the purchase of verified legal information in the online shop within the scope of executed sale and purchase contract appears to be a striking example of the phenomenon described above (Sushkova, 2019).

The abovementioned facts give us an opportunity to give serious thought to the possibility of development of a mechanism to improve legal awareness and legal culture of e-commerce entities within the framework of Internet communication.

4 Conclusion

In our opinion, the development of a personalized program which would take into account measures to improve educational products for entrepreneurs with regard to the issues of doing business in virtual space, improving their legal education and culture, will be considered effective (Azizov & Arkhipov, 2014). Moreover, alongside with these procedures, it is important to prepare legal provisions with regard to the maintenance of appropriate cultural and legal standards on the Internet, for the entities under consideration in particular.

While determining the content, we believe that this regulatory act should take into account the following directions:

- an act as a tool of self-discipline and as a tool for the judicial and other authorities in respect of the aspect of the source of necessary information;
- it is important to formalize the standards of cultural and legal conduct of business entities on the Internet, and the importance of following the spirit and the letter of the law by entrepreneurs;
- to establish that responsibility for violation of behavioral rules which is documented in the elaborated act shall extend to the entire pool of representatives of e-commerce in accordance with the existing legal framework of the country, as well as provisions of international law.

From the perspective of implementation of the effect of suggested act, certain checklists can be created that would document major violations specifying business entities.

In conclusion, it is worth noting that efficient legal regulation in the Internet is considered to be of paramount importance for the development of legal culture of entrepreneurs; in many countries, this issue is still unresolved to date. We believe that the State should turn its attention to the development of high-quality content within the framework of legal information and creation of a legal environment which would include legal policies, ideas, and opinions, within the online community.

References

Abdrakhmanov, D. V. (2018). Legal certainty as a guarantee for the exercise of the constitutional and legal foundation of the information society in the Russian Federation. *Yurist, 7*, 59–70.

Azizov, R. F., & Arkhipov, V. V. (2014). Relations on Internet in WEB 2.0 format: A problem of consistency between network architecture and legal regulation. *Zakon, 1*, 90–104.

Belykh, V. S., & Bolobonova, M. O. (2020). Concept, importance and trends of digital law development. *Yurist, 1*, 5–14.

Grigoriev, A. V. (2020). The exercise of the constitutional right of citizens to manage the affairs of State amid digitalization. *Zhurnal Rossiyskogo Prava, 2,* 45–57.

Gruntovskii, I. I. (2018). Legal culture of society as a basis for the formation of a legal environment for business. *Bezopasnost Biznesa, 2,* 12–18.

Ivanova, K. A. (2018). Modern conception of the right of citizens to freedom of expression in cyberspace. *Konstitutsionnoe i Munitsipalnoe Pravo, 5,* 36–39.

Malko, A. V., Isakov, N. V., Mazurenko, A. P., Smirnov, D.A., & Isakov, I. N. (2018). Legal policy as a means to improve lawmaking process. *Astra Salvensis, 6*(1), 836–837.

Naumov, V. B. (2018). Negative patterns in the formation of the conceptual framework in the field of Internet regulation and identification. *Informatsionnoe Pravo, 1,* 32–39.

Rozhkova, M. A. (2018). *Internet Law: A collection of articles. M.: Statut.*

Shatilina, A. S. (2018). Human rights on the Internet: The issue of recognition of the to access the Internet. *Legal Precedents of the European Court on Human Rights, 1,* 38–45.

Sushkova, O. V. (2019). Pressing issues in copyright protection practice in business on the Internet. *Predprinimatelskoe Pravo. Appendix "Pravo I Biznes", 3,* 26–31.

Modern Trends in the Development of Environmental Emergencies Legislation: Theoretical and Legal Aspects

Eleonora S. Navasardova, *Natalya G. Zhavoronkova*, *and Vyacheslav B. Agafonov*

1 INTRODUCTION

Ecological and biological safety is a complex and not fully studied subject of legal regulation. The problem is that, on the one hand, there are fairly obvious studied and classified issues, on the other hand, the most complicated and, therefore, potentially hazardous elements are outside the law—genetics, bioengineering, and global infrastructure projects. We are talking about unknown, but quite real situations, events, facts that can lead to a global catastrophe, and were unknown in the past.

Among the environmental hazards, creating a threat of emergencies, the biological and genetic safety stands out, but currently there is no

---

E. S. Navasardova (✉)
North Caucasian Federal University, Stavropol, Russia

N. G. Zhavoronkova · V. B. Agafonov
Moscow State Law University (MSAL), Moscow, Russia

V. B. Agafonov
National University of Oil and Gas (Gubkin University), Moscow, Russia

© The Author(s), under exclusive license to Springer Nature Switzerland AG 2021
E. G. Popkova and B. S. Sergi (eds.), *Economic Issues of Social Entrepreneurship*,
https://doi.org/10.1007/978-3-030-77291-8_21

single systematized legislative and regulatory, and methodological framework that allows to identify, take into account, determine and classify all possible features and conditions for assigning some or others risks and threats to an emergency of a natural and, in particular, biological disaster.

2 Materials and Method

To shed a light on modern approaches to the study of the problems of improving the legislative and regulatory framework in the area of population and territories protection from emergencies caused by environmental and biological threats, a comparison of various methods of legal regulation and management was made, including the dialectical, logical, predictive method, as well as the method of system analysis.

The implication of these methods made it possible to carry out a comprehensive legal analysis of the current legislation, documents of state strategy planning, bills of federal laws and to develop a theoretical and legal doctrine for ensuring environmental and biological safety in emergency situations, and on the basis of which to formulate package proposals for improving the current legislation.

3 Results

According to the article 1 of the Draft Federal Law No. 850485-7 "On Biological Safety of the Russian Federation" (reviewed and adopted by the State Duma of the Federal Assembly of the Russian Federation in the 1st reading on January 21, 2020), the biological safety of the Russian Federation is defined as a state of population and environmental protection from the influence of dangerous biological factors, with an acceptable level of biological risk.

Also in the Draft Law a number of other important terms and definitions are provided, in particular, such as a dangerous biological factor, biological risk, an acceptable level of biological risk, biological threat (hazard), etc., but in the Federal Law dated December 21, 1994 No. 68-FZ "On Protection of Population and Territories from Natural and Man-Made Emergencies" these types of hazards and special measures to prevent them are not spelled out.

Porfiriev B. N. identifies seven indicators, the presence of which makes it possible to qualify an emergency: the time factor, socio-ecological, psychological, political, economic, managerial, and multiplicative (Porfiriev, 1991).

We can add a few more criteria, for example, emotional, informational, synergetic, since an emergency is also a revision of development paradigms.

Starostin S. A. characterizes emergency situations as dangerous phenomena that threaten the expressive interests of the individual, society and the state, or leading to heavy casualties, material losses, disruption of the living conditions of people, natural damage (Starostin, 2000).

According to Bogolyubov S. A. zones of an environmental disaster as a type of the territory of unfavorable ecological situation are the result of a long-term temporary negative impact on the natural environment (Bogolubov, 2002), while, in addition to zones of ecological disasters and zones of environmental emergency, i.e. officially declared zones of unfavorable ecological situation, other emergencies arise and there are other places with an unfavorable state of the environment, suggesting appropriate lawmaking (Bogolubov, 2010).

In general, we agree with these definitions. But it seems to us that the approach to defining the concept of an ecological emergency should be somewhat different. It can be compared with the provisions of the documents on environmental safety, where several threats and risks are highlighted (Navasardova & Kolesnikova, 2016).

But even using the concept of "environmental safety", one should keep in mind the broader context of environmental emergencies (EES). And this concept, as evidenced by the documents of the European Union and other international organizations, is fundamentally different from other "emergencies". What are these differences?

Firstly, environmental emergencies can be not only dangerous for people, their danger in the fundamental meaning of the sustainability of nature, biodiversity, and balance;

Secondly, environmental emergencies are global, at its core (even if they are localized within the region) and have enormous latency, interdependence, fluidity, and delayed consequences;

Thirdly, we can hardly monitor environmental problems not as separate manifestations of crises (water, land, biological, technological,

biological, territorial, etc.), but as a "disease" or symptoms of a disease of a whole organism. An environmental emergency is possibly a diagnosis of a terminal illness;
Fourthly, any local ecological emergency has signs and typology such as natural, biological, and technological for its definition, but in essence it is directly relevant to the environmental safety.

In addition to the term "environmental emergency", other definitions are used in the scientific literature and regulatory legal acts, for example, "emergency circumstances", "crisis situation".

In our opinion, these are theoretically interesting, but practically unimportant differences. Officially, there is a slightly different formula "Protection of the Population and Territories from Emergencies", which does not differentiate between circumstances, situations and in some way "depersonalizes" the main criteria of an emergency.

So, Stepanov A. G., defines "extraordinary circumstances" as a form of actions of the state authorities of the Russian Federation, the state authorities of the constituent of the Russian Federation, business entities during the period of localization and settlement of processes and phenomena in the natural environment, technological and social spheres (Stepanov, 2002), as well Kropacheva A. V. gives the concept of a "crisis situation", which is characterized by a high degree of complexity and poses an immediate threat to national security (Kropacheva, 2016).

But environmental safety, and the introduction of a state emergency as a following, must be measurable, for example, by setting a period of time or certain parameters to be achieved. The goal can be measured not only by using quantitative methods, but also qualitative indicators, for example, preserving biocenosis, passing through environmental certification, discovering new resource saving technologies. It is also advisable to organize environmental monitoring and (or) analysis of technological progress in achieving goals, and update, as necessary, potential or current environmental and economic changes that may affect the life quality and the ecology quality (Zhavoronkova & Shpakovsky, 2015).

The main regulatory legal act in the field of prevention and elimination of emergency situations is the Federal Law of December 21, 1994, No. 68-FZ "On Protection of Population and Territories from Natural and Man-Made Emergencies." In addition, a number of norms are contained in the Federal Laws of 9.01.1996, No. 3-FZ "On Radiation Safety of

MODERN TRENDS IN THE DEVELOPMENT ... 231

the Population", of 15.05.1991, No. 1244-I "On Social Protection of Citizens Who Were Exposed to Radiation as a Result of the Disaster at Chernobyl Atomic Electric Power Station" and etc. The provisions of these legislative acts were developed and concretized in the decrees of the Government of the Russian Federation and orders of the Ministry of Emergency Situations of Russia, and the Ministry of Natural Resources of Russia (see: Orders of the Ministry of Natural Resources of the Russian Federation of March 28, 1996, No. 113 "On Approval of Requirements for Materials Submitted for State Environmental Expertise for the Assignment of Certain Areas of the Russian Federation to the Zones of an Ecological Emergency or Ecological Disaster ", dated February 6, 1995, No. 45" On the Approval of the "Temporary procedure for declaring a territory an environmental disaster area").

The existing scientific approach, according to which the Federal Law "On Protection of Population and Territories from Natural and Man-Made Emergencies" fully covers all the signs and conditions for determining environmental emergencies, is deeply flawed.

In our opinion, both list of measures, the response mechanism and the provision on qualifying an emergency situation are outmoded and require revision. When the Law "On Protection of Population and Territories from Natural and Man-Made Emergencies" focuses on prohibitive, restrictive, "military" measures without taking into account the reaction of the population, economy, and business, without clarifying the consequences and assessing the degree of guilt (responsibility) of the governing and dedicated agencies, the law needs absolute adaptation.

The Federal Law of January 10, 2002 No. 7-FZ "On Environmental Protection" also does not contain a clear definition of an environmental disaster zone, upon that the following criteria are still current—"Criteria for assessing the ecological situation of territories to identify zones of an environmental disaster and zones of ecological emergency" (approved by the Ministry of Natural Resources of the Russian Federation on November 30, 1992), which provide for features of an environmental disaster zone, corresponding to the content of the Law "On Environmental Protection" approved in 1991.

In this regard, we should assent to the opinion of. Khludeneva N. I, according to which the norms establishing the legal status and legal regime of environmental disaster zones on the territory of the Russian Federation are an example of the omissions in the Environmental Law (Khludeneva, 2014), i.e. As Boltanova E. S. rightly notes, in fact, the legislator has abandoned the term "zone of an environmental emergency" in favor of a broader concept. The environmental emergency zone is now considered as a type of disaster zone, which is characterized by causing environmental harm (Boltanova, 2017).

4 Conclusion

We will formulate key conclusions and proposals based on the results of the study.

1. Environmental emergencies have been, are and will be. Moreover, recent events indicate their growth and consequences that are significant for the population, economy and nature.
2. Legislation on emergency situations levels all the emergency situations, without highlighting the fundamental features and differences between them. Meanwhile, environmental emergencies have a pronounced unique context, affecting not only the interests of human, but also nature.
3. There are practically no emergencies without environmental consequences. Any man-caused, industrial, natural, and other situation in one degree or another negatively affects the environment. On the other hand, nature recovers very quickly at the accident and disasters scenes, forming a new biocenosis.
4. Distinguishing a special grade (level) of ecological emergencies in the legislation also requires the adoption of a group of legislative acts and making amendments to the existing legislation, starting from the strategy planning acts to the technological and city-planning norms.
5. As the legislative practice shows, a significant gap in the legislation on emergency situations is a narrowly specialized approach from the standpoint of accidents, disasters, their localization and elimination of consequences. In fact, the key points are tasks of the conceptual type, including observation, examination, preventive inspections, and control of parameters.
6. The most important factor for the environmental emergencies typology should be not the degree (size) of damage, but the speed of response, the situation analysis, the application of a risk-oriented approach, the assignment of an immediate decision-making algorithm, criteria and principles of responsibility not for

the non-elimination of consequences, but for not taking identifying and preventive actions.

7. The environmental emergency to one degree or another is related to the global environmental problems. An effective response requires the global monitoring (data exchange) and the global response protocols. Within the framework of national jurisdictions, an urgent (immediate) databank, an interdepartmental monitoring of the environmental state, the involvement of public and expert organizations in the environmental state's examination are required.

8. Since the quantity, scale and magnitude of damages from the environmental problems will increase, and an adequate response mechanism has not been created yet, it is necessary to prepare proposals for a vertically integrated insurance environmental fund for disasters through environmental payments, fines, and deductions.

9. The "ideology" of environmental emergencies should be based not only and even not so much on the damage caused to the population, but on the potential, predictable and quantifiable value of eliminating the consequences along the entire environmental and economic chain. Methodologically, it should be clear that preventing the situation is much cheaper than allowing it to happen.

10. The legislation on environmental emergencies should provide for the option of mandatory use of "stress tests (method)", in which the most general and fundamental methods of measuring damage (situation process) from the negative to the catastrophic are given. The key element in the legislation should be an element of personal responsibility for the environmental miscalculations, both in city-planning and in any other planning of the location of the powers of production.

Acknowledgements This work was carried out with the financial support of the Russian Foundation for Basic Research, project 20-511-00015 Bel_a "Legal problems of the formation of a single ecologically safe space of the Member States of the Eurasian Economic Union", and project 18-29-14034/19 "Legal support of the environmental safety of the Arctic region under implementation of genomic technologies".

REFERENCES

Bogolyubov, S. A. (2002). *The procedure for assigning regions of Russia to zones of ecological emergency and zones of ecological disaster* (p. 197). Moscow Publishing Group NORMA-INFRA-M.

Bogolyubov, S. A. (2010). *Lawmaking in the field of ecology* (p. 528).

Boltanova, E. S. (2017). Legal regime of zones of ecological disaster zones and emergencies. *Environmental Law, 1*, 33–39.

Khludeneva, N. I. (2014). *Defects of legal regulation of the environmental protection* (p. 172), Monograph. Moscow Publishing Group NORMA-INFRA-M.

Kropacheva, A. V. (2016). On the concept of emergency situations. *Russian Investigator, 24*, 30–33.

Navasardova, E. S., & Kolesnikova, K. V. (2016). On the flaws in environmental legislation that feed corruption. *Criminology Journal of Baikal National University of Economics and Law, 10*(1), 185–193.

Porfiriev, B. N. (1991). *Management in emergency situations: Problems of theory and practice* (p. 135). VINITI.

Starostin, S. A. (2000). *Management bodies of internal affairs in emergencies (legal and organizational aspects): Dis. ... d-r of law sciences*. M. (p. 469).

Stepanov, A. G. (2002). *The training of employees of internal affairs bodies and units of management in emergencies: A training manual*. M (p. 31). Academy of Management of MIA of Russia.

Zhavoronkova, N. G., & Shpakovsky, Y. G. (2015). Legal aspects of ensuring environmental safety of the fuel and energy complex of modern Russia. *Oil Economy, 8*, 122–124.

Special Aspects of Formation of Legal Awareness in an Information Society: The Role of Mindset

Alexandr A. Volkov, *Tatyana F. Maslova*,
Valeriy V. Meleshkin, *Andrey M. Salny*,
and Galina V. Stroi

1 INTRODUCTION

At present, the concept of information society has been defined not only in science, where it is descriptive of the civilizational phase of social reality, but also in public policy. This points to institutionalization of culture of such social order where the creation and use of information is recognized as the main development factor. This serves as a basis for forming new sociocultural elements and making changes in the functioning of all areas of society with a focus on values, knowledge, and technologies related to the acquisition and consumption of information, and norms of digital culture. Thus, Decree of the President of the Russian Federation No. 203 of May 9, 2017 "On the Strategy for the Development of the Information Society in the Russian Federation for 2017–2030" presents the focus

---

A. A. Volkov (✉) · V. V. Meleshkin · A. M. Salny
North-Caucasus Federal University, Stavropol, Russia

T. F. Maslova · G. V. Stroi
Stavropol State Pedagogical Institute, Stavropol, Russia

© The Author(s), under exclusive license to Springer Nature
Switzerland AG 2021
E. G. Popkova and B. S. Sergi (eds.), *Economic Issues of Social Entrepreneurship*,
https://doi.org/10.1007/978-3-030-77291-8_22

on strengthening the interrelation between the economic and sociocultural conditions of life of citizens and the level of use and accessibility of information (Website of the President of the Russian Federation, 2017). It is emphasized that "the Russian Federation is on the threshold of a new, progressive stage in the development of modern civilization, which is characterized by the dominance of knowledge, science, technology and information in all spheres of life, including the interaction of citizens, economic entities, and public authorities" (Lubskii, 2018). Current information society gives rise to new opportunities for access to the regulatory framework, increasing the level of legal awareness and legal culture based on the Russian mindset drawing on the tasks arising from Decree of the President of the Russian Federation No. Pr-1168 of May 4, 2011 "Basic Principles of State Policy of the Russian Federation for the development of legal literacy and legal awareness of citizens", as well as Federal Law of the Russian Federation No. 324-FZ of 21.11.2011 "On free legal assistance in the Russian Federation" (as amended on 28.11.20–15 under No. 358-FZ).

2 Materials and Method

The promotion of modernization processes on an information and digital basis contributes to progressive changes in the interests of society and the individual. The introduction of digital technologies gives rise to new opportunities for recognition of intelligence, professional abilities of an individual, consideration of past experience for his/her career with minimum participation of experts to increase the objectivity of the assessment. The adoption of the project "Modern digital educational environment" by the Government of the Russian Federation paves the way for the systematic improvement of the quality of lifelong education with a view to expanding the digital educational space. Digital technologies based on virtual reality allow for the creation and practical application of simulators that can be unconnected to a particular working place, multiplying the variety of employed technologies; at the same time, online education capabilities are implemented, blended learning can be organized, and other directions of formal and informal education are established (Zhuzhgov et al., 2019).

Thus, informatization and digitalization transform social life of people, opening up new vistas for expanding and deepening competences, knowledge and skills. However, in the context of transformations, there has

SPECIAL ASPECTS OF FORMATION OF LEGAL... 237

been an increasing need to search for ways and means of achieving the target goals, judging from peculiarities of social reform entailing various consequences. Taking into account the dynamic and nonlinear nature of the modernization process, the status and results of which depend on a variety of factors, it is expedient to refer to the theory of risk that explains the current state of contemporary society. It claims that "in addition to the fact that modern technologies release irreversibly destructive forces which usually act latently, these technological innovations concurrently create socially dangerous situations" (Beck, 2000).

Thus, the advent of computer equipment and the further development of IT technologies have contributed to the formation of a new type of crime. Cyber-crimes have emerged: for example, hackers can hack into banking systems, interfere in public affairs, delete votes cast by citizens for specific candidates, hack into educational systems, etc.

The state of informatization and digitalization risks is influenced by the degree of preparedness of society and the individual to the involvement in the reform processes and their ability to overcome negative consequences. Such preparedness is based on culture of society and its subjects, where legal culture holds a special place. Amid the confrontation between traditional and innovative movements in society, it is legal culture that contributes to preventing the risks of social destabilization, is treated as a factor supporting social stability in a state of changes. Traditionally, information was provided to society by state institutions. The emergence of social networks and the Internet has made it possible to establish direct public contacts and create mechanisms for communication among citizens at various levels, both national and international, i.e. the State, having lost this privilege, has not only gained benefits in certain fields of the economy, politics and law, but also faced certain threat to democracy and public security, since such mediators as the editor and the censor between the speaker and the public are gone. Once again, the contradiction between the national law to restrict public information and global possibilities to disseminate it in online communities foregrounds the issues of legal culture, legal awareness, and the role of mindset of citizens. New trends in the development of law are emerging with the advent of the technological factor—Twitter, Facebook etc.; the main features of law are beginning to lose their former meaning, such as a system of universally binding rules authorized by the State, that express the political will and are enforced by the State, since every State from the moment of its emergence is aimed at introducing the law as an equal measure for all citizens, which is conditioned by the need to remove the judgmental factor (Streltsov, 2006). In the context of these problems, we are confronted with the concepts of consciousness, morality, ethic, national consciousness, spirit, people, mindset, and culture.

The culture of information society where the legal component is distinguished, is transmitted by way of diffusion, formalized into collective knowledge and relations; interiorized into individual consciousness, objectifying legal awareness and legal thinking; good behavior, reproduces the results of good behavior in action and interaction (Andreeva & Yatsenko, 2017). This emphasizes the nature of social relations (functional, motivational) and relations of information society, where legal relations and informational relations can be distinguished. Legal relations demonstrate the interaction of participants united by an interest in a definite goal, as well as the methods (approaches) of introducing these relations in the framework of legal provision with the achievement of an unambiguous result; information relations give rise to the need for legal regulation in the field of information and communication activity, mediated by legal awareness, legal thinking through learning and understanding information reality. The groups of information relations include, in particular, "spiritual, in which information in the form of facts affects the mental state of the subjects, shaping their world view" (Arutiunian et al., 1996).

The peculiarity of information legal relations is openness and transparency; therefore, they involve each and all legal entities: individuals, non-governmental organizations, legal entities, public authority, both at the discretion of the participants of relations, and beyond will of one of the parties, because the distribution of information can be addressless and enforced, and the content of legal relations can be both public, civil and mixed. Under these conditions, the role of legal culture and legal awareness in the regulation of legal relations increases dramatically. A new direction in legal education is emerging—informational and legal education. It stems from the fact that if formerly the legal fact was conditioned by a fragment of a specific life circumstance and gave rise to legal relations that, according to Isakov (1998), represent a material legal phenomenon, then in our case it is referred to nonmaterial legal phenomena (Bachilo, 2018).

SPECIAL ASPECTS OF FORMATION OF LEGAL... 239

Legal awareness in the information society treats social activity on development and use of information and digital technologies, acquisition and distribution of information as useful, lawful (or socially harmful, unlawful) activity; on the possibility of transferring legal information, its uniform interpretation, etc.; on the interaction within the legal framework. The level of development of legal awareness in society can be regarded as the guarantee of successful modernization processes.

3 RESULTS

Global changes related to the emergence of digital technologies, change the collective concepts of worldview. The emerging images of external environment with the use of the TV and the Internet give rise to a new type of thought—clip thinking as a phenomenon of the era of information technologies. Clip worldview consists of a variety of disparate facts, events, and phenomena that are in constant motion, creating an informational kaleidoscope that develops a need for the "effect of novelty, curiosity" in an individual. That said, when an individual acquires new information, the so-called reference reflex referred to by Pavlov as "What's wrong?" gets involved as a preventive mechanism which should be followed by the research and cognitive activity to open up novelty, awareness and experience of events and facts. However, since we obtain new ready-made knowledge in a short period of time, followed by another knowledge, we cannot understand information, because semantic fields have no time to get involved and form the associative bond. However, this may produce "the effect of interrupted activity" or the Zeigarnik effect, which indicates that if the informational action of understanding is not completed, it is remembered better than the completed action.

On this account, one can see the opposite of conceptual thinking, which is based on laying the emphasis on essential attributes of objects, in-depth analysis and synthesis. Clip thinking is more focused on the understanding of short information. This deteriorates the properties of attention: concentration and switchover capability, affecting the clarity of consciousness, which does not fully reveal the essence of this phenomenon. All of the above, among other things, affects the distortion of image of law and the outcomes of legal thinking.

We shall enlarge upon the nature of these phenomena. We should primarily point out that legal awareness is a complex structure. While its ideological aspect concerns knowledge and understanding of legal phenomena, its legal psychology is based on legal feelings and experiences reflected in the emotional-volitional sphere of an individual exercising legal relations. Informal factors determining the quality of legal awareness may include mindset which is an inherent invisible feature of any person, society, which can be observed in stigmatization, thinking standards, legal and nonlegal decisions made, individual, group, or mass behavior which penetrates (interiorizes) the inner world of an individual and manifests itself in law-abidance, patriotism, ambitiousness, religiousness, freethinking, laziness, conformism, cosmopolitism, legal nihilism etc.

We estimate mentality of a person through presented mental phenomena and processes, states and properties. We should point out that mentality of a person is represented not only by the conscious, but also by the unconscious. The anticipation of the future allows us to "repair our cart in December and remember our sledge in July"; sometimes they say: "Had I known where I would fall, I wouldn't have come to that place at all" etc. Anticipation is carried out via two channels, namely the conscious and the unconscious. Since the concept of "conscious" cannot fully describe the past of mentality of a person, the scholars opted for the term "mindset" instead. In psychology, the most established scientific term is the concept of attitude as an unconscious willingness to perceive people, events, facts in a strictly defined way, i.e. in a manner of speaking in this case the past determines the present and the future. If we treat mindset as manifestation of the past basic attitudes ("one law for the rich, and another for the poor"), then we have a distorted perception of modern law, which can be compensated by the mass, group, and individual legal awareness, which has formed in the present and is more dynamic and ductile in terms of law. The compensation abilities of legal awareness as a regulator of adaptation to current legal reality ("a law is a law") are diverse at the level of law making, administration, and enforcement. They develop under certain specific conditions and are reproduced within the framework of an interiorized culture of an individual.

Historically, Russian statehood was built from the top-down. Contemporary society adopted from supreme power taxes orthodox religion, kulak elements, private land ownership, capitalism, Soviet power, socialism, collective farms, plants, factories, banks, democracy, constitution, legal state etc. The rigid vertical power structure created a double-minded attitude of the population as a personality trait. One mind is for others (in logic, the term "concept" is considered in two ways—through "value" and "meaning"; it can be represented in the form of "thesis-antithesis" scheme), while the other mind is for oneself ("meaning"). Hence, there is a well-known saying "one cannot know the inside of a man's mind". And if some new developments (innovations) have not been transformed through the system of collective experiences, "have not been boiled in the cauldron" of the unconscious collective, then the other mind ("meaning") will not accept this. Thus, Orthodoxy which was enforced 1,000 years ago by the princely power as the new state religion that promised "paradise in heaven", was very quickly—in 70 years—replaced by the Soviet idea of communism, according to which "we will have heaven on earth" when we build it (the apologists of this idea promised that "your children will live under communism").

The lack of trust to an "abstract official" as a representative of authority has developed for centuries. Against this background, only the trust to a "cater cousin" was developed, as indicated by the people's proverb "one hand washes another". As can be seen from the prevalence of Russian practice of solving legal issues through personal relations, this is becoming the norm of legal awareness in Russian society. For example, today, when the question is the social ladder through which a young person can make a career for himself/herself, many people feel that they need such "cater cousin".

As we can see, personal relations are an alternative to the law in regulation of public relations, which is considered by some citizens to be more effective in solving legal issues. Hence, the term "micromanagement" emerged, giving rise to negative attitude towards law, legal nihilism, subjectivism, and infantilism. This phenomenon is nothing new. We can take Article 6 of the Constitution of the USSR on the "guiding force of the CPSU" as an example. Following this Article in practice has demonstrated that it is actually accompanied by micromanagement. The "micromanagement" model made a transition from the elite of autocracy to the elite of Soviet power, and then to the present elite. That is, the scenario which is inherent in the mindset of the people is repeated endlessly in the practice of the past, the present and the future with the participation of different "actors". We may consider the manifestation of a special alterable attitude towards government as a common example of this. For example, a decrease in the level of trust in the activities of government institutions compared to 2012 can be inferred by opinion surveys. For example, this criterion for the Federation Council of the Russian Federation Dropped from 41 to 34%, while for the State Duma of the Russian Federation it dropped from 48 to 40%, these indicators dropped from 41 to 37% for the Government of the Russian Federation. Local authorities (city and district) are also characterized by a significant decrease in the trust criterion from 45 to 34%, while political parties have shown a decrease from 48 to 41% (REGNUM News Agency, 2018).

Some authors try to attribute this phenomenon to the lack of "good" laws which could stabilize social development. Many existing laws are not effective in practice, either because there is no social stability or because the state budget is currently unable to enforce them from the economic point of view.

According to the present realia, the politicized slogans of the perestroika-minded period about universal human values and the transition to the rational legal awareness of Russians can be considered as legal idealism which was not confirmed in the realia of the mindset.

4 Conclusion

Research conducted in the South of Russia (Russian Science Foundation, 2017) on the study of mental programs and patterns of social behavior of various population groups has shown that not only the rights of an individual living in a legal state, but also the features of the mechanisms of implementation of law through the rule of law and the independence of judicial authorities were included with the basic values in the liberal pattern of social behavior in the legal sphere. This social behavior pattern covers 10% of the population surveyed. At the same time, 50% of respondents, drawing on the value of law, believe that order in the state is more important than human rights. Thus, we can find proof to this opinion, for example, in 58.3% residents of Stavropol Krai, who find the factor of strong state power more important; it was as low as 40.6% in the residents of Crimea. The leading positions regarding the independence of the Russian Federation from other Western countries in the realm of politics and economics were shown by 37.3% of respondents in Stavropol Krai and 37.5% in Crimea (the all-Russian figure is 37%).

Special attention should be paid to the choice of social equity as the main value by the citizens of Stavropol Krai—50.0% and the Republic of Adygea—45.1% (that said, the all-Russian figure is much lower and is as low as 36%).

However, comparative studies of the image of law in France and Russia have shown that law and responsibility serve as the main criteria of visions of the image of law for the French as values based on the principles of equality, solidarity, and freedom.

Law, justice and responsibility represent the transformation of social justice for Russians through equality, the good, and solidarity. For Russians, the law, responsibility and justice embody the good, equality, and retribution for actions committed. We might as well say that the law in different countries, despite the different mindsets of the peoples, is a common point of reference which defines the general rules of the game for both the Government and the population. The structure and content of legal awareness in the information society reflect the strategies for the modernization of society, its development based on scientific achievements in information and technology, and the interpretation of legal phenomena related to them, distinguishing the estimates and attitudes of people with regard to legal reality.

Legal and informational public relations arising from informatization, digitalization and IT development are reflected in legal awareness:

1. The development of legal awareness of the citizens of the information society in Russia is affected by the mindset which has developed in the context of rigid vertical of power, ambiguous attitude towards power, and the underdevelopment of civil society.
2. Morality, virtue as an acknowledged element of mindset for the Russian population still serves as a criterion of public relations. The law becomes effective only if it is consistent with morality and virtue.

References

Andreeva, O. A., & Yatsenko, O. V. (2017). Transformation of legal awareness in the context of informatization of public relations in the Russian Federation: Development strategies. *Bulletin of the Taganrog Institute of Management and Economics, 1*(25), 54–57.

Arutiunian, M. Y., Zdravomyslova, O.M., & Kurilski-Ozhven, S. (1996). *Images of law in Russia and France: A learning guide*. M. Aspekt Press.

Bachilo, I. L. (2018). *Information law: A textbook for the academic bachelor's degree*, 5th ed., Revised and enlarged. M. Yurait.

Beck, U. (2000). *Risikogesellschaft. Auf dem Weg in eine andere Moderne*. M. Progress-Traditsiya.

Isakov, V. B. (1998). *Legal facts in Russian law. A learning guide.* M. Yustitsinform Legal Publishing House.

Lubskii, A. V. (2018). Modal patterns of social behavior and features of social integration of Crimea into the mental diversity of Russian society. *Gumanitariy Yuga Rossii, 7*(3), 60–76. https://doi.org/10.23683/2227-8656.2018.3.4).

REGNUM News Agency. (2018). *Sociologists claim that the citizens of the Russian Federation have lost confidence in government institutions.* https://regnum.ru/news/polit/2494482.html. Accessed May 20, 2020.

Russian Science Foundation. (2017). Russian Science Foundation grant card No. 16–18–10387. *Mental programs and patterns of social behavior in Russian society* (2016–2017). https://rscf.ru/contests/search-projects/16-18-10387/. Accessed May 20, 2020.

Streltsov, A. A. (2006). *The content of information relations. Conceptual problems of information law* (pp. 29–38). Under the editorship of I. L. Bachilo. M. Institute of State and Law of the Russian Academy of Sciences.

Website of the President of the Russian Federation. (2017). Decree of the president of the Russian Federation No. 203 of 09.05.2017. *On the strategy for the development of the information society in the Russian Federation for 2017–2030.* http://static.kremlin.ru/media/acts/files/0001201705100002.pdf. Accessed May 20, 2020.

Zhuzhgov, I. V., Volkov, A. A., Salnyy, A. M., Kulikova, T. B., & Ryasnyanskaya, N. A. (2019). *Legal space monitoring: Theoretical and legal aspects,* Vol. 35, 20, (pp. 2337–2362). Opcion.

The Use of Digital Technologies in Civil Proceedings

Galina O. Belanova, Svetlana I. Mukhametova, Alexey P. Chizhik, and Vera P. Kutina

1 Introduction

The widespread introduction of digital technologies in social relations is a trend in global social development. Publicity principle, which has traditionally existed in Russian civil proceedings and holding a special place in the system of principles, is interpreted in a slightly different way at present, providing unimpeded access to justice through the submission of

---

G. O. Belanova (✉) · S. I. Mukhametova
North Caucasian Federal University, Stavropol, Russia
e-mail: Belanova-G@yandex.ru

S. I. Mukhametova
e-mail: msud@mail.ru

A. P. Chizhik
Moscow Institute of Economics, Moscow, Russia
e-mail: achizhik@yandex.ru

V. P. Kutina
Saint Petersburg Law Academy, St. Petersburg, Russia
e-mail: Kutiny@mail.ru

© The Author(s), under exclusive license to Springer Nature
Switzerland AG 2021
E. G. Popkova and B. S. Sergi (eds.), *Economic Issues of Social Entrepreneurship*,
https://doi.org/10.1007/978-3-030-77291-8_23

documents and participation in a court session via the Internet. Unimpeded access to justice and transparency of the entire court system is of paramount importance in the establishment of a legal State. The use of increasingly sophisticated and diverse digital technologies in civil proceedings allows simplifying and speeding up the civil proceedings process in court, which definitely ensures the efficiency of judicial activity.

Today, the judiciary reform aimed at modernizing the existing general jurisdiction court system has been implemented in the Russian Federation pursuant to the Federal Target Program "Development of the Russian judiciary system for 2013 – 2020". Pursuant to decree of the President of the Russian Federation No. 204 of 07.05.2018 "On National Goals and Strategic Objectives of the Russian Federation through to 2024", an objective has been set to speed up the introduction of digital technologies in the economy and social sphere (Kasevich et al., 2019). As a result, these two areas of State activity make it possible to create an IT infrastructure in the field of judicial proceedings.

2 Materials and Method

In order to implement the Strategy for development of the information society in the Russian Federation for 2017–2030 and the Target Program "Development of the Russian judiciary system for 2013 – 2020" the sphere of administration of justice in civil actions is undergoing increasingly perceptible changes involved with the introduction of digital technologies. In this regard, many regulatory acts are adopted to enshrine and regulate both the changes in general and certain procedural actions. The authors of this research used a general scientific dialectical method, which made it possible to reveal the essence of such concept as "e-justice". The logical methods of analysis and synthesis for the study of provisions of law regulating procedural actions in electronic form were widely used. Analogy method and comparative legal method were also used to study best practices of foreign countries in the introduction of digital technologies in court proceedings.

3 RESULTS

3.1 The Concept of e-justice in the Russian Federation

Rapid development of information and communication technologies throughout the world and their introduction in all fields of activities of contemporary society has necessitated the legal regulation of activities involving the introduction and the use of digital technologies. The sphere of administration of justice does its part in this global process as well (Smirnov et al., 2020).

Over the last years, the Russian Federation has adopted a significant number of statutory acts regulating the procedure for the introduction of digital technologies in civil proceedings. The legal framework for their introduction included such acts as Federal Law No. 149-FZ of 27.07.2006 "Concerning Information, Information Technologies, and Information Protection", Federal Law No. 63-FZ of 06.04.2011 "Concerning Electronic Signatures".

Furthermore, it is necessary to point out that the first step on this way was taken by arbitration courts, when the introduction of the electronic system for the commencement of actions and the submission of other documents to the courts was started in 2010. In our opinion, this is due to the fact that when adjudicating disputes arising the in the field of business activity, arbitration courts, just as the entire business, were forced to focus on the introduction of sophisticated technologies.

In furtherance of the provisions of Federal Laws, regulatory acts were adopted to regulate various aspects of court records in digital form. Judicial Department at the Supreme Court of the Russian Federation amended its earlier instructions on record management in district courts, in courts of the constituent entities of the Russian Federation, and in arbitration courts regarding the maintenance of automated court records with the use of the State Automated System Pravosudie. Similar instructions were approved for the newly created general jurisdiction courts of appeal and cassation.

All regulatory and practical activities are carried out in pursuance of the Target Program "Development of the Russian judiciary system for 2013 – 2020" approved by the Government of the Russian Federation. Within this program, provision was made for a wide range of activities aimed at informatization of the judiciary system (Malko et al., 2018). These activities should be pursued in several areas. The first area involves unimpeded access of citizens to information about activities of the courts of the Russian Federation, the second area involves the implementation of court proceedings in electronic form, i.e., the introduction of electronic court proceedings, and the third area involves the development of e-justice.

Everything is clear with the first two areas—it is mainly a case of switching from hard-copy forms to digital forms. Unfortunately, it is not yet possible to completely renounce the use of hard-copy documents, since it complicates records management in many cases.

The third area, e-justice, has given rise to numerous opinions regarding its essence and interpretation of this concept as such. It appears that the opinions of many Russian scholars and practitioners have formed under the influence of the concept that was formulated in the Recommendations of the Committee of Ministers of the Council of Europe No. CM/Rec (2009)1 concerning e-democracy for the member states of the Council of Europe. Paragraph 38 of this document defines e-justice as "the use of information and communication technologies in the administration of justice", and further: "It includes electronic communication and data exchange, as well as access to judicial information". This is the definition of e-justice that Ovchinnikov and Antonov (2016) adhere to; further, they point out that e-justice has been fully implemented in the system of arbitration courts.

The same attitude in the definition of the concept of e-justice is assumed by Zarubina and Novikova (2017). They believe that e-justice is an electronic form of interaction between courts and parties to the proceedings, which includes electronic procedural actions, electronic documents, and electronic support to the proceedings.

In our opinion, in this case it is only about electronic records management, not about e-justice. E-justice is a broader and more complex category, which should include not only the formation of a civil case in digital format, but also examination of a case on its merits.

At present, certain procedural actions in civil proceedings can be committed digitally. First of all, this is the commencement of an action in the court, which is aimed at initiation of proceedings; notifying the parties to the proceedings on the place and the time of the court session; the use of electronic documents (conditionally "electronic", because its hard-copy equivalent is required) as evidence, executing and sending judicial acts to concerned parties in the form of electronic documents. These actions are examined by such authors as (Solokhin, 2019).

Kirillov (2018) argues that the entire judiciary system is an e-justice system in a broad sense, since audio recordings are made during the trial, and adopted judicial acts are created as electronic documents.

In our opinion, it is wrong to reduce the concept of e-justice to a mere execution of documents service documents in electronic form and remote proceedings.

Civil justice means the consideration and resolution of civil law conflicts arising from material legal relations, in a special legal form. Judging from this general concept, it may be concluded that the concluding stage of the entire process is an intellectual activity of a judge to deliver a judgment. Therefore, while the operation of thinking for the delivery of legitimate and reasonable judgment is done by a man rather than by a machine (technology, Artificial Intelligence etc.), one cannot suggest the presence of e-justice. We share the opinion of scientists such as Beliakova (2019) and Reshetniak and Smagina (2017) on this point.

At the same time, solid steps have long been taken towards the development of Artificial Intelligence. In the field of law, some firms have started using the so-called self-learning chat bots with elements of Artificial Intelligence (Pravo.ru-300 Ranking, 2018). Thus, Russian RuMoneyBack can be used to get legal advice on various legal issues, to register electronic digital signature, or to submit the documents to the general jurisdiction court.

Today, in some courts in the United States, when deciding on whether to release a criminal defendant on bail, the judges began using the Artificial Intelligence System. This system, which is referred to as the Public Security Assessment, uses the analysis of thousands of court cases to decide on whether there is a risk of failure of accused person to appear in court and whether there is a need to keep them in custody (Zaplatina, 2019). Legal issues that arise during the proceedings must be resolved under the law, as well as the principles of equity, which can only be done with the participation of a man (Baieva et al., 2019). For example, the American judge Posner (1998) believes that Artificial Intelligence and other automated systems can only be used for helping judges, including for revealing their own prejudicial views.

Being fully supportive of this position, we believe that digital technologies should serve only as a tool to facilitate routine technical activities of a man, not to replace a man in the performance of intellectual activity, especially such important and socially desirable as administration of justice.

3.2 Classification of Digital Technologies in Civil Proceedings

Different digital technologies are used in civil proceedings at present. First of all, the communication between the court and the parties to civil proceedings is carried out via the Internet, using specialized systems—SAS Pravosudie, Moi Arbitr, as well as regular e-mail and text messaging systems. The choice of a digital instrument to be chosen depends on the procedural action to be taken. Hence, relevant digital technologies differ in terms of their functional and procedural purposes. Since the use of digital technologies in civil proceedings becomes increasingly diverse, we believe that their classification is not only of applied but also of practical interest.

Some studies have already been carried out in this area. For example, Neznamov (2019) proposes to range digital technologies into classes according to their interaction with information as follows:

- information recording, storage and displaying technologies;
- information transmission technologies;
- information processing technologies.

In this particular case, the author groups the digital technologies according to their technical substance and includes certain actions of the court, court personnel, and the parties to the civil proceedings, with each particular group.

Another alternative of the classification of digitally committed procedural actions may be effected depending on the stage of the process.

The actions that are carried out electronically at the stage of the initiation of proceedings may include the submission of a claim and other documents to the court.

The automated system for the receipt of documents and their distribution to judges contributes, among other things, to the fight against corruption (Galstyan et al., 2019).

At the stage of preparation of a case for trial, documents may be submitted via the Internet, and evidence may be submitted in the form of an electronic document. Further, the parties to the proceedings are notified of the listing for trial using the means of electronic communication.

At the stage of judicial examination—investigation of electronic evidence; taking certain legal proceedings via video conferences; conduct

THE USE OF DIGITAL TECHNOLOGIES ...   251

of the trial via web conference; performance and execution of judicial acts in the form of a digitally signed electronic document.

As a matter of fact, each of the verification stages of the proceedings, such as the appeal proceedings, cassational and supervision proceedings also consists of the initiation of proceedings, the preparation for the examination of complaints, and the delivery of judgment. Therefore, all digitally committed actions in the court of primary jurisdiction are similarly committed in the courts of superior jurisdiction.

As a result, we deal with a variety of homogeneous objects—legal proceedings that are committed digitally—and their use depends, first, on their role in civil proceedings, and second, on the stage of civil or arbitration procedure.

3.3   The Use of Digital Technologies in the Activity of Civil Courts

The transition from traditional forms of judicial proceedings to informatization of the justice process was beginning in all legal systems of foreign countries in the same way—from the conversion of documents in hard copy to electronic form and their submission to the court in this form.

As keeping of paper records became increasingly expensive, ideas related to the conversion of documents to electronic form have started to emerge. The idea of submitting documents to the courts in electronic form first appeared in the United States in the late 80s of the last century (Litvinova, 2013).

This idea was implemented step by step, and was enshrined in legislation in the United States in 2004, when the Federal Rules of Civil Procedure was adopted. This statutory act regulated a common procedure for the submission of applications to the courts through the registry and in hard copy. However, the courts were also given the right to provide in their regulations for the possibility of filing documents using the electronic means which still had to meet technical standards determined by the judicial conference of the United States. Since that time, the courts in the United States have started gradually switching to electronic document flow and introducing specialized information systems. An example of such systems is the global system "Case Management/Electronic Case Files" (CM/ECF), which is based on PACER and is designed for the submission of documents to the courts in electronic form. The introduction of the system was completed by March 2006, primarily in district courts and in bankruptcy courts (Reshetniak, 2016).

The United Kingdom has started using the electronic form for the submission of documents to the courts since 2002. The documents were submitted through the specialized centers Money Claim Online and Claim Production Centre. Such form for the submission of documents was introduced gradually—first for the claims for the recovery of money to the amount not exceeding 100,000 lb sterling, and then for the defense to the claim by the defendant. Later it became possible to track the progress of the procedure via the Internet

The Russian Federation took the path of digitalization of court proceedings much later than advanced European countries and the United States. As noted above, the possibility of judicial recourse by completion of an electronic form first appeared in the Russian Federation in 2010. Changes were made in the Arbitration Procedure Code of the Russian Federation. Thus, Part 1 of Article 125 of the Arbitration Procedure Code of the Russian Federation provides for the submission of the statement of claim to the court via the Internet by completing the form on the official website of the arbitration court. The same applies to documents enclosed with the statement of claim (Part 2 of Article 126 of the Arbitration Procedure Code of the Russian Federation).

In order to submit documents to the arbitration courts, one should have a personal account in the Moi Arbitr system. Personal account can be signed in for the submission of documents in electronic form using the verified profile in the Unified Identification and Authentication System (UIAS). The Public Services Portal can be used for that end.

In addition to statements of claim, other statements, for example, claims for the recovery of mandatory payments, statements on corporate disputes, statements on establishment of facts of legal value etc. may be submitted to the arbitration court in electronic form. The statements of defense, counter-actions, certain applications, appeal petitions and cassation petitions, petitions for the supervisory review of a judicial act in a court of supervision, and some other documents may also be submitted in electronic form.

The same system for the commencement of actions and submission of other claims is provided for in the general jurisdiction court system. In this case, electronic documents should be submitted via the official website of the court which is located on the web portal of the SAS Pravosudie on the Internet. The procedure is spelled out in Order No. 251 of Judicial Department at the Supreme Court of the Russian Federation

"Concerning the approval of the procedure for the submission of electronic documents to the federal general jurisdiction courts, including in the form of an electronic document" of 27.12.2016.

Electronic documents have been increasingly often used as evidence in civil proceedings. Once again, the arbitration court was the first on the way to this achievement. The possibility of production of evidence obtained by facsimile, electronic or other means of communication and signed by e-signature, to the court, is provided for in Part 3 of Article 75 of the Arbitration Procedure Code of the Russian Federation and Part 1 of Article 71 of the Civil Code of the Russian Federation. It must be noted that such documents are fairly often used in arbitration practice today, since the court resolves economic disputes, including corporate disputes (Sagalaeva et al., 2019). However, there is still no regulation of the procedure for the examination of such evidence in court session, and there are no regulatory provisions that would define accurate criteria for determining the validity of an electronic document.

One of criteria of validity of an electronic document is the presence of e-signature; the procedure for the use of e-signature is spelled out in Federal Law No. 63-FZ of 06.04.2011 "Concerning Electronic Signatures". As a general rule, not all pieces of evidence that are presented to the court have e-signature in judicial practice.

The falsification of electronic documents is not ruled out as such due to the fact that there is a growing number of cybercrimes committed with the use of digital technologies (Abdulgaziev et al., 2019).

Thus, decisions on whether to accept electronic evidence, verify their validity and examine them are made on a case-by-case basis at the discretion of the judge.

Until recently, the courts of the Russian Federation have selectively involved concerned parties and their representatives, as well as witnesses, experts, specialists, and interpreters via videoconferencing (Article 151.1 of the Civil Code of the Russian Federation, Article 153.1 of the Arbitration Procedure Code of the Russian Federation).

In the context of the threat of distribution of coronaviral infection COVID-19 in the territory of the Russian Federation, the courts have urgently begun to use digital technologies for litigation. The first attempts of litigation with the use of Whatsapp draw criticism of lawyers and were considered unsuccessful. However, the Supreme Court of the Russian Federation offered a new remote litigation system was the first to test it.

This procedure for holding the court session online shall be as follows: The parties to the proceedings must file an application in electronic form via the official website of the court on the web portal of SAS Pravosudie to hold the court session via web conference. Personal identification can be performed using the Public Services Portal. The parties to the proceedings connect to the videoconferencing server of the court by following the link received from the court. The parties to the proceedings can use any gadget with built-in camera and microphone—personal computer, tablet, or smartphone.

We believe that these methods of civil proceedings will be widely used in the future even after the threat of distribution of new coronaviral infection COVID-19 is overcome. However, legislators are faced with the need to enshrine this procedure in procedural legislation and regulate it in detail.

4 Conclusion

Intensified digitalization of civil proceedings allows significantly simplifying and speeding up the process of the administration of justice, thus establishing an e-justice system in a staged manner. However, the proceedings in a case and delivery of a judgment are based on the intellectual and thinking activity of the judges, and they are still indispensable to such an extent. Contemporary society must think to what extent digital technologies can be introduced into the field of justice, and whether it is worth driving this course to extremes by replacing the judges with Artificial Intelligence.

Despite the fact that countries throughout the world use different legal orders, all developed countries have an ongoing intensive process of the introduction of digital technologies in court proceedings. In these conditions, irrespective of differences, all judiciary systems face similar issues, which are as follows.

1. Since the documents that are submitted to the courts contain confidential information, it is necessary to ensure protection of personal data as well as the secrecy of information (state, personal, banking, etc.).
2. It should be made possible to verify the authenticity of electronic documents submitted to the courts and to prevent the falsification of such documents.

THE USE OF DIGITAL TECHNOLOGIES ... 255

3. It is essential that equal access to the court is ensured for individuals of different income levels who cannot afford buying high-tech computers.
4. It is necessary to ensure access to justice and adequate protection of interests for individuals without legal training and knowledge of information technology.

Some of these issues are already being addressed in our country, though the rate and effectiveness of addressing them could be improved.

REFERENCES

Abdulgaziev, R. Z., Alsultanov, M. R., Mamichev, V. N., Sarukhanyan, A. R., Sostin, D. I., & Sukhorukova, A. N. (2019). Social causation of criminalization of cyber crime committed with the use of information technology. *International Journal of Advanced Trends in Computer Science and Engineering, 8*(5), 2459–2463.

Baieva, N. A., Vysheslavova, T. F., & Lukinova, S. A. (2019). The principle of justice in social security law. *Journal of Advanced Research in Dynamical & Control Systems, 11*(08), 2754–2759.

Beliakova, A. V. (2019). The development of digital technologies in the justice system as a way to speed up judicial proceedings in the Russian Federation. *Arbitrazhnyi i Grazhdanskii Protsess, 12,* 50–56.

Bhorat, Z. (2017). *Do we still need human judges in the age of artificial intelligence?* https://www.opendemocracy.net/en/transformation/do-we-still-need-human-judges-in-age-of-artificial-intelligence/ (data accessed: 21 June 2020).

Galstyan, I. S., Klukovskaya, I. N., Gabrilyan, R. R., Aparina, O. U., & Semenov, V. E. (2019). Problems of definition and consolidation of the principles of anti-corruption policy in the modern world. *Dilemas Contemporáneos: Educación, Política y Valores, 7*(1), 101.

Kasevich, E. V., Atayan, G. Y., Amvrosova, O. N., Stankevich, G. V., & Kara-Kazaryan, T. V. (2019). Perspectives on the use of new information and communication technology (ICT) in the modern economy. *Advances in Intelligent Systems and Computing,* 439–445.

Kirillov, A. E. (2018). The jurisdictional basis of e-justice. *Vestnik Grazhdanskogo Protsessa, 1,* 220–228. https://doi.org/10.24031/2226-0781-2018-8-1-220-228

Litvinova, N. N. (2013). Electronic documents: Selection, use and safekeeping. *Avtomatizirovannaya Biblioteka: Dostizheniya, Novatsii, Perspektivy, 4,* 313–319.

Malko, A. V., Isakov, N. V., Mazurenko, A. P., Smirnov, D. A., & Isakov, I. N. (2018). Legal policy as a means to improve lawmaking process. *Astra Salvensis, 6*(1), 833–842.

Neznamov, A. V. (2019). On the classification of digital technologies in the civil procedure. *Rossiyskii Yuridicheskii Zhurnal (electronic Supplement), 3*, 27–35.

Ovchinnikov, V. A., & Antonov, Y. V. (2016). E-justice as an e-democracy project: Prospects for implementation in Russia. *Gosudarstvennaya Vlast i Mestnoe Samoupravlenie, 5*, 3–7.

Posner, R. (1998). The problematics of moral and legal theory. *Harvard Law Review, 111*(1637), 1642–1646.

Pravo.ru-300 Ranking. (2018). *Chats, bots, and services: Legaltech market in Russia.* https://pravo.ru/story/203790/ (data accessed: 21 June 2020).

Reshetniak, V. I. (2016). Electronic form for the submission of documents to the court (experience of foreign civil proceedings). *Advokat, 4*, 61–69.

Reshetniak, V. I., & Smagina, E. S. (2017). *Information technologies in civil proceedings (Russian and foreign experience): A textbook. M.: Gorodets.*

Sagalaeva, E. S., Melnikova, M. P., Shevchuk, S. S. , Komarevceva, I. A., & Landina, O. V. (2019). On the legal nature of domestic documents of the corporation. *Revista dilemas contemporáneos: educación, política y valores, VII,* Edición Especial, 113.

Smirnov, D. A., Tereshchenko, E. A., Botasheva, L. E., Trofimov, M. S., Melnikova, V. A., & Dolgopolov, K. A. (2020). Digital jurisprudence. *Revista Inclusiones, 7*(1), 273–283.

Solokhin, A. E. (2019). E-justice: Features, problems and prospects. *Zakon, 6,* 193–208.

Zaplatina, T. S. (2019). Artificial intelligence in the matter of delivery of judgments, or AI judge. *Bulletin of the Kutafin Moscow State Law University, 4,* 160–168. https://doi.org/10.17803/2311-5998.2019.56.4.160-168

Zarubina, M. N., & Novikova, M. M. (2017). Revisiting the essence of e-justice in the Russian Federation. *Administrator Suda, 1,* 9–12.

Legal and Regulatory Framework for the Creative Industries in a Digital Age

Ivan A. Bliznets, *Viktoriia S. Savina*, *and Ilia A. Gribkov*

1 INTRODUCTION

In contemporary information society, intellectual property, including copyright items, is one of the most important intangible assets, particularly in the modern digital economy. We can unequivocally assert that the nature of intellectual rights to the results of intellectual activity and the means of individualization is private, while the rights to scientific, literary and artistic works (both existing and newly created) acquire the property of market assets, including cost, and act as a subject of transaction. Today, copyright- and related rights-protected items are incorrectly considered to be a purely legal category, since they are already treated as an extremely

---

I. A. Bliznets (✉)
Institute of International Law and Economics named after A.S. Griboyedov, Kutafin Moscow State Law University, Moscow, Russia
e-mail: bliznets@mail.ru

V. S. Savina
Russian State Academy of Intellectual Property, Moscow, Russia
e-mail: savin-viktoriya@yandex.ru

I. A. Gribkov
World Intellectual Property Organization, Geneva, Switzerland
e-mail: ilya.gribkov@wipo.int

© The Author(s), under exclusive license to Springer Nature Switzerland AG 2021
E. G. Popkov and B. S. Sergi (eds.), *Economic Issues of Social Entrepreneurship*,
https://doi.org/10.1007/978-3-030-77291-8_24

valuable asset belonging to citizens, legal entities, organizations, institutions and enterprises, state-owned corporations, being a basis for the dynamic development of a wide range of industries and foreign trade. It is they that have started to provide significant increase in value added, number of jobs, often and often becoming a significant item of government revenues from the exports of such rights. According to the statistics of the World Intellectual Property Organization (WIPO), the proportion of intangible capital is 30.4 per cent, which is about twice the amount of physical capital. On a global scale, intangible capital has increased by 75 per cent over the recent 10 years and currently it amounts to about 6 trillion US dollars. (World Intellectual Property Report, 2017). This is indicative of great importance of intellectual property these days, as noted in other studies of WIPO. (Report of the Advisory Committee on Enforcement of Copyright, 2014). Today, copyright is an integral part of our daily life; moreover, we are faced with completely new forms of works (3d models, holographic objects, visualizations, etc.) that could not have been imagined as recently as 10 years ago. Copyright items fill the vast majority of e-commerce industries, including the video game industry (World Intellectual Property Report, 2017) and the manufacturing of the most sophisticated computer products. According to WIPO, revenues from such activities amount to 31.3% of revenues in e-commerce overall. Protection of new forms of creation along with explosive development of digital technologies gave impetus to exchange of knowledge, which also increased the benefits of copyright.

2 Materials and Method

General scientific and specific scientific methods have been used during this research, in particular, comparison method, descriptive method, interpretation method, methods of formal and dialectical logic, legal dogmatic method, simulation method, systemic functional method, induction and deduction method, method of formal logic, and system approach.

The methodological basis of the research consists of general scientific and specific scientific methods, in particular: comparative legal method which allowed us to compare legal provisions of different universal and regional (at the level of the CIS) of international treaties regulating the intellectual property issues; historical method that allowed to track the evolution of legal provisions and organizational decisions on the subject of research, in their development; empiric method for the study of legislation and practical organization of the processes of enforcement of intellectual rights to the results of creative activity, and the means of individualization of goods, works, services and enterprises equivalent to them; systemic analysis method, analog method, formal legal method and logical method which were used to systematize available empirical data and to describe the scientific results that were obtained during this research for their further use.

3 RESULTS

First of all, the infrastructure of creative industries should be described. It consists of a network of institutions which can be classified according to the delimitation of types of creative work. In accordance with the Report on principal directions and results of operations of the Ministry of Culture of the Russian Federation in 2018 and the tasks for 2019, there are currently 94,423 cultural establishments in Russia. According to the types of activity, their structure is as follows: the most numerous categories are organizations providing library services (42,803 institutions), followed by cultural and leisure institutions (42,579 institutions), art schools for children (4,955 institutions), museums (2,742 institutions), theaters (649 institutions), concert organizations (350 institutions), culture and leisure parks (305 institutions), zoos (31 institution), and, finally, circus organizations (9 institutions) (Official website of the Ministry of Culture of the Russian Federation, 2020).

Works that are copyright protected are characterized by features that are inherent in public goods, being favorable to society as a whole, which can be enjoyed by all members of society at the same time. This by no means reduces the value of these items, so no competitive relations arise here.

The research that has been conducted over the last years lead us to the conclusion that Russia has successfully established the basis of national civil legislation in the field of intellectual property which fully complies with the standards of major international treaties in this field (Berne Convention, 2003; Geneva Convention, 1999; Rome Convention, 2005; TRIPS Agreement, 2012, etc.).

At the same time, researchers rightly point out that copyright is improving today, dynamically perfecting exclusive rights to the modes of commercialization, and this is largely responsible for an imbalance, a state of insufficient protection of personal nonproperty rights and interests of authors and even "endangers proper protection of the attribution and integrity of the works" (Bliznets et al., 2014; Matveev, 2017).

Within this framework, today, the Russian Federation has focused on creating an effective regulatory mechanism of copyright protection.

The adoption of Part 4 of the Civil Code of the Russian Federation "Exclusive rights to the results of intellectual activity and means of individualization" (Civil Code of the Russian Federation, 2006) in 2006 made it possible to ensure compliance of the Russian civil legislation with the main international legal principles of protection of intellectual rights. This was further facilitated by Russia's accession to a number of other treaties that are highly relevant to the digital age (WIPO Copyright Treaty, 1996; WIPO Performances and Phonograms Treaty, 1996). In addition, prerequisites were formed for Russia to ratify the Agreement on Trade-Related Aspects of Intellectual Property Rights (TRIPS) (TRIPS Agreement, 2012) and join the WTO (World Trade Organization).

In our opinion, the next stage should be the large-scale introduction of copyright (copyright items) into the economic turnover. This fact is pointed out by a wide range of researchers.

It is also necessary to raise awareness among citizens of their rights and obligations with regard to intellectual property imposed on both copyright holders and users.

We would like to lay emphasis on the two important documents which were adopted by the Ministry of Science and Higher Education of the Russian Federation and the Ministry of Economic Development of the Russian Federation, and it is invincible belief that they will contribute to the significant impact of copyright on the fulfillment of objectives of the capitalization of businesses and organizations, their extended introduction into the economic turnover. It is a case of policy in the field of intellectual property for universities and research establishments, as well as on Recommendations on the management of exclusive rights to the results of intellectual activity and the means of individualization in Russian regions.

We would like to inform the readers that the Russian State Academy of Intellectual Property, with a view to performing a government task, has started a research on the topic: "The contribution of copyright to the economy of the Russian Federation. The role of creative industries", (for information—similar researches are conducted by many countries on a regular basis). We believe that the research into the economy of copyright will help to describe the features of copyright and assess its impact on the economy of the Russian Federation.

We would also like to point out that a strictly legal approach to the assessment of efficiency of the legal and regulatory framework for the legal relations in the field of copyright involves the risk of separation of copyright from the economic consequences, arising from the application of legal norms created through lawmaking. Again, the use of a strictly economic approach may give rise to certain errors in the results of the analysis of the creative component inherent in many production processes in the national economy of Russia. All these processes must be inextricably connected.

The research carries out the analysis of sectors of the economy directly related to the use of copyright items (creative industries) that can be grouped today according to the main criterion—the level of dependence on the degree of utilization of copyright- and related rights-protected items. These include:

1. the primary industries which are directly related the copyright (publishing, music, literature, theater, photography, cinema, advertizing, collective management of copyright and related rights, education, science, information services, development of software etc.);
2. interdependent industries (manufacture of computer or other equipment—TV sets, radio sets, musical instruments, diverse copy machines, physical media for recording of works and performances, manufacture of publishing and printed products etc.);
3. industries that are partly related to copyright (architecture, design, cabinetry, jewelry etc.);
4. the so-called non-specific industries which are auxiliary in nature (support industries, including telephony, Internet, transportation, wholesale trade, retail trade, etc.).

All abovementioned groups cover economic sectors that have been investigated at this stage.

In contemporary information society, particular emphasis should be made on the role of copyright and related rights, which is clearly illustrated by the added value that is created in relevant industries and has an impact on gross domestic product (GDP) at that.

When we are governed by established procedures, primarily the WIPO methodology, we should point at such basic indicators as the added value, employment, and foreign trade volume which ensure economic growth and determine the extent of the contribution of copyright to the economy of any state.

In this regard, many states are constantly carrying out research activities, identifying the contribution of creative industries to the national economies (the United States of America, Finland, the Netherlands, the United Kingdom, etc.).

For example, based on available statistics, the contribution to the economy of the United States is more than 12% of GDP, while in the advanced European countries it is close to this figure, amounting to about 12% of GDP. Unfortunately, for Russia we only have information for 2004—this is 6.06% of GDP.

Current practice of recent years shows that there are still trends in the world, such as constant increase in the contribution to the creation of value added and the number of jobs, as well as the presence of outstanding dynamics in the development of cultural and information sectors (much higher than in other fields of the economy).

When we carry out the research study of the contribution of copyright-based industries to the economy on a regular basis, we can actually assist in the realization of potential of creative and information sectors of society.

In the context of future research activities, we would also like to make a point of the following. The analysis of the field of protection of exclusive rights to the results of intellectual activity (works, performances, phonograms) on trademarks and other means of individualization, including the fight against counterfeiting and piracy, shows the following. Today, it is clear that the number of offenses in the field of intellectual property has significantly increased over the last two decades. The increase in the volume of production of counterfeit goods significantly destabilizes the domestic consumer market, leading to the spread of crime and the expansion of illicit trafficking of money and, as a result, has a negative impact on the investment climate in the country.

As a result of the large-scale sale of counterfeit goods, consumers suffer serious damage (not only material but also moral). In addition, the business reputation of bona fide producers is being damaged. According to statistics of the Ministry of Economic Development, the Ministry for Industry and Trade, and the Ministry of Internal Affairs of the Russian Federation, damage caused annually to holders of copyright and related rights amounts to several billion US dollars, while the losses of state budget as a result of nonpayment of taxes during the production of counterfeit goods amount to hundreds of millions rubles. No wonder that the representatives of the International Intellectual Property Alliance point out that copyright infringements are still extremely widespread in Russia—losses amounted to more than 1.7 billion US dollars in 2004. Five years ago, this organization filed a petition to the United States Government to stop or suspend the distribution of trade preferences worth several hundred million dollars a year to the Russian Federation until the issues related to the protection of intellectual property are successfully solved and the progress is achieved in the fight against the production and distribution of counterfeit goods infringing the copyright to disks, books, and other protected items.

All of the above constitutes a clear demonstration of the urgency of the problem of legal and regulatory framework for the copyright protection and the fight against violation of law in this field that society is facing in this day and age.

Of course, the legislator and the law enforcement agencies undertake attempts to improve the situation in this field; their activities on prevention and fight against copyright infringement and the distribution of counterfeit goods in the territory of Russia are gradually increasing the number of offenses detected.

However, the share of counterfeit goods, especially copies of computer software, audio-visual and musical works, is still quite high in the economic turnover. In general, the manufacture and distribution of counterfeit consumer products is still the most challenging problem.

In our opinion, in order to efficiently handle the current situation in the field of creative industries, a comprehensive method is needed for the monitoring of condition of the production and distribution of counterfeit goods within Russia, as well as the systemic analysis of the issues of statutory regulation and stopping the illegal economic turnover in the field of intellectual property in Russia.

Current situation in the field of legal copyright regulation is largely due to the lack of a unified approach to the legal treatment of acts related to infringement of their copyright, on the part of the law enforcement agencies in different constituent entities of the Federation. Furthermore, existing legislative gaps cause considerable difficulties in the process of adjudication of civil and criminal cases by the general jurisdiction courts, which often allows offenders to escape from due punishment.

Taking into consideration the above, we consider it highly effective and expedient to create a particular system of indicators for the market of audio and video products, copies of computer software, products in the field of creative industries labeled by the means of individualization of goods, works, services and enterprises protected by law, and to introduce this system in the production sector.

The use of this system of indicators can significantly bring down the level of infringements of copyright and related rights, stop the production and distribution of counterfeit goods, make prosecution more effective, establish control over the manufacture of legal products, etc.

In addition, these indicators assist in an unbiased assessment of the current condition of the production and distribution of counterfeit goods in the territory of Russia, as well as forecasting of future development trends in these phenomena. They allow demonstrating the measures taken by the to combat infringements of rights in this field, increasing the level of interest of copyright holders in the fight with infringements of their rights, and developing the domestic market.

Today, the development of a highly efficient legal mechanism for the enforcement and protection of intellectual rights is a highly relevant issue for the Russian Federation. Russia's accession to the main international law acts in this field has helped to ensure the compliance of Russian legislation with international standards of intellectual property protection.

4   Conclusion

When we study the impact of copyright on the national economy, it is expedient to point out a highly significant role of copyright in promotion of the welfare of citizens as well as the growth in prosperity of the entire society as a whole, since the mentioned categories are directly relevant to the realization of creative potential. Copyright significantly influences the processes of redistribution of income of individuals and legal entities through the payment of royalty fees and taxes, since each change in this system entails changes in the income structure of different market actors. Copyright is not only aimed at ensuring the normal functioning of the market economy, but also acting as a very valuable asset of a number of enterprises, as well as an indicator of the economic well-being of the state as a whole. We have reason to believe that this trend will become increasingly more entrenched, and the role of intellectual property (intangible assets) in the global economy will be steadily increasing.

The economic indicators such as added value, employment, as well as development of foreign trade, allow assessing the extent of contribution of copyright to the strengthening of the national economy.

In our opinion, the principal directions of conducted research should be as follows:

1. To assess the economic significance of copyright within the framework of state statistical monitoring of full-scale measurement of gross domestic product created in industries based on the use of copyright.
2. To solve the main problem—to determine the actual economic contribution of copyright-related industries to the Russian economy: total production, GDP, and employment of population.
3. The research all over the world uses a methodology which divides copyright branches into four groups in accordance with the level of dependence on the copyright items: the primary industries, interdependent industries, industries that are partly related to copyright, as well as the so-called non-specific support industries.

In conclusion, we would like to observe that understanding of the current processes in society, the focus of the State and business on the issues involved with intellectual property will certainly have an impact on the creation of an efficient economy based on digital technologies with the use of achievements in knowledge. This, in turn, will give advantages for attracting investment and involving intangible assets in the capital of businesses and organizations.

Acknowledgements The article was prepared as part of the state assignment on the topic 3-GZ-2020 of the thematic plan of research of the Federal State Budgetary Educational Institution of Higher Education and Research of the Russian Academy of Geography for 2020 "Contribution of copyright to the economy of the Russian Federation. The role of creative industries".

References

Agreement on Trade-Related Aspects of Intellectual Property Rights (TRIPS) (Signed in Marrakesh on 15.04.1994) (as amended on 06.12.2005). (2012). *Collection of legislative acts of the Russian Federation, 37* (appendix, part VI), 2818–2849, (appendix, part V), 2336–2369.

Berne Convention for the Protection of Literary and Artistic Works of 09.09.1886 (as amended on 28.09.1979). (2003). *Biulleten Mezhdunarodnykh Dogovorov, 9.*

Bliznets, I. A., Leontiev, K. B., Revinskii, O. V., Kazmina, S. A., Mukhopad, V. I., Smirnova, V. R., Mukhamedshin, I. S., Vidiakina, O. V., & Savina, V. S. (2014). *Practical tools for the commercialization of the results of intellectual activity.* M.: FSBEI HVE RSAIP.

Civil Code of the Russian Federation (Part Four) No. 230-FZ of 18.12.2006. (2006). *Collection of legislative acts of the Russian Federation, 52* (Part 1), p. 5496.

Geneva Convention for the Protection of Producers of Phonograms Against Unauthorized Duplication of Their Phonograms (Geneva, October 29, 1971). (1999). *Biulleten Mezhdunarodnykh Dogovorov, 8.*

Matveev, A. G. (2017). *Copyright system in Russia: Regulatory and theoretical models: Thesis ... of the Doctor of Legal Sciences: 12.00.03.* M.: Russian State Academy of Intellectual Property.

Official website of the Ministry of Culture of the Russian Federation. (2020). https://www.mkrf.ru/documents/ob-itogakh-raboty-ministerstva-kultury-rossiyskoy-federatsii-v-2018-godu-i-zadachakh-na-2019-god/ (data accessed: 12 April 2020).

Report of the Advisory Committee on Enforcement of Copyright of the World Intellectual Property Organization "Systemization of new business models that are used to distribute the copyright content". (2014). WIPO/ACE/9/19 // www.wipo.net/ (data accessed: 12 April 2020).

Rome Convention for the Protection of Performers, Producers of Phonograms and Broadcasting Organizations (Rome, October 26, 1961). (2005). *Biulleten Mezhdunarodnykh Dogovorov, 7.*

WIPO Copyright Treaty of December 20, 1996 (Original text). (1996). http://www.wipo.int/wipolex/ru/treaties/text.jsp?file_id=295439/ (data accessed: 22 February 2020).

WIPO Performances and Phonograms Treaty of December 20, 1996 (Original text). (Together with "Agreed statements concerning the WIPO Copyright Treaty"). (1996). http://www.wipo.int/treaties/ru/text.jsp?file_id=295578/ (data accessed: 28 February 2020).

WIPO. (2017). *World intellectual property report 2017 intangible capital in global value chains.* https://www.wipo.int/edocs/pubdocs/en/wipo_pub_944_2017.pdf (data accessed: 12 February 2020).

Modern International Experience and Prospects for the Development of Social Entrepreneurship

Reformation of the Social Support System for a Family, Mother/Fatherhood and Childhood as a Factor of Social and Economic Welfare of the Russian Society

Elena S. Vologdina and *Olga A. Kuzmina*

1 INTRODUCTION

Family, mother/fatherhood and childhood form an interrelated system of constitutional values which have direct influence on reproduction of population, successive alternation of generations and a decent living level of population in general (Rakitina et al., 2018).

A social support system for a family, mother/fatherhood and childhood functions in Russia under current conditions. However, mortality rate prevails over birth rate among indicators related to natural population change.

According to the data of the Russian Federal State Statistics Service the mortality rate was half as much as birth rate in January–February 2020 (for the first two months of 2019 mortality rate exceeded birth rate

---

E. S. Vologdina (✉) · O. A. Kuzmina
Komsomolsk-Na-Amure State University, Komsomolsk-on-Amur, Russia
e-mail: Vologdina-el@yandex.ru

O. A. Kuzmina
e-mail: petr0va@mail.ru

© The Author(s), under exclusive license to Springer Nature Switzerland AG 2021
E. G. Popkova and B. S. Sergi (eds.), *Economic Issues of Social Entrepreneurship*,
https://doi.org/10.1007/978-3-030-77291-8_25

by 1.3 times); such exceedance was equal to 1.5–2.4 times in 41 federal subjects of the Russian Federation (The Federal state statistics service, 2020). The number of deaths exceeded the number of births by 1.3 times for the same period of time in Khabarovsk Krai (The official web-site of Khabarovsk Krai Government, 2020). The birth rate consistently fails to provide population growth.

2 Methodology

The methodological basis of the study was formed by comparative legal, chronological and sociological methods.

Authors of the study analyzed the legal base with regard to the results of sociological studies in order to check the efficiency of the social support system for a family, mother/fatherhood and childhood.

The theoretical basis of the study is formed by transactions of Ageeva (2020), Kulikova (2020), Troshkina (2019), Matveeva et al. (2019), Maleeva (2019).

3 Findings

Strategic objectives of the country related to the social and economic development, as well as to the demographic development.predetermined the development of some core documents (ConsultantPlus, 2018). They include national / regional projects and programs of support to families with children.

Forms of the social support in Russia include privileges, services, in-kind and monetary aid (ConsultantPlus, 1995, 2006, 2014). Since 2008 an indexation procedure related to the allowances for parents has existed in the Russian Federation (Table 1).

The Decree No. 61 dated January 29th, 2020 approved the indexation coefficient of social allowances in amount of 1.03 for current year (in 2019 that coefficient was 1.043) (ConsultantPlus, 2020).

In 2020 the sum of a child care benefit for the first child is not less than 3375,77 rubles, for the second and further ones is 6751,54 rubles. While in 2007 the amount of that benefit did not exceed 700 rubles without taking into consideration a priority and a number of children.

Since 2007 the state has initiated new lump sum allowances after a birth or an adoption of the second and a subsequent child, i.e. a maternity capital. In terms of an annual indexation the amount of the stated capital

Table 1 Federal benefits and compensatory allowances for families with children

Types of benefits	Benefit amount in 2020, RUB	Regulatory Legal Act
1. A lump sum benefit when a child is born / or handovered to a family (application for the benefit shall be done not later than within 6 months from the day of a child's birth)	18,004.12/ 137,566.13	The Federal Law No. 81-FZ dated 19.05.1995 "On state benefits for citizens with children" (as of 08.06.2020)
2. A lump sum benefit for women registered at early pregnancy	675.15	
3. Monthly maternity benefit until a child is 1.5 years old: - for the first child - for the second and subsequent children Maximum amount	3,375.77 6,751.54 13,503.10	
4. Prenatal benefit	675.15	
5. A lump sum benefit to a pregnant wife of a military man who is called up for service	28,511.40	

(continued)

Table 1 (continued)

Types of benefits	Benefit amount in 2020, RUB	Regulatory Legal Act
6. A monthly benefit to a child of a military man who is called up for service	12,219.17	
7. A monthly benefit to a child of a military men and employees of some federal executive bodies who died or were missing in action	2,402.31	The Decree of the Russian Federation Government No. 481 dated 30.06.2010 "On a monthly benefit to a child of a military men and employees of some federal executive bodies who died or were missing in action" (as of 11.12.2019)
8. A summer health-improving rest benefit for children of certain categories of military men and employees of some federal executive bodies who died or were missing in action, or who acquired disabilities in case of mission execution under the conditions of an armed conflict	25,196.92	The Decree of the Russian Federation Government No. 1051 dated 29.12.2008 (as of 26.07.2019)

Source It is compiled by Vologdina E. S. on the basis of data received from ConsultantPlus (2020)

REFORMATION OF THE SOCIAL SUPPORT ...   273

raised from 250 thousand rubles up to 466,617 thousand rubles. (since 2007 till 2020). The sum of this lump sum allowance was increased by 1.9 times or by 86.6% (ConsultantPlus-2, 2017).

The latest changes of a lump sum allowances amount let a maternity capital increase up to 150 thousand rubles for the second child. Since 2020 a family has the right for getting an increased allowance in case of not having got a maternity benefit for the first two children.

A family is allowed to spend maternity benefit money for buying, building or reconstruction of a housing, for education of a child or for integration or adaptation of children having disabilities, for a saving part of a maternal pension or monthly allowances for law-income families (ConsultantPlus-1, 2017). Easing of requirements related to the spending maternal capital money for private construction was included into the new law. When earlier only individual housing construction was allowed for families on their plots, since that year building erection is also permitted on a garden plot. As for today maternity capital validity is prolonged up to the end of 2026.

Since 2011 on behalf of the initiative of the federal authorities, regional ones began introducing additional measures of a social support for families with children. It was a positive reinforcer for families willing to have children.

Regional policy in this sphere is based on a social and demographic situation and budget capabilities of a region (Makar, 2020).

Since 2011, the regional maternal (family) capital in the Khabarovsk Territory has become an innovation. Parents can use it after the birth or adoption of the third kid, then for subsequent children. The Amount of this lump sum allowance was 200,000 rubles for children born before 01.01.2019 and 250,000 rubles for children born after 01.01.2019.

The lump sum benefit is provided in the region when the second and each subsequent child is born. One of parents has the right for the benefit. The amount of the benefit is 5000 rubles.

Pursuant to the Decree of the Russian Federation President No. 204 dated May 7th, 2018 (ConsultantPlus, 2018) the Khabarovsk Krai ministry has developed a regional project "Financial support of families in case of children birth" (Khabarovsk Krai population welfare ministry, 2019) and monitors it. The regional project "Financial support of families in case of children birth" is aimed at achieving one of the main objectives related to demographic development of the country, i.e. at the increase of a birth coefficient up to 1.7 all over Russia and up to 2.02 in the region by 2024.

A main objective of the project is the development of an economic independence of a family with children and the improvement of the families state support system.

Support of families within the framework of the project is performed Support for families within the project is carried out depending on the order of birth of the child. Each month, one of the parents receives payments for the first-born, electronically issued immediately after registration with the registry office. After registering the birth of the third child and so on, parents also issue a monthly allowance until the child is three years old.

The right for the monthly allowance is provided to the families in which the first child is born, if income amount per one family member is not more than 30,656 rubles. (since 01.01.2018). Amount of the benefit is 15248 thousand rubles. The allowance is awarded for the period until the child is 3 years old. When the third child and subsequent children are born (adopted) after December 31st, 2012, the monthly allowance is provided to one of (adoptive) parents in the families having an average income which does not exceed the average income of people in the region (in 2020 it is 39,083.70 rubles). The amount of the benefit is 15,248 rubles. The allowance is awarded beginning with the birth of a third child or subsequent children until a child is three years old, if application for the allowance was provided within a year after the birth of the third child or subsequent children. The above-mentioned allowance provides support of multi-child families due to the increase of the dependency load on employable family members.

Multi-child families of Khabarovsk Krai can obtain a land plot for free since November 2010. Such regional solution allows families to create their own subsistence farming for food needs satisfaction, as well as for human assets retaining in the Far East.

Since July 2019 additional measures of social support for families with children are established in the region in form of a lump sum allowance due to the birth of the first child and a regional maternity (family) capital due to the birth of the second child (Consultant Plus, 2019).

A lump sum allowance due to the birth of the first child is awarded to the Russian Federation citizens living in the territory of Khabarovsk Krai in case of the first child birth providing that a child is a citizen of the Russian Federation and is born after January 1st, 2019.

The allowance for children is paid off in amount of a doubled living wage for the second quarter of the year preceding the year of application for the above-mentioned allowance awarding. In 2020 its amount is RUB 30,362.

Families, in which the second child is born after January 1st, 2019, have a right for a regional maternity (family) capital. The amount of the allowance for children born before 01.01.2020 is RUB 135,907.8, and RUB 139,985.10 for children born after 01.01.2020.

The law of Khabarovsk Krai No. 58 dated March 20th, 2020 "On amending the law of Khabarovsk Krai "On additional measures of support for families with children on the territory of Khabarovsk Krai" and the decree of the Khabarovsk Krai government No. 146-pr dated April 10th, 2020 "On approval of awarding and payment of a monthly allowance for a child of three to seven years old inclusive" was adopted to execute the decree of the Russian Federation president No. 199 dated March 20th, 2020 (ConsultantPlus, 2011).

The right for allowance is awarded to the families having average income which is less than the living wage set in the region for the second quarter of the year preceding the year of application. In 2020 it is less than 14,369 rubles per one family member.

The amount of a monthly allowance per each under-age person at the age of 3 to 8 years old is a half of the living wage set for the second quarter of the year preceding the year of application. The amount of the allowance will be 7,590.5 rubles per month in 2020.

In Sweden, public payments are paid by parents before minors reach the age of 16 (Business Sweden, 2019). The German Government can allow families to support children up to the age of majority, moreover, provide monthly assistance to adults (up to 25 years old) studying in schools and universities (European Union, 2019). Child benefits are not paid off in the USA; in that country tax remissions are provided for (Lee et al., 2020).

As for today regional measures aimed at the position improvement of mothers willing to work and upbring their children are implemented in Khabarovsk Krai. The program includes activities and described is a procedure for retraining mothers raising children from birth to three years of age on vacation. An important milestone of the program is the opportunity to improve the qualifications of unemployed mothers whose children have not yet gone to primary school. Complex of measures within the framework of Khabarovsk Krai program "Retraining and professional improvement of women being on a childcare leave until a child is three years old, as well as of nonworking women having children and applied to employment service bodies in order to find a job for the period till 2024" (The official web-portal of legal information, 2019). Such retraining is carried out under the auspices of the larger national project "Demography."

In 2019 during a childcare leave until a child is three years old, 94 women were trained according to the programs of vocational education and additional vocational education in order to recover knowledge and skills lost in the childcare leave, to acquire a new profession, to ease the work place adaptation period, to improve the employment possibility upon accomplishment of the maternity leave (the number of trained women exceeded the annual control indicators by one third).

Training was performed with the assistance of an employment service in relation to the following professions (specialities): procurement specialist, accountant, hairdresser, HR manager, manicure specialist, records manager, computer operator with study of various application software, confectioner, HSE specialist, kindergarten teacher, junior kindergarten teacher, speech-language pathologist, employment service specialist, kindergarten teacher assistant, dietitian, social worker, Russian language teacher, vocational education manager and others.

State contracts for women training have been concluded with 21 institutions providing educational activities, such as: Federal State-Financed Educational Institution of Higher Education "Komsomolsk-na-Amure State University", Non-state Educational Private Institution of Higher Vocational Education "Amur Institute of Agricultural Economics and Business", Independent Noncommercial Organization of Further Vocational Education "Knowledge Center "Professional", Independent Noncommercial Educational Organization of Further Vocational Education "Pacific Higher School of Economics and Management" and others.

Remote training based on the programs of further vocational education with application of electronic technologies has been organized for 30 women living in remote areas (Okhotskiy area, Nikolaevskiy area, Sovetsko-gavanskiy area, Ulchskiy area, Verkhnebureinskiy area, Solnechniy area, area named after P. Osipenko, Nanaiskiy area, Bikinskiy area, Vyazemskiy area, area named after Lazo).

1,089.41 thousand rubles from the regional budget were spent for organization of professional education and further vocational education of women in 2019.

REFORMATION OF THE SOCIAL SUPPORT ... 277

A targeted social assistance is provided in the region on the basis of social contracts (4140 families were provided with the targeted social assistance for the sum of RUB 52.8 million in 2019). Difficult life situation has been overcome by 1,773 families.

The implementation of the poverty rate decrease plan has been started in the region. According to the preliminary evaluation done by the regional ministry of economic development, in 2019 the population having income under the living wage was 10.7% of total population in the region (in 2018 it was 12.2%).

Recreation and rehabilitation of children from low-income families, children with disabilities and children from families being in a socially dangerous situation are provided in order to help families to improve their financial situation and overcome a difficult life situation (31.5 thousand of children are provided with organized recreation of various kinds including 2359 children from families being in a socially dangerous situation). The expenses were RUB 134.1 million (and RUB 135.4 million in 2018).

Due to the execution of a complex state support measures, the number of multi-child families was increased by 1,178 families during 2019 (by 1,357 families during 2018 and by 1,894 families during 2017) and now is equal to 17,910 families that is on 7.0% more than in 2018.

However according to the data of the Russian Federal State Statistics Service the number of residents in the region whose income was less that the living wage was equal to 10.7% in 2019.

4 Conclusions

A family is the most important social and economic resource of the future; however, its capabilities cannot be fulfilled in full without a state and regional support.

Social support for a family, mother/fatherhood and childhood is one of the top priorities for preservation of the country national security. A social state is interested in keeping a social stability in the society, economic well-being both across the country in general and in its regions in particular (Vologdina et al., 2020).

Khabarovsk Krai is a region with a difficult demographic situation where a key role is played by migration outflow of the population. The migration flows exceed the indicators of natural decline in the population by one third (Zubkov, 2019). Level of living is one of the conditions related to a regional attractiveness and population retaining. Due to this fact it seems appropriate to increase the age range from three to sixteen years inclusive when awarding a monthly child allowance. According to the allowance awarding procedure, the amount of a family average income shall not be more than 1.5 of the living wages which is set for employable part of Khabarovsk Krai population for the second quarter of the year preceding the year of application for the above-mentioned allowance awarding.

The proposed measures will allow to increase the number of people getting such a benefit by the improvement of living conditions for families with children alongside with the retaining of social support targeting and its efficiency from the viewpoint of the poverty rate decreasing among families with children, and among all population of the region in general, will cease the population outflow and facilitate the birth rate stimulation.

REFERENCES

Ageeva, E. V. (2020). Improvement of approaches to spending funds of social protection of citizens with children. *Business Education Law*, 1(50), 122–126.

Business Sweden. (2019). *The Swedish social security system*. https://www.bus iness-sweden.com/globalassets/services/learning-center/establishment-gui des/the-swedish-social-security-system.pdf (data accessed: 23 March 2020).

ConsultantPlus. (1995). The Federal law no. 81-FZ dated 19.05.1995 "On state benefits for citizens with children" (as of 08.06.2020). http://www.consul tant.ru/document/cons_doc_ LAW_6659/ (data accessed: 23 August 2020).

ConsultantPlus. (2006). The Federal law no. 256-FZ dated 29.12.2006 "On additional state support measures for families with children" (as of 01.03.2020) (as amended, valid since 15.04.2020). http://www.consultant. ru/document/cons_doc_LAW_64872/ (address date: 20 May 2020).

ConsultantPlus. (2011). The law of Khabarovsk Krai no. 112 dated 27.07.2011 "On additional support measures for families with children on the Khabarovsk Krai territory" (as of 11.04.2020). http://www.consultant.ru/regbase/cgi/ online.cgi?req=doc&base=RLAW011&n=56123#026976950774290276 (data accessed: 10 May 2020).

ConsultantPlus. (2014). The Decree of the Russian Federation government no. 1618-r dated 25.08.2014 "On approval of the state family policy concept in the Russian Federation for the period till 2025". http://www.consultant.ru/ document/cons_doc_LAW_167897/ (data accessed: 20 April 2020).

ConsultantPlus. (2018). The Decree of the Russian Federation president no. 204 dated 7.05.2018 "On national purposes and strategic objectives related to the Russian Federation development for the period till 2024 (as

REFORMATION OF THE SOCIAL SUPPORT ... 279

of 19.07.2018)". http://www.consultant.ru/document/cons_doc_LAW_297 432/ (data accessed: 23 March 2020).

ConsultantPlus. (2019). The Decree of Khabarovsk Krai government no. 39-pr dated 12.02.2019 "On additional measures related to birth support in Khabarovsk Krai" (as of 14.11.2019). http://www.consultant.ru/regbase/cgi/online.cgi?req=doc&base=RLAW011&n=136600#09408403462774253 (data accessed: 23 March 2020).

ConsultantPlus. (2020). The Decree of the Russian Federation government no. 61 dated 29.01.2020 "On approval of allowances, benefits and compensations indexation in 2020". http://www.consultant.ru/document/cons_doc_LAW_344133/ (data accessed: 23 May 2020).

ConsultantPlus-1. (2017). The federal law no. 418-FZ dated 28.12.2017 "On monthly allowances for families with children" (as of 24.04.2020) (as amended, valid since 05.05.2020)". http://www.consultant.ru/document/cons_doc_LAW_286470/ (data accessed: 23 March 2020).

ConsultantPlus-2. (2017). The order of Russian ministry of labour no. 889n dated December 29th, 2017 "On approval of a procedure related to monthly allowances paying off due to the birth (adoption) of the first child and/or the second child, application for the mentioned allowances awarding, as well as a list of documents (information) required for monthly allowances awarding due to the birth (adoption) of the first child and/or the second child". http://www.consultant.ru/document/cons_doc_LAW_287721/ (data accessed: 11 May 2020).

European Union. (2019). Your social security rights in Germany. http://ec.europa.eu/social/main.jsp?catId=849&langId=en (data accessed: 23 March 2020).

Khabarovsk Krai Ministry of Population Social Protection. (2019). The regional project "The financial support of families when children are born". https://mszn.khabkrai.ru/Deyatelnost/Gosudarstvennye-programmy/Regionalnyj-proekt-quot-Finansovaya-podderzhka-semej-pri-rozhdenii-detej-quot- (data accessed: 23 April 2020).

Kulikova, A. M. (2020). Theoretical basis of a social support system for families, motherhood and childhood. *Policy, Economy and Innovations, 1*(30), 2.

Lee, B. R., Battalen, A. W., Brodzinsky, D. M., & Goldberg, A. E. (2020). Parent, child, and adoption characteristics associated with post-adoption support needs. *Social Work Research, 44*(1), 21–32.

Makar, S. V. (2020). The demographic situation in Russian and the social infrastructure. *Population, 1*, 67–75.

Maleeva, T. M., & Smolina, I. G. (2019). A proper child benefit. *Economic Policy, 14*(3), 54–69.

280 E. S. VOLOGDINA AND O. A. KUZMINA

Matveeva, T. P., Pavlovskaya, Yu. V., & Kuznetsova, N. A. (2019). A multi-child family and the state. *Humanitarian, Social and Economic, and Social Sciences, 1*, 79–82.

Rakitina, N. E., Filipova, A. G., & Kupryashkina, E. A. (2018). The new research focuses in childhood sociology. *Sociological Studies, 3*(407), 86–93.

The Federal State Statistics Service. (2020). *Information on social and economic situation in Russia.* Demography. https://gks.ru/bgd/free/B20_00/Main. htm (data accessed: 23 March 2020).

The official web-portal of legal information. (2019). The decree of Khabarovsk Krai government no. 538-pr dated 12.12.2019 "On organization of vocational and additional vocational education for women being in a childcare leave until the child is three years old and nonworking women with children of preschool age". http:// publication.pravo.gov.ru/Document/View/2700201912160 014 (data accessed: 23 March 2020).

The official web-site of Khabarovsk Krai government. (2020). *Demographic evolution.* https://www.khabkrai.ru/khabarovsk-krai/Razvitie-kraya/50274 (data accessed: 23 March 2020).

Troshkina, I. N., & Smolina, I. G. (2019). State family policy as a basis for modern family functioning (regional aspect). *Social Dynamics, 11*, 20–43.

Vologdina, E. S., Kuzmina, O. A., & Matyuschko, A. V. (2020). Experience of implementing state policy on life and adaptation of families of agricultural migrants from the European part of Russia to the far East in the 20–30s of the 20th century. *Advances in Economics, Business and Management Research, 128*, 584–588. https://doi.org/10.2991/aebmr.k.200312.084

Zubkov, V. V. (2019). Migration viewpoints of people: Declared tendency or objective reality. *Authority and Management in the East of Russia, 2*(87), 85–92.

Methodological Foundations of an Expanded Understanding of the Economic Mechanism of the Modern Socio-Economic System of Russia

Elena E. Nikolaeva and *Vadim V. Soldatov*

1 Introduction

Every socio-economic system has its own specific mechanism of functioning, the study of which is currently not very popular in economic theory.

Although the topic of the economic mechanism is constantly touched upon through the issues of management, integration, interconnections and interactions, it isn't considered comprehensively, it is often about the functioning of the market and the impact of the state regulatory mechanism on it. In the Soviet scientific literature of the 60–80s years of the twentieth century, the term «economic mechanism» was interpreted by most authors as «a method of organizing and implementing management of social production with its inherent forms of using economic laws,

---

E. E. Nikolaeva (✉) · V. V. Soldatov
Ivanovo State University, Ivanovo, Russia
e-mail: dvn2002@yandex.ru

V. V. Soldatov
e-mail: vv_soldatov@rambler.ru

© The Author(s), under exclusive license to Springer Nature Switzerland AG 2021
E. G. Popkova and B. S. Sergi (Eds.), *Economic Issues of Social Entrepreneurship*,
https://doi.org/10.1007/978-3-030-77291-8_26

methods and means of management» in the context of the specific stage in the development of a socialist economy (Porokhovsky (Ed.), 1989). This topic was developed by L. I. Abalkin (Abalkin, 1973, 1986), Yu. M. Osipov (Osipov, 1987, 1994), B. A. Medvedev (Medvedev, 1976, 1983) and others. The modern economy is becoming more complex under the influence of the emergence of new forms and types of economic activity and their management, the process of digital transformation of the economy and society, the action of new political, social, environmental factors in the global economy as a whole and its separate parts. All this leads to the need for an expanded understanding of the economic mechanism of the socio-economic system.

2   Materials and Methods

The methodological foundations of the expanded interpretation of the economic mechanism of understanding are, firstly, the interconnection and interaction of political economy, institutionalism and economic policy and, secondly, the system-reproduction approach. The synthesis of political economy and institutionalism acts as a unity of essential (endothermic) and superficial (exoteric) economic processes, such as the opening of economic laws and their institutionalization (Babaev & Babaev, 2013; Babaev & Nikolaeva, 2018). Institutions can, through the subjective activities of people, influence objective processes, for example, environmental standards through prices and fines force enterprises to improve technological processes taking into account the laws of production and nature. Ideas close to this methodological approach are developed by L. A. Karaseva (Karaseva, 2017). Within the framework of this methodological approach, the economic mechanism is presented as a logical chain: interactions—relations—economic laws—institutions—management decisions.

The systemic reproductive approach allows us to reveal the elements, structures of the economic mechanism, their functions, integrative processes, a system of direct and feedback connections. This approach includes such methodological principles as consistency, integrability, reproducibility and contradictions.

3 RESULTS

The extended economic mechanism of the national economy, which is interpreted as a system of spontaneous and consciously regulated dialectical interactions, acting as a set of methods, projects that ensure the movement of subjects and objects as self-development and under the influence of external forces should be considered in various aspects. The Russian economic mechanism is manifested through the economic activity of subjects (households, firms, the state and foreign partners) because the socio-economic system of Russia is multilevel.

The mechanism of functioning of the economy presupposes movement, i.e., the interaction of self-development and controlled development, the result of which is a product in natural and monetary terms, subject to distribution, exchange and consumption. The economic mechanism ensures the knowledge and implementation of economic laws in the unity of their technological (human connection with nature) and social and labor sides (relations between people in the labor process), manifests itself through the formation of institutions and the institutional environment, determining the behavior of business entities. Within the framework of the synthesis of political economy and institutionalism, the economic mechanism is the interconnection of the aggregate of productive forces, including science, economic relations and institutions. The center of economic activity is a person who interacts with nature, other people and the society as a whole, he is influenced by non-economic ("superstructure") factors and influences the socio-economic system by himself and therefore the mechanism of functioning of the system should be interpreted as a unity of natural, technical -economic, social processes. The economic mechanism in the context of the digital transformation of society is the interaction of the real and virtual economies. For Russian society, the spatial aspect is extremely relevant, which implies the interpretation of the economic mechanism as a set of interconnected territorial entities that ensure the integrity of the socio-economic system. The final result of the economic mechanism is the resolution of the contradictions existing in the country, the coordination of the interests of the subjects, the tendency towards balance and stability of the economic system and its adaptation to constantly changing conditions (Babaev & Nikolaeva (Ed.), 2019; Nikolaeva, 2019).

The multilevel economic mechanism provides analysis for it within the framework of macroeconomics (programming, forecasting, development of strategies, the formation of comprehensive target programs, economic development of territories, etc.), and it's also applied to the mesoeconomics (regional economy), which has a significant significance, because each of the 85 regions of the country has its own natural-climatic and socio-economic characteristics, the specifics of the mechanism of functioning. As you can know, the regional economy is an open system of social reproduction. The elements of the regional territorial system are combined into extremely complicated complexes and subsystems, among which the municipal level is especially important, which is legally defined as self-governing, but in fact, significantly dependent on external financial injections due to limited own funds, which gives rise to many socio-economic and environmental problems. Therefore, it's important to ensure the combination of self-development and self-government of municipalities with the influence of the regional and federal levels and the local interests with national interests.

The main feature of the current stage of development of the world economy is the contradictory unity of two main processes: globalization and de-globalization of industrial production. The localization of national production becomes the main means of resolving this contradiction in these conditions. The main form of manifestation of the localization of cotton production in our country is the creation of an innovative textile and industrial cluster, which is located within the boundaries of the Upper Volga regions, a set of textile and clothing industries for the manufacture, processing, sale of all types of fabrics and disposal of waste from these activities and also the industrial enterprises of the financial and social infrastructure to ensure their functioning.

To increase the competitiveness of production within this cluster, not only the actions of individual entrepreneurs who introduce modern materials and technologies are needed, but also the functioning of a whole set of mechanisms that contribute to the realization of the competitive advantages of technologically related enterprises. These include the next ones:

- The interaction of enterprises of the cotton, linen, chemical industry with research organizations and specialized universities to create materials with predetermined properties and deep processing of waste;

METHODOLOGICAL FOUNDATIONS OF AN EXPANDED ...   285

- The development of various forms of public–private partnerships for the implementation of the investment process in innovative activities by private and state structures of various levels;
- On this basis, the implementation of the modernization of manufacturing enterprises of the textile and clothing industries using the latest technologies, including digital;
- Training by educational institutions of the regions of personnel, which are necessary for the enterprises of the cluster, receptive to modern innovations;
- Opening of specialized enterprises for the production of innovative fabrics and designer garments and the placement of cluster enterprises as close as possible to the places of processing and sale of its products (Nekrasova & Soldatov, 2017).

The development of the modern economy is substantially going along the path of the formation of cluster-like formations (complexes of the national economic or regional level). Cluster formation (creation and development of territorial-production complexes) requires the creation of a single management body, which is of an intersectoral nature. Regional clusters are structures that introduce elements of planning into the functioning of a territory and they also ensure its comprehensive development as a socio-economic system. Ivanovo State University is actively developing this issue on the example of the sewing and textile logistics cluster and the recreational and tourist cluster of the Vladimir, Ivanovo, Kostroma and Yaroslavl regions (Babaev (Ed.), 2013; Nikolaeva (Ed.), 2017; Nekrasova, 2013; Soldatov & Nekrasova, 2016).

The digital transformation of society leads to the formation of a virtual sector of the economy, which assumes a number of functions of the real sector—information entrepreneurship, electronic money, online stores, electronic government, distance employment, etc. New technologies contribute to a change in technological processes at enterprises. These phenomena significantly affect the economic mechanism and increase the share of such a component as self-movement, self-regulation in it. Technologies 4.0 make the opportunities for creating different-sized production, bring diversity to economic activities and accelerate the implementation of production processes. But due to the fact that digitalization also generates negative consequences for the economy and for the person, the development of a «controlled economy», new methods of state influence that are adequate to the requirements of the laws of nature and economics and also the creation of an institutional environment adequate to these requirements is required.

4 Conclusions and Recommendations

In this case, we focused only on some aspects of an expanded understanding of the economic mechanism and drew attention to the fact that when analyzing the driving forces of the economy, the social division of labor should be considered not only as the sectoral and territorial, but also as cluster-like, and it's necessary to develop interregional and inter-municipal cooperation for this. The cluster, being a product of the interaction of a complex of production, financial, scientific and other mechanisms, introduces elements of planning into the self-developing regional system of social reproduction. The economic mechanism of the modern Russian economy is becoming more complex and requires a broad understanding at all levels of the socio-economic system.

Acknowledgements The material was prepared with the financial support of the Russian Foundation for Basic Research, scientific project No. 19-010-00329 "Theoretical and methodological foundations of an expanded understanding of the economic mechanism in the modern economy" (2019–2020).

References

Abalkin, L. (1973). *Economic mechanism of a developed socialist society.* Thought.
Abalkin, L. I. (Ed.). (1986). *The economic mechanism of social formations.* Thought.
Babaev, B. D., & Babaev, D. B. (2013). The Relationship of political economy and institutionalism—An important direction for improving economic and theoretical knowledge. *Journal of Economic Theory. No., 2,* 84–93.
Babaev, B. D. (Ed.). (2013). *Actual problems of regional economy and the intensification of territorial factor in the socio-economic development: The* (scientific). Pressto.
Babaev, B. D., & Nikolaeva, E. E. (2018). Conceptual framework of the region research as an open economic system: Synthesis of political economy and institutionalism. Vestnik Permskogo universiteta. Seria Ekonomika = Perm Uni-versity Herald. *Economy, 13*(2), 159–176. DOI: https://doi.org/10.17072/1994-9960-2018-2-159-176.

METHODOLOGICAL FOUNDATIONS OF AN EXPANDED ... 287

Babaev, B. D., & Nikolaeva, E. E. (Eds.). (2019). *Expanded concept of the economic mechanism of the modern socio-economic system of Russia: Theoretical and methodological foundations* (scientific). Ivan. state University.

Karaseva, L. A. (2017). Institutional illusion and the real problems of the economic mechanism of the Russian economy. Vestnik of Tver state University. *Economics and Management, 1*, 24–31.

Medvedev, B. A. (1976). *Socialist production. Political and economic re-search.* Ekonomika.

Medvedev, B. A. (1983). *Management of socialist production: Problems of theory and practice.* Politizdat.

Nekrasova, I. V. (2013). Coordination of interests of participants of the territorial-industrial textile complex. *Modern Science-Intensive Technologies. Re-Gional Supplement. No., 4*(36), 96–102.

Nekrasova, I. V., & Soldatov, V. V. (2017). The place of the innovative textile cluster in the conditions of globalization of the world economy (on the example of the Ivanovo region). *Multilevel Social Reproduction: A Question of Theory and Practice., 12*(28), 114–119.

Nikolaeva, E. E. (Ed.). (2017). *Regional reproduction: Fundamental ques-tions of theory and practice (based on the materials of the upper Volga regions)* (scientific). Ivan. State University.

Nikolaeva, E. E. (2019). The content of the concept of "economic mecha-nism" in the economic literature. *Multilevel Social Reproduction: A Question of Theory and Practice., 16*(32), 28–38.

Osipov, Yu. M. (1987). *Economic mechanism of state-monopoly capital-ism.* Moscow state University publishing House.

Osipov, Yu. M. (1994). *Fundamentals of the theory of economic mecha-nism.* MSU publishing House.

Porokhovsky, A. A. (Ed.). (1989). *Economic laws and intensification of economy.* Moscow state University publishing House.

Soldatov, V. V., & Nekrasova, I. V. (2016). Innovative textile cluster as the main direction of development of the textile industry. *Modern Science-Intensive Technologies. Regional Supplement. No., 3*(47), 154–157.

Transforming Business Ethics in the Coronavirus Pandemic

Liudmila P. Sidorova and *Timur M. Khusyainov*

1 INTRODUCTION

Today, the coronavirus pandemic, as a global epidemic in its nature and scope, has brought about the same global changes in all aspects of human life and society as a whole. The impact of COVID-19 on health and education system, on social and cultural space, on economies of individual countries and on the world economy is undoubtedly unprecedented. One by one, the world's three largest economies—China, Europe, and the US—have been severely affected. The closure of large and small enterprises in many countries has damaged the global economy, affecting primary producers in Latin America and Africa, as well as Asian supply chains (Nicola, 2020). Stock markets collapsed, tourist flows, major business conferences, events, festivals, and tournaments were cancelled or rescheduled as a result of the spread of the virus. Life of the whole planet has been put on hold.

L. P. Sidorova (✉) · T. M. Khusyainov
National Research University Higher School of Economics, Nizhny Novgorod, Russia
e-mail: lsidorova@hse.ru

T. M. Khusyainov
e-mail: timur@husyainov.ru

© The Author(s), under exclusive license to Springer Nature Switzerland AG 2021
E. G. Popkova and B. S. Sergi (eds.), *Economic Issues of Social Entrepreneurship*,
https://doi.org/10.1007/978-3-030-77291-8_27

Perhaps one of the areas most directly affected by the coronavirus pandemic, causing a lot of new problems, is ethics. Many issues and ethical dilemmas have emerged that have either become more acute or have been created by the crisis itself—from the allocation of limited resources and the prioritization of aid, public health surveillance (Hamid, 2020), physical separation, rights and obligations of health care workers prior to clinical trials. This, in turn, is complicated by the different characteristics of health systems and the unique cultural and socio-economic conditions of countries. However, the ethical issues raised by COVID-19 do not concern only health care.

The crisis caused by the pandemic has presented business community with a number of challenges not only of an economic but also of an ethical nature. The decisions that business leaders are now swiftly making will have a significant impact and will determine the direction of business ethics in general after the crisis phase.

2 Materials and Method

In the light of COVID-19, the following issues have become the most pressing and relevant in the area of business ethics: how to make decisions in accordance with the values and stated principles of the organization; how to remain loyal to business objective of maximizing profits without infringing the rights and interests of employees and other interested parties; how to make strategic decisions with short time frames and limited cash flow; how business can best interact with the local community and government; whether it is necessary to support the most vulnerable during a pandemic categories of staff, suppliers and customers, etc.

Such problems, which companies certainly faced before the pandemic, are now on the front lines and require urgent responses and solutions from the business community. As D. Samuelson, Vice-president of the Aspen Institute in the United States, noted, the crisis is not worth "wasting". She believes that "Covid-19 is a chance for business leaders to renegotiate their contract with society". The Professor of Strategy in Business School, the University of Nevada's Business Ethics Expert, O. Won-Yong, draws attention to the fact that already more and more companies, aware of the importance of taking responsibility for their employees, customers and society, are shifting their views from those of the University of Nevada "joint-stock capitalism" on "interested capitalism", and after the pandemic the level of corporate social responsibility must inevitably rise (Bruzda, 2020).

In view of scale and seriousness of the unfolding crisis, companies of all sizes and different sectors are currently facing a number of unprecedented challenges, the solution of which requires clarity and unconventional thinking, focusing on objectives, Commitment to international standards and norms, concerted efforts and collective action.

One of the most pressing issues of business ethics in the light of the coronavirus was the issue of respect for the rights of staff, within which several issues could be identified. The Institute for Human Rights and Business published a survey on compliance of human rights in companies during a pandemic, the first part of which highlights how the pandemic has affected human rights situations: the issue of proportionality of regulatory measures, vulnerability of women, migrant workers, manifestations of xenophobia in society (The Institute for Human Rights & Business, 2020).

3 Results

Today, technology can greatly assist governments in controlling the spread of the virus. For example, mobile network operators can provide data on the movement of people infected with Covid-19 and violating self-isolation. It is also possible to track passengers of flights via a cell phone in case they are detected and informed in due course. For example, Vodafone has provided data to European governments to better understand people's movements. The company notes, however, that such use must be reasonable and lawful, and therefore only anonymous data is provided. New applications, such as those that alert users when they are near someone who may be infected with the virus, pose serious human rights concerns. Vodafone recommends that applications meet four conditions: they must be independent of operators or other private companies; be developed by national health authorities; require individual consent; and State institutions must justify why the Annex is necessary and that it is in conformity with the law.

The problems faced by migrant workers during the crisis became particularly acute (Overcrowded, 2020). Since migrant labor is mainly required in areas that do not involve remote work, such as construction, taxi services, etc. a lot of them were out of work and literally on the verge of starvation. Migrants generally do not have the same rights as citizens of the host country, which exacerbated the situation. Having lost their jobs, some have been forced to leave their homes, and in many countries they lack adequate health insurance and other benefits, including unemployment insurance. In some cases, migrant workers have either been quarantined or faced restrictions in the form of closed borders that prevent them from returning home. For example, a group of domestic migrant workers in India had to walk hundreds of kilometers to return home when their employers left them homeless and without wages, and public transport was restricted (Frayer & Pathak, 2020).

Since most governments in the pandemic are solely or more supportive of their citizens, it is the companies that should pay attention to the rights of migrant workers working for them, seek to ensure their safety and provide the same level of support that is provided to civilian staff.

Covid-19 has had a significant impact on working women. This category of staff was most vulnerable during the period of the pandemic-induced quarantine. This is related to the role of women in many modern societies, as they bear a disproportionate share of the domestic burden, which includes, in addition to paid work, domestic care, child-rearing and caring for their families. The so-called "Third Shift" or emotional labor can also be distinguished. This is the additional cognitive work involved in the planning and organization of the entire family order, and the main fear and concern for the risk of infection of family members falls on their shoulders.

Also, the influence of traditional hierarchical roles in the family, where men enjoy greater privileges, means that even if the family has a personal computer, a woman working from home can access it for fewer hours than a man (Morrow, 2020). Businesses should be aware of this vulnerable situation of working women and pay special attention to women who are forced to work from home.

In addition to the fact that some women in the coronavirus are at risk of losing their jobs, women may be the only earners in the family, because they who work in those vital areas that continue to work outside the home: medical personnel, sales workers and others.

Of course, the virus is indiscriminate and affects all people. Wealth, religion, sex, physical condition, or social status does not confer immunity on individuals or groups. But it is already clear that COVID-19 disproportionately affects the poor, in part because they lack the resources to take adequate precautions. The WHO Global Preparedness Monitoring Board has shown how the poorest suffer during a massive outbreak (Brundtland et al., 2019). The WHO report notes that outbreaks of disease are destroying the entire health system, and reduced access to health services leads to even higher mortality and further economic decline. The negative impact is particularly severe in the fragile and vulnerable conditions in which poverty, poor governance, weak health systems, and lack of trust in health services, Specific cultural and religious aspects and sometimes ongoing armed conflict make the outbreak of the disease much more complex. Businesses offering consumer credit or essential products and services should be particularly attentive to consumers from economically weaker segments of the population.

The COVID-19 crisis has highlighted the importance of rights such as the rights to equality, livelihood, security, housing and food, etc. It is clear that social, economic and cultural human rights must first and foremost be protected by the State, by providing assistance and support to citizens in times of pandemic. However, not all countries have the same resources and not all societies are at the same stage of development. Therefore, governments in some cases are actually unable to meet their obligations (due to lack of resources or the nature of the crisis) (Khoo & Lantos, 2020) while in others they simply do not want to do so.

Companies that are able to act are therefore often expected to play a more important role in helping the State protect human rights, even if they have no legal obligation to do so. In the current context, companies operating in the countries most affected by the pandemic have a special responsibility to care for their employees and others affected by their activities.

The "United Nations Guiding Principles on Business and Human Rights" do not explicitly mention specific rights, such as the right to health or the responsibility of business in emergency or other crisis situations. However, if one looks at the basic principles of corporate responsibility for human rights set out in this guidance, it becomes clear what actions are expected from business.

Business enterprises should respect human rights, including the right to health, avoid human rights violations and address adverse human rights impacts. The responsibility to respect human rights is a universal standard of expected behavior for all business enterprises, wherever they operate. Addressing adverse human rights impacts entails taking appropriate measures to prevent, mitigate and, where appropriate, redress. Business enterprises may make other commitments or engage in other activities to support and promote human rights that can contribute to the realization of these rights. However, this does not compensate for the lack of respect for human rights in their activities (Subasinghe & Breese, 2020).

These basic principles have become more relevant and have been used by the business community as one of the main guidelines used in the development of institutional policies in the field of human rights during the Covid-19 crisis.

This means a number of measures, which include, for example, the provision of safe and healthy working conditions if the work is not remote and must be performed in the office or in the workplace; Protection of workers from the effects of the virus through special equipment, as well as masks, disinfectants for employees who can interact with a large number of people in their work (courier services, banks, supermarkets, pharmacies and other enterprises). Such protection should be offered to all workers, even those who are contractors or subcontractors. Where working remotely is possible, companies must provide staff with the necessary facilities, equipment and technology to work from home.

If workers are sick, companies should, to the possible extent, provide a paid leave, taking measures to ensure access to health care. Some companies were forced to downsize during the ongoing COVID-19 outbreak, but opted to lay off their employees, providing them with more benefits than with cuts. Some company executives have decided to cut or forgo salaries this year as a sign of solidarity and commitment to staff welfare. In an economic downturn, it takes much longer for people to find new jobs. Therefore, the companies least affected by the crisis should give priority to recruiting the newly unemployed in order to reduce unemployment and support the affected people.

As an example of responsible corporate behavior, one can look at the measures taken by one of the world's largest employers, the giant American retailer Walmart. It has 1.5 million employees. In response to the COVID-19 crisis, Walmart took a number of measures to protect its employees. These include emergency leave policies and support for workers with COVID-19; Provision of telemedicine services for staff; Strengthening of sanitary measures, including the installation of plexiglas on cash registers to prevent transmission of the virus; Disinfection of purchases and carts; temperature measurement; Staff masks and gloves, hourly cash bonuses and other measures to protect customers and staff.

Microsoft has expressed concern about cyber attacks on hospital systems in Paris, Italy, Thailand, the United States, and even the World Health Organization. As supporting measures, the company provided Accountguard with medical service providers, including hospitals, medical facilities, clinics, laboratories, and pharmaceutical and medicinal biological companies and companies manufacturing medical equipment for safety (Burt, 2020).

Although there are government security instructions for COVID-19, not all companies follow them. The actions of tea plantation owners in India could be considered as an example of irresponsible business in a pandemic. Twenty-five thousand tea collectors sued the Supreme Court for non-payment of wages during quarantine. Workers were on the verge of starvation and had to return to work in the midst of a pandemic. Tea plantation owners claim that paying wages during isolation without any help from the state would be a "titanic" task (Lalwani, 2020).

In May 2020, Mcdonald's employees in Chicago filed a class-action lawsuit against the network, accusing it of failing to comply with the government's orders and, as a result, endangering employees and their families. They noted that the company did not provide hand sanitizer, gloves and masks and did not notify its employees when one of the employees contracted coronavirus (Hals, 2020).

4 Conclusion

The response to the ongoing COVID-19 crisis was guided by a number of factors. These include laws and regulations, including international standards, as well as expectations from employees, customers, investors and society at large. The actions of the business community were also based on well-known good practices of responsible behavior, ethical codes and company policies, and the values of executives ("Business and COVID-19", 2020).

It is worth noting that there is no clear set of rules or general guidance from the international community. This is not surprising; pandemic is a unique situation, and there are no ready-made solutions. But companies can learn from each other about what to do and what not to do.

It should be noted that some of the measures identified, recommended and proposed are more suitable for large companies with a presence in many countries and considerable resources. The introduction of a number of measures would entail significant costs for companies, which may not be feasible in practice, and it is not to be expected that each company would implement all of these recommendations, as the crisis has put the survival of many companies at risk.

The following principles can form the basis of responsible business in emergency situations such as Covid-19, and are consistent with recognized practices of responsible business conduct and business ethics.

1. Prepare. The risks associated with the company and its personnel, as well as the impact on the community in its area of operations and other stakeholders, need to be identified.
2. Do no harm. Companies should examine their practices to determine whether they are at risk of contributing in any way to the spread of the pandemic. It should also be determined whether their behavior increases pressure on health systems. Some business operations must continue during a crisis, but this requires a responsible adjustment of the workplace. It was important to create or maintain an environment in which staff, contractors or suppliers would not feel threatened by being able to postpone work and seek medical treatment. People have a responsibility not to spread the virus, and companies have a responsibility to prevent its spread as much as possible.
3. Ensure that there is no discrimination. As the COVID-19 spread, in some countries there was an increase in the number of cases of racism against people of Asian origin or people who appear to be different from the general population (Devakumar, 2020: Yang et al., 2020). Violence or non-violent discrimination was reported in several countries (Yearby & Mohapatra, 2020). This may occur at the workplace or during work meetings. Companies should take all reasonable steps to protect employees who are stigmatized or attacked, physically or verbally. Companies should have a policy of "zero" tolerance for such discrimination, aggression, intimidation or harassment of employees, consumers, customers or partners. Strict disciplinary measures should be taken in cases involving company personnel. Channels for reporting cases of discrimination or threat should be provided. In determining who may be exposed to the virus, companies should follow only scientific information and evidence. No decisions should be made about the risks to people based on race, faith, gender, etc.

Business should be guided by the ethics of duty to assist in crisis situations such as COVID-19. For a company, compliance with responsible business standards in response to the COVID-19 crisis can ensure that its business solutions avoid and eliminate potential adverse impacts on the company and its supply chain. COVID-19 is a real test of how companies can be more resilient and adaptable, as well as better in the long run.

REFERENCES

Brundtland, G. H., et al. (2019). *Global preparedness monitoring board a world at risk.* https://apps.who.int/gpmb/assets/annual_report/GPMB_annualreport_2019.pdf (accessed 20 July 2020).

Bruzda, N. (2020). *COVID-19 and the ethical questions it poses.* https://www.unlv.edu/news/release/covid-19-and-ethical-questions-it-poses (accessed 12 July 2020).

Burt, T. (2020). *Protecting healthcare and human rights organizations from cyberattacks.* https://blogs.microsoft.com/on-the-issues/2020/04/14/accountguard-cyberattacks-healthcare-covid-19/.

Business and COVID-19. (2020). *Business and COVID-19: Response framework and action mapping tool.* Available at https://businessfightspoverty.org/business-and-covid-19/ (accessed 20 July 2020).

Devakumar, D., et al. (2020). Racism and discrimination in COVID-19 responses. *The Lancet, 395*(10231), 1193–1194. https://doi.org/10.1016/S0140-6736(20)30792-3.

Frayer, L., & Pathak, S. (2020). *Coronavirus lockdown sends migrant workers on a long and risky trip home.* https://www.npr.org/822642382 (accessed 20 July 2020).

Hals, T. (2020). *U.S. workers hit McDonald's with class action over COVID-19 safety.* https://reut.rs/2yhxuFf (accessed 20 July 2020).

Hamid, H., et al. (2020). Current burden on healthcare systems in low- and middle-income countries: Recommendations for emergency care of COVID-19. *Drugs Ther Perspect, 36*(8), 355–357.

Institute for Human Rights and Business. (2020). *Respecting human rights in the time of the covid-19 pandemic: Examining companies' responsibilities for workers and affected communities.* https://www.ihrb.org/focus-areas/covid-19/report-respectinghuman-rights-in-the-time-of-covid19 (accessed 12 July 2020).

Khoo, E. J., & Lantos, J. D. (2020). Lessons learned from the COVID-19 pandemic. *Acta Pædiatrica, 109*(7), 1323–1325. https://doi.org/10.1111/apa.15307.

Lalwani, V. (2020). *One reason why tea garden employees went back to work despite Covid-19 fears—Hunger.* https://scroll.in/article/960142/ (accessed 20 July 2020).

Morrow, A. (2020). *'Not just a health issue': How Covid-19 is quietly eroding women's rights.* https://www.rfi.fr/en/france/20200326-coronavirus-domestic-violence-gender-perspectives (accessed 20 July 2020).

Nicola, M., et al. (2020). The socio-economic implications of the coronavirus pandemic (COVID-19): A review. *International Journal of Surgery, 78,* 185–193. https://doi.org/10.1016/j.ijsu.2020.04.018.

Overcrowded reception centres and informal settlements make migrants vulnerable to COVID-19. https://ec.europa.eu/migrant-integration/news/overcrowded-reception-centres-and-informal-settlements-make-migrants-vulnerable-to-covid-19 (accessed 20 July 2020).

Subasinghe, R., & Breese, H. (2020). *COVID-19 and the corporate duty to respect human rights: It's time for the business community to step up.* https://clck.ru/QK8Zm (accessed 20 July 2020).

Yang, C.-C., et al. (2020). Discrimination and well-being among Asians/Asian Americans during covid-19: The role of social media. *Cyberpsychology, Behavior, and Social Networking, 1–6.* https://doi.org/10.1089/cyber.2020.0394.

Yearby, R., & Mohapatra, S. (2020). *Structural discrimination in covid-19 workplace protections.* https://ssrn.com/abstract=3614092 (accessed 20 July 2020).

The System of Compliance Management of Corporate Social Responsibility

*Pavel A. Kanapuhin, Larisa M. Nikitina,
and Dmitry V. Borzakov*

1 INTRODUCTION

In the modern economic paradigm, company management is directly related to the proper, complete and timely fulfilment of requirements of a wide range of stakeholders. Company executives all over the world have been pointing out difficulties in monitoring changes that are in process in the highly turbulent external environment (Bogoviz & Sergi, 2018; Goyal & Sergi, 2015; Goyal et al., 2015, 2016) and introduce specialized compliance systems that allow increasing the level of confidence in the future regulatory landscape of their activities.

Compliance is most often interpreted as combating violations of current legislation (Primakov, 2019). Therefore, most companies are traditionally focused on compliance risks in such areas as corruption and fraud management, countering money laundering and terrorism financing, protection of personal data, compliance with antitrust laws, etc. (KPMG, 2016).

P. A. Kanapuhin (✉) · L. M. Nikitina · D. V. Borzakov
Voronezh State University, Voronezh, Russia
e-mail: kanapukhin@econ.vsu.ru

L. M. Nikitina
e-mail: nikitina@econ.vsu.ru

© The Author(s), under exclusive license to Springer Nature Switzerland AG 2021
E. G. Popkova and B. S. Sergi (eds.), *Economic Issues of Social Entrepreneurship*,
https://doi.org/10.1007/978-3-030-77291-8_28

Considering the fact that regulatory bodies, customers, employees, shareholders, and investors around the world continue placing increasingly higher demands on the transparent and ethical conduct of companies, harmonization of the impact of business on society and the environment, the concept of compliance is gradually transformed. Experts increasingly agree that compliance is interdisciplinary in nature and defines a mechanism to ensure conformity of activities with different standards contributing to enhancement of reliability and sustainability of the company. Thus, according to ISO 19600 standard "Compliance management system. Guiding principles", compliance means fulfilment of all requirements applicable to an organization, both those that are mandatory and those that it opts to fulfill. Therefore, compliance management can be defined as an in-house management system that ensures compliance of activities with parameters of the institutional space—mandatory and voluntary (beyond statutory provisions) and establishes a legitimate platform for interaction of all stakeholders.

In this regard, it should be emphasized that Corporate Social Responsibility (CSR) is the most general category of management theory describing voluntary socially significant business activity (Blagov, 2010; Borzakov & Nikitina, 2019). At the same time, compliance with legal requirements is not excluded from CSR and is an essential but not sufficient condition for achieving the status of a responsible company. In addition, in many countries of the world, CSR becomes the field of state regulation based on the use of combinations of mandatory and optional provisions. First of all, issues related to environment protection, observance of human rights, occupational safety and occupational health and safety, disclosure of reliable nonfinancial information shall be subject to legislative regulation.

CSR management is still included with management tasks that are difficult to formalize. Modification of CSR management technologies based on compliance management will allow structuring the complex institutional environment of CSR and harmonizing procedures related to compliance with social, economic and environmental requirements, both voluntary and mandatory, for the benefit of numerous stakeholders. In our opinion, specification and clarification of the methodological support for the solution of this problem appears to be highly relevant.

2 Methodology

CSR management methodology has various theoretical underpinnings that have been consistently developed to explain how the originally intrinsically regulatory concept can be implemented in the company's practical activities. The theories of Corporate Social Sensitivity (CSS), Corporate Social Activity (CSA), stakeholders, and sustainable development are described as some of the best-known theories in the academic literature.

The theory of CSS most adequately describes CSR management technologies from the perspective of ensuring compliance of company's activities with different and varying requirements. Back in the early 70's of the twentieth century, even before the term "compliance" was introduced and obtained a wide circulation, such authors as R. Ackerman, S. Sethi, and A. Carroll explored the problem of "bridging the gap in legitimacy" of companies by monitoring compliance of their business strategies with public requirements. In their writings, the mentioned authors viewed the company as a living organism that responded to external stimuli, and pointed to such essential elements of compliance management as concernment and moral choice of executive management, development of methods of organizational training and adaptation of personnel. According to the authors of the theory of CSS, the company should not simply adapt, but should prevent challenges and potential risks of non-compliance with legal provisions, requirements of market forces, and social norms, values and expectations before their codification as legal requirements (Ackerman, 1973; Carroll, 1979; Sethi, 1975), which is reflective of the modern comprehension of the role of compliance in management of an organization.

Subsequently, CSS processes were integrated in the theory of corporate social activity. Using the CSA model proposed by J. Wood, we can treat the effectiveness of CSS through the study of the company's motivation to sensitivity to social problems and the measurement of performance of commitments (Wood, 2009).

Other theories have significantly contributed to the development of scientific approaches to CSR management as well. For example, the provisions of stakeholder theory have served as a basis for the personalization of actors of CSR (Nikitina, 2011) and the risks of non-compliance with their interests have been identified. The theory of sustainable development has described the content of three key areas of corporate sustainability and social responsibility: economic, social and environmental. At the beginning of the new decade, this approach was extended to include the management (or institutional) dimension (Skolkovo IEMS, 2016). We have used the conceptual provisions of these theories to reveal the content of the CSR management system based on management compliance.

A comprehensive approach to management implies considering the elementary composition of the phenomenon under consideration—subjects and objects to management, which in the context of CSR are most developed in the theory of stakeholders, as well as the mechanism ensuring their effective interaction. The management mechanism in the management theory is most often characterized through the consistent implementation of management cycle stages—functions of the management process: planning, organization, incentivization, and control (Mangutov, 1975). The continuous improvement cycle known as PDCA (plan—do—check—act), which is included in most ISO standards, including ISO 19600 "Compliance management system", ISO 31000 "Risk management", ISO 26000 "Guide on social responsibility", is also used to characterize the management mechanism.

In compliance management practice, companies most often use a three-component model of functions of the compliance management process which involves their consistent implementation to prevent and identify the dangers of violation of approved requirements and responding to their consequences (Cherepanova, 2016).

The above functions reflect the key procedures of the "life cycle" of compliance and have an increased focus on the proactive approach to compliance risk management in terms of threat prevention procedures (Table 1). We believe that this model can be successfully adapted to CSR.

3   RESULTS

Relations arising during the implementation of CSR are difficult to formalize; they cover a wide and dynamic range of issues related involving balancing the interests of different groups of stakeholders (Blagov, 2010; Nikitina, 2011), which clearly causes difficulties in the practice of management of this domain of relations and prevents the prevalence of responsible behavior. The relevance and complexity of this issue can hardly be overestimated, since at the present stage efficient CSR management

THE SYSTEM OF COMPLIANCE MANAGEMENT... 303

Table 1 Compliance management functions and their content

Function	Content
Preventing	– compliance risk identification and assessment;
	– comprehensive adequate inspection;
	– development and actualization of the Code of Conduct;
	– incentivization and training;
Identifying	– monitoring and audit;
	– channels for the provision of information;
	– incident detection;
Responding	– internal investigations;
	– responsibility and discipline;
	– corrective actions;
	– assessment of efficiency;
	– internal and external reporting

mechanism becomes one of determinants of sustainable development of the company.

In our opinion, the implementation of the compliance management system (primarily functions and procedures) will make it possible to formalize the CSR management process from the perspective of sensitivity and assuring compliance with requirements, including the establishment of the necessary procedures to monitor responsible behavior.

The main elements of the CSR compliance management system include objects and subjects of management as well as mechanism that ensures their interaction through consistent implementation of functions to prevent and identify risks of violation of assumed obligations in the field of CSR and respond to their consequences.

The company and its stakeholders which are regarded as participants of the system of mutual relations which all of them influence and none of them can fully control (Nikitina, 2011; Wood, 2009), act as the subjects of management in the proposed system. For CSR compliance management, the circle of stakeholders goes beyond the range of primary interaction of the company and includes such groups as, for example, employees of suppliers, local communities, or abstract future generations. By identification of a stakeholder, the company acknowledges the validity of its claims and is legitimized itself due to implementation of compliance procedures in their relationship to it. Hence, the category "subjects of management" in this case unites those who implement CSR directly on behalf of the company and its addressees.

The object of CSR compliance management consists of a wide range of requirements, which includes voluntary commitments within the scope of adopted charters, memorandums, codes, and guidelines of authoritative international, national and industry-specific non-governmental organizations, over the statutorily prescribed minimum. The acknowledged and best-known international standards in the field of CSR include the United Nations Global Compact, 17 sustainable development goals, ISO 14000, ISO 26000 standards, etc. (Borzakov & Nikitina, 2019).

As have been noted above, CSR is increasingly being used as a tool of state policy. However, the vector of government regulatory policy in this sphere is often oriented to achieve a balance in direct regulation and self-regulation systems.

France became the first state in Europe which adopted the Law on CSR in business in 2017 to place one hundred largest companies of the country under an obligation to have their own CSR plan and monitor its implementation by parent company and affiliated companies, as well as contracting parties bound by financial relations. The company that violated this law will be fined to the amount of up to 10 million Euros (TASS, 2017).

Nevertheless, governments in most countries avoid direct legal instruments of enforcement of responsible behavior and aim at encouraging the companies to follow the statutory standards in order to obtain certain incentives in the future. Economic measures include tax incentives and subsidies for companies that use energy saving solutions and renewable energy sources that facilitate the development of responsible consumption and participate in charity (Borzakov & Nikitina, 2019).

At present, legal requirements related to disclosure of nonfinancial information have obtained the widest circulation. According to the report by Carrots and Sticks, state regulation in this field operates in at least 52 countries (Carrots & Sticks, 2016). Fines and sanctions for failure to submit or late submission of nonfinancial information vary from country to country: e.g. up to 1,500 euros in Portugal, up to 150,000 euros in Italy, more than 100,000 euros in Latvia (Feoktistova et al., 2019).

In Russia, there is also an outlined tendency towards reinforcement of state policy in the field of CSR, which is reflected in such important legislative initiatives as the introduction of the Draft Federal Law "On nonpublic financial reporting", the adoption of amendments to laws "On charitable activity and volunteering" and "On the development of small and medium businesses in the Russian Federation".

The compliance management process is a consistent implementation of prevention, identification and response functions. We shall give consideration to the key features of implementation of abovementioned functions in the context of CSR.

(1) *Implementation of the risk prevention function in the CSR compliance management system.*

The point of reference in compliance management is represented by procedures of identification and assessment of compliance risks. Wide variety of relevant fields and areas of implementation of CSR requires systematization of emerging compliance risks.

CSR compliance risks should be primarily classified by spheres of responsibility. Pursuant to the theory of sustainable development, we can identify compliance risks related to economic, social, environmental and management responsibility of the company. The management sphere is connective and includes the risks arising from the inability of management and staff of the company to adequately perceive requirements in social, economic and environmental spheres.

In the scope of spheres of CSR mentioned above, compliance risks can also be grouped according to the degree of voluntariness of imposed requirements.

Compliance risks related to failure to comply with mandatory and voluntary legal requirements in the field of CSR include: noncompliance with current legislation, including the absence of timely changes or adjustments in the activities of the organization in line with new requirements (mandatory legislative minimum of CSR, the non-compliance with which excludes the company from the list of socially responsible companies); risks of possible litigation against the company on the part of stakeholders; adverse changes in specialized legislation, leading to an increase in operational expenditures for irresponsible companies, etc.

Compliance risks related to failure to comply with nonbinding requirements in the field of CSR include: improper conduct and unfair practices of management and staff in their relations with stakeholders; inconsistency of accepted standards of CSR with stakeholders' expectations, based on the role, scale of activity, and growth potential of the company; misleading information that can cause serious damage to reputation; the use of CSR as a "camouflage" for unfair practices (for example, "greenwashing") etc.

The compliance technologies make it possible to identify the risks that arise due to extension of areas of responsibility of the company to its stakeholders. In particular, the management of the company's impact on suppliers is one of consistent trends in the development of CSR for the recent years. In order to disseminate the practice of responsible supply chain, compliance management provides for special procedures of integrated checkouts of contractors (due diligence), which will make it possible to avert the risks of bringing them to joint responsibility for their activity (or inactivity) in legal and reputational sense. Selected partners are obliged to declare their consent to comply with requirements of CSR in order to start or continue cooperation, for example by signing the appropriate code of conduct.

All identified CSR compliance risks are assessed from the perspective of probability of infliction of damage and its specific size. With this information, the managers can develop and implement the subsequent compliance procedures, reflecting the order of precedence of threats, and efficiently distribute limited resources (Borzakov & Nikitina, 2019). It is important to understand that CSR compliance risk assessment must be carried out on a regular basis due to the high rate of changes in the interests of stakeholders.

According to J. Wood, social responsibility is borne on behalf of the company by particular individuals who constantly make their choice and decisions, both insignificant and vital (Wood, 2009). Risk factors for companies in this case include the absence of management interest ("authoritative tone"), lack of awareness of the importance of ethics and compliance by employees in their everyday activities, lack of skilled professionals, inefficient selection and adaptation of the staff, negative staff morale.

In this regard, the crucial task of CSR management is to create such organizational context in which every employee would be aware of the need to act in compliance with applicable requirements and would be supplied with reliable compliance management tools to enable making responsible decisions in the performance of their official duties, in other words, internal compliance culture of CSR. In practice, however, the employee is more often treated as an addressee of CSR, and less often—as a participant of certain activities (such as volunteerism) and even less often—as its direct everyday performer.

The code of conduct is a fundamental document of the compliance management system. Unlike codes of ethics, corporate conduct and

CSR which most often form the internal regulatory framework of CSR management, codes of conduct include not only ideological part (description of the mission, common vision and core values of CSR as well as basic ethical principles of interaction with stakeholders), but also the regulatory part which establishes the rules of working behavior and minimum procedures intended to reduce compliance risks (Cherepanova, 2016; Karpovich & Truntsevskii, 2016).

It is the code of conduct that contributes to the formation of responsible decision-making culture in employees by setting clear rules and algorithms. Therefore, their content must be consistently worded in the form that would be understandable for the maximum number of employees, so that each of them could clearly understand what behavior is expected of them and how their decisions influence the level of CSR.

Development of violation prevention culture is achieved by development of the code of conduct, and, more importantly, ensuring its performance. Therefore, all new employees are obliged to familiarize themselves with the code of conduct and undergo the orientation training. In addition, regular scheduled trainings should be conducted, while unscheduled trainings should be conducted in case of introduction of changes in legislation, the Code and other internal documents.

(2) *Implementation of the identification and response function in the CSR compliance management system.*

The fundamental role in the CSR management system is played not only by the procedures involved with the formation and approval of an internal legal framework for responsible behavior, but also the procedures to ensure the timely and complete fulfilment of obligations that are related to the implementation of compliance risks.

In order to pinpoint the problems before they cause serious damage, companies introduce internal whistleblowing mechanisms thanks to which every employee may rest assured that they have somewhere to report the detected violation and that their report will be taken seriously and the necessary measures will be taken. Popular tools for the provision of information and consulting include "hotlines", e-mail messages, checklists, or web portals and chat bots.

Taking into account the specific nature of CSR compliance risks, the compliance management system may include maintenance of whistleblowing mechanisms not only for internal, but also for external stakeholders. This will make it possible to promptly receive information about violations (or their threat), to provide consulting support, and to receive feedback from all stakeholders, rather than from company employees only. The importance of feedback from external stakeholders is also due to the fact that modern information technologies facilitate the exchange and dissemination of information about socially responsible practices of the company.

Following the detection of an incident and/or the receipt of a solid message concerning the imminent or completed violation, the company initiates an internal investigation first, since unsafe information may lead to serious damage to business reputation of a company.

Any incident proved of violation of rules established must be followed by appropriate response. Staff members must be responsible for their actions. Therefore, responsible employees should be rewarded and promoted in their careers. Irresponsible behavior must have clear and apparent negative consequences for the employees. It is important that the cause and effect relationship between the violator's behavior and the sanctions of the executives is reasonable and obvious to other employees (Cherepanova, 2016).

After the company completes its investigation, it must develop appropriate corrective actions, which, in line with ISO 19600, may include: termination or alteration of project participation; reimbursement of unlawful payments; disciplinary action against responsible employees; provision of information to the authorities; taking measures to change the compliance management system with a view to preventing similar violations.

At present, there are universal standards of assessment of compliance management efficiency that can be used for various areas of compliance risks, including CSR. For example, "Compliance metrics handbook" (Convercent, 2016), "High-quality ethics & compliance program. Measurement framework" (ECI, 2018) etc. In connection with changes in claims of stakeholders selected efficiency assessment parameters should be updated at regular intervals, or they will lose their effectiveness with regard to disclosure of violations.

Information that concerns the issues of CSR and compliance is included in the category of nonfinancial reporting, publication of which has become an established practice of companies all over the world. The companies openly provide their stakeholders with information about their responsible practice—target goals, achieved results, and projected plans—in special sections of annual reports, within the framework of integrated reporting, or by preparing special reports in the field of CSR (Borzakov & Nikitina, 2019).

Public reporting contributes to the preservation of the "operating license", proving to regulators and the general public that the compliance risk management system conforms to the nature of company's activity and functions properly. Requirements of such international standards as GRI Standards, United Nations Global Compact, 17 sustainable development goals are used for the compilation of nonfinancial reports.

4 Conclusions

In a climate of the integration of compliance risks in CSR in the company management system, compliance management can be generally described as an in-house system which ensures compliance of activities of an organization with parameters of the institutional framework within which it operates.

Consistent implementation of action to prevent, identify and respond to compliance risks allows harmonizing and streamlining internal processes and increasing efficiency of the CSR management system by means of:

- creation of a centralized source and system of dissemination information on legislative provisions, best standards and best industry practices, in-house instructions, as well as codes of conduct and amendments to them;
- enhancement of communications and monitoring of activities to provide a more accurate picture of the behavior of employees and other stakeholders;
- adoption of clear behavior algorithms as well as possibilities of taking adequate response measures;
- introduction of procedures allowing to perform prompt and thorough investigation of alleged offense, and to assess the overall efficiency of operation of the compliance risk management system;
- prevention of preparation and publication of false or inaccurate reports.

Efficient transformation of CSR management technologies based on theory and practice of compliance risk management is impossible without the development of internal compliance culture. Here, compliance serves as an integrating principle which enables interaction of all managerial functions. It forms the necessary behavior patterns due to which the company gains the ability to perceive with ease the problems of society as they develop.

The implementation of compliance management functions in CSR contributes to the development of culture of responsible behavior, provides the company with reasonable assurance that there are no violations, prevents bringing to responsibility, and improves its trustworthiness and business reputation.

REFERENCES

Ackerman, R. (1973). How companies respond to social demands. *Harvard Business Review, 51*(4), 88–98.

Blagov, Y. (2010). *Corporate social responsibility: Concept evolution* (p. 272). Publishing House "Vysshaya Shkola Menedzhmenta".

Bogoviz, A. V., & Bruno S. S. (2018). Will the circular economy be the future of Russia's growth model? In S. S. Bruno (Ed.), *Exploring the future of Russia's economy and markets: Towards sustainable economic development* (pp. 125–141). Emerald Publishing Limited.

Borzakov, D., & Nikitina, L. (2019). *Management control of corporate social responsibility: Regulatory, informational and methodological support* (p. 270). Publishing House of the VSU.

Carroll, A. (1979). A three-dimensional conceptual model of corporate performance. *The Academy of Management Review, 4*(4), 497–505.

Carrots and Sticks. (2016). *Global trends in sustainability reporting regulation and policy—2016.* Available at https://www.carrotsandsticks.net/wp-content/uploads/2016/05/Carrots-Sticks-2016.pdf. Accessed May 7, 2017.

Cherepanova, V. (2016). *Compliance program of an entity: A how-to guide* (p. 288). Infra–M.

Convercent. (2016). *Compliance metrics handbook.* Available at https://www.convercent.com/resource/convercent-guide-compliance-metrics-handbook.pdf. Accessed December 12, 2017).

ECI. (2018). *High-quality ethics & compliance program: Measurement framework.* Available at https://www.ethics.org/high-quality-compliance-program-framework/. Accessed April 23, 2018.

Feoktistova, E., Alenicheva, L., Kopylova, G., Ozerianskaya, M., Purtova, D., & Khoniakova, N. (2019). *Analytical review of corporate nonfinancial reporting: 2017–2018* (p. 104). December 10, 2020. Russian Union of Industrialists and Entrepreneurs.

THE SYSTEM OF COMPLIANCE MANAGEMENT... 311

Goyal, S., & Sergi, B. S. (2015). Social entrepreneurship and sustainability—Understanding the context and key characteristics. *Journal of Security & Sustainability Issues, 4*(3), 269–278.

Goyal, S., Sergi, B. S., & Jaiswal, M. (2015). How to design and implement social business models for base-of-the-pyramid (BoP) markets? *European Journal of Development Research, 27*(5), 850–867.

Goyal, S., Sergi, B. S., & Jaiswal, M. P. (2016). Understanding the challenges and strategic actions of social entrepreneurship at base of the pyramid. *Management Decision, 54*(2), 418–440.

ISO 19600. *Compliance management systems. Guidelines.* Available at https://www.iso.org/obp/ui/#iso:std:iso:19600:ed-1:v1:en:term:3.13. Accessed February 11, 2016.

Karpovich, O., & Truntsevskii, Y. (2016). *Theory and modern practices of compliance. Global models of counteracting criminal threats: A monograph* (p. 407). Unity-Dana.

KPMG. (2016). *International study of the compliance function.* Available at https://home.kpmg/content/dam/kpmg/ru/pdf/2017/07/ru-ru-international-compliance-survey.pdf. Accessed October 10, 2019.

Mangutov, I. (1975). *Organizer and organizational activity* (p. 312). Publishing House of Leningrad State University.

Nikitina, L. (2011). *Corporate social responsibility system in Russia: Content, development factors, management mechanism* (p. 300). Voronezh State Pedagogical University.

Primakov, D. (2019). *Special types of compliance: Anti-corruption, banking, sanction, asset tracing* (p. 270). Infotropik Media.

Sethi, S. (1975). Dimensions of corporate social performance: An analytical framework. *California Management Review, 17*(3), 58–64.

Skolkovo IEMS. (2016). *Sustainable development in Russia: Guidance for transnational corporations.* Available at https://iems.skolkovo.ru/downloads/documents/SKOLKOVO_IEMS/Research_Reports/SKOLKOVO_IEMS_Sustainable_Business_Lab_Research_2016-07-13_ru.pdf. Accessed July 7, 2016.

TASS. (2017). *France has formalized corporate social responsibility.* Available at http://tass.ru/plus-one/4077436. Accessed May 12, 2018.

Wood, J. (2009). Corporate social activity: A reconception. *Bulletin of St. Petersburg State University, 3*, 38–74.

Legal Regulation of Modern Forms of Social Services in the Russian Federation

Nataliya A. Baieva, *Valentina I. Mineeva*, *and Igor E. Nelgovsky*

1 INTRODUCTION

To implement the concept of a decent human life, which is declared as the goal of the Russian welfare state in Article 7 of the Constitution of the Russian Federation, the state takes certain measures, both economic and legal.

The right to social support is enshrined in Article 39 of the Constitution of the Russian Federation. Realization of social rights by citizens contributes to the achievement of a decent standard of human life. However, the legal consolidation of social rights is not enough; their implementation by the subjects of public relations directly depends on the economic capabilities of the state and on the political will of the country's

---

N. A. Baieva (✉)
North-Caucasian Federal University, Stavropol, Russia

V. I. Mineeva
Branch of the Russian Technological University MIREA in the City of Stavropol, Stavropol, Russia

I. E. Nelgovsky
North-West Branch of the Russian State University of Justice, St. Peterburg, Russia

© The Author(s), under exclusive license to Springer Nature Switzerland AG 2021
E. G. Popkova and B. S. Sergi (eds.), *Economic Issues of Social Entrepreneurship*,
https://doi.org/10.1007/978-3-030-77291-8_29

314 N. A. BAIEVA ET AL.

leadership. In a social state, the authorities cannot but interfere in the processes related to the material welfare of citizens, the state must ensure social stability in society with the help of legal mechanisms, enshrine the guarantees of social rights of citizens in the norms of law, take a differentiated approach to determining the level of social security and protect vital human rights.

2 Materials and Method

The authors will consider the organizational legal forms of social security in Russia during the period of building socialism, when the main principles of social security were the principles of universality, diversity and non-equivalence, as well as the organizational legal forms of social security in modern Russia. Economic realities dictate the need to involve the business community in the social sphere, and the state adopts the rules of law that govern this type of social relations. When considering the development of such a form of social security as social entrepreneurship, the authors used research methods such as historical, logical, induction, deduction, comparative legal analysis and synthesis, analogies and other methods of scientific knowledge.

3 Results

The types and organizational legal forms of social security depend on socio-economic relations in society. For example, in Soviet Russia in Article 43 of the Constitution of the RSFSR of 1977, citizens were guaranteed material security in old age, in the case of illness, complete or partial disability, as well as loss of a breadwinner. Funding of the social rights enshrined in the Constitution was carried out through certain forms of social support. At the expense of social insurance of workers, employees and collective farmer workers, benefits for temporary disability were paid. Old age pensions, disability and loss of a breadwinner were financed by the state and collective farms. The state guaranteed employment for citizens who have partially lost their ability to work, and also took care of the elderly and the disabled.

In the Soviet period, the specific features of social security were their distributive nature, special subjects of these relations, the presence of special public funds, with the help of which the financing of types of social services was provided, the purpose of providing was to compensate for the wages lost for various reasons. The nature of these relations had all the signs of alimentarity, which meant that a state institution endowed with the appropriate powers by the state must provide the subject of legal relations with the type and amount of social security in accordance with the law without any counter material obligation, that is, free of charge. An equalizing approach in determining the amount and type of social support, the presence in the law of departmental and other privileges in the distribution of social benefits - were the characteristic distinctive features of the Soviet period. (Baieva, 2017).

Economic relations in the field of social security in the Russian Federation after the adoption of the 1993 Constitution have undergone changes and are characterized by the presence of various organizational legal forms, as well as the presence of contractual relations. The social security system in the Russian Federation has a number of essential features, which include: (1) organizational legal methods of distribution of the compound social product are established by the state; (2) the legislation contains lists of social risks recognized by the state as the basis for the assignment of types of social security; (3) the definition in the laws of the group of individuals entitled to certain types of social security; (4) the establishment by the state of a minimum level of social support, below which it cannot be provided (Navasardova, 2018).

Organizational legal forms of social security implementation in the Russian Federation are characterized by certain features, which include, first, the method of forming financial sources for social security; secondly, the range of individuals who are entitled to social security from certain sources of funding; third, types of social security for a certain range of subjects; fourth, the system of bodies endowed with certain powers in the sphere of realization of the social rights of citizens.

The issues of financing social security both in modern Russia and in other countries, including the EU, are the most discussed and relevant. Article 39 of the Constitution of the Russian Federation defines the sources of funding - these are budget appropriations, compulsory social insurance, funds from charitable foundations and citizens, and additional forms of social security. Currently, the most widespread and, probably, the most effective organizational legal form of social security in the Russian Federation is compulsory social insurance, the legal definition of which is enshrined in the Federal Law of July 16, 1996 "On Bases of Compulsory Social Insurance." The essence of compulsory social insurance is the creation by the state of a system of legal and other measures aimed at lightening the changes in the financial situation of citizens for reasons beyond their control, such as old age, illness, loss of a breadwinner, disability, pregnancy and childbirth, work-related injury or occupational disease, and others.

This law legally established the principles on which the compulsory social insurance system in the Russian Federation is built and developed. These include: the stability of the entire financial system of compulsory social insurance, depending on the receipts of insurance payments and the proportional distribution of funds among the payers of insurance contributions on an equivalent basis; the universality of compulsory social insurance (not only subjects of labor relations are insured); guaranteed social rights of the insured, regardless of the financial position of the insurer and the policyholder; the guarantees of targeted funds using; independence of the financial system of compulsory social insurance; a ban on the withdrawal of resources from funds for other needs not related to social security; availability of a control system, including public, over the spending of funds.

Compulsory social insurance is directly related to the system of social protection of the population, which, in turn, is aimed at leveling the material situation of socially vulnerable and economically weak communities, creating a certain level of security and safety by limiting violations of general legal, constitutional principles of equality and equity (Smirnov, 2015). Thus, compulsory social insurance is one of the most effective organizational legal forms of social security implementation. The rates of insurance payments for compulsory social insurance are established by the Federal Law, and the rates are differentiated based on the economic capabilities of the payers. One of the basic principles of compulsory social insurance is the universal compulsory nature of social insurance and the availability of insured individuals to implement their social guarantees.

Objective economic reasons (regular crises in the economy and, as a consequence, the growth of unemployment, bankruptcy of enterprises, the closing up of business by individual entrepreneurs) force the state to look for new forms that can be used to involve representatives of the business community in the social sphere (Klyukovskaya, 2018). Following the principle of social responsibility, in a market economy, entrepreneurs should be involved in the social sphere and provide social support to citizens in need. Social entrepreneurship is a promising direction in the development of new socio-economic elements in the field of social services.

In Europe, social entrepreneurship began to develop actively in the late 80s of the XX century. With the growth of GDP per capita, at this time it became clear that the issues of improving the quality of life and creating a decent standard of living for the population are becoming a priority, and this entailed the need to search for new forms of corporate social responsibility (Carrol, 2010).

In the EU countries, social entrepreneurship is considered as the activity of organizations that produce goods and services (including creating new jobs) to provide for their members or society as a whole. Using innovative methods and technologies, social enterprises are involved in solving social problems of society. Socially oriented entrepreneurial activity, which is carried out on an innovative basis, creates favorable conditions for the formation of a social services market.

A new breath in the development of social entrepreneurship in the world began in 2006 after the Nobel Peace Prize was awarded to a social entrepreneur for the creation of the Grameen Bank microcredit organization.

Social entrepreneurship is actively developing in Russia. Before the legislative assignment of the concepts of "social entrepreneurship" and "social enterprise", the norms of subordinate acts were in force - orders of the Ministry of Economic Development on subsidies to regions to support small and medium-sized businesses (Petrov, 2018). These documents indicated the priority of the development of social entrepreneurship. This indicates the interest of the state in the development of small and medium-sized businesses, the purpose of which is socially oriented activity, expressed in the promotion of employment of citizens who are recognized as socially vulnerable (disabled people, large families, single mothers, minors, etc.), as well as the production of goods and services of social orientation (education of elderly people, social services at home, creation of private gerontological centers, psychological support and medical care for the minors, etc.)

In order to develop small and medium-sized businesses, on the initiative of the Ministry of Economic Development of the Russian Federation, innovation centers of the social sphere were created, aimed at attracting entrepreneurs to this field of activity, as well as promoting the implementation of social projects developed by the state.

In the modern theory of social security, this idea is considered as a social innovation, involving the activities of entrepreneurs aimed at creating favorable conditions for the formation of a market for social services. For the same purposes, the Agency for Strategic Initiatives has developed a guideline "Access Support for the non-governmental organizations to the provision of services in the social sphere."

In 2019, in the Federal Law of July 24, 2007 No. 209-FZ "On the Development of Small and Medium Scale Entrepreneurship in the Russian Federation" new terms appeared - social entrepreneurship and social enterprise, which were previously absent in Russian legislation. The first one is understood by the legislator as entrepreneurial activity aimed at achieving socially useful goals, contributing to the solution of social problems of citizens and society and carried out in accordance with the conditions provided for by this law. The second is a small or medium sized business entity operating in the field of social entrepreneurship. The legislator formulated the following goals of social entrepreneurship in article 24.1 of the law, firstly, it is to provide employment to citizens in need of support, namely: (a) disabled people and persons with disabilities; (b) single and (or) parents with many children raising minor children, including children with disabilities; (c) pensioners and citizens of pre-retirement age (within five years before the onset of the age that gives the right to an insurance old age pension, including those assigned ahead of schedule); (d) graduates of orphanages under the age of twenty-three; (e) individuals released from prison and having an unexpunged or outstanding conviction; (f) refugees and forced migrants; (g) low-income citizens; (h) people experiencing homelessness and without occupation; (i) other citizens recognized in need of social services; secondly, it is the sale of products made by citizens in need of support; thirdly, it is the manufacture of goods (performance of work, provision of services) for the rehabilitation or social adaptation of citizens in need of support; fourthly, these are activities aimed at achieving socially useful goals and contributing to the solution of social problems of society (services of a family psychologist; services for organizing leisure and education for children; medical and social assistance to children who have difficulties in social adaptation and learning; services of private museums, theaters, libraries, archives, studio schools, creative workshops, botanic gardens and zoos, houses of culture, houses of folk art); services related to the preservation and protection of national identity; publishing services related to education, science and culture.

The procedure for recognizing an organization as a social enterprise is developed by the Ministry of Economic Development of the Russian Federation. As of April 17, 2020, the Federal Tax Service of Russia entered into the Unified Register of Small and Medium Sized Businesses information on the status of a social enterprise for 1197 legal entities and individual entrepreneurs. It is difficult to say whether this is little or much for a country like the Russian Federation, the main thing is that the consolidation of the provision on social entrepreneurship and its criteria in the law gave the necessary impact for the legal activity of such subjects of law. However, it should be noted that according to the norms of Law No. 209-FZ "On the Development of Small and Medium Sized Enterprises in the Russian Federation", only small and medium sized business entities can be subjects of social entrepreneurship, and what about the legal status of large organizations and corporations? Their activity in this area is not legalized (Smirnov, 2018). The state, having developed a set of legal means to attract large business entities, for example, city-forming enterprises, into the sphere of social entrepreneurship, would solve a number of serious problems in this area, first of all, it is attracting additional funds for social services, and secondly, the creation of atmosphere of mutual support and responsibility for those who need this support (Abdulgaziev, 2018).

Another omission of the legislator is the absence of norms on social entrepreneurship in the Civil Code of the Russian Federation. In the Civil Code of the Russian Federation, there was no such organizational legal form of a legal entity as a social enterprise. It follows from this that the status of a social enterprise remains uncertain, and this does not contribute to the development of this form of social security and the effective implementation of the state's social policy.

Article 24.1 of Law No. 209-FZ contains a provision on the necessity for state support for social entrepreneurship entities. State authorities and local self-government bodies, in accordance with the powers established by this Federal Law and other federal laws, may provide support to small and medium sized businesses carrying out activities in the field of social entrepreneurship that meet one or more of the conditions listed in the law. However, the law does not contain criteria by which state authorities or local self-government bodies will choose to whom and to what extent this support will be provided, and in what cases and on what grounds to refuse such support (Drozdova, 2019). It would be necessary to formulate this norm in a mandatory form and supplement the law with provisions on the grounds for refusing measures of state support to social enterprises.

Modern economic realities dictate the need to discuss in society the issues of the procedure for the provision of services in the social sphere and their quality, the expansion of both economic and financial autonomy of organizations providing such services, and a correlated reduction in the costs of the corresponding budgets. Some authors believe that the task of public administration is twofold. On the one hand, the state needs to create favorable conditions for the development of the service sector by removing regulatory and law enforcement obstacles, and on the other hand, it is important to ensure not only the availability, but also the appropriate quality of services - a quality that meets the modern needs of citizens.

4 Conclusion

Thus, at present, innovative concepts in the field of social services are being developed and implemented with elements of economic policy as an integral part of the right to social security. Social entrepreneurship combines social mission, economic efficiency and entrepreneurial innovation. The foundation of social entrepreneurship is the creation of social enterprises, the purpose of which is different from the goals of ordinary organizations and is to create social good. The state can transfer some of the powers in the social sphere to entrepreneurs, which will reduce administrative costs and time spent on implementing social programs. However, for the development of social entrepreneurship in the Russian Federation there are certain difficulties associated with its legal regulation. First, according to the law, only small and medium sized enterprises can be subjects of social entrepreneurship, and the legal status of large organizations and corporations in this area is not defined. Secondly, such an organizational legal form of a legal entity as a social enterprise did not appear in the Civil Code of the Russian Federation. Therefore the status of a social enterprise remains uncertain, and this does not contribute to the development of this form of social security and the effective implementation of the state's social policy. Thirdly, state authorities and local self-government bodies, in accordance with the powers established by law, can provide support to small and medium sized enterprises carrying out activities in the field of social entrepreneurship, which meets one or more of the conditions listed in the law. At the same time, the law lacks criteria by which the above-mentioned authorities will determine the amount of such support and specific individuals, who need it, as well as in what cases and on what grounds to refuse such support. This norm should be formulated in a mandatory form, and the law should be supplemented with provisions on the grounds for refusing measures of state support to social enterprises.

Since social security is under the joint jurisdiction of federal and regional authorities, at the regional level it is necessary to specify the forms and types of support for social enterprises, which will have a positive impact on the development of social entrepreneurship and will contribute to the implementation of the social policy of the Russian Federation.

REFERENCES

Abdulgaziev R. Z., Zhukova T. G., Sukhorukova A. N., Mamichev V. N., Arshinov A. S., & Alsultanov M. R. (2018). Family welfare as a basis of fighting crime. *Amazonia investiga*, (17), 143–149.

Baieva, N. A., Burkin, D. O., Vysheslavova, T. F., & Lukinova, S. A. (2017). The concept of the social state and its implementation in the Russian Federation. *Journal of Advanced Research in Law and Economics, 8*(27), 1446–1455.

Barkov A. V. (2012). Social entrepreneurship in the context of the formation of a legal model of the social services market. http://www.center-bereg.ru/n790.html (Accessed on May 20, 2020).

Baymatov P. N. (2014). The constitutional right of citizens of the Russian Federation to social security: New economic policy. Constitutional and municipal law, Part 9.

Carrol A. B., Shabana K. M. (2010). The business case for corporate social responsibility: A review of concepts, research and practice. *International Journal of Management Reviews*, pp.85–105.

Drozdova A. M., Balakireva L. M., Vorotilina T. V., Makarova E. V., & Meleshkin, V. V. (2019). Legal awareness and legal culture as elements and means for the implementation of a mechanism for ensuring the legal impact. *Opcion, 35*(19), 2922–2934.

Klyukovskaya I. N., Cherkashin E. Y., Gabrilyan R. R., Semenov V. Y., & Melekayev R. K. (2018). Methodological basis of the theoretical and legal research of integration processes in modern states. *International Journal of Engineering and Technology, 7*(4.38), 261–264.

Malko, A. V., Isakov, N. V., Mazurenko, A. P., Smirnov, D. A., & Isakov, I. N. (2018). Legal policy as a means to improve lawmaking process. *Astra Salvensis, 6*(1), 833–842.

Navasardova, E. S., Nutrikhin, R. V., Zinovyeva, T. N., Shishkin, V. A., & Joludeva, J. V. (2018). Codification of the natural resource legislation in the

Russian Empire. *Journal of Advanced Research in Law and Economics, 9*(1), 183–193.

Petrov N. V., Petrova I. V., & Fedorovskiy A. P. (2018). The russian law effectiveness and sociocultural context. *The Turkish Online Journal of Design, Art and Communication*, pp. 978–981.

Smirnov, D. A., & Strus, K. A. (2015). General scientific analysis of implementation of principles of law in the contemporary Russian legal basis. *Indian Journal of Science and Technology, 8*(S10), 2–10.

Roick, W. (2013). *Economics, finance and social insurance law.* Albana Publisher.

Social Entrepreneurship as a Subject of the Market Economy and Consumer Society: Essence, Specifics and Tendencies of Development

Aleksei V. Bogoviz⊙

1 Introduction

Social entrepreneurship is one of the most popular economic subjects; however, it faces the largest number of difficulties, which makes it very contradictory. The notion "social entrepreneurship" has not been clearly defines by the modern economic science. The narrow treatment includes in social entrepreneurship only those subjects of entrepreneurship that provide public benefits for free during implementation of non-profit activities. This envisages the balance of social companies at the brink of unprofitability and their existence due to charity, sponsorship from private investors, and grants from government.

The wide treatment allows including in social entrepreneurship all subjects of entrepreneurship that manifest corporate social responsibility. In this case, for a company to be included in the list of subjects of social entrepreneurship, its activities must have at least one of the following features: realization of socially important goods and services, which could

---

A. V. Bogoviz (✉)
Independent Researcher, Moscow, Russia

© The Author(s), under exclusive license to Springer Nature Switzerland AG 2021
E. G. Popkova and B. S. Sergi (eds.), *Economic Issues of Social Entrepreneurship*,
https://doi.org/10.1007/978-3-030-77291-8_30

potentially include any products that are in high demand in society, responsible HR management (in addition to the full compliance with labor law), and implementation of socially important events, in particular in the sphere of social support and environment protection.

The problem of underdevelopment of a clear scientific notion of the essence of social entrepreneurship as an economic category, which hinders its research, statistical accounting, measuring, monitoring, and control, and state and corporate management, is not solved due to uncertainty of the social entrepreneurship's functioning in the conditions of the market economy and consumer society. The hypothesis of this research is as follows: behavior of social entrepreneurship in the market economy is determined by the influence of competition and dictates by consumer society – since the social market economy is not formed in the modern economic systems and remains at the level of a scientific concept, due to which non-profit initiatives should be directly (in responsible entrepreneurship) or indirectly (in non-profit entrepreneurship) justified from the commercial point of view.

This research aims to determine the essence, specifics, and tendencies of development of social entrepreneurship as a subject of market economy and consumer society.

2   Literature Review

Both treatments of the essence of social entrepreneurship are studied in the modern scientific works. Canestrino et al. (2019), Hassan (2020), Lorenzo-Afable et al. (2020), and Maalaoui et al. (2020) define social entrepreneurship as a subject of non-profit activities, using the narrow treatment.

Contrary to them, such authors as Alpidovskaya and Popkova (2019), Popkova et al. (2020), Popkova (2017), Popkova and Sergi (2019), Popkova and Sergi (2020a), Popkova and Sergi (2020b), and Zavyalova et al. (2018) include in social entrepreneurship all companies that manifest corporate social responsibility, using the wide treatment.

Literature review has shown that there is a scientific discussion on the topic of the nature of social entrepreneurship. In the existing works and publications, the position of social entrepreneurship in the conditions of the market economy and consumer society has been insufficiently studied and has not been clearly determined in the economic science. Here we try to fill this gap.

3 Methodology

Regression analysis is used to check the offered hypothesis. We determine regression dependence (building regression curves) of the social entrepreneurship index, according to the materials of the Rating of social entrepreneurship in 2020 by the Institute of Scientific Communications (2020), based on the dataset "Social entrepreneurship in the global economy: a path from virtual evaluations to big data – 2020", on the factors of the market economy and consumer society:

– buyer sophistication;
– extent of market dominance.

Both factors are reflects in the Global Competitiveness Report 2019, compiled by the World Economic Forum (2020). The hypothesis is deemed proved if positive (direct) regression dependencies of the described indicators are determined. This will mean that the market mechanism (extent of market dominance) and consumer society (buyer sophistication) stimulate corporate social responsibility (the wide treatment of social entrepreneurship). In case of negative (reverse) regression dependencies, the hypothesis is disproved, and the narrow treatment of social entrepreneurship as a subject of non-profit activities, which does not depend on market's stimuli, is accepted.

To obtain the most precise and correct results, we perform this research in view of the generally accepted categories of countries – by the example of top 10 developed countries and top 10 developing countries, according to the Rating of social entrepreneurship in 2020, compiled by the Institute of Scientific Communications (2020). The basic statistical data for the research are shown in Table 1.

4 Results

To check the offered hypothesis, let us use regression curves that are built separately for developed (Fig. 1) and developing (Fig. 2) countries.

As shown in Fig. 1, increase of buyer sophistication by 1 point in developed countries leads to reduction of the level of social entrepreneurship's development by 0.1935 points. Increase of the level of extent of market dominance by 1 point leads to reduction of the level of social entrepreneurship's development by 0.4251 points. Therefore, the market

326 A. V. BOGOVIZ

Table 1 Statistics of social entrepreneurship in developed and developing countries, where it is most developed, and the factors of the market economy and consumer society in 2020, points 1–100

Category	Country	Social entrepreneurship index	Buyer sophistication	Extent of market dominance
Top 10 developed countries	1. New Zealand	84.173	53.30	52.70
	2. USA	73.238	68.80	70.60
	3. Singapore	72.114	63.50	63.80
	4. UK	70.496	62.10	60.20
	5. Canada	70.452	59.50	59.00
	6. Netherlands	67.478	62.70	70.60
	7. Australia	64.166	51.10	54.60
	8. Switzerland	62.699	66.90	80.10
	10. Germany	61.14	62.20	71.70
	11. Sweden	60.923	57.90	63.70
Top 10 developing countries	9. Russia	61.147	41.20	44.40
	12. Taiwan (China)	59.981	61.70	70.50
	13. Hong Kong (China)	59.406	71.30	64.40
	21. India	54.086	49.80	53.80
	23. Malaysia	52.959	62.90	67.40
	30. Brazil	49.027	43,10	46.20
	31. UAE	48.035	62.40	66.90
	33. Thailand	47.193	55.40	43.80
	35. South Africa	46.878	47.0	46.20
	38. China	46.685	58.20	58.90

Source compiled by the authors based on Institute of Scientific Communications (2020), World Economic Forum (2020)

economy and consumer society in developed countries do not determine the functioning and development of social entrepreneurship, which is a subject of non-profit activities.

As shown in Fig. 2, increase of buyer sophistication by 1 point in developing countries leads to growth of the level of social entrepreneurship's development by 0.0827 points. Increase of the level of extent of market dominance by 1 point leads to growth of the level of social entrepreneurship's development by 0.1535 points. It should be noted that correlation coefficients are rather small in both cases, constituting 1.92% and 7.81%, accordingly. Therefore, the market economy and consumer society in

SOCIAL ENTREPRENEURSHIP AS A SUBJECT OF THE MARKET ECONOMY ... 327

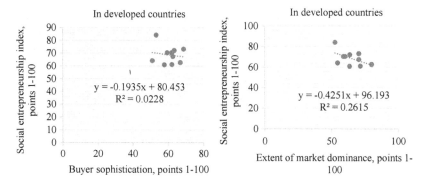

Fig. 1 Regression curves of the dependence of social entrepreneurship's development on extent of market dominance and buyer sophistication in developed countries in 2020 (*Source* Calculated and built by the authors)

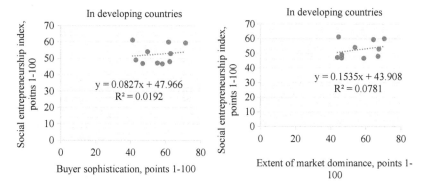

Fig. 2 Regression curves of the dependence of social entrepreneurship's development on extent of market dominance and buyer sophistication in developing countries in 2020 (*Source* Calculated and built by the authors)

developing countries determine – to a certain extent – the functioning and development of social entrepreneurship, which is a subject of corporate social responsibility.

Taking into account the analyzed experience of developed and developing countries, it is possible to see the two following universal tendencies of social entrepreneurship's development as a subject of the market economy and consumer society. The first tendency is connected to general progress of social entrepreneurship and reduction of barriers for business activity subjects' joining it. Since the limits of social entrepreneurship are unclear, it becomes more accessible for a wide circle of the subjects of entrepreneurship around the world, each of which could select the most suitable form of conducting social entrepreneurship: implementation of non-profit initiatives or measures of corporate social responsibility.

The second tendency consists in emergence of a new direction of social entrepreneurship's activities, which is in high demand by the market and is popular in the business environment, in the conditions of the COVID-19 pandemic and crisis: support for healthcare through financing of social insurance and provision of medical services to employees, allowing for remote work, creation of expanded sanitary requirements, etc. This direction appeared in 2020 and will be probably topical during the pandemic (2021–2022) and in the post-pandemic period (until 2025 and after that). Most of the companies around the world joined this direction, which led to popularization of social entrepreneurship and ensured its domination in the structure of entrepreneurship.

5   Conclusion

The results of the performed research proved the offered hypothesis only partially, demonstrating the essential incorrectness of its setting. It has been determined that both wide and narrow treatments of social entrepreneurship are met in the modern business practice. This allows formulating a universal definition of social entrepreneurship as a subject of business activity, which functions in the conditions of extent of market dominance, reacts flexibly to the signals of the market economy and requirements of consumer society, and conducts corporate social responsibility and/or non-profit activities.

As the empirical experience of 2020 has shown, non-profit social entrepreneurship dominates in developed countries, and responsible social entrepreneurship dominates in developing countries. The determined specifics of developed and developing countries should be taken into account during state and corporate management of social entrepreneurship's development. The latest universal tendencies of social entrepreneurship's development include the increase of its accessibility (reduction of entering barriers), achievement of its popularity, and emergence of a new direction in the conditions of the COVID-19 pandemic and crisis in 2020 – support for healthcare. The specified essence of social entrepreneurship determines the foundations of its scientific concept and opens expanded opportunities for its further research.

REFERENCES

Alpidovskaya, M. L., & Popkova, E. G. (2019). Marx and modernity: A political and economic analysis of social systems management. A volume in the series Popkova, E. G. (Ed.), Advances in Research on Russian Business and Management. Information Age Publishing.

Canestrino, R., Ćwiklicki, M., Di Nauta, P., & Magliocca, P. (2019). Creating social value through entrepreneurship: The social business model of La Paranza. *Kybernetes, 48*(10), 2190–2216. https://doi.org/10.1108/K-03-2018-0135.

Hassan, H. M. K. (2020). Intention towards social entrepreneurship of university students in an emerging economy: The influence of entrepreneurial self-efficacy and entrepreneurship education. *On the Horizon, 28*(3), 133–151. https://doi.org/10.1108/OTH-04-2020-0012.

Institute of Scientific Communications. (2020). Dataset "Social entrepreneurship in the global economy: a path from virtual evaluations to big data – 2020": Rating of social entrepreneurship in 2020. https://iscvolga.ru/data3 (Accessed on November 8, 2020).

Lorenzo-Afable, D., Lips-Wiersma, M., & Singh, S. (2020). 'Social' value creation as care: The perspective of beneficiaries in social entrepreneurship. *Social Enterprise Journal, 16*(3), 339–360. https://doi.org/10.1108/SEJ-11-2019-0082.

Maalaoui, A., Le Loarne-Lemaire, S., & Razgallah, M. (2020). Does knowledge management explain the poor growth of social enterprises? Key insights from a systematic literature review on knowledge management and social entrepreneurship. *Journal of Knowledge Management, 24*(7), 1513–1532. https://doi.org/10.1108/JKM-11-2019-0603.

Popkova, E., DeLo, P., & Sergi, B. S. (2020). Corporate social responsibility amid social distancing during the COVID-19 crisis: BRICS vs. OECD countries. Research in International Business and Finance. https://doi.org/10.1016/j.ribaf.2020.101315.

Popkova, E. G. (2017). Economic and legal foundations of Modern Russian Society. A volume in the series Popkova, E. G. (Ed.), Advances in Research on Russian Business and Management. Information Age Publishing.

Popkova, E. G., & Sergi, B. S. (2019). Social entrepreneurship in Russia and Asia: Further development trends and prospects. *On the Horizon, 28*(1), 9–21. https://doi.org/10.1108/OTH-09-2019-0065.

Popkova, E. G., & Sergi, B. S. (2020a). Human capital and AI in industry 4.0. Convergence and divergence in social entrepreneurship in Russia. *Journal of Intellectual Capital*, *21*(4), 565–581. https://doi.org/10.1108/JIC-09-2019-0224.

Popkova, E. G., & Sergi, B. S. (2020b). Human capital and AI in industry 4.0. Convergence and divergence in Social Entrepreneurship in Russia. *Journal of Intellectual Capital*. https://doi.org/10.1108/JIC-09-2019-0224.

World Economic Forum. (2020). The Global Competitiveness Report 2019. https://www.weforum.org/reports/global-competitiveness-report-2019 (Accessed on November 8, 2020).

Zavyalova, E. B., Studenikin, N. V., & Starikova, E. A. (2018). Business participation in implementation of socially oriented Sustainable Development Goals in countries of Central Asia and the Caucasus region. *Central Asia and the Caucasus, 19*(2), 56–63.

Corporate Social Responsibility as a Criterion of Assigning Commercial Business to Social Entrepreneurship in the Market Economy

Svetlana V. Lobova, Aleksei V. Bogoviz, and Alexander N. Alekseev

1 INTRODUCTION

Social entrepreneurship is very important for building a social market economy. However, social companies – which number is too small – cannot fully provide all the necessary public and socially important economic benefits. That's why the initial concept of establishment of high barriers and strict criteria for social companies in their narrow treatment as subjects of non-commercial activities is being changed. A new concept of social entrepreneurship is formed; it is based on its wide treatment and envisages involvement of wide groups of commercial companies.

S. V. Lobova (✉)
Altai State University, Barnaul, Russia

A. V. Bogoviz
Independent Researcher, Moscow, Russia

A. N. Alekseev
Financial University Under the Government of the Russian Federation, Moscow, Russia

Plekhanov Russian University of Economics, Moscow, Russia

© The Author(s), under exclusive license to Springer Nature Switzerland AG 2021
E. G. Popkova and B. S. Sergi (eds.), *Economic Issues of Social Entrepreneurship*,
https://doi.org/10.1007/978-3-030-77291-8_31

The mechanism of involving commercial business in social entrepreneurship is corporate social responsibility. It envisages voluntary implementation and popularization (information and marketing support) of socially important initiatives by business – the ones that go beyond the standard (mandatory) requirements of the existing law. Corporate social responsibility could be manifested in the form of higher quality of products, as compared to the standard required by the law, improved labor conditions for employees, or observation of higher ecological standards than is adopted in the country.

Though the theory of corporate social responsibility is rather simple at the fundamental level, the problem is that its implementation and determination in practice are complicated due to the absence of unified quantitative indicators for its measurement and, accordingly, dye to impossibility to develop its regular, mass, and official statistical accounting. Thus, the issue whether corporate social responsibility contributes to economy's social development remains open.

The purpose of this chapter is to determine the possibility to use corporate social responsibility as a universal criterion of assigning commercial business to social entrepreneurship in the market economy. The hypothesis of the chapter is as follows: corporate social responsibility could be implemented for commercial purposes and ensure only economic advantages – that's why it does not necessarily ensure the social effect; manifestation of corporate social responsibility cannot be considered a universal criterion of assigning commercial business to social entrepreneurship in the market economy.

2 Literature Review

The issues of manifestation of corporate social responsibility in entrepreneurship are studied in the works Akbari and McClelland (2020), Baranova (2015), Jeffrey et al. (2019), Glazova (2015), Kelley et al. (2019), Natsubidze (2015), Sekhon and Kathuria (2019), and Smetanina (2015).

The issues of development of social entrepreneurship are considered in the works Alpidovskaya and Popkova (2019), Bogoviz (2019), Bogoviz et al. (2019), Bogoviz et al. (2020a), Bogoviz et al. (2020b), Popkova et al. (2020), Popkova (2017), Popkova and Sergi (2019), Popkova and Sergi (2020a), Popkova and Sergi (2020b), and Zavyalova et al. (2018).

We see that corporate responsibility and social entrepreneurship are rather developed concepts in economics. However, these concepts exist separately, and there are no logical connections between them. The possibility to use corporate social responsibility as a criterion of assigning commercial business to social entrepreneurship in the market economy has not been determined, which is a research gap.

3 Methodology

To check the offered hypothesis, we formed a selection of countries, which includes developed (top 10) and developing (top 10) countries with the highest level of commercial entrepreneurship's development, according to Global Entrepreneurship Index ranking (2019), compiled by The Global Entrepreneurship and Development Institute (GEDI, 2020). It is inexpedient to perform the research by the example of countries with developed commercial entrepreneurship, since the probability of obtaining distorted and imprecise data is high. That's why we selected counties with dominating commercial entrepreneurship, which guarantees the most correct and precise results of the research. The characteristics of the selected countries are shown in Fig. 1.

As shown in Fig. 1, the level of development of commercial entrepreneurship among developed countries is much higher, constituting 76.03 on average, while its average value in developing countries is 47.77 points. Correlation analysis is used to check the hypothesis. It allows determining the level (values of correlation coefficients) and character ($\pm$ sign of correlation coefficients) of the connection between the manifestations of corporate social responsibility, which are accessible to commercial business, and advantages of social entrepreneurship. The hypothesis is deemed confirmed if low (below 50%) or negative (<0) correlation for most of the indicators is determined.

The manifestations of corporate social responsibility, which are accessible to commercial business, are such indicators as share of protected employment, keeping employees, benefits for redundant workers, stimulation of unions, and multi-stakeholder collaboration – from the dataset "Social Entrepreneurship in the World Economy: a Path from Virtual Scores to Big Data – 2020" (Institute of Scientific Communications, 2020b).

The advantages of social entrepreneurship are reflected by such indicators as quality of life index, happy life index, and sustainable development

Fig. 1 Global Entrepreneurship Index (2019) in the selected countries, points 1–100 (*Source* Built by the authors based on GEDI [2020])

index – from the dataset "Big data of the modern global economy: a digital platform for intellectual analytics – 2020" (Institute of Scientific Communications, 2020a). The statistical basis of the research is shown in Table 1.

4 Results

To determine the possibility and conditions of using corporate social responsibility as a criterion of assigning commercial business to social

CORPORATE SOCIAL RESPONSIBILITY AS A CRITERION ... 335

Table 1 Manifestations of corporate social responsibility, which are accessible to commercial business, and advantages of social entrepreneurship in developed and developing countries in 2020

Category of countries	Country	Manifestations of corporate social responsibility that are accessible to commercial business					Advantages of social entrepreneurship		
		Share of protected employment, %	Keeping employees, points 1–100	Benefits for redundant workers, points 1–100	Stimulation of unions, points 1–100	Multistakeholder collaboration, points 1–100	Quality of life index, points 1–200	Happy life index, points 1–10	Sustainable development index, points 1–100
Developed countries	USA	96.2	71.8	100.0	70.6	73.9	176.77	6.892	74.5
	Switzerland	91.0	80.4	87.3	85.2	72.1	196.08	7.480	78.8
	Canada	89.3	60.9	87.5	67.5	63.8	169.42	7.278	77.9
	UK	87.0	66.4	89.0	66.1	65.5	166.73	7.054	79.4
	Australia	89.3	39.1	83.3	59.7	54.5	189.73	7.228	73.9
	Denmark	94.9	70.4	100.0	81.0	69.5	196.47	7.600	85.2
	Iceland	92.0	71.5	81.3	74.1	62.6	188.12	7.494	79.2
	Ireland	89.1	51.4	78.3	69.6	62.8	158.34	7.021	78.2
	Sweden	93.8	43.1	78.3	77.7	72.0	180.52	7.343	85.0
	France	92.6	44.5	81.3	54.1	58.3	156.10	6.592	81.5
	Hong Kong (China)	94.1	80.6	96.5	77.5	65.8	99.58	5.430	n/a
Developing countries	Taiwan (China)	100.0	62.0	76.3	73.2	61.8	146.59	6.446	n/a
	Chile	75.9	34.4	51.300	59.3	44.8	123.80	6.444	75.6

(continued)

Table 1 (continued)

Category of countries	Country	Manifestations of corporate social responsibility that are accessible to commercial business					Advantages of social entrepreneurship		
		Share of protected employment, %	Keeping employees, points 1–100	Benefits for redundant workers, points 1–100	Stimulation of unions, points 1–100	Multistakeholder collaboration, points 1–100	Quality of life index, points 1–200	Happy life index, points 1–10	Sustainable development index, points 1–100
	Qatar	n/a	69.6	60.0	70.2	65.8	164.29	6.374	66.3
	UAE	99.2	69.3	99.4	71.4	63.1	158.32	6.825	69.7
	Turkey	72.0	42.6	46.3	47.3	43.1	126.46	5.373	68.5
	China	56.2	57.700	51.3	59.6	57.3	99.87	5.191	73.2
	Saudi Arabia	97.1	61.6	58.8	68.0	56.7	151.75	6.375	64.8
	South Africa	90.3	31.3	89.0	36.4	52.6	135.75	4.722	61.5
	Russia	94.7	51.1	72.1	56.5	49.5	104.05	5.648	70.9

Source Compiled by the authors

entrepreneurship in the market economy, let us use the results of correlation analysis (Fig. 2 (developed countries) and Fig. 3 (developing countries).

As shown in Fig. 2, only one manifestation of corporate social responsibility, which is accessible to commercial business, in developed countries – stimulation of unions – shows large positive connection with the advantages of social entrepreneurship in 2020: quality of life (66.44%) and level of happiness in society (77.85%).

As shown in Fig. 2, two manifestations of corporate social responsibility, which are accessible to commercial business, in developing countries show large positive connection with the advantages of social entrepreneurship in 2020: protected employment/ quality of life (52.07%) and stimulation of unions / level of happiness in society (67.20%).

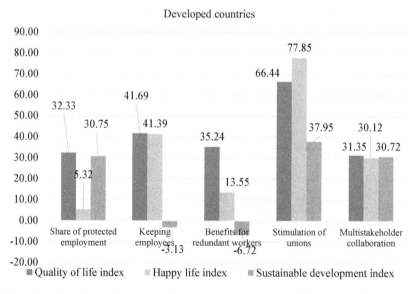

Fig. 2 Correlation between the manifestations of corporate social responsibility, which are accessible to commercial business, and the advantages of social entrepreneurship in developed countries in 2020, % (*Source* Calculated and built by the authors)

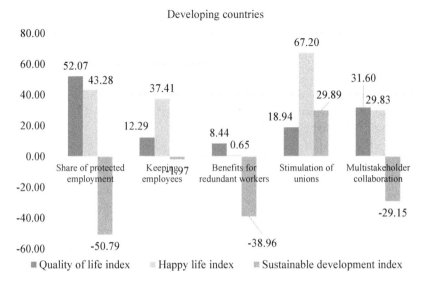

Fig. 3 Correlation between the manifestations of corporate social responsibility, which are accessible to commercial business, and the advantages of social entrepreneurship in developing countries in 2020, % (*Source* Calculated and built by the authors)

To determine the general connections between the studied indicators, let us consider arithmetic mean of correlation coefficients from Figs. 2 and 3 (Fig. 4).

As shown in Fig. 4, neither of the generalized coefficients of correlation reached or exceeded 50%. The most vivid social advantages ensure such manifestations of corporate social responsibility, which are accessible to commercial business, as stimulation of unions (60.74% in developed countries and 38.68% in developing countries) and keeping employees (26.65% in developed countries and 15.91% in developing countries).

The most vivid social advantages, which are provided by the totality of the manifestations of corporate social responsibility, which are accessible to commercial business, are increase of happiness level (33.64% in developed countries and 35.68% in developing countries) and growth of population's quality of life (41.41% in developed countries and 24.67% in developing countries).

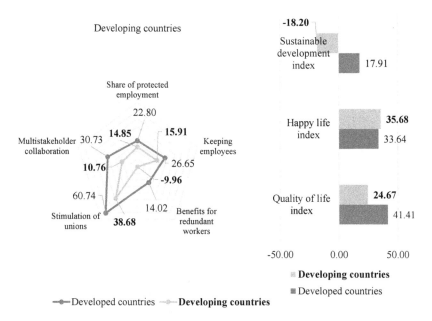

Fig. 4 Generalized correlation between the manifestations of corporate social responsibility and the advantages of social entrepreneurship in developed and developing countries in 2020, % (*Source* Calculated and built by the authors)

5 Conclusion

It is possible to conclude that solid and sufficient proofs to support the offered hypothesis have been collected. It has been shown – by the example of developed and developing countries with the most developed commercial business – that corporate social responsibility does not always ensure social advantages. That's why assigning commercial business to social entrepreneurship by the criterion of the implemented initiatives in the sphere of corporate social responsibility is rather an exception than a rule.

This conclusion stimulates the development of the social entrepreneurship concept through specifying its criteria. Corporate social responsibility cannot be used as a universal criterion of assigning commercial business to social entrepreneurship in the market economy. However, corporate social responsibility plays an important role in the process of transition of commercial business to the sphere of social companies and thus requires further research and state management.

REFERENCES

Akbari, M., & McClelland, R. (2020). Corporate social responsibility and corporate citizenship in sustainable supply chain: a structured literature review. *Benchmarking: An International Journal, 27*(6), 1799–1841. https://doi.org/10.1108/BIJ-11-2019-0509.

Alpidovskaya, M. L., & Popkova, E. G. (2019). Marx and modernity: A political and economic analysis of social systems management. A volume in the series Popkova, E. G. (Ed.), Advances in Research on Russian Business and Management. Information Age Publishing.

Baranova, I. V. (2015). Possibilities of using online marketing for improving the educational system in the conditions of formation of the knowledge economy. In E. G. Popkova (Ed.), INSSCCOM15. IV All-Russian online seminar-conference "Online marketing in the conditions of a crisis". https://www.archilab.online/konferentsii-2015-goda/43-2015-iv/492-vozmozhnosti-primeneniya-internet-marketinga-dlya-sovershenstvovaniya-sistemy-obrazovaniya-v-usloviyakh-formirovaniya-ekonomiki-znanij (Accessed on June 5, 2020).

Bogoviz, A. V. (2019). Cluster mechanism of marketing optimization on the basis of systemic interaction between the internet of thing and social networks. In E. G. Popkova, (Ed.) Ubiquitous Computing and the Internet of Things: Prerequisites for the Development of ICT. Springer. https://doi.org/10.1007/978-3-030-13397-9_95.

Bogoviz, A. V., Kletskova, E. V., Sultanova, M. K., Lavrova, E. V., & Shapoval, E. V. (2019). The new concept of social justice in the globalizing economy. *Growth Poles of the Global Economy: Emergence, Changes and Future Perspectives, 3*(1), 1001–1008.

Bogoviz, A. V., Lobova, S. V., & Alekseev, A. N. (2020). Social development versus economic growth: Current contradictions and perspectives of convergence. *International Journal of Sociology and Social Policy*. https://doi.org/10.1108/IJSSP-03-2020-0061.

Bogoviz, A. V., Shokhnekh, A. V., Petrenko, E. S., & Milkina, E. A. (2020). Social effectiveness of the market economy: Measuring and management. *International Journal of Sociology and Social Policy*. https://doi.org/10.1108/IJSSP-03-2020-0060.

Glazova, M. V. (2015). Determinants of improving the process of development and making of managerial decisions by modern companies in the crisis conditions. In E. G. Popkova (Ed.), INSSCCOM15. IV All-Russian online seminar-conference "Online marketing in the crisis conditions". https://

CORPORATE SOCIAL RESPONSIBILITY AS A CRITERION ... 341

www.archilab.online/konferentsii-2015-goda/43-2015-iv/493-determina nty-sovershenstvovaniya-protsessa-razrabotki-i-prinyatiya-upravlencheskikh-res henij-sovremennymi-predpriyatiyami-v-usloviyakh-krizisa (Accessed on June 5, 2020).

GEDI: The Global Entrepreneurship and Development Institute. (2020). Global Entrepreneurship Index rankings. https://thegedi.org/global-entrepreneur ship-and-development-index/ (Accessed on November 10, 2020).

Institute of Scientific Communications. (2020a). Dataset "Big data of the modern global economy: a digital platform for intellectual analytics – 2020". https://iscvolga.ru/data1 (Accessed on November 8, 2020).

Institute of Scientific Communications (2020b). Dataset "Social Entrepreneur-ship in the World Economy: a Path from Virtual Scores to Big Data – 2020". https://iscvolga.ru/data3 (Accessed on November 8, 2020).

Jeffrey, S., Rosenberg, S., & McCabe, B. (2019). Corporate social responsibility behaviors and corporate reputation. *Social Responsibility Journal, 15*(3), 395–408. https://doi.org/10.1108/SRJ-11-2017-0255.

Kelley, K. J., Hemphill, T. A., & Thams, Y. (2019). Corporate social respon-sibility, country reputation and corporate reputation: A perspective on the creation of shared value in emerging markets. *Multinational Business Review, 27*(2), 178–197. https://doi.org/10.1108/MBR-07-2017-0047.

Natsubidze, A. S. (2015). Online marketing as a means of ensuring sustainability of entrepreneurial structures in the food market of Russia in the crisis conditions. In E. G. Popkova (Ed.), INSSCCOM15. IV All-Russian online seminar-conference "Online marketing in the crisis conditions". https:// www.archilab.online/konferentsii-2015-goda/43-2015-iv/496-internet-mar keting-kak-sposob-obespecheniya-ustojchivosti-predprinimatelskikh-struktur-na-rynke-produktov-pitaniya-rossii-v-usloviyakh-krizisa (Accessed on June 5, 2020).

Popkova, E., DeLo, P., & Sergi, B. S. (2020). Corporate social responsibility amid social distancing during the COVID-19 crisis: BRICS vs. OECD coun-tries. Research in International Business and Finance. https://doi.org/10. 1016/j.ribaf.2020.101315.

Popkova, E. G. (2017). Economic and Legal Foundations of Modern Russian Society. A volume in the series Popkova, E. G. (Ed.), Advances in Research on Russian Business and Management. Information Age Publishing.

Popkova, E. G., & Sergi, B. S. (2019). Social entrepreneurship in Russia and Asia: Further development trends and prospects. *On the Horizon, 28*(1), 9–21. https://doi.org/10.1108/OTH-09-2019-0065.

Popkova, E. G., & Sergi, B. S. (2020a). Human capital and AI in industry 4.0. Convergence and divergence in social entrepreneurship in Russia. *Journal of Intellectual Capital, 21*(4), 565–581. https://doi.org/10.1108/JIC-09-2019-0224.

Popkova, E. G., & Sergi, B. S. (2020b). Human capital and AI in industry 4.0. Convergence and divergence in social entrepreneurship in Russia. *Journal of Intellectual Capital*. https://doi.org/10.1108/JIC-09-2019-0224.

Sekhon, A. K., & Kathuria, L. M. (2019). Analyzing the impact of corporate social responsibility on corporate financial performance: Evidence from top Indian firms. *Corporate Governance, 20*(1), 143–157. https://doi.org/10.1108/CG-04-2019-0135.

Smetanina, A. I. (2015). Online marketing as a perspective tool of development of virtual entrepreneurship in modern Russia. In E. G. Popkova (Ed.), INSSCCOM15. IV All-Russian online seminar-conference "Online marketing in the crisis conditions". https://www.archilab.online/konferentsii-2015-goda/43-2015-iv/494-internet-marketing-kak-perspektivnyj-instrument-raz vitiya-virtualnogo-predprinimatelstva-v-sovremennoj-rossii (Accessed on June 5, 2020).

Zavyalova, E. B., Studenikin, N. V., & Starikova, E. A. (2018). Business participation in implementation of socially oriented sustainable development goals in countries of central Asia and the caucasus region. *Central Asia and the Caucasus, 19*(2), 56–63.

Non-commercial Organizations as Subjects of Social Entrepreneurship in the Market Economy

Vladimir S. Osipov©, Elena L. Pozharskaya,
Aleksei V. Bogoviz©, and Alexander N. Alekseev©

1 INTRODUCTION

Non-commercial organizations play an important role in the modern economy, which is connected to overcoming the "market gaps". Large competition leads to entrepreneurial subjects' striving to implement the projects that are connected to large commercial profit and are characterized by the largest investment attractiveness. However, there remain a lot

---

V. S. Osipov (✉)
Moscow State Institute of International Relations (University) of the Ministry of Foreign Affairs Russian Federation, Moscow, Russia

E. L. Pozharskaya
Plekhanov Russian University of Economics, Moscow, Russia
e-mail: Pozharskaya.EL@rea.ru

A. V. Bogoviz
Independent Researcher, Moscow, Russia

A. N. Alekseev
Financial University Under the Government of the Russian Federation, Moscow, Russia

© The Author(s), under exclusive license to Springer Nature   343
Switzerland AG 2021
E. G. Popkova and B. S. Sergi (Eds.), *Economic Issues of Social Entrepreneurship,*
https://doi.org/10.1007/978-3-030-77291-8_32

of popular – in society and economy – projects, which are underrated or unattractive for commercial entrepreneurship.

These could be projects that are aimed at creation of public benefits – e.g., development of infrastructure or urban development. In this case, there's a need for large-scale investments with a large return period and limited opportunities for receiving income or profit. These could be also projects on provision of socially important goods and services with fixed (by government) prices and high requirements to quality. Expenditures for their creation and realization are high, and the possibilities of return are limited – therefore, the investment risks are high.

Though government can independently implement such projects, this leads to an excessive burden on the state budget and low effectiveness of project management, which, in its turn, leads to lost social advantages. A more attractive alternative is stimulation of development of non-commercial entrepreneurship, which is oriented at implementation of projects with reduced commercial attractiveness.

The advantage of non-commercial organizations is, firstly, separation from government. In some cases, this requires state co-financing, and in other cases donations from sponsors are sufficient – which allows reducing the burden on state budget.

Secondly, high effectiveness of management and high quality, regardless of the level of prices. Being a special form of private entrepreneurship, non-commercial organizations demonstrate the necessary (but inaccessible for government) flexibility, observing the requirements of state and society from the positions of the number of goods and services, their quality, and prices.

However, the above advantages are not ensures and require substantiation in each separate case. This causes a problem of uncertainty of the role of non-commercial organizations in the modern market economy. We offer the following hypothesis: non-commercial organizations play two roles in the market economy: economic (improving economic indicators) and social (improving social indicators). The goal of this research is to study the role of non-commercial organizations as subjects of social entrepreneurship in the market economy.

2 Literature Review

Social significance of non-commercial organizations, which is connected to their stimulation for increase of population's quality of life and living standard, is emphasized in the works Alkire (née Nasr) et al. (2019), Baranova (2015), Duarte Alonso et al. (2020), Dubova (2015), Fakoussa et al. (2020), Glazova (2015), Urban (2020), Natsubidze (2015), and Smetanina (2015).

Economic advantages of the functioning and development of non-commercial organizations are considered in the works Alpidovskaya and Popkova (2019), Bogoviz (2019), Bogoviz et al. (2019), Bogoviz et al. (2020a), Bogoviz et al. (2020b), Popkova et al. (2020), Popkova (2017), Popkova and Sergi (2019), Popkova and Sergi (2020a), Popkova and Sergi (2020b), and Zavyalova et al. (2018).

The large number of the existing publications allows stating that the considered problem has been sufficiently elaborated. Gap analysis has determined the absence of a solution to the set problem – due to the lack of the systemic character with the published works and the subsequent role and value of non-commercial organizations for the modern market economy. This gap is to be filled by this research.

3 Methodology

Correlation analysis is used to check the offered hypothesis and to determine the connection between the indicators of non-commercial organizations' development and the indicators of their potential contribution to development of society and economy. The indicators of non-commercial organizations' development are the number of non-commercial companies, share of non-commercial companies, index of information disclosure, and charity index, according to the materials of the dataset "Social Entrepreneurship in the World Economy: a Path from Virtual Scores to Big Data – 2020" (Institute of Scientific Communications, 2020b).

The indicators of potential economic contribution are the global competitiveness index 4.0, innovations index, and rate of economic growth. The indicators of potential social contribution are quality of life index, happy life index, and sustainable development index. The source of the information and empirical data is the dataset "Big data of the modern global economy: a digital platform for intellectual analytics – 2020" (Institute of Scientific Communications, 2020a).

The hypothesis is deemed proved if there are large (more than 70%) positive values of the coefficients of correlation with the indicators of social and economic contribution. The research is performed separately for developed (by the example of Major Advanced Economies – G7) and developing (by the example of BRICS) countries in 2020. The initial data are presented in Table 1.

4 Results

To determine the detailed contribution of non-commercial entrepreneurship to social and economic development of the modern economic systems with the domination of market relations, let us consider the detailed results of correlation analysis of the data from Table 1 (Figs. 1 and 2).

As shown in Fig. 1, in developed countries (shown by the example of G7) non-commercial organizations contribute poorly to development of economic systems. Large positive values of correlation coefficients are observed only with one indicator of non-commercial organizations – charity index: with happy life index (87.47%) and rate of economic growth (75.33%). Despite the poor contribution, it is manifested in the social and economic spheres.

As shown in Fig. 2, in developing countries (as shown by the example of BRICS) non-commercial organizations contribute a lot to development of economic systems. Large positive values of correlation coefficients are observed with the whole range of indicators: between charity index and quality of life index (social contribution: 86.75%), between share of non-commercial organizations and quality of life index (social contribution: 76.19%), between information disclosure index and innovations index (economic contribution: 74.54%), between number of non-commercial companies and rate of economic growth (80.90%), between innovations index (88.64%) and global competitiveness index 4.0 (70.57%) – economic contribution. Like in developed countries, the contribution of non-commercial organizations in developing countries is manifested in the social and economic spheres.

For the purpose of systemic reflection of the obtained results, let us use the generalized (averaged) coefficients of correlation in view of the considered groups of countries.

As shown in Fig. 3, in developed countries (shown by the example of G7) non-commercial organizations contribute the most to acceleration of economic growth (52.93% on average), increase of global competitiveness (31.62%), and acceleration of economy's innovative development (45.12%). Domination of economic contribution, in which the key role belongs to charity (42.18%), is very clear.

Table 1 Statistics of non-commercial organizations and their potential social and economic contribution in the countries of G7 and BRICS in 2020

Group of countries	Country	Indicators of development of non-commercial organizations				Indicators of potential contribution of non-commercial organizations					
		Number of non-commercial companies	Share of non-commercial companies, %	Information disclosure index, points 1–100	Charity index, points 1–100	Global competitiveness index 4.0, points 1–100	Innovations index, points 1–100	Economic growth rate, %	Quality of life index, points 1–200	Happy life index, points 1–10	Sustainable development index, points 1–100
Countries of G7	Canada	1,190.0	0.770	8.0	55.0	79.6	53.88	1.843	169.42	7.278	77.9
	France	736.0	0.110	8.0	30.0	78.8	54.25	1.749	156.10	6.592	81.5
	Germany	634.0	0.170	5.0	43.00	81.8	58.19	1.415	184.30	6.985	81.1
	Italy	310.0	0.300	7.0	33.0	71.5	46.30	0.800	143.81	6.223	75.8
	Japan	3,336.0	0.120	7.0	23.0	82.3	54.68	0.846	176.46	5.886	78.9
	UK	1,511.0	0.540	10.0	54.0	81.2	61.30	1.606	166.73	7.054	79.4
	USA	7,696.0	1.440	7.0	58.0	83.7	61.73	2.121	176.77	6.892	74.5
Countries of BRICS	Brazil	373.0	n/a	5.0	28.0	60.9	33.82	1.954	103.87	6.300	70.6
	China	2,388.0	0.030	10.0	16.0	73.9	54.82	6.000	99.87	5.191	73.2
	India	1,383.0	0.370	8.0	26.0	61.4	36.58	7.791	115.41	4.015	61.1
	Russia	312.0	0.340	6.0	21.0	66.7	37.62	1.500	104.05	5.648	70.9
	South Africa	344.0	n/a	8.0	36.0	62.4	34.04	2.198	135.75	4.722	61.5

n/a – no data in the source.

Source compiled by the authors based on Institute of Scientific Communications (2020a), Institute of Scientific Communications (2020b)

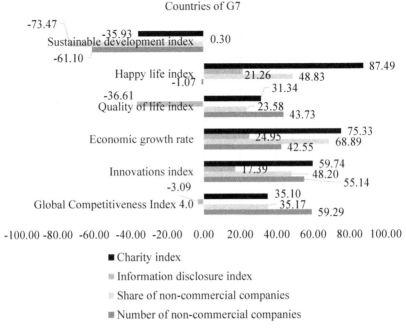

Fig. 1 Cross correlation between the indicators of non-commercial organizations and the indicators of their potential social and economic contribution in the countries of G7 in 2020, % (*Source* Calculated and built by the authors)

In developing countries (shown by the example of BRICS), non-commercial organizations contribute the most to increase of quality of life (34.50%) and acceleration of economic growth rate (24.15%). We see a clear combination of social and economic contribution, in which the key role belongs to information disclosure (24.10%) and number of non-commercial companies (31.64%).

5 Conclusion

Thus, the offered hypothesis has been proved on the whole: non-commercial organizations do contribute to social and economic development. However, it is manifested mostly in developing countries (shown by

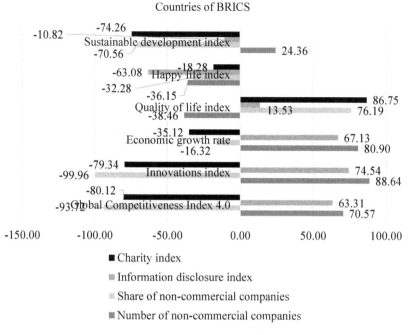

Fig. 2 Cross correlation between the indicators of non-commercial organizations and the indicators of their potential social and economic contribution in the countries of BRICS in 2020, % (*Source* Calculated and built by the authors)

the example of BRICS), where non-commercial initiatives are differentiated and ensure a complex of positive effects for society and economy. Due to this, developing countries implement a traditional model of development of non-commercial organizations, which envisages them providing public benefits and socially important economic benefits.

In developed countries (shown by the example of G7), the influence of the current market relations lead to the situation when non-commercial organizations do not perform their social mission and make only the economic contribution to development of economic systems, which is connected to acceleration of economic growth, innovative development, and increase of economy's global competitiveness. Non-commercial initiatives are limited by charity, which is implemented within a specific

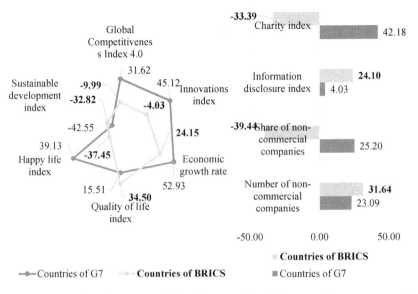

Fig. 3 Generalized cross correlation between the indicators of non-commercial organizations and the indicators of their potential social and economic contribution in the countries of G7 and BRICS in 2020, % (*Source* Calculated and built by the authors)

(non-traditional) model of development of non-commercial organizations, which envisages provision of only socially important economic benefits.

The determined differences in the models of development of non-commercial organizations in developed and developing countries specified the concept of social entrepreneurship and formed a scientific basis for independent development of the economic policy and corporate strategies by non-commercial organizations in these groups of countries with refusal from the routine use of international experience for accounting the specifics of functioning and development of social entrepreneurship in each separate economic system.

References

Alkire (née Nasr), L., Mooney, C., Gur, F. A., Kabadayi, S., Renko, M., & Vink, J. (2019). Transformative service research, service design, and social entrepreneurship: An interdisciplinary framework advancing wellbeing and social impact. *Journal of Service Management, 31*(1), 24–50. https://doi.org/10.1108/JOSM-05-2019-0139.

Alpidovskaya, M. L., & Popkova, E. G. (2019). Marx and modernity: A political and economic analysis of social systems management. A volume in the series Popkova, E. G. (Ed.), Advances in Research on Russian Business and Management. Information Age Publishing.

Baranova, I. V. (2015). Possibilities of using online marketing for improving the educational system in the conditions of formation of the knowledge economy. In E. G. Popkova (Ed.), INSSCCOM15. IV All-Russian online seminar-conference "Online marketing in the conditions of a crisis". https://www.archilab.online/konferentsii-2015-goda/43-2015-iv/492-vozmozhno sti-primeneniya-internet-marketinga-dlya-sovershenstvovaniya-sistemy-obrazo vaniya-v-usloviyakh-formirovaniya-ekonomiki-znanij (Accessed on June 5, 2020).

Bogoviz, A. V. (2019). Cluster mechanism of marketing optimization on the basis of systemic interaction between the internet of thing and social networks. In Popkova, E. G. (Ed.), Ubiquitous Computing and the Internet of Things: Prerequisites for the Development of ICT. Springer. https://doi.org/10.1007/978-3-030-13397-9_95.

Bogoviz, A. V., Kletskova, E. V., Sultanova, M. K., Lavrova, E. V., & Shapoval, E. V. (2019). The new concept of social justice in the globalizing economy. *Growth Poles of the Global Economy: Emergence, Changes and Future Perspectives, 3*(1), 1001–1008.

Bogoviz, A. V., Lobova, S. V., & Alekseev, A. N. (2020). Social development versus economic growth: Current contradictions and perspectives of convergence. *International Journal of Sociology and Social Policy*. https://doi.org/10.1108/IJSSP-03-2020-0061.

Bogoviz, A. V., Shokhnekh, A. V., Petrenko, E. S., & Milkina, E. A. (2020). Social effectiveness of the market economy: Measuring and management. *International Journal of Sociology and Social Policy*. https://doi.org/10.1108/IJSSP-03-2020-0060.

Duarte Alonso, A., Kok, S. K., O'Brien, S., & O'Shea, M. (2020). The significance of grassroots and inclusive innovation in harnessing social entrepreneurship and urban regeneration. *European Business Review, 32*(4), 667–686. https://doi.org/10.1108/EBR-05-2019-0102.

Dubova, Y. I. (2015). Online marketing as a component of the market activities of Russia's regions in the crisis conditions. In E. G. Popkova (Ed.), INSS-CCOM15. IV All-Russian online seminar-conference "Online marketing in the crisis conditions". https://www.archilab.online/konferentsii-2015-goda/ 43-2015-iv/495-internet-marketing-kak-sostavnoj-element-marketingovoj-deyatelnosti-regionov-rossii-v-usloviyakh-krizisa (Accessed on June 5, 2020).

Fakoussa, R., O'Leary, S., & Salem, S. (2020). An exploratory study on social entrepreneurship in Egypt. *Journal of Islamic Accounting and Business Research, 11*(3), 694–707. https://doi.org/10.1108/JIABR-02-2017-0023.

Glazova, M. V. (2015). Determinants of improving the process of development and making of managerial decisions by modern companies in the crisis conditions. In E. G. Popkova (Ed.), INSSCCOM15. IV All-Russian online seminar-conference "Online marketing in the crisis conditions". https://www.archilab.online/konferentsii-2015-goda/43-2015-iv/493-determina nty-sovershenstvovaniya-protsessa-razrabotki-i-prinyatiya-upravlencheskikh-res henij-sovremennymi-predpriyatiyami-v-usloviyakh-krizisa (Accessed on June 5, 2020).

Institute of Scientific Communications (2020a). Dataset "Big data of the modern global economy: a digital platform for intellectual analytics – 2020". https://iscvolga.ru/data1 (Accessed on November 8, 2020).

Institute of Scientific Communications (2020b). Dataset "Social Entrepreneurship in the World Economy: a Path from Virtual Scores to Big Data – 2020". https://iscvolga.ru/data3 (Accessed on November 8, 2020).

Natsubidze, A. S. (2015). Online marketing as a means of ensuring sustainability of entrepreneurial structures in the food market of Russia in the crisis conditions. In E. G. Popkova (Ed.), INSSCCOM15. IV All-Russian online seminar-conference "Online marketing in the crisis conditions". https://www.archilab.online/konferentsii-2015-goda/43-2015-iv/496-internet-mar keting-kak-sposob-obespecheniya-ustojchivosti-predprinimatelskikh-struktur-na-rynke-produktov-pitaniya-rossii-v-usloviyakh-krizisa (Accessed on June 5, 2020).

Popkova, E., DeLo, P., & Sergi, B. S. (2020). Corporate social responsibility amid social distancing during the COVID-19 crisis: BRICS vs. OECD countries. Research in International Business and Finance. https://doi.org/10.1016/j.ribaf.2020.101315.

Popkova, E. G. (2017). Economic and legal foundations of modern russian society. A volume in the series Popkova, E. G. (Ed.), Advances in Research on Russian Business and Management. Information Age Publishing.

Popkova, E. G., & Sergi, B. S. (2019). Social entrepreneurship in Russia and Asia: Further development trends and prospects. *On the Horizon, 28*(1), 9–21. https://doi.org/10.1108/OTH-09-2019-0065.

Popkova, E. G., & Sergi, B. S. (2020a). Human capital and AI in industry 4.0. Convergence and divergence in social entrepreneurship in Russia. *Journal of Intellectual Capital, 21*(4), 565–581. https://doi.org/10.1108/JIC-09-2019-0224.

NON-COMMERCIAL ORGANIZATIONS AS SUBJECTS ... 353

Popkova, E. G., & Sergi, B. S. (2020b). Human capital and AI in industry 4.0. Convergence and divergence in social entrepreneurship in Russia. *Journal of Intellectual Capital.* https://doi.org/10.1108/JIC-09-2019-0224.

Smetanina, A. I. (2015). Online marketing as a perspective tool of development of virtual entrepreneurship in modern Russia. In E. G. Popkova (Ed.), INSSCCOM15. IV All-Russian online seminar-conference "Online marketing in the crisis conditions". https://www.archilab.online/konferentsii-2015-goda/43-2015-iv/494-internet-marketing-kak-perspektivnyj-instrument-raz vitiya-virtualnogo-predprinimatelstva-v-sovremennoj-rossii (Accessed on June 5, 2020).

Urban, B. (2020). Entrepreneurial alertness, self-efficacy and social entrepreneurship intentions. *Journal of Small Business and Enterprise Development, 27*(3), 489–507. https://doi.org/10.1108/JSBED-08-2019-0285.

Zavyalova, E. B. Studenikin, N. V., & Starikova, E. A. (2018). Business participation in implementation of socially oriented Sustainable Development Goals in countries of Central Asia and the Caucasus region. *Central Asia and the Caucasus, 19*(2), c. 56–63.

.

Systemic Scientific Vision of Social Entrepreneurship in the Unity of Its Manifestations: As Non-commercial and Socially Responsible Business

Vladimir S. Osipov, *Veronika V. Yankovskaya,*
Elena N. Akimova, *and Svetlana V. Lobova*

1 INTRODUCTION

Development of social entrepreneurship is slowed down by the gaps in its scientific concept, which hinders the proclaimed transition of the modern scientific systems to the social market economy. One of the gaps is incompletion of the methodological provision for identification of social entrepreneurship, for its differentiation from other forms

---

V. S. Osipov (✉)
Moscow State Institute of International Relations (University) of the Ministry of Foreign Affairs Russian Federation, Moscow, Russia

V. V. Yankovskaya
Plekhanov Russian University of Economics, Moscow, Russia

E. N. Akimova
Moscow Region State University, Mytishchi, Russia

S. V. Lobova
Altai State University, Barnaul, Russia

© The Author(s), under exclusive license to Springer Nature   355
Switzerland AG 2021
E. G. Popkova and B. S. Sergi (eds.), *Economic Issues of Social Entrepreneurship,*
https://doi.org/10.1007/978-3-030-77291-8_33

of entrepreneurship, and monitoring and control of its development. The existing economic literature does not clearly determine the place of social entrepreneurship in the system of classification of subjects of entrepreneurship. Thus, social entrepreneurship exists separately, and its limits are not clearly determined.

Another gap is connected to underdevelopment of the approach to state management of social entrepreneurship's development. The sources of its development are not determined. There are two alternative points of view regarding this issue. According to the first one, social entrepreneurship develops better in the conditions of market freedom, for natural competitive stimuli are crested for implementing socially important business initiatives. According to the second one (quite opposite), social entrepreneurship could be created and developed only under the pressure of state regulation, since it is a "market gap".

Two research tasks are solved in order to reach the set goal. 1st task: developing a methodological approach to classification of companies in the process of building the social market economy and specifying the place in it and the criterion of social entrepreneurship. 2nd task: identifying the key source of social entrepreneurship's development and determining the prospects of improving its state management. The research is based on the method of correlation analysis.

2 LITERATURE REVIEW

General issues of functioning and development of social entrepreneurship are studied in the works Badzim et al. (2015), Baranova (2015), Bogoviz et al. (2019), Bogoviz et al. (2020a), Bogoviz et al. (2020b), Boyazitov (2015), Dubova (2015), Tran Van Thuy Anh (2015), Popkova et al. (2020), Popkova and Sergi (2019), Popkova and Sergi (2020). Noncommercial manifestations of social entrepreneurship are studied in the works Corduneanu and Lebec (2020), Dumalanede et al. (2020), and Maletzky and Grosskopf (2020),

Socially responsible manifestations of social entrepreneurship are studied by such authors as Bhattacharyya and Jha (2020), Bhattacharyya (2020), and Chen et al. (2020). As the performed literature overview has shown, despite the comprehensive elaboration of the manifestations of social entrepreneurship, the scientific and methodological basis of its measuring and state management is not accurate and requires further attention.

SYSTEMIC SCIENTIFIC VISION OF SOCIAL ENTREPRENEURSHIP ... 357

3 Methodology

We offer and use a new classification of entrepreneurship's subjects by the criterion of their contribution to formation of the social market economy. The classification is given in Table 1, with criteria of assigning business structures to various subjects of entrepreneurship.

According to the authors' classification, the following subjects of entrepreneurship are distinguished:

- commercial entrepreneurship, which does not contribute to formation of the social market economy. It includes companies that implement socially responsible initiatives, the correlation between which and the indicators of the social market economy is less than 15%, and companies, which implement non-commercial business initiatives, the correlation between which and the indicators of the social market economy is less than 35%;
- provisionally social entrepreneurship, which contributes moderately to formation of the social market economy. They include companies that realize socially responsible initiatives, the correlation between which and the indicators of the social market economy is 15%–30%, and companies that realize non-commercial business initiatives, the correlation between which and the indicators of social market economy is 35%–70%;

Table 1 Classification of subjects of entrepreneurship by the criterion of their contribution to formation of the social market economy

Implemented initiatives, which provide the contribution to formation of the social market economy	Commercial entrepreneurship: does not contribute to formation of the social market economy	Provisionally social entrepreneurship: contributes moderately to formation of the social market economy	Social entrepreneurship: contributes significantly to formation of the social market economy
Socially responsible business initiatives	correlation* below 15%	correlation* 15%–30%	correlation* above 30%
Non-commercial business initiatives	correlation* below 35%	correlation* 35%–70%	correlation* above 70%

*with indicators of social market economy.
Source Developed and compiled by the authors

- Social entrepreneurship, which contributes significantly to formation of the social market economy and is its main driver. They include companies that realize socially responsible initiatives, the correlation between which and the indicators of the social market economy is more than 30%, and companies that realize non-commercial business initiatives, the correlation between which and the indicators of the social market economy is more than 70%.

The indicators social market economy are as follows: quality of life index, happy life index, and sustainable development index, which values for 2019 (as of year-end, current as of 2020) are taken from the dataset "Big data of the modern global economy: a digital platform for intellectual analytics – 2020" (Institute of Scientific Communications, 2020a).

The indicators that reflect socially responsible initiatives of business are stimulation of unions and multistakeholder collaboration. The indicators that reflect non-commercial business initiatives are share of non-commercial companies and charity index. These indicators are taken from the dataset "Social Entrepreneurship in the World Economy: a Path from Virtual Scores to Big Data – 2020" (Institute of Scientific Communications, 2020b).

To determine which approach to state regulation is the most favorable for development of social entrepreneurship, we study correlation between indicators, which reflect socially responsible and non-commercial initiatives of entrepreneurship, and indicators of social market economy in countries with different levels of economic freedom according to the 2020 Index of Economic Freedom (Country Ranking) by The Heritage Foundation (2020). The data on the selected countries are given in Fig. 1.

Statistics of social entrepreneurship and the social market economy in the selected countries are shown in Table 2.

4 Results

To form a systemic scientific vision of social entrepreneurship in the unity of its manifestations – as non-commercial and socially responsible business – let us consider detailed (Figs. 2, 3, and 4) and generalized (Fig. 5) results of correlation analysis of the materials from Table 2.

As shown in Fig. 2, non-commercial business initiatives (share of non-commercial companies and charity index) contribute the most to

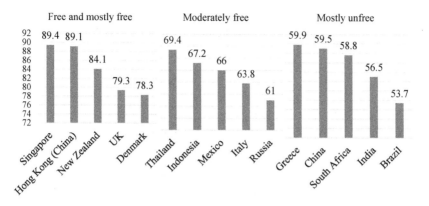

Fig. 1 Index of economic freedom for groups of countries in 2020, points 1–100 (*Source* Built by the authors based on The Heritage Foundation, [2020])

formation of the social market economy in free and mostly free countries, while socially responsible business initiatives are insignificant.

As shown in Fig. 3, only share of non-commercial companies contributes moderately (66.92%) to formation of the social market economy in moderately free countries.

As shown in Fig. 4, business initiatives are insignificant in mostly unfree countries. It should be noted that correlation between share of non-commercial companies is distorted due to deficit of statistics and it cannot be taken into account.

As shown in Fig. 5, non-commercial business initiatives in free and mostly free countries contribute a lot (71.38%) to formation of the social market economy, while this contribution decreases in the course of decrease of market freedom.

5 Conclusion

Thus, we have formed a systemic scientific vision social entrepreneurship in the unity of its manifestations: as non-commercial and socially responsible business; and developed a new classification of subjects of entrepreneurship by the criterion of their contribution to formation of the social market economy, according to which criteria of assigning business structures to various subjects of entrepreneurship are offered,

Table 2 Statistics of social entrepreneurship and the social market economy in countries with different levels of economic freedom

Category of countries by the level of economic freedom	Country	Quality of life index, points 1–200	Happy life index, points 1–10	Sustainable development index, points 1–100	Stimulation of unions, points 1–100	Multistakeholder collaboration, points 1–100	Share of non-commercial companies, %	Charity index, points 1–100
Free and mostly free	Singapore	146.09	6.262	69.6	85.3	66.0	0.390	35.0
	Hong Kong (China)	99.58	5.430	n/a	77.5	65.8	n/a	n/a
	New Zealand	183.07	7.307	79.5	67.9	61.4	0.790	57.0
	UK	166.73	7.054	79.4	66.1	65.5	0.540	54.0
	Denmark	196.47	7.600	85.2	81.0	69.5	n/a	44.0
Moderately free	Thailand	104.54	6.008	73.0	64.9	52.1	n/a	42.0
	Indonesia	101.90	5.192	64.2	58.0	59.7	n/a	50.0
	Mexico	122.44	6.595	68.5	59.1	45.3	0.030	28.0
	Italy	143.81	6.223	75.8	49.4	45.6	0.300	33.0
	Russia	104.05	5.648	70.9	56.5	49.5	0.340	21.0
Mostly unfree	Greece	135.61	5.287	71.4	50.3	34.9	n/a	16.0
	China	99.87	5.191	73.2	59.6	57.3	0.030	16.0
	South Africa	135.75	4.722	61.5	36.4	52.6	n/a	36.0
	India	115.41	4.015	61.1	58.4	53.3	0.370	26.0
	Brazil	103.87	6.300	70.6	44.1	44.3	n/a	28.0

Source Compiled by the authors based on Institute of Scientific Communications (2020a), Institute of Scientific Communications (2020b)

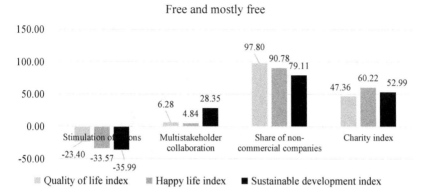

Fig. 2 Correlation between business initiatives and the indicators of social market economy in free and mostly free countries, % (*Source* Calculated and built by the authors)

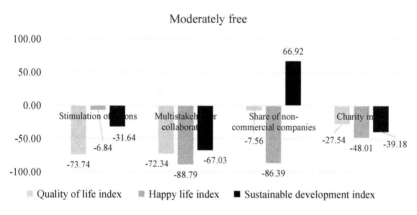

Fig. 3 Correlation between business initiatives and the indicators of social market economy in moderately free countries, % (*Source* Calculated and built by the authors)

with distinguishing commercial entrepreneurship, provisionally social entrepreneurship, and social entrepreneurship.

As the economic analysis has shown, development of social entrepreneurship requires the increase of the level of economic freedom. At present, it is insufficiently high even in countries with high level of

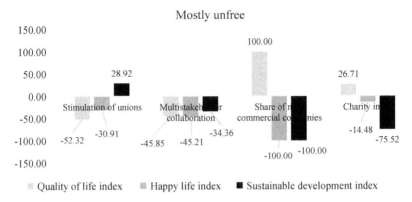

Fig. 4 Correlation between business initiatives and the indicators of social market economy in mostly unfree countries, % (*Source* Calculated and built by the authors)

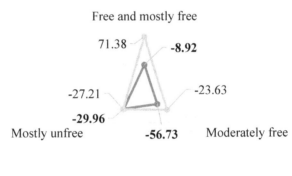

Fig. 5 Correlation between business initiatives and the indicators of social market economy in countries with different levels of economic freedom, % (*Source* Calculated and built by the authors)

economic freedom to stimulate the development of social entrepreneurship. Thus, further deregulation for the purpose of forming the social market economy is recommended.

REFERENCES

Badzim, P. V., Abramova, N. V., & Farvazova, A. R. (2015). Study of the social and economic potential of oil and gas enterprises. In E. G. Popkova (Ed.), INSSCCOM15. VI All-Russian online seminar-conference "Research of state support for region's investment attractiveness". https://www.archilab.onl ine/konferentsii-2015-goda/45-2015-vi/525-issledovanie-sotsialno-ekonom icheskogo-potentsiala-predpriyatij-neftegazovoj-otrasli (Accessed on June 5, 2020).

Baranova, I. V. (2015). Socio-cultural background of education system development in modern Russia. In E. G. Popkova (Ed.), INSSCCOM15. VII All-Russian online seminar-conference "The modern socio-cultural and legal foundations of the Russian society". https://www.archilab.online/konfer entsii-2015-goda/46-2015-vii/532-sotsio-kulturnye-predposylki-razvitiya-sis temy-obrazovaniya-v-sovremennoj-rossii (Accessed on June 5, 2020).

Bhattacharyya, S. S. (2020). Explicating firm international corporate social responsibility initiatives. *Review of International Business and Strategy, 30*(4), 515–536. https://doi.org/10.1108/RIBS-05-2020-0055.

Bhattacharyya, S. S., & Jha, S. (2020). Explicating micro foundations of corporate social responsibility: A moderated-mediation study of customer, investor and employee roles. *International Journal of Ethics and Systems, 36*(4), 619–640. https://doi.org/10.1108/IJOES-05-2020-0073.

Bogoviz, A. V., Kletskova, E. V., Sultanova, M. K., Lavrova, E. V., & Shapoval, E. V. (2019). The new concept of social justice in the globalizing economy. *Growth Poles of the Global Economy: Emergence, Changes and Future Perspectives, 3*(1), 1001–1008.

Bogoviz, A. V., Lobova, S. V., & Alekseev, A. N. (2020). Social development versus economic growth: Current contradictions and perspectives of convergence. *International Journal of Sociology and Social Policy.* https://doi.org/10.1108/IJSSP-03-2020-0061

Bogoviz, A. V., Shokhnekh, A. V., Petrenko, E. S., & Milkina, E. A. (2020). Social effectiveness of the market economy: Measuring and management. *International Journal of Sociology and Social Policy.* https://doi.org/10.1108/IJSSP-03-2020-0060

Boyazitov, D. R. (2015). Economic and legal aspects of state management of region. In E. G. Popkova (Ed.), INSSCCOM15. VII All-Russian online seminar-conference "The modern socio-cultural and legal foundations of the Russian society". https://www.archilab.online/konferentsii-2015-goda/46-2015-vii/533-ekonomiko-pravovye-aspekty-gosudarstvennogo-upravleniya-regionom (Accessed on June 5, 2020).

Chen, J. -Y., Lim, S. -J., Nam, H. -J., & Phillips, J. (2020). Local culture as a corporate social responsibility multiplier: Confucian values' mediation

364 V. S. OSIPOV ET AL.

between firm policies and employees' attitude. *Asia-Pacific Journal of Business Administration*, *12*(3/4), 387–407. https://doi.org/10.1108/APJBA-04-2019-0088.

Corduneanu, R., & Lebec, L. (2020). People in suits: A case study of empowerment and control in a non-profit UK organization. *Journal of Public Budgeting, Accounting & Financial Management*, *32*(3), 511–528. https://doi.org/10.1108/JPBAFM-06-2019-0098.

Dubova, Y. I. (2015). Modern Socio-cultural Foundations of Russian Regions Territorial Marketing. In E. G. Popkova (Ed.), INSSCCOM15. VII All-Russian online seminar-conference "The modern socio-cultural and legal foundations of the Russian society". https://www.archilab.online/konferent sii-2015-goda/46-2015-vii/531-sovremennye-sotsio-kulturnye-osnovy-territ orialnogo-marketinga-regionov-rossii (Accessed on June 5, 2020).

Dumalanede, C., Hamza, K., & Payaud, M. (2020). Improving healthcare services access at the bottom of the pyramid: The role of profit and non-profit organisations in Brazil. *Society and Business Review*, *15*(3), 211–234. https://doi.org/10.1108/SBR-10-2018-0118.

Institute of Scientific Communications. (2020a). Dataset "Big data of the modern global economy: A digital platform for intellectual analytics – 2020". https://iscvolga.ru/data1 (Accessed on November 11, 2020).

Institute of Scientific Communications. (2020b). Dataset "Social Entrepreneurship in the World Economy: A Path from Virtual Scores to Big Data – 2020". https://iscvolga.ru/data3 (Accessed on November 11, 2020).

Maletzky, M., & Grosskopf, S. (2020). Personnel mobility in German non-profit organizations – An institutional perspective. *Journal of Global Mobility*, *8*(3/4), 353–380. https://doi.org/10.1108/JGM-04-2020-0028.

Popkova, E., DeLo, P., & Sergi, B. S. (2020). Corporate social responsibility amid social distancing during the COVID-19 crisis: BRICS vs. OECD countries. Research in International Business and Finance. https://doi.org/10.1016/j.ribaf.2020.101315.

Popkova, E. G., & Sergi, B. S. (2019). Social entrepreneurship in Russia and Asia: Further development trends and prospects. *On the Horizon*, *28*(1), 9–21. https://doi.org/10.1108/OTH-09-2019-0065

Popkova, E. G., & Sergi, B. S. (2020). Human capital and AI in industry 4.0. Convergence and divergence in social entrepreneurship in Russia. *Journal of Intellectual Capital*, *21*(4), 565–581. https://doi.org/10.1108/JIC-09-2019-0224.

The Heritage Foundation. (2020). 2020 Index of Economic Freedom: Country Ranking. https://www.heritage.org/index/ranking?version=738 (Accessed on November 11, 2020).

Tran Van Thuy Anh. (2015). Plans and infrastructure support of the Vietnamese state for the development of tourism in particular in Sapa. In E. G. Popkova

(Ed.), INSSCCOM15. VI All-Russian online seminar-conference "Research of state support for region's investment attractiveness". https://www.arc hilab.online/konferentsii-2015-goda/45-2015-vi/526-plany-i-podderzhka-infrastruktury-vetnamskogo-gosudarstva-dlya-razvitiya-turizm-v-chastnosti-v-g-sapa (Accessed on June 5, 2020).

Contribution of Education and Personnel Management to the Development of Social Entrepreneurship

Project Activities as One of the Tools Unlocking the Students' Potential

Anna Storozheva and Elena Dadayan

1 Introduction

The relevance of the topic of our scientific research is due to the increase in work on the implementation and conducting of the project works of students, educational programs.

We need to note that the main objective of this study, to prove that thoroughness, comprehensiveness and criticality of the project work of the students is aimed at ensuring the quality of training of young professionals, is a tool unlocking the creative potential of the student, which ultimately affects the assessment of quality of educational programs by the state and society, and is the key to confidence in taught majors (clusters of majors) on the part of professional communities, other social groups and society as a whole.

Let us turn to the etymology of the word "project." The project should be understood as a set of interconnected activities aimed at obtaining unique results in the conditions of time and resource constraints. It is no coincidence that at present, the concepts of "project" and "project activity" are quite popular in education. For example, in the schedule of

---

A. Storozheva (✉) · E. Dadayan
Federal State Budgetary Educational Institution of Higher Education, Krasnoyarsk State Agrarian University, Krasnoyarsk, Russia

© The Author(s), under exclusive license to Springer Nature Switzerland AG 2021
E. G. Popkova and B. S. Sergi (eds.), *Economic Issues of Social Entrepreneurship*,
https://doi.org/10.1007/978-3-030-77291-8_34

secondary schools there is such a subject as project activity. Some federal state higher education standards contain project blocks. For example, Federal State Educational Standard of Higher Education for a major 38.05.01 Economic Security (specialty level)[1] contains the first block of professional competencies, which is merged into the group "Calculation and project economic activity" and includes positions aimed at forming a virtually complete range of economist skills, including the development of project solutions (Gorokhova, 2019).

Despite the fact that the main professional educational program in the field of law studies (40.03.01 Bachelor's training; 40.04.01 Master's training) do not contain the discipline of "project activity" as a discipline (module), which is mandatory for the development of students, regardless of the direction (profile) of the bachelor's program or the master's program, which is mastered by the student, teachers treat performing design work (development of tasks) in the study of disciplines aimed at forming professional competences, quite seriously. The quality and high efficiency of the educational programs implemented by the higher educational institution are evidenced by many indicators, which are evaluated not only by state accreditation, but also by professional and public acclaim. The latter determines the compliance not only with Russian state standards, but also with the standards of foreign countries, European in particular (ESG-ENQA1), and with the demands of professional standards and the needs of the labor market (Letyagina et al., 2020). We believe that project activity is one of those tools that not only reveal the creative and practical potential of students, but also show that the university on a systematic and planned basis, taking into account the current trends and tendencies in higher education, creates conditions and gives the students the opportunity to prove themselves, understand their human resources and find a decent place of employment after graduation.

2   Methodology

Not many scientific papers have been devoted to the problem of project activity in higher educational institutions implementing the direction of

---

[1] Order of the Russian Ministry of Science and Education dated 16.01.2017 N 20 "On the approval of the federal state educational standard of higher education in the specialty 38.05.01 Economic Security (specialty level)". Consultant Plus Information and Search System.

law training, to date. Most of the research and work on the implementation of the project activities by students takes place in the pedagogical field (secondary and secondary special education).

Acquainting students with the field of scientific knowledge begins much earlier and is carried out at all levels of education. Educational organizations, being focused on the development of cognitive interests, intellectual and creative interests of students, actively involve them in research and project work (Barabanova et al., 2019). The case value of the project can be viewed in two ways: from the student's point of view and from the teacher's point of view. From the point of view of the student (learner), a project gives the opportunity to do something interesting in groups or alone, make the most of own opportunities, prove oneself, try own hand, apply knowledge, etc. From the point of view of the teacher (instructor), a project is an integrative didactic means of development, learning and education, which allows to establish and develop specific abilities, skills and competences, including problematization (consideration of the problematic situation, highlighting existing contradictions, formulating the problem and sub problems, setting goals and objectives, etc.) (Pakhomova, 2005). The main aspects of theory and practice of projects (project activities of educators and students of educational institutions) are conceptual foundations of the project method, project typology, design methods, project structure, design requirements, presentation and defense rules, etc. proposed by Yakovleva N. F. (Yakovleva, 2014). The project approach to the formation of pedagogical and legal competences among law students is one of the educational technologies for the formation of such competencies (Zernov et al., 2019). Grudtsina L. Y. believes that there is a need to develop training programs on project activities (Grudtsina et al., 2009).

Belova T. G. notes that project activity is defined by its multifunctional focus, during which the student masters not only basic knowledge, but also key competencies; all this contributes to multilateral personal development (Belova, 2008). Any project is aimed at students acquiring the skills required to supplement their knowledge independently, to navigate in the rapid flow of information (Vokhmentseva, 2011).

As for project activities in foreign countries, educational systems of different countries have accumulated a lot of experience in the use of the project method in training, which allows to bring the theoretical material closer to real life (Kazun & Pastukhova, 2018; Penkovskikh, 2010; Retivykh, 2008).

372 A. STOROZHEVA AND E. DADAYAN

Table 1 Student questionnaire results

Study year	Yes, I used to	No, I did not participate	I'm not interested in project activity/project activity is quite complex
2nd	45	25	10
3rd	83	15	7
4th	91	5	2

Then, the authors of the study conducted a survey (questionnaire) of students in the field of law studies from second to fourth year, where one of the points of the questionnaire was the following question: "Did you get to participate in the projects offered by the faculty of the institute?" The results of the survey can be seen in Table 1.

Based on the data provided, the authors have interviewed 283 students, including 80 students in the 2nd year, 105 people in the 3rd year, and 98 in the 4th year.

The qualitative indicators show that 56% of students were involved in project activities in the 2nd year, 31% did not participate in projects and 13% knew about the projects available, but were not interested in them. In the third year, 79% of the respondents participated in the projects, 14% did not participate and 7% were not interested in project activities or believed that project activities are quite complex and beyond the power of a student. In the 4th year, 93% participated in projects, 5% did not participate and 2% were not interested in such an activity and did not see its prospects. We believe that by the 4th year students approach the project activities more meaningfully and see (note) serious prospects for such work, including for future employment.

In addition, we note that by their graduation from the university, only 5% did not participate in the project activities, and this indicates that performance of students is quite high.

Thus, we see that 77% of the total number of people surveyed are actively involved in the project activity, 16% do not participate and 7% are not interested in such a topic.

The analysis of the scientific literature shows that at present there is not enough theoretical and empirical basis for the scientific and practical justification of project activities in the university in the field of law studies. Such statement is based on pedagogical sciences. However, despite the small volume and results of these works, we should note that in general, the problem of a comprehensive study of the influence of such a tool as a project on the disclosure of the student's creative potential does not raise doubts and has all the prospects for further analysis and detailed consideration.

3 RESULTS

The authors of this work are teaching civil law at the Department of Civil Law and Process of the Law Institute of Krasnoyarsk SAU and very actively use the technique of creating educational projects. Some of the projects are aimed at effectively assimilating and applying the theoretical norms of civil law in practice. Students, for example, are invited not only to study theoretical material, but also to prepare analytical information on the application of a particular institution of civil law, for example, in judicial practice. To do this, the student is offered to study and analyze court rulings. Most often, we offer students to perform such work in mini-groups of 4–5 people. Like this, we present freedom of choice to the learners already at the initial stage of the project. The students themselves, without the intervention of the teacher, form mini-groups (subgroups). Students select the head of the subgroup and determine the mode of its work within the time frame set by the teacher for the project work. Here, students approach the realization (acquisition), for example, of such competencies as the ability to make optimal managerial decisions, the ability to manage a team, the ability to work in a team, the ability to organize and self-study, the ability to improve the level of own professional competence, the ability to apply legal acts, implement the norms of material and procedural law in professional activities, the ability to legally correctly qualify facts and circumstances.[2]

Next, we propose that students submit their findings (analyzed information) in the form of an analytical table and defend the result in front of colleagues in the study group.

[2] Order of the Russian Ministry of Science dated 14.12.2010 N 1763 (Ed. May 31, 2011) "On the approval and introduction of the federal state educational standard of higher professional education in the direction of training 030900 Law (qualification (degree) Master's)"; Order of the Russian Ministry of Science dated 01.12.2016 N 1511 (Ed. January 11, 2018) "On the approval of the federal state educational standard of higher education in the direction of training 40.03.01 Law (bachelor's level)". Consultant Plus Information and Search System.

Examples of analytical tables.
Analytical table 1.
Task 1. Make a table on the topic: "Vindication lawsuit." The table is based on an analysis of 4–5 court rulings.

Court name, date, No	Plaintiff/defendant	The subject of the lawsuit	The grounds of the lawsuit

Note: Based on the court papers analyzed, establish:

1. grounds for a vindication claim;
2. conditions for the satisfaction of the claim;
3. evidence under study.

Analytical table 2.
Task 2. Make a table on the topic: "Compensation for losses upon elimination of obstacles in the exercise of property rights." The table is based on an analysis of 2–3 court rulings.

Court name, date, No	Plaintiff/defendant	The subject of the lawsuit	The grounds of the lawsuit

Note: Based on the court papers analyzed, establish:

1. grounds for filing a negatory claim;
2. conditions for satisfying a negatory claim;
3. evidence under study.

In addition to the educational process, teachers of the department contribute to the development and implementation of student projects and during the course of their practice.[3] The university has the right to

---

[3] Dadayan E. V., Storozheva A. N. To the question of the implementation of competence project activities in the educational practice of students in the field of law/Modeling

determine independently specific types of practices, their goals, objectives, programs and forms of reporting. For example, we are already developing recommendations for each student for completing an individual assignment. In these recommendations, depending on the chosen place of internship, we offer students different options for project activities and supporting documents. It can be the development of drafts of the founding documents of the legal entity, templates of documents, etc. Of course, we understand and are aware that not every student is ready to independently and creatively implement his task (develop a project) and immediately start independent work in practice. It seems that any activity requires experience and repetition of a particular procedure, sometimes even working according to a template and a model. However, this fact in no way diminishes the fact that we, as teachers, were unable to teach the student to work, design, and create. We believe that we have taught the student, first of all, the algorithm of how to do it and directed, and sometimes motivated the learner to manifest independence by performing project work, showed that working following a template or a model should take into account all the actual circumstances for making a competent and balanced decision. In short, we have taught not to be afraid of independence and the manifestation of initiative. Although the results are not always positive.

The analysis of the project works shows whether the learner is prepared for independent practical work or whether there are any gaps in theoretical preparation that require adjustments in the formation of project tasks and establishing the level of their complexity. It also reveals the negatives, weaknesses and deficiencies that need to be upgraded, improved and addressed.

Identified inconsistencies:

1. Not all students are ready to perform project work, including independent work and teamwork.
2. Many students follow the pattern (template), not noticing and sometimes not realizing that in a given situation it is necessary to show a total of knowledge and to deviate from the example.

and design in the educational environment: a collection of materials of V All-Russian (with international participation) scientific, practical, and methodological conference for scientific educational community/Ed. I. A. Artemyev, V. O. Belevtsova, N. D. Dudina.—M.: GBPOU Moscow State Educational Complex, 2020. 114–116.

3. Many projects are submitted outside the deadline.
4. Many projects have a formal, far from creative, approach to execution.

This is illustrated later in Fig. 1.

During the academic year (2019–2020), students were asked to perform 15 civil law projects. The project work was carried out by 6 subgroups (mini-groups). Without violations or virtually without violating the deadlines (or violation of deadlines was of the maximum allowable nature) performed 50% (exactly half) of subgroups. As for the quality of the submitted works, 66% of subgroups crossed the three-point threshold for the quality of work. 33% of subgroups failed or mishandled (showed a formal approach) their project work.

As project assignments, we offered tasks for the search and analysis of court rulings, independent compilation of legal documents, as well as preparation of a research project (research) on the application of separate norms of the Civil Code of the Russian Federation.

To complete this task, the students had to analyze and establish:

1. Essence (relevance, novelty) of the problem;

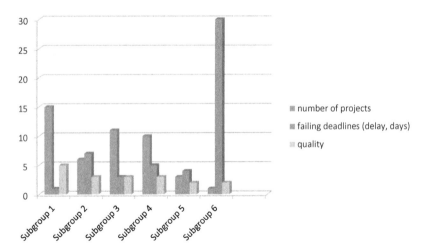

Fig. 1 Analysis of the quality of performed projects by the subgroups of students

PROJECT ACTIVITIES AS ONE OF THE TOOLS ...   377

2. How this problem is solved in theory (to analyze the views of scientists studying the subject);
3. How this problem is addressed in practice (confirmed by examples of court rulings);
4. Whether this problem exists in the legislation of foreign states (if so, how this problem was solved by a foreign legislator), on the example of 3–5 states;
5. Conclusion (own opinion, recommendations, proposals).

We would like to note that, despite the negative ones available, and we believe that these are workable and can be eliminated, in most cases the project activity gives its positive results and is one of the effective tools for assessing the quality of the future graduates, their compliance with modern requirements and relevance for the needs of society and potential employer.

We annually interview graduates of the Department of Civil Law on many issues. One such question is: "What forms (educational technologies) in practical activities do you remember and how do you think they will affect your future life prospects (employment)?".

We interviewed 275 graduates (during 2018, 2017, 2016) (Table 2).

The analysis shows that 91% of students support traditional practice (question–answer), 2% consider such educational technology optional, 7%

Table 2   Graduate survey results

Forms of training	Gained experience, see further prospects (employment, admission to master's degree, etc.)	Such forms are not mandatory, it was enough to practice in the traditional form	The form of choice of the type of educational technology is the prerogative of the teacher (I am not fit to give an assessment)
Traditional practice (question–answer)	250	5	20
Solving problems	188	17	70
Project activities	230	10	35
Making mini-cases, solving tests	90	85	100
Discussion	147	30	98

of respondents believe that the choice of educational technology is the prerogative of the teacher. As for problem solving, 68% of respondents see the prospects of this form of practice organization. In this analysis, we are undoubtedly most interested in how graduates evaluated the project activity and we see that 84% of graduates understand that project activity is important not only in the study of specific disciplines, but also in further practical activities.

Nevertheless, it should be noted that the majority of respondents still prefer traditional practice (question–answer) without any initiative and activity. But this does not mean that the students were not involved in the project activities, but only shows the not quite successful result of such activities, which in no way is an obstacle to their further professional development.

For example, over the past 3–5 years, graduates of the Department of Civil Law and Process of the Law Institute of Krasnoyarsk SAU have been successfully employed in various law enforcement organizations and institutions. We will list the data on the employment of graduates in the Court of Arbitration of the Krasnoyarsk Region as of April 20, 2020 (15 people became assistant judges and 5 people judges). Here we see, among other things, our merit in teaching students to learn. Through the application of various educational technologies, including the project work, students have formed not only an individual educational trajectory, but above all, have understood (revealed) their potential, which allowed many to facilitate their career growth and to gain self-confidence.

4 Conclusions/Recommendations

Summing up our research, we can draw the following conclusions:

1. It appears that the project is a set of interconnected activities aimed at obtaining unique results in the context of the implementation of a professional educational program in the field of law, and project activities are activities related to the initiation, preparation, implementation and completion of projects. This is, first of all, an independent educational and cognitive activity of students, aimed at obtaining scientific knowledge, which has signs of novelty and theoretical and/or practical significance.

2. Project activities are one of the tools to unlock the potential of the learner. The application of well-defined criteria and the most objective procedures for evaluating student projects always corresponds to the planned results of training, the goals of the major and current goal (current, intermediate or final control of students' knowledge). Performing project work, especially group work, requires a certain concentration from learners, the ability to find common ground, smooth out conflicts, etc. This is undoubtedly an effective educational technology, which is one of the tools for identifying the potential of the student.
3. An inadequate, according to the teacher, result of the project activity is also a result that will not pass without a trace for the student. At least the students, although they will not find the right answer to the questions posed by the teacher, will nevertheless try to work independently, will get additional knowledge on the subject studied, will think about the effective organization of their working time.
4. Forms of project presentation can be not only speakers and defense of the project at the seminar (including at a research seminar with the participation of invited practitioners), but also further publication of theses, articles, speeches at scientific conferences, participation in the competitions, as well as writing coursework on problems (materials collected in the process of writing project work) solved as a result of the project.
5. The teacher is not a bystander to the process of project creation by students. The main task of the teacher is to accompany the learner (from setting the task to the final result) to ensure the creation of an understandable and accessible algorithm (mechanism) of the self-studying activity of the learner and try to involve more students in the process.

REFERENCES

Barabanova, S. V., Peshkova (Belogoirtseva), H. V., Baranov, I. V., Menkenov, A. V., Selezneva, A. H., Chernus, N. Yu, Belyaev, M. A., Zenkov, M. Yu, & Kotukhov, S. A. (2019). *Comment on the Federal Law of December 29, 2012 No 273-FZ*. "On Education in the Russian Federation" (itemized)/ Prepared for the System Consultant Plus.

380 A. STOROZHEVA AND E. DADAYAN

Belova, T. G. (2008). *Research and project activities of students in modern education* (pp. 76–82). Bulletin of the A. I. Herzen Russian State Teachers' University.

Gorokhova, S. S. (2019). On the legislative provision of improving the professional standardization of specialists in the financial market. *Russian Justice, 9*, 56–59.

Grudtsina, L. Yu., Spector, A. A., & Tumanov, E. V. (2009). *Scientific and practical commentary on the Federal Law of July 24, 2007 No. 209-FZ. "On the development of small and medium-sized enterprises in the Russian Federation" (itemized).* "YURCOMPANY".

Kazun, A. P., & Pastukhova, L. S. (2018). Practices of the application of the project method of training: Experience of different countries. *Education and science, 20*(2).

Letyagina, E., Storozheva, A., & Dadayan, E. (2020). *Self-examination as the main mechanism that universities use to assess the quality of implementation of educational programs: Modern requirements.* ICEST 2020 International Conference on Economic and Social Trends for Sustainability of Modern Society.

Pakhomova, N. Yu. (2005). The method of educational project in an educational institution: M.:ARCTI.

Penkovskikh, E. A. (2010). Project method in domestic and foreign teaching theory and practice. *Education Issues.* Issue 4.

Retivykh, M. V. (2008). Formation and development of the project method in the national and foreign pedagogical theory and practice. *Herald of the Bryansk State University, 1*, 24–31.

Vokhmentseva, E. A. (2011). *Project activities of students as a means of forming key competences.* Topical tasks of pedagogy: Materials of I International Scientific Conference (Chita, December 2011). Chita: Young Scientist Publishing House, pp. 58–65. https://moluch.ru/conf/ped/archive/20/1390/. Accessed May 3, 2020.

Yakovleva, N. F. (2014). *Project activities in the educational institution [Electronic Resource]: A textbook* (2nd ed., 144p.). Ster. - M.: FLINTA.

Zernov, V. A., Kozhanov, T. A., Svistunov, A. A., Simonyan, K. V., & Tyrtyshny, A. A. (2019). Project approach to the formation of pedagogical and legal competences among law students. *Constitutional and Municipal Law, 9*, 11–17.

Socio-Economic Aspects of Digital Maturity Management of HR-System in Transport Company

Tatiana V. Aleksashina[ID]*, Victoria I. Smagina*[ID]*, and Karina V. Fionova*

1 Introduction

According to the McKinsey Global Institute, the growth process of the digital economy will be comparable in scale to the industrial revolution of the eighteenth-nineteenth centuries, which radically changed the world and updated the development paradigm itself. In 2017, the digital revolution entered a decisive phase - every second inhabitant of the Earth connected to the Internet. The economic effect of digitalization for the Russian economy can increase the country's GDP by 4.1–8.9 trillion rubles by 2025 (McKinsey Digital Russia: a new reality, 2017).

The implementation of the state program "Digital Economy in Russia" suggests development are the following: markets and spheres of activity, platforms and technologies, the environment (conditions) for the effective interaction between market entities and activities (SAP, 2019). The dominant elements in the development of manufacturing companies are

---

T. V. Aleksashina (✉) · V. I. Smagina · K. V. Fionova
Russian University of Transport, Moscow, Russia

© The Author(s), under exclusive license to Springer Nature Switzerland AG 2021
E. G. Popkova and B. S. Sergi (eds.), *Economic Issues of Social Entrepreneurship,*
https://doi.org/10.1007/978-3-030-77291-8_35

381

the use of large amounts of data, information and communication technologies (ICT), artificial intelligence, cloud technology, the Internet of things, energy storage technology (PWC, 2019).

According to the analytical report "Digital Transformation in Russia" prepared by kmda.pro, in 2018 the transport sector is "catching up" in this direction. The main objective of the development of the transport industry involves the formation of a single transport space in Russia based on the balanced development of an efficient transport infrastructure and is associated with the transition to the "leaders" quadrant (KMNDA.RPO: Digital transformation in Russia, 2018).

Research in the field of digital transformation of the personnel management system is relatively young. E. Kostenko (2018) considers the reasons for the transformation of approaches and technologies of personnel management in the digitalization era, I. Epishkin and D. Osipov (2019) highlight HR digitalization trends taking into account the impact of the transformation of the business environment. If we talk about digital maturity, then this is the state in which the digital transformation of the organization reaches the limit, i.e. the company is in a permanent state of optimizing the production and economic system for digital solutions (Babynina, 2018). It is noteworthy that as a guideline for self-assessment of the digital maturity of the company, the organizational culture and personnel (Galeva, 2019).

The active phase of the application and development of digital technologies in activities on a par with telecommunication companies and the banking sector is demonstrated by railway transport and the key player for this sector - Russian Railways. According to expert estimates, the economic effect of digital transformation for the company will be up to 150 billion rubles, and for the country's economy and partners, positive externalities will range from 400 to 500 billion rubles (Cnews, 2019). The scope of the digital transformation of Russian Railways is impressive: the Strategy provides for the implementation of more than 50 projects focused on the application of advanced domestic innovative developments based on digital technologies such as storage and management of "big" data, distributed registries, industrial Internet of Things, quantum computing and others.

However, these estimates provide only a fragment description of the situation. In the context of the digital transformation of the company, a large amount of work falls on human resources (HR) specialists (50% of the labor operations are related to information), which provide integration of data from various internal sources and carry out a huge amount of work on primary data processing (Popov et al., 2019). The implementation of the digitalization process is primarily associated with the work of the personnel unit. Its aim is to transform the model of interaction with the "internal" client and to organize a convenient digital environment for employees. Highlight features of digitalization in personnel management system as a stand-alone unit promotes the development of digital thinking throughout the company, carrying out work for a cultural shift in the direction of cooperation within the organization and is a "pioneer" in the use fundamentally new effective and comfortable tools based on the best digital solutions. This can ensure the high quality of HR processes and their significant contribution in business performance indicators.

Therefore, the scientific task of the article is connected with the analysis of the uniformity of digital transformation in personnel management within the enterprise and the determination of break points. Thus, the study expands the following research areas:

1. Stages of digital maturity of the personnel management system and their characteristics
2. Features of manifestation and the degree of "digital" load for HR specialists in the conditions of digital transformation of personnel management functions
3. Factors contributing to the digital workload of human resources in Russian Railways.

2 Materials and Method

The methods used in this study include formal and informal surveys, surveys and studies of the transport industry by analyzing statistical reports, observing, comparing, and ranking.

The questionnaire developed by the authors presents questions related to the characteristics and stages of the digital maturity of the enterprise personnel management system:

- The level of knowledge and understanding of strategic objectives and corporate values;
- Level of knowledge of digital competencies;

384 T. V. ALEKSASHINA ET AL.

- The level of "digital" load on employees involved in the implementation of the concept of digitalization of personnel management functions; and
- The depth of digitalization in the organization.

Uniformity Analysis Implementation of the digital personnel management transformation within the enterprise is based on the identification and determination of the digital maturity stages in the enterprise personnel management system (Table 1). The initial selection of the criteria is based on the digitalization models described above, and then adjusted through unfinished surveys of HR managers of the studied organization.

The study involved 40 employees of the company. About 50% of respondents aged 35 to 44 years with work experience of 10 years or more – 59%. The main characteristics of the sample are presented in Table 2.

For the purposes of the study, the survey was conducted among employees of the personnel department of the Company, which, although the process model does not apply to the main business processes, is at the same time present in all structural divisions and often takes on the function of relaying information from higher hierarchical levels of management.

3 RESULTS

More than 80% of respondents are familiar with the Digital Transformation Strategy of Russian Railways 2025, 25% of respondents have a knowledge and understanding of strategic goals and corporate values that meet expectations, 55% understand and is working according to this document. More than 50% of all respondents have digital competencies, and the majority of them (75%) hold leadership positions. It is worth noting that there is a significant discrepancy in the stages of digitalization, depending on the position held. In more detail, the ratio of understanding of digitalization goals and the level of digital competences in the context of employee categories is presented in Table 3.

The distribution of respondents' opinions related to the characterization of personnel business processes in the context of determining the digital maturity of the enterprise personnel management system is presented in Fig. 1.

SOCIO-ECONOMIC ASPECTS OF DIGITAL MATURITY ...   385

Table 1   The stages of the digital transformation of personnel management within the enterprise

Criteria	Stage of chaotic development	Stage of active development	Proactive Development Stage	Integrated stage development
Knowledge and understanding of strategic attitudes and corporate values	Does not meet expectations	Improvement required	Meets Expectations	Exceeds Expectations
Characteristics of HR business processes	Not structured, no automation	Partially Automated and Standardized	Fully Automated, Standardized	Continuous automation involves maximum simplification and interconnection of personnel processes
Data Storage Features	On paper	In electronic form with duplication on paper, several data warehouses	The transition to electronic document management has been completed, but several local databases are possible	Unified cloud data storage throughout the organization, the use of blockchain technology
Digital competency	Level of understanding, level of denial	A basic level	Middle level	Strong level
Current digital technology	Missing or unsystematic application of separate software products with duplication in paper	Applications of many different systems for different processes	Single entry point, single platform, mobile access from any device	Unified interface in many applications, VR/AR and chat bots
Information load of employees	Perception at the level of acceptable standards	Perception is above the maximum permissible norms, digital overload is characteristic	Perception at the level of maximum permissible standards, a decrease in the digital load is characteristic	Perception at the level of acceptable standards

(continued)

386   T. V. ALEKSASHINA ET AL.

Table 1 (continued)

Criteria	Stage of chaotic development	Stage of active development	Proactive Development Stage	Integrated stage development
Digitalization depth	Realization of the creative potential of individual leaders	At the level of t op-management	At all levels of management	The digitalization process everywhere includes leaders at all levels as well as performers

Source Author's compilation based on Deloitte (2018), McKinsey (2017), Otkritie Bank (2019), and Urban Sky Digital (2017)

Table 2 The main characteristics of the sample

Specifications	%	Specifications	%
Age groups		*Work experience in the company*	
Under 24 years old	10	Less than 1 year	12.5
25–34 years old	25	1 to 5 years	12.5
35–44 years old	45	5 to 10 years	32.5
45–55 years old	17.5	10 to 15 years	17.5
More than 55 years old	2.5	More than 15 years	25.0
Gender			
Male	15		
Female	85		
Categories of respondents			%
HR/HR Specialist			50
Head of Sector/HR Department			35
Head of Human Resources, Deputy Head of the Linear Enterprise for Social and Personnel Issues			15

Source Author's compilation

In the 1st place, HR business processes are characterized by regulation of the main functional blocks and concentration of decision-making at the top level. To a lesser extent, but there is a transition to a service model of personnel management. If we compare the result with the theoretical approaches, research of other scientists (Urban Sky Digital, 2017), and synchronize the results with the types of digital maturity, in this study it is impossible to unambiguously distinguish the stage of "digital" maturity of the company.

SOCIO-ECONOMIC ASPECTS OF DIGITAL MATURITY ... 387

Table 3 Understanding the goals of digitalization and ownership of digital competencies by employee category

	HR/HR Specialist (%)	Head of Sector/HR Department (%)	Head of Human Resources, Deputy Head of the Linear Enterprise for Social and Personnel Issues (%)
Knowledge and understanding of strategic attitudes and corporate values			
Does not meet expectations	20	29	0
Improvement required	65	57	17
Meets Expectations	10	14	33
Exceeds Expectations	5	0	50
Digital competency			
Level of understanding	80	29	0
A basic level	5	43	67
Middle level	10	7	17
Strong level	5	21	17

Source Author's compilation

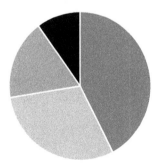

- regulation of the main functional blocks of the personnel management system, concentration of decision-making at the top level

- HR processes are connected and standardized, there is a transition to a service model of personnel management

- HR business processes are automated and integrated among themselves into a single system, roadmaps for the implementation of HR initiatives

- personnel processes are not formalized and not structured, development occurs mainly due to the realization of the creative potential of individual informal leaders

Fig. 1 Characterization of the personnel business processes of the Company (*Source* Author's compilation)

The increasing trend of the load volume as a part of the digital transformation concept of personnel management was noted by 87.5% of the employees surveyed. Respondents associated the "digital" overload with the following characteristics (Table 4), which are worth considering in more detail by category of respondents.

We see on Table 4 that a high level of digital "overload" is observed at all levels considered in the company, however, the leaders of HR sectors and departments have the highest values, and not at a higher level of management. In part, this is the result of unequal manifestations of digitalization processes at various personnel levels. At the same time, specialists of the functional subsystem of personnel management, being at a lower stage of digitalization, have not had experience the digital "overload" yet on themselves.

The study of the factors associated with the digital workload in professional activities among the personnel involved in the digitalization of the personnel management of the company gave the following results. The ranking list of the respondent's election on this issue is in Table 5.

It is characteristic of the maximum positive inequality (e.g. human error minimization or the decline in personal productivity of labor) that respondents do not often have digital factors in the work process, and a negative deviation together with the negative consequence of the factor

Table 4 Characteristics of "digital" overload by employee category

Digital overload features	Distribution of respondents' answers by category		
	HR Specialist (%)	Head of Sector/HR Department (%)	Head of Human Resources, Deputy Head of the Linear Enterprise for Social and Personnel Issues (%)
Constant "inclusion" in the workflow (24 × 7 mode)	65	92.9	83.3
More information noise and distractions	65	57.1	50
Arithmetic mean	65	75	67

Source Author's compilation based on E. Diener et al. (2020) and D. Chen and Z. Wang (2014)

Table 5 Factors associated with digitalization and the frequency of its occurrence in the workplace

	Factors associated with digitalization (%)	Often occur in the workplace (%)	Inequality (%)
Duplication of information, for example, the need for combined accounting on paper and in an automated system	83	85	−3
Simplification of the procedures	70	70	0
Constant "inclusion" in the workflow	68	80	−13
Many automated control systems that are not integrated into a common information system	65	70	−5
Human error minimization	65	55	10
Simplicity and accuracy of information	63	60	3
Large general unstructured data, for example, individual nonalgorithmic requests from users	63	68	−5
Many communication channels	60	55	5
Long process of obtaining information and bureaucratization of processes	60	75	−15
Enhanced planning and control	58	63	−5
Lack of necessary programs and applications	55	50	5
There are no clear instructions for completing the task	55	50	5

(continued)

Table 5 (continued)

	Factors associated with digitalization (%)	Often occur in the workplace (%)	Inequality (%)
The increase in organizational gaps (bottlenecks in the activities of structural units)	53	53	0
Manifestation of the "tired of changes/innovations" behavior	53	63	−10
Lack of vision and understanding of digitalization processes in the company at my level	48	50	−3
The decline in personal productivity of labor	48	33	15
Weak interaction between departments	45	55	−10
Lack of data to complete tasks	43	53	−10
Frequent equipment breakdowns	38	40	−3
Tensions in the team	38	45	−8
Free time for more creative tasks	35	40	−5
The increasing likelihood of finding a new job	30	50	−20

Source Author's compilation based on E. Diener et al. (2020) and D. Chen and Z. Wang (2014)

indicates a risk factor for inhibiting the transition to a higher stage of the organization's digital maturity.

Respondents almost unanimously (83%) associate the process of digital transformation in the enterprise with duplication of information. 25% of repetitions from different recipients are observed, the situation is complicated by the need to maintain a combined workflow on paper and in an automated system.

Most of the parameters of the digital load are associated with information overload of employees, but to varying degrees, the largest gap is in the reduction of personal productivity. At the same time, 70% of respondents do not associate digital processes and the likelihood of finding a new job. This may be a hidden signal for the company of reduced employee loyalty and, as a result, manifest opportunistic behavior.

Thus, the uncertainty of digital transformation more relates to organizational and managerial barriers, and to a lesser extent, to social factor.

For the most part, three groups of indicators of digital personnel services are not in demand:

- Work in ACS (automatic control of employee movement and motivation)—60%;
- Work with a career portal—49%;
- Formation of HR-dashboards (HR-reporting)—41%.

As it turned out, access to these resources is not limited, but a number of experts do not see the need for them or there is no time to study them.

4 Conclusions

In the course of the study, we concluded that the implementation of the digital transformation of personnel management within the researched organization is unequal, primarily related to the uncertainty of requirements and expectations. A mismatch between the subjective assessment of the level of digital competencies and understanding of the strategic goals and objectives of digitalization in the organization.

The digital maturity level of HR business processes development is active; however, there are points of removable gaps in which the conditions for the uniformity of the digital transformation of personnel management within the enterprise are not violated.

The first break point is the level of the structural unit of the Russian Railways: among ordinary employees, there is often a lack of understanding of digitalization goals and specific requirements for skills. Inconsistency of the subjective level of competencies and understanding of the goals and objectives of digitalization in the organization at the linear level: some of the line managers are unfamiliar with the digital transformation strategy of the Company; however, 45% of them claim to have the required digital competencies. For comparison, at the level of directorates, knowledge of the strategy and compliance with competencies are fully implemented. Among specialists, the vast majority are not familiar with the strategy and do not see for themselves and do not understand the content of the required digital competencies, and there is no linear relationship with the experience and age on this issue (Table 3).

The opinion is refuted that managers are more involved in the processes of digital transformation of HR than ordinary employees who do not associate professional activity only with the fulfillment of tasks and assignments from managers (Table 4).

The second point of the gap is the spread across the elements of digital services: Formation of HR dashboards (HR reporting), Work on a career portal, Work in ACS (automation of management of employee movements and motivation). Some employees use these services with different frequencies, and some claim that they cannot accessed them at all (Table 6).

Table 6 The choice of digital personnel services by frequency of demand

Digital HR services	Share of respondents by frequency of demand		
	Often (once a week or more) (%)	Rarely (once a month or less) (%)	Never (%)
Work with the service portal	64	31	5
Use of ECDO (electronic document management)	87	10	3
Work in ACS (automatic control of employee movement and motivation)	12	28	60
Training on the electronic platform	33	62	5
Work with a career portal	13	38	49
Formation of HR-dashboards (HR-reporting)	33	26	41
Using automated staff assessment tools	49	28	23

Source Author's compilation

The main factors of digital overload in work are associated with duplication of business processes. There are practically no statements about equipment failures and the need for additional programs or applications, which can signal that the level of automation has been passed. The work with a large amount of non-algorithmic data and the presence of automated control systems that are not integrated into the general information system can be the main points of growth and opportunities for increasing the level of digital maturity in the Company. However, it is worth noting that it is necessary to explore the social factors within the organization. It signals, according to the staff, that digitalization cannot influence (the probability of searching for a new job, a manifestation of the behavior of "fatigue from changes / innovations" and lack of free time for more creative tasks), but may indicate a high level of burnout (which may require further evaluation as part of the additional study) (Table 5). In addition, to move to a higher level of digitalization of the personnel management system, careful examination of the identified organizational and structural features that employees often encounter is required: weak interaction between departments and a long process of obtaining information.

REFERENCES

JOURNAL ARTICLES

Chen, D., & Wang, Z. (2014). The effects of human resource attributions on employee outcomes during organizational change. *Social Behavior and Personality: An International Journal, 42*(9), 1431–1443 (13).

Diener, E., Thapa, S., & Tay, L. (2020). Positive emotions at work annual review of organizational psychology and organizational behavior. *Annual Reviews, 7,* 451–477.

Galeva, T. (2019). Digital maturity of an enterprise: Methods of assessment and management.*Bulletin of UGNTU. Science, Education, Economics. Series "Economics", 1*(27), 38–52.

Kostenko, E. P. (2018). Modern trends in personnel management: Domestic and foreign experience. *Journal of Economic Regulation* (Issues of Economic Regulation), (9/4), 107–123.

Popov, E. V., Semyachkov, K. A., & Moskalenko, Yu. A. (2019). Comparative evaluation of the digital potential of enterprises Management in Russia and abroad, (3), 70–75.

Conference Proceeding

Babynina, L. S. (2018). *Training for the digital economy. Lomonosov readings-2018. Section of Economic Sciences.* "Digital Economy: Man, Technology, Institutions": A collection of articles, 472–479.

Epishkin, I. A., & Osipov, D. V. (2019). Aspects of the use of digital- technology of personnel management during the period of digital transformation Digital transformation in the economy of the transport complex: Materials of the international scientific-practical conference, 117–122.

Internet Resources

CNEWS. (2019). *Approved the construction plan of the "digital railway" in Russia.* https://cnews.ru/news/top/2019-03-21_rzhd_poluchila_plan_s troitelstva_tsifrovoj_zheleznoj. Accessed March 15, 2020.

Deloitte. (2018). *Global human capital trends.* https://hctrendsapp.deloitte. com/. Accessed March 15, 2020.

KMDA.RPO. (2018). *Digital transformation in Russia analytical report based on the results of a survey of Russian companies.* https://drive.google.com/file/ d/1k9SpULwBFt_kwGyrw08F0ELI49nipFUw/view. Accessed March 15, 2020.

McKinsey. (2017). *Digital Russia: A new reality.* https://www.mckinsey.com/ ~/media/McKinsey/Locations/Europe%20and%20Middle%20East/Russia/ Our%20Insights/Digital%20Russia/Digital-Russia-report.ashx. Accessed March 15, 2020.

Otkritie Bank. (2019). *Small business digitalization index.* https://www.open. ru/about/press/44331. Accessed March 15, 2020.

PWC. (2019). *Overview of transport and logistics development trends in 2019.* https://www.pwc.ru/ru/transportation-logistics/assets/obzor-tenden tsiy-razvitiya-transporta-i-logistiki-v-2019.pdf. Accessed March 15, 2020.

SAP. (2019). *Digital transformation HR experience of Russian companies.* https://sapnow.ru/. Accessed March 15, 2020.

Urban Sky Digital. (2017). *Digital maturity audit.* https://www.urbansky.dig ital/. Accessed March 15, 2020.

Digital Economy Influence on the Formation of Staff Competencies

Anna E. Belolipetskaya⊙, Tatyana A. Golovina⊙,
Irina L. Avdeeva⊙, and Andrey V. Polyanin⊙

1 Introduction

The relevance of the work is created by the rapid development of the digital economy. According to GIV-25 forecast data, the digital economy is estimated at 23 trillion US dollars. By 2025 85% of world applications for companies will be stored in cloud platforms, 86% of multinational companies will implement artificial intelligence, and the share of big data will grow to 80% (McKinsey, 2017).

The rapidly growing volume of information determines the demand for artificial intelligence technologies and high-speed processing of big data.

The modern economy is embarking on a new innovative stage of development, and a person with his potential, knowledge, creative thinking and experience is becoming increasingly important. In the context of the development of the fourth scientific and technological revolution and global digitalization familiar processes are getting transformed and simplified (Keshelav et al., 2017). This happens in almost all areas of human life, including the management of human resources.

More and more global companies are rapidly introducing various models of digital personnel competencies in order to quickly adapt the

---

A. E. Belolipetskaya (✉) · T. A. Golovina · I. L. Avdeeva · A. V. Polyanin
Central Russian Institute of Management, Branch of RANEPA, Orel, Russia

© The Author(s), under exclusive license to Springer Nature
Switzerland AG 2021
E. G. Popkova and B. S. Sergi (eds.), *Economic Issues of Social Entrepreneurship,*
https://doi.org/10.1007/978-3-030-77291-8_36

company to a changing external environment. More competitive the company is better the company and personnel meet the requirements of the modern world.

Digitalization of business actively affects the knowledge, skills and abilities of HR managers, as the organizational tasks and processes are automated, and therefore the personnel is required to have more developed competencies in the field of digital technologies. The human resources departments are today no longer just an executor, but a kind of business partner who renders services to provide business with qualified personnel and to develop this personnel. Therefore, to maintain the work of HR departments, to minimize risks at all stages of the selection, training and development of employees, to build effective interaction with staff, new digital competencies are now urgently needed.

2 Materials and Method

A special contribution to the study of the digital economy, the formation of new technological structures, electronic business models, the introduction of digital technologies and the development of digitalization was made by the works of the following scientists and professional communities: Don Tapscott, Boston Consulting Group, International Bank for Reconstruction and Development.

Issues of increasing labor productivity, human resource management, challenges and risks in the development of the labor market are considered by Digital McKinsey specialists, foreign scientists F. W. Taylor, P. Drucker, leading scientists of the Laboratory of Economic Forecasting of the Russian Academy of Sciences.

In publications and scientific developments of foreign and Russian scientists and economists, the issue of forming a personnel competency model is mainly considered without studying the risks and prospects of digitalization processes and their impact on the activities of business structures.

The implementation of breakthrough technological projects in the digital economy creates a demand for specialists who possess a set of tough, flexible and special digital competencies.

3 Results

A "smart" society is being formed little by little, based on the values of human orientation, flexibility, creativity, and a new institutional environment favorable for the development of digitalization. The digital economy, which arose in the 80s of the twentieth century with the advent of personal computers, today transforms society, states, consumer behavior, innovative policies, organizations and their business models, and changes the role of a person in an organization and its profession (Kolosnitsyna, 2016).

The new economy is characterized by features that require other tools necessary for the sustainable development of organizations in this new economy (Vidas-Bubanja and Bubanja, 2016).

Under these conditions, the situation is that a small group of organizations that create 1–5% of GDP takes into account the challenges of the digital economy and transforms under new conditions, in contrast to them there are the a lot of organizations (70% of GDP) that do not respond correctly to digital changes and for this reason the lose step by step their competitiveness (*Apps run the world*).

The key, thanks to the development of information technologies, the advent of the Internet, and rapidly developing technological progress as a whole, has become the trend of economic transformation and digitalization, which entailed the transformation of all market players and their behavior (Domrachev et al., 2016).

The concept of "digital economy" was formulated in 1995 and according to various sources, the authorship is attributed to American scientist from the University of Massachusetts Nicholas Negroponte and/or Canadian specialist in business and consulting Danald Tapscott. The latter, however, describes it in his works as changing people's way of life under the influence of information and communication technologies (ICT). In his opinion, it is the snowballing growth of data communication that is the basis of the new economy, and it is itself the main engine of globalization (Tapscott, 1995).

When considering the position of the digital economy in the global economy as a whole, the following picture emerges (Fig. 1).

The core of the DE is the technology sector of the information technologies (ICT sector), which includes companies in the IT industry segment that produce hardware and software. Within the framework of this core, the economy allows the development of new business models,

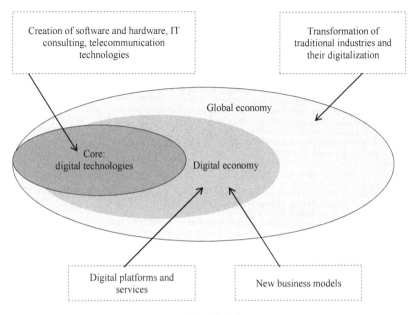

Fig. 1 Digital economy as part of the global economy

digital services, and platforms that make it possible to have new types of economic activities. However, since DE and traditional industries have a mutual influence on each other, which leads to global changes, its borders are blurred (*Digital-HR—A step into the future*).

The interaction of the digital economy and the global market economy is realized in two main directions. First of all, the digital economy, consisting of a combination of new industries, is a rapidly growing part of the global economy in its classical sense. The development of technology has led to the emergence of new markets (mobile communications, Internet services, online gaming industry, etc.)—this is a direct impact. Secondly, technology has changed the industries which have existed for hundreds of years, the activities of established economic entities (for example, the replacement of analog working mechanisms with digital ones). However, it is still early to talk about turning the economy into a digital one, since, according to experts, the digital economy will depend on the traditional one for another 10–15 years (Dobrynin, 2016).

In addition to the characteristics of the digital economy, some authors distinguish three of its levels (Fig. 2).

The digitalization, as well as the sustainability of an organization, has a complex characteristic: design thinking, new business models, production chains, etc.—everything is interconnected (Kupriyanovskiy et al., 2016). Hence it is logical to assume that this complex effect of digitalization factors puts the organization in the conditions of global transformation, encompassing its entire existence, from a business model and organizational structure to changing marketing tools with a view to its sustainable development (Samostroenko, 2017).

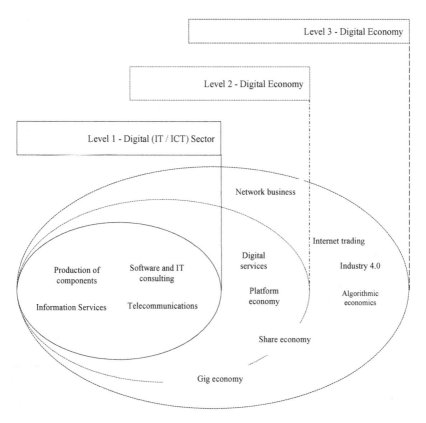

Fig. 2 Levels of the digital economy

In the context of globalization and the development of the digital economy, the pace of development of science, technics, technology is too high, but it is impossible to get greater benefits only at their expense. There is a need to constantly develop and use a more powerful human potential. It's from here that that the development of a humanistic paradigm came, which is based on the idea that a person is the main subject of the organization and a special management object that cannot be considered as a resource spent by the organization. The paradigm is confirmed by studies by foreign scientists, according to which, a 10 percent increase in the cost of professional staff training gives an increase in labor productivity of 8.5%, and the same increase in capital investments enhances the growth in labor productivity by only 3.8%. However, scientific thought achieved such results during almost a century, having gone through several stages of development.

The competencies are stable parts of the personality that can predetermine person's behavior in many situations, and they predict good or bad performance, measured using a specific criterion, for example, financial one.

The concept of "competency" is much deeper than "knowledge, skills," they underlie professional activity and have a direct impact on its success. To assess competencies, the levels of its development are distinguished and the specified level is assigned to a specific employee. In order to make the competencies assessment to affect positively the personnel management system, it is necessary to conduct an analysis from the point of view of certain principles, for example, exhaustibility, concreteness, modernity, etc.

Competencies are most often studied in the framework of the formation of the so-called competency model.

The competency model reflects the vision what need for human resources will appear in the future and which competencies need a greater attention from the management to carry out its development, and what is more the competency model helps to plan human resources and create a personnel reserve on a long-term basis.

Let us present in Fig. 3 the basic principles that must be followed when creating a competency model in a digital economy.

The development of trends and modern trends seems for many to be a threat in terms of replacing human labor with automated processes and robotization of activity (Bersin). The fears that the introduction of robots will lead to an increase in unemployment are clearly manifested

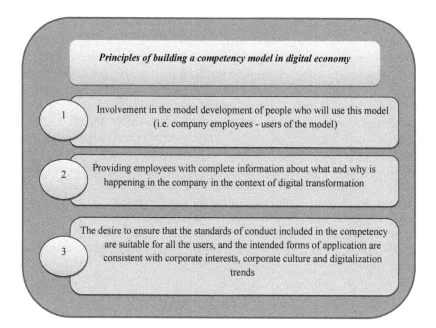

Fig. 3 The basic principles of the formation of a competency model in digital economy

in industry. The introduction of new technologies puts some workers in a vulnerable position. Robots are implemented in the automotive, electrical and electronic industries, as well as in mechanical engineering and metallurgy (Taylor, 2016). Not only heavy industry workers are facing the staffing cut, but also the employees in the financial sector, most of whose work consists in calculations based on ready-made formulas. So, for example, in the largest bank of Russia—Sberbank, 35% of decisions on granting loans are made by artificial intelligence and transaction features (Sizova and Khusyainov, 2017).

However, this experience is not so justified at the moment. According to the World Bank's 2019 World Development Report, new technologies create more jobs than they are crowding out (*Big Data analytics for dummies*). Of course, machines replace manual routine labor, thereby creating a problem for average skilled personnel who will have to compete for low-paying jobs (Loshkareva et al., 2011).

The positive point is the emergence of a large number of new professions related to management, or rather, to the training of autonomous systems based on artificial intelligence (robots and computers). In addition, existing trends and the transformation of work tasks lead to the evolution of existing skills and professions, preserving jobs. For example, in the recent past, the professions related to typing and editing text were transformed, specialists switched from typewriters to computers.

Nowadays the scientific and technological progress, eliminating the need for workers engaged in routine labor, creates jobs in new high-tech industries. A person becomes an active user of various gadgets, uses them for work, as well as for solving their domestic and financial issues. Technology require from employees to obtain new skills and competencies indispensable in the labor market. Therein the most promising employee in the labor market is one who combines different types of skills. The proof of these changes are the new requirements for professional qualifications.

4 Conclusion

Thus, the study determined that the influence of trends on all the spheres of human activity is irreversible. Ubiquitous digitalization leads to a transformation of society, which consists in improving the standard of living in general, automating routine processes, and developing the "Internet of Things". All this entails the need to develop cognitive abilities, ability to work with a large amount of data and continuously develop in order to "keep pace" with the changing world. At the same time, the future of labor activity is not completely clear for the reason that the technological development, on the one hand, contributes to the development of innovative production, and accordingly, the demand for professions related to IT technologies and analytics will increase. On the other hand, automation and robotization can replace a person in production, and employees who do not want to get new knowledge and adopt modern technologies in their current work may remain non-demanded. Taking into account the fact that future employment of the population is not precisely defined, states need to reconsider issues that impede job creation, while emphasizing the consideration of options for protecting vulnerable categories of citizens.

DIGITAL ECONOMY INFLUENCE ON THE FORMATION ... 403

Further research requires interlinking the formation of digital competencies of business entities and the strategy of digital transformation, gaps between the target and the existing level of digital maturity.

Acknowledgements The reported study was funded by RFBR, project number 19-310-90036.

References

Apps run the world [Electronic Resource]. Top 10 HCM software vendors and market forecast 2016–2021. https://www.appsruntheworld.com/top-10-hcm-software-vendors-and-market-forecast/

Bersin, J. *Predictions for 2016: A bold new world of talent, learning, leadership, and HR technology ahead* [Electronic Resource]. https://www.bersin.com/Practice/Detail.aspx?id=19445/

Big Data analytics for dummies. Alteryx Special Edition John Wiley & Sons, Inc. Copyright © 2013.

Digital-HR—A step into the future [Electronic Resource]. https://www.hr-director.ru/article/67046-digital-hr-shag-budushchee-18-m3/

Dobrynin, A. P. (2016). Digital economy—Various ways to the effective application of technologies (BIM, PLM, CAD, IOT, Smart City, BIG DATA and others). *International Journal of Open Information Technologies, 4*(1), 4–11.

Domrachev, A. A., Evtushenko, S. N., Kupriyanovskii, V. P., & Namiot, D. E. (2016). On innovative initiatives of the EEA member states in the field of building a global digital economy. *International Journal of Open Information Technologies, 9*, C.24–33.

Keshelav, A. V., Budanov, V. G., Rumyantsev, V. Yu., et al. (2017). *Introduction to the digital economy* (28 p.). VNIIGeosystem.

Kolosnitsyna, M. A. (2016). Total automation. *The Human Resources Times Magazine*, No. 30, pp. 11–15.

Kupriyanovskiy, V. P., Namiot, D. E., & Sinyagov, S. A. (2016). Cyber-physical systems as a basis of digital economy. *International Journal of Open Information Technologies, 4*(2), 18–25.

Loshkareva, E., Luksha, P., Ninenko, I., Smagin, I., & Sudakov, D. (2011). *Skills of the future. What you need to know and be able to in a new complex world* (314 p., p. 17).

McKinsey. (2017). *Digital Russia: A new reality* [Electronic Resource]. http://www.tadviser.ru/images/c/c2/Digital-Russia-report.pdf

Samostroenko, G. M. (2017). "Digital" inheritance as a factor in the development of entrepreneurship in the field of personal data protection / G.M.

Samostroenko, E.P. Sulima. *Central Russian Herald of Social Sciences*, 1(12), 252–258.

Sizova, I. L., & Khusyainov, T. M. (2017). Labor and employment in the digital economy: Problems of the Russian labor market. *Tomsk State University Journal. St. Petersburg un-that. Sociology*, T. 10(4), 376–396.

Tapscott, D. (1995). *The digital economy: Promise and Peril in the age of networked intelligence* (342p.). McGraw-Hill.

Taylor, E. (2016). Labor in the global digital economy: The cybertariat comes of age. *Radical Philosophy*, 60–62.

Vidas-Bubanja, M., & Bubanja, I. (2016). *The future of digital economy in SEE countries* (Case study: Croatia, Macedonia, Montenegro, Serbia, Bosnia and Herzegovina). 2016 39th International Convention on Information and Communication Technology, Electronics and Microelectronics (mipro) 2016, 1515–1520.

Electronic Services as Components of the Future Education

Tatiana E. Lebedeva⑩, Maria P. Prokhorova⑩,
Tatyana V. Krylova⑩, Svetlana A. Vinogradova⑩,
and Marina V. Lebedeva⑩

1 INTRODUCTION

Digitalization is the most important global trend of the last decade, covering all sectors and spheres of human life (Abdrakhmanova et al., 2019). Digital technology is recognized as a major competitive advantage for countries in the international arena (Gros, 2016). Digitalization in the modern sense is interpreted differently: as an objective process of changing analog technologies to digital, as a characteristic of a new social situation, as a new way of creating, transmitting, processing and storing information, as a new paradigm of thinking and transmitting information (Keshelava et al., 2017). The digitalization process involves

---

T. E. Lebedeva (✉) · M. P. Prokhorova · T. V. Krylova
Minin Nizhny Novgorod State Pedagogical University, Nizhny Novgorod, Russia

S. A. Vinogradova
The Russian Presidential Academy of Nation Economy and Public Administration (Dzerzhinsk Branch), Dzerzhinsk, Russia

M. V. Lebedeva
Linguistic University of Nizhny Novgorod, Nizhny Novgorod, Russia

© The Author(s), under exclusive license to Springer Nature Switzerland AG 2021
E. G. Popkova and B. S. Sergi (eds.), *Economic Issues of Social Entrepreneurship*,
https://doi.org/10.1007/978-3-030-77291-8_37

405

the widespread use of artificial intelligence technologies, neural networks, which allow creating information systems with analytical and predictive functions (Lebedeva et al., 2016). Through digital technology will automate most processes, and apply artificial intelligence to make decisions. The "digital economy" is also manifested in the spread of mobile, cognitive and cloud technologies, the "Internet of things" and "Big data" technologies (Keshelava et al., 2017).

In the educational system, digitalization has led to a fundamental change in the meaning of the technology of organization, and education. These changes are related to:

- Formation and development of full-fledged electronic educational environments in educational institutions using all the achievements of digital reality;
- Widespread open online courses in higher education and their integration into the educational process of universities; and
- Individualization of educational trajectories in accordance with the needs of students (Gruzdeva et al., 2020; Klochkova & Sadovnikova, 2019).

All this testifies to the relevance of studying the issue of student's digital skills in Russia. Since the topic of ownership and development of digital skills of students is a rather broad topic, in this paper we will focus only on the sociological aspect of the study on the use of the Internet by students of Russian universities.

2 MATERIALS AND METHOD

Currently, the issue of the component composition of the digital educational environment is debatable (Pons et al., 2015; Zawacki-Richter et al., 2019). Research of the electronic educational environment is devoted to the research of E. L. Vartanov, A. Yu. Uvarov, O. V. Bashirina and others. So in the research of O. V. Bashirina, Yu. G. Kotenkov, A. V. Kuznetsova, E. V. Ogorodnikov, I. V. Robert, T. N. Suvorova A. V. Uvarov, I. V. Chernov, the main role is given to subjective and methodological components, and the remaining components, such as software and hardware, are auxiliary (Safuanov et al., 2019).

E. V. Chernobay believes that the digital educational environment should include a value-semantic component, which is consisting of the goals and objectives of the organization in the project process in a digital educational environment, program-methodological (normative support for the functioning of the educational system), information and knowledge (the learner's competence complex), communication (interaction of subjects of the educational process in the digital educational environment [DEE]) and technological modern teaching aids in DEE (Petrova & Bondareva, 2019).

O. V. Bashirina notes that in the digital educational environment, such a unit as effectively corrective should be included that performs the functions of evaluating the diagnosis and correcting the student's educational trajectory (Vaganova et al., 2019, 2020b). The authors agree with the point of view of A. V. Uvarov who believes that the structure of the digital educational environment should include an information block that includes information systems, services, tools that are used to solve certain problems (Gruzdeva & Tukenova, 2019, Gruzdeva et al., 2020).

Services such as in Moodle, 1C has been used in universities for a long time and allow to track the changes of student and teacher population to determine their rating. Collaboration of participants of the educational process is facilitated by the information sharing service, which is available in the personal account for both students and teachers (Petrova & Bondareva, 2019; Shkunova et al., 2019).

In fact, there are a lot of electronic services and tools for creating a digital educational environment, and their saturation depends on the technical and financial capabilities of the educational organization Gruzdeva et al. (2018).

Purpose: to study the level of student's use of digital technologies and services in educational activities.

Research objectives:

- Explore the main directions of the use of Internet resources by educational organizations;
- To explore the digital technologies that students use to obtain education in Nizhny Novgorod and conduct a comparative analysis with data on the Russian Federation;
- Evaluate the relevance of digital services for students of the University of Minin; and
- Identify barriers to the use of digital technology for learning.

At the first stage, a survey was conducted using standard Google forms. The survey was conducted in December 2019–January 2020. The total number of respondents was 135 people. The survey mainly involved respondents aged 15–24 years (92.6% of the sample), living in Nizhny Novgorod (91.9%), the rest in the Nizhny Novgorod region, 63% of women and 37% of men, most of them work (indicated 87.4%) and 96.3% are currently studying.

At the second stage, conclusions were formulated regarding the degree of use of digital technologies and electronic services by students during their studies in Nizhny Novgorod and the national average.

3 RESULTS

At the beginning of the study, it was necessary to find out what digital technology opportunities were used by students in their education. For this purpose, several questions were formulated regarding the availability of a site and specialized services in the educational organization that automate the provision of educational services and process maintenance (educational, managerial, etc.). More detailed information is presented in Table 1. The data obtained during the survey allow us to conclude that all educational organizations have a functioning website (93.3% of respondents are aware of this), while in the country as a whole only 44% of organizations have a website. Educational organizations make extensive use of the Internet to provide educational services, in particular, to digitalize the educational process and remotely implement educational programs (in the form of electronic courses) (70.4%), provide corporate email (80%), and conduct events (webinars, video conferences) (27.4%), providing access to electronic databases, libraries (32.6%), tuition and related services (65.9%). Comparing the results with Russian indicators, we can conclude that there is an intensive development of electronic educational environments of educational organizations that represent a wide range of services using digital technologies—from presenting certificates to the complete automation of management processes and the formation of large databases. This once again confirms the great importance of the development of digital skills among students.

Next, we turn to the results of a study on the use of digital technologies and electronic services at the University of Minin.

First, we describe the main electronic services presented on the electronic platform of the University of Minin.

ELECTRONIC SERVICES AS COMPONENTS OF THE FUTURE EDUCATION 409

Table 1 Main directions in educational organizations

Internet usage directions	Response rate, in % (according to a sample of 135 young people, 2019–20 years) in the Nizhny Novgorod region	Response rate, in % (according to 2017 data RF, age 15–74 years) (Abdrakhmanova et al., 2019)
Using email	80	83.1
Search for information on the network	71.1	82.1
Educational services	70.4	*
Vocational training (refresher courses)	43	*
Video conferencing, webinars	27.4	38.1
Telephone conversations over the Internet/VoIP	11.9	36.6
Subscription to access electronic databases, and digital libraries for a fee	32.6	29.1
Online tuition and related services	65.9	*
Using cloud services	23.7	*
Difficult to answer (not studying)	3	*

*Research on these parameters was not conducted

So, acquaintance with the electronic services of the University of Minin begins with students at a time when they are still planning to become students.

The university has a service "Entrant", which allows to remotely submit documents, get an answer to a question from the admissions committee, choose your own profession from the many areas presented in the university using the EGE calculator, sign up for interesting master classes as part of career counseling events, vacation schools and much more.

Further, entering the first year, the student receives a username and password for access to your personal account and becomes a full member of the Electronic Information and Educational Environment (EIOS) of the University of Minin.

EIOS is represented by electronic services and electronic educational content of educational courses (Moodle, MOOK, Wiki, etc.).

From the personal account, the student gets access to services such as Portfolio, which is filled throughout the entire period of study (Vaganova et al., 2020a). This service includes such sections as: Autobiography, educational activities, research and project activities, personal and professional development, social, sports, cultural and creative activities.

Using the "Reference Window" service you can ask for necessary help and learn about its status.

For the convenience of students, the "Electronic Information Resources" service is available, which allows them to reserve the necessary literature both on the subscription and in the reading rooms of the University of Minin.

For students who study on a commercial basis, the service "Tuition Payment" is available, which will indicate the contract number, payment terms, availability of deposit, or penalty.

The service, which is relevant for students every day, is an electronic schedule.

Also, each student has an electronic test book, which is integrated with the student's curriculum, and the student always has the opportunity to see their learning outcomes and upcoming forms of final reporting events.

My account opens access to educational courses at the University of Minin, as mentioned earlier, electronic courses are presented on the Moodle platform, are used as didactic support for students in all disciplines, all profiles and areas of training.

So, for example, a course can be represented by lecture material, a number of tasks, test items, etc.

In addition to these courses, presented in Moodle, which students use constantly, there are courses, training/retraining—these are open MOOC courses. Students can also use the MOOC service to expand their professional competencies (Sinyagina & Artamonova, 2018).

A study among full-time students showed that 91% of students turn to electronic services every day, 80% of respondents indicate accessible and necessary content, 89% indicate relevant information; 67% of respondents complete assignments daily using Moodle e-courses.

The undisputed leader in the visit is the electronic schedule directory (100% note the convenience of finding a group, audience, teacher); 92% of respondents actively use the service of ordering the necessary information and 83% of the literature in the library. Results of demand by students of Minin University of electronic services during the month are presented in Fig. 1.

ELECTRONIC SERVICES AS COMPONENTS OF THE FUTURE EDUCATION

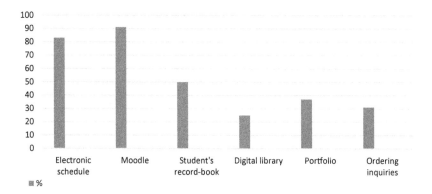

Fig. 1 Demand for electronic services for a month by students of the University of Minin

The data presented in Fig. 1 confirm the results of a questionnaire survey.

A study conducted among part-time students is also very interesting for analyzing and comparing the degree of use of individual services with full-time education.

So, 98% of respondents of correspondence courses use electronic services. This high rate is due to the fact that about 60% of students at the University of Minin live in the regional center and travel to the city, for example, for solving one organizational issue, it can take a sufficient amount of time. Therefore, they consider the electronic services to be the ideal solution not only to organizational issues but also to issues directly related to training. So the use of the Moodle electronic platform and electronic educational and methodological complexes provides an opportunity for part-time students to quickly perform the necessary tasks, to be in constant consultation mode with teachers, to quickly learn about the necessary educational information, everyone has the opportunity to ask a question using the chat or the training course forum.

If needed, then students can always turn to electronic and/or video lectures. In addition, part-time students, even living in different cities, have the opportunity to work in micro-groups, for example, when developing a training project. All of the above confirms the relevance and high demand for electronic services by students at the university.

412 T. E. LEBEDEVA ET AL.

Table 2 Factors constraining the use of the Internet in Education

Factors constraining Internet use	Response rate, in % (according to a sample of 135 young people, 2019–20 years) in the Nizhny Novgorod region
No need (unwillingness to use, no interest)	43
For security and privacy reasons	29.6
Lack of technical connectivity	13.3
High connection costs	9.6
Lack of internet skills	4.5

The authors were convinced that electronic services are popular with students of the Minin University, however, there are always those who are negative about the process of digitalization in education and turn to these technologies because of necessity only. Therefore, at the end of the study, the authors were interested in obstacles to the use of digital technologies for learning, and the results are presented in Table 2.

Thus, the most important factors constraining students' use of the Internet are lack of interest in educational services (43%), security and privacy concerns (29.6%), and lack of skills to work online (only 4.5%).

This indicates the need to clarify the relevance and feasibility of using digital technologies in education and compliance with security protocols when using them.

4 CONCLUSION

Our study allows us to conclude that digitalization is already firmly entrenched in modern education. University students actively use all kinds of electronic services, which greatly simplify not only the solution of organizational issues, but also optimize educational activities. Education is becoming more flexible, remote, and mass.

The results of the survey suggest that:

- Students make extensive use of the capabilities of digital technology and the Internet for learning, and this trend of digitalization of all processes will only intensify;

- Educational organizations are actively developing electronic learning environments and electronic services that automate the educational process;
- Most students are ready for distance learning with the support of a course manager; and
- Despite the fact that the detected level of use of electronic services by students is higher than the national average, it is necessary to diagnose and monitor the adequacy of this level.

The prospects of this study are to clarify the capabilities of various educational technologies that provide the greatest efficiency in digital education.

REFERENCES

Abdrakhmanova, G. I., et al. (2019). *Digital economy: 2019: A brief statistical digest.* HSE.

Gros, A. (2016). The design of smart educational environments. *Smart Learning Environments, 3,* 15. https://doi.org/10.1186/s40561-016-0039-x

Gruzdeva, M. L., Smirnova, Zh. V., & Tukenova, N. I. (2018). The use of Internet services in teaching technology. *Vestnik of Minin University, 6*(1) (22), 8.

Gruzdeva, M. L., & Tukenova, N. I. (2019). Analysis of the current state of research and development in the field of building information and educational environments of higher educational institutions. *Vestnik of Minin University, 7*(2), 1.

Gruzdeva, M. L., Vaganova, O. I., Kaznacheeva, S. N., Bystrova, N. V., & Chanchina, A. V. (2020). Modern educational technologies in professional education. *Lecture Notes in Networks and Systems, 73,* 1097–1103.

Keshelava, A. B., Budanov, V. G., & Rumyantsev, V. Yu. (2017). *Introduction to the digital economy.* VNII Geosystem, 28 p. http://spkurdyumov.ru/upl oads/2017/07/vvedenie-v-cifrovuyu-ekonomiku-na-poroge-cifrovogo-bud ushhego.pdf. Accessed 30 November 2019.

Klochkova, E. N., & Sadovnikova, N. A. (2019). Transformation of education in the context of digitalization. *Open Education, 23*(4), 13–23.

Lebedeva, T. E., Okhotnikova, N. V., & Potapova, E. A. (2016). The electronic educational environment of the university: Requirements, opportunities, experience and prospects of use. *World of Science, 4*(2), 22.

Petrova, N. P., & Bondareva, G. A. (2019). Digitalization and digital technologies in education. *World of Science, Culture, Education, 5*(78), 353–355. https://doi.org/10.24411/1991-5497-2019-00138

Pons, P., Catala, A., & Jaen, J. (2015). Customizing smart environments: A tabletop approach. *Journal of Ambient Intelligence and Smart Environments, 7*(4), 511–533.

Safuanov, R. M., Lehmus, M. Yu., & Kolganov, E. A. (2019). Digitalization of the education system. *Vestnik UGNTU. Science, Education, Economics. Series: Economics, 2,* 108–112. https://doi.org/10.17122/2541-8904-2019-2-28-108-113

Shkunova, A. A., Prokhorova, M. P., Labazova, A. V., Belousova, K. V., & Bulganina, A. E. (2019). Implementation of blended learning technology using LMS MOODLE. *Innovative Economics. Prospects for Development and Improvement, 2*(36), 108–115.

Sinyagina, NYu., & Artamonova, E. G. (2018). Digitalization of education: Determining priorities. *Personality Education, 3,* 10.

The Global Competitiveness Report 2018. https://www.classcentral.com/report/mooc-stats-2018. Accessed 30 November 2019.

The OECD handbook for innovative learning environments, OECD. Publishing Paris 2017. https://www.oecd.org/education/the-oecd-handbook-for-innovative-learning-environments-9789264277274-en.htm. Accessed 18 November 2019.

Vaganova, O. I., Bulaeva, M. N., Meteleva, L. A., Popkova, A. A., & Vezetiu, E. V. (2020a). Portfolio as an educational technology in the educational process of a university. *Amazonia Investiga, 9*(25), 356–361.

Vaganova, O. I., Rudenko, I. V., Lapshova, A. V., Bulaeva, M. N., & Popkova, A. A. (2020b). Psychological and pedagogical foundations for interaction technologies implementation at the university. *Amazonia Investiga, 9*(25), 362–368.

Vaganova, O. I., Lebedeva, T. E., Prokhorova, M. P., Smirnova, Zh. V., & Shkunova, A. A. (2019). Pedagogical support of the educational and information environment. *Espacios, 40*(2), 21–28.

Zawacki-Richter, O., Marín, V. I., Bond, M., et al. (2019). Systematic review of research on artificial intelligence applications in higher education—Where are the educators? *International Journal of Education Technology in High Education, 16,* 39. https://doi.org/10.1186/s41239-019-0171-0/

Theoretical and Methodological Foundations of the Research Modernization Processes in Traditional Societies as an Integral Part of Ensuring National Security

Andrey I. Gorelikov

1 Introduction

With the change in the country sociopolitical system, the idea of the functions of historical science, its theoretical and methodological aspects began to change. The formation of the new Russia is marked by the formation of the concept of state national security. The National security strategy of the Russian Federation of 2009 and 2015 as well as the Federal law "On security" of 2010 states that one of the main tasks of national security in modern Russia is to protect, create conditions for observance and apply public relations, as stipulated in the Constitution of the Russian Federation (ConsultantPlus, 2014, 2015, 2020).

National security means the condition of stable development of the individual, society and the state, guaranteed implementation and protection of the interests of the Russian Federation. An important conclusion is made that a successful solution to ensuring national security requires a comprehensive approach, development of basic provisions of the theory

---

A. I. Gorelikov (✉)
Komsomolsk-na-Amure State University, Komsomolsk-on-Amur, Russia

© The Author(s), under exclusive license to Springer Nature
Switzerland AG 2021
E. G. Popkova and B. S. Sergi (eds.), *Economic Issues of Social Entrepreneurship*,
https://doi.org/10.1007/978-3-030-77291-8_38

of national security, and search for effective ways to assess the level of national security of the Russian state.

Considering the process of searching for theoretical and methodological approaches in Russian historical science, academician Kovalchenko (1995) paid attention to the fact that with the change in the socioeconomic and ideological situation, issues of methodology and theory of history have become extremely relevant. He pointed out the need to review many theoretical and methodological aspects of formation theory.

The analysis of numerous scientific literature shows that the works of specialists dealing with the problem of national security focus on the disclosure of economic, political, social, environmental and other factors that pose threats to national security (Artyomov et al., 2005).

In the article, the author identifies ideological and methodological issues for building a view on ensuring national security.

2   MATERIALS AND METHOD

A very important aspect of the methodological situation was the problem of choosing explanatory models of the historical process. Instead of the prevailed in the Soviet historical science Marxist theory there were proposed civilization, modernization and other theories.

In the course of the research, the author has widely applied provisions of the concept of sustainable development and basic principles of improving the system of ensuring national security. Relying on the doctrinal developments of the theory of modernization made it possible to sufficiently present the overall picture of national security provision at the transition stage of the indigenous small-numbered peoples of the Far East from traditional to industrial society.

Methodological pluralism in science, which is characteristic of modern historiography, has revealed a tendency for historians to become increasingly aware of the need to develop a universal cognitive apparatus for the study of complex historical processes. In the works of Dameshek (2007), methods of comparative historical analysis were applied and made it easier to understand the place of the Far East not only in the history of Russia, but also in the Asia–Pacific region.

It is noteworthy that in foreign historiography, there is an effort to highlight positive aspects of the state's national policy towards small indigenous peoples as an integral part of ensuring national security (Armstrong, 1965). The contribution of regional historians into solving theoretical and methodological problems related to the transition of traditional societies to a new stage of development as national security has significantly increased (Batten, 2012). New methodological approaches to explaining the past of small indigenous peoples of the vast region have been tested on the actual material. An essential observation is made that with the rapid acceleration of the pace of changes in public life, the search for new methodological approaches to the study of Russian history, a large-scale and deep reinterpretation of the history of the Fatherland and its key problems and events becomes relevant (Gallyamova, 2006). This conclusion underlines the relevance of the study of the degree of changes in ethnic societies under the influence of Russian modernization.

The change of the research paradigm and the revision of the theoretical foundations of historical science in recent times have highly raised the question of the scientific formulation of the variability of interpretative concepts and the construction of models of historical processes and the research of the state national policy as a mechanism for implementing the concept of national security of traditional societies.

According to the author, the conceptual approach from the point of view of modernization theory expresses the need for a comprehensive use of all state resources on targeted complex programs (economic, political, sociocultural, medical, etc.) and specific measures to ensure national security.

One of the most important methods of obtaining scientific knowledge is a systematic approach that is successfully applied in the study of processes related to the individual, society and the state. No less significant methodological approach in the study of national security is the value approach. It should be particularly noted that the formation of national interests is based on national values under the influence of long-term trends in the social development of indigenous peoples. To increase the objectivity of the obtained knowledge, the author applied general scientific methods of cognition (Collins & Kunz, 2009).

Defining the essence of social changes, a number of authors propose to consider such changes that are not limited to a quantitative increase in any parameters but lead to the modernization of these parameters and to a change of the way society is organized. The last of these fundamental changes was called modernization in science. Modernization is a long historical process spanning several centuries, when people made the transition from a traditional, mainly agricultural, society to a

418 A. I. GORELIKOV

modern, industrial society as a component of ensuring national security (Poberegnikov, 2006).

3 RESULTS

In modern Russian social science, the most popular are civilization and modernization theories. In the scientific views of prominent proponents of the theoretical concept of modernization, a special place is occupied by its application in the course of research on the reform processes taking place in Russia (Akhmetova, 2015, 2017). First of all, it concerns studying specific transformations in the sociopolitical, economic, social, and other spheres as part of ensuring national security. Without an in-depth analysis of the processes taking place at the micro level, it is impossible to answer the question of how successfully Russia can cope with the challenges facing it at the present stage (Tikhonova, 2008).

The relevance of this issue, in our opinion, is determined by the fact that Russian historiography, having overcome mainly the stereotypes of the Soviet period, has come to a holistic reinterpretation of the ethnic history of indigenous peoples within the framework of Russian modernization. Based on the methodological basis of the theory of modernization, it becomes possible to more thoroughly and comprehensively consider all the subtleties of civilizational influence on traditional societies as an integral part of ensuring national security.

It is known that the theory of modernization developed in the 1950s–1960s as one of the explanatory concepts of socio-historical development on the way to historical progress. During this period, various analytical trends merged into a single interdisciplinary concept, which proved to be very productive in explaining the development of transitional societies. In the context of new knowledge, modernization theory contains a different system of attitudes, where knowledge is understood not as a description of happening events, but as an intervention of modernization in historical processes. Such approach to the study of modernization in the economic, political, and sociocultural spheres of the life of indigenous peoples during the transition period is reduced to revealing the constructive relations of the state and ethnic societies as an integral part of ensuring their national security.

Based on an in-depth understanding of the National security strategy of the Russian Federation, the central part in ensuring in the transition of traditional societies to industrial development includes the following

THEORETICAL AND METHODOLOGICAL FOUNDATIONS ... 419

processes: the pre-possession of innovation over tradition; the secular nature of social life; the formation of democracy; a dedicated personality; a preference for individual values; the industrial character of mass education; a preference for worldview representation; and knowledge of exact Sciences and technologies, etc. (Fedotova, 2002).

It should be noted that with the entry into industrial society, various aspects of modernization among indigenous peoples constitute a process of unified structural change and are inseparable from national ones. Due to the general orientation of the Russian historical process, it is not only possible but necessary to consider modernization among indigenous peoples as a phenomenon of civilizational scale.

The study of modernization processes in traditional societies in the historical retrospect of national security reveals the use of technical achievements of modernization by the Soviet state while simultaneously denying democratic forms of organization and human rights. Under the strict regulation the government sought to temporarily adapt some of the technical, scientific, and cultural achievements for the progressive development of traditional societies, which gave rise to a tendency to dissolve indigenous small-numbered peoples in a single socialist space.

Krasilshchikov (1998) and Vishnevsky (2010) justify the concept of the Soviet model of modernization, its structure and elements as an objective necessity, a continuation of the policy of Imperial modernization. Krasilshchikov comes to the conclusion that changes in the country were accelerated, the ground was formed for the upcoming leap, which later took root in the Soviet, and in fact, Soviet-Slavic mobilization model of modernization-industrialization. According to Gavrov (2004), imperial modernization in Russia is carried out primarily in the name of stabilizing and preserving the basic characteristics of the Empire, which is served both by foreign cultural borrowings and by achieving the competitiveness of individual elements of the cultural-civilizational system.

Consequently, the model of accelerated conservative modernization came across with, first of all, the historical conditions where the peoples of Russia, including the indigenous peoples of the Far East, found themselves.

Today the concept of modernizing Russia hardly raises doubts about its relevance. Now there is a general understanding of modernization as a process of changes in social, political, economic and spiritual systems that ensure the transition of indigenous peoples from traditional to industrial societies. The specifics of the Soviet model of modernization, if we do not take into account the ideological design of social practice, consisted in a significant degree of state intervention through political and economic impact on the life of indigenous peoples.

From the point of view of the modernization theory, Krasilshchikov (1993) drew the attention of researchers to the fact that:

- in the social sphere - the division of functional roles performed by different individuals in society, especially the division between responsibilities in social production, politics and the family, the division of private and public life;
- in the economy—the use of technology based on the use of scientific (rational) knowledge, the emergence of secondary (industry, trade) and third (services) sectors of the economy, the deepening of the social and technical division of labor, the development of the market for goods, money and labor;
- in the political sphere—the formation of centralized states and at the same time the separation of powers, the inclusion of the broad masses of the population in the political process, the formation of conscious interests of various social groups; and
- in the spiritual sphere—differentiation of cultural systems and value orientations, the spread of literacy, the development of information dissemination tools, and the introduction of large groups of the population to cultural achievements.

In our opinion, the selected factors reflect the features of the theoretical and methodological approach to the study of the specifics of the implementation of national security in the regional dimension. It should be noted that the concept of national security was not used at this stage.

In the Soviet period the concept of state security considered social relations in unity and interdependence as the security of the state, society and the individual among the most important components. The fundamental factor of ensuring security was to subordinate the interests of the individual and society to the interests of the state. Particular attention was paid to the need to develop appropriate legal acts that reflect the degree of protection of the state's interests.

The next stage of imperial modernization in the "execution" of the Brezhnev leadership contained sufficient conservatism aimed at preserving

THEORETICAL AND METHODOLOGICAL FOUNDATIONS ... 421

the existing situation in the country. The power of the state was recognized as comprehensive, and human rights, the individual and society were not considered as priority objects.

The modern concept of the National security strategy of the Russian Federation was considered on the basis of the provisions of article 2 of the Constitution proclaimed that "man, his rights and freedoms are of the supreme value" (ConsultantPlus, 2020). The individual becomes the main object of national security of the state. A fundamentally new relevance in the subject field needs new theoretical and methodological approaches. The author of the article suggests using the theory of modernization as a methodological basis.

The applied experience of studying the state-conducted pre-formations in traditional societies allows us to conduct a historical analysis of human activity in various spheres and consider modernization processes in traditional societies as an integral part of ensuring national security in the transition to an industrial society.

The application of theoretical and methodological approaches to the modernization concept allows us to organically include the processes of renewal among small ethnic groups in the context of large-scale changes in the Russian social and political system of the period under study, makes it possible to clearly define the characteristics of the modernization of the traditional way of life of indigenous peoples within the framework of the transformed" old " ethno-tribal traditional system, and identify the features of relations and connections among ethnic societies, get a clear idea of the specific impact of each modernization model in the course of the national security implementation of the Soviet state. No less significant, which is especially important for multinational Russia, in the study of national security assessment is the value approach. Its application allows us to consider both fundamental state values and national interests – interethnic peace and harmony, unity of cultures, preservation of traditions. In this topic, the state national policy in relation to the indigenous peoples of the North, Siberia and the Far East acts as a part of ensuring national security.

The specifics of the implementation of the state national policy in relation to ethnic societies are a clear example of the impact of Russian modernization.

4 Conclusion

The mechanism of implementation of national security by the state in relation to small indigenous peoples was a multi-level system of organizational links, methods, tools and values that determined its formation. The implementation of national security included an analysis of the mechanisms by which indigenous peoples were integrated into the General political, economic, socio-cultural and legal system of the state.

The modernization approach to the study of the problem, in contrast to the approaches used in previous studies of the historical development of indigenous peoples, is more flexible in relation to the studied reality. It is more productive when studying the regional dynamics of transformation of ethnic societies. The modernization approach creates prerequisites for comparing different variants of the transition of ethnic societies from traditional to modern ones, identifying common and special features in the course of these processes. It assumes a scheme of historical development in the form of movement from primitive to more complex structures of social existence. This is reflected in the modeling of the modernization process as radical and comprehensive transformations, generating processes of structural differentiation, industrialization, social mobility, national identification, media dissemination, literacy and education, the formation of modern political structures, and the growth of political participation (Poberegnikov, 2006). The modernization approach allows us to consider traditional societies as a subsystem of the international or national community of the peoples of the Russian state, explains the principles of national security formation in relation to small indigenous peoples, and makes it possible to trace the change in the status of these peoples in the context of the national security policy implemented by the state.

At the same time, the integration process was accompanied by the formation of national values of national security, goals and interests of man, society and nature. The main indicator of the complex and ambiguous historical process of the complete transition of traditional societies to industrial societies is the preservation of national conditions of their existence, the realization of their interests, culture and traditions.

The state guaranteed the protection of ideals, values and traditions, way of life, family, as well as normal life, ethnicity, language and religion, and fundamental freedoms as part of ensuring national security.

THEORETICAL AND METHODOLOGICAL FOUNDATIONS ... 423

REFERENCES

Akhmetova, A. V. (2015). Modernization of ethnocultural processes in the national areas of the Far East (1920s–1930s years). *Bylye Gody, 37*(3), 766–774.

Akhmetova, A. V. (2017). Transformation of ethnocultural development of indigenous peoples in the conditions of socialist modernization of the Far East in 1920–1970s: Problems of historiography. *Contributions to Economics* (9783319454610), 553–558. https://doi.org/10.1007/978-3-319-45462-7_53

Armstrong, T. (Ed.). (1965). *Russian settlement in the North.* University of Cambridge.

Artyomov, E. T., Golovnev, A. V., & Poberezhnikov, I. V. (2005). Problems of Social Transformation in History. *New and Contemporary History, 1,* 248–252.

Batten, Br. (2012). Strengthening aboriginal community wellbeing. *Cosmopolitan Civil Societies Journal, 4*(3), 54–77.

Collins, J., & Kunz, P. (2009). Ethnicity and public space in the city: Ethnic precincts in Sydney. *Cosmopolitan Civil Societies Journal, 1*(1), 39–70.

ConsultantPlus. (2014). *The constitution of the Russian Federation* (adopted by popular vote on 12/12/1993) (taking into account the amendments introduced by the Laws of the Russian Federation on amendments to the Constitution of the Russian Federation of 30/12/2008 N 6-FKL, of 30/12/2008 N 7-FKL, of 05/02/2014 N 2-FKL, of 21/07.2014 N 11-FKL). http://www.consultant.ru/document/cons_doc_LAW_28399/. Data accessed 08.05.2020.

ConsultantPlus. (2015). *Decree of the President of the Russian Federation of December 31, 2015 N 683.* On the National Security Strategy of the Russian Federation. http://www.consultant.ru/document/cons_doc_LAW_191669/. Data accessed 08.05.2020.

ConsultantPlus. (2020). *Federal Law of 28/12/2010 N 390-ФЗ.* On safety (as amended on 02/06/2020). http://www.consultant.ru/document/cons_doc_LAW_108546/. Data accessed 08.05.2020.

Dameshek, L. M. (Ed.). (2007). *Siberia within the Russian Empire.* New Literary Review.

Fedotova, V. G. (2002). Non-classical modernizations and alternatives to modernization theory. *Problems of Philosophy, 12,* 4–16.

Gallyamova, L. I. (2006). *Modern tendencies in the study of national history.* Proceedings of the Institute of History, Archeology and Ethnography of the Peoples of the Far East, Series Domestic History, 13, Vladivostok: Dalnauka, pp. 7–12.

Gavrov, S. N. (Ed.). (2004). *Modernizing for the Empire. Socio-cultural aspects of modernization processes in Russia.* URSS.

Kovalchenko, I. D. (1995). Theoretical and methodological problems of historical research. *Notes and Reflections on New Approaches. New and Contemporary History, 1*, 3–12.

Krasilshchikov, V. A. (1993). Modernization in Russia on the threshold of the 20th century. *Problems of Philosophy, 3*, 41–44.

Krasilshchikov, V. A. (Ed.). (1998). *Keeping up with the past century: Russia's development in the 20th century from the point of view of world modernizations.* ROSSPEN.

Poberezhnikov, I. V. (Ed.). (2006). *Transition from traditional to industrial society: Theoretical and methodological problems of modernization.* ROSSPEN.

Tikhonova, N. E. (2008). Socio-cultural modernization in Russia (Experience of empirical analysis). *Domestic Science and Modernity, 2*, 6–9.

Vishnevsky, A. G. (Ed.). (2010). *Sickle and ruble: Conservative modernization in the USSR.* GU-VSE.

Additional Vocational Teacher Education in the Field of the Formation of a Safety Culture in Transport in the Era of Intelligent Machines

Galina S. Kamerilova, *Marina A. Kartavykh*, *Elena L. Ageeva*, *Marina A. Veryaskina*, *and Irina A. Gordeeva*

1 INTRODUCTION

Information vector of social development, justified in the twentieth century (E. Toffler, D. Bell), defined the modern transition to the powerful promotion of digital technology, and intelligent machines. These technologies have gained rapid and large-scale distribution and have identified the growing role of continuing professional education of teachers. According to Federal Law dated December 29, 2012 No. 273-FL "On Education in the Russian Federation", the focus of additional professional education is determined by its ability to satisfy professional needs, ensuring the adequacy of advanced training for students in the changing conditions of professional activity and the social environment

---

G. S. Kamerilova (✉) · M. A. Kartavykh · E. L. Ageeva · M. A. Veryaskina · I. A. Gordeeva
Minin Nizhny Novgorod State Pedagogical University, Nizhny Novgorod, Russia

© The Author(s), under exclusive license to Springer Nature Switzerland AG 2021
E. G. Popkova and B. S. Sergi (eds.), *Economic Issues of Social Entrepreneurship*,
https://doi.org/10.1007/978-3-030-77291-8_39

425

(9, 2012). The main characteristics of the information society, according to E. Toffler, are the "end of constancy" and "escalation of acceleration". It is additional education that is called in these conditions to provide the opportunity for teachers to acquire new competencies that are in demand in the era of intelligent machines. The author believes that illiterate in the twenty-first century will not be those who cannot read and write, but those who cannot learn and relearn (Toffler, 2002). High dynamism of the development in information, communication technologies, and digital technologies determine rapid re-equipment of educational processes and procedures. This, on the one hand, forms a new quality of education, on the other, cause a stressful situation among students and teachers, the need for rapid adaptation (Khangeldieva, 2018). A. G. Asmolov, E. D. Shekhter, A. M. Chernorizov believe that the usual adaptation strategies stop working; the ability to "pre-adapt"—readiness for changes becomes in demand, because according to the author, "there will be no other era than the era of change" (Asmolov et al., 2017).

These provisions most directly relate to additional professional teacher education in the field of developing a safety culture for children in transport, which has been implemented on the basis of the MOOC digital educational platform for four years at the Nizhny Novgorod State Pedagogical University named after K. Minin commissioned by the Russian Ministry of Education and Science as part of the federal program "Improving Road Safety in 2013–2020". Further education courses are conducted using the electronic educational resource on teaching children how to behave safely on roads created by the Russian Ministry of Education (http://eor.edu.ru), as well as the Road Without Danger portal (bdd-eor.edu.ru).

In addition, the development and implementation in the electronic educational environment of a practice-oriented project to improve the qualifications of teachers in the field of creating a safety culture in transport was based on the ideas of education informatization (I. B. Gosudarev, S. A. Dochkin, I. G. Zakharova, D. V. Zemlyakov, V. M. Ilkevich, Yu V. Karjakin, I. A. Kolesnikova, A. M. Novikov, I. V. Robert, A. G. Sukiyazov, A. D. Ursul, Yu A. Schrader), the formation of an electronic educational environment (Dochkin, 2010; Gosudarev, 2014; Novikov, 2009; Zemlyakov et al., 2016). Information and communication technologies (ICT) provide interactivity, multimedia effect, diverse computer modeling, broad communication, and time saving routine actions. In the framework of this current direction, the position of academician I.V.

Robert, who identifies the so-called transfer-integrative areas of new scientific knowledge, which are subject disciplines or areas enriched with ideas of informatization and practical tools of information and communication technologies (Robert, 2012). In our case, this is a culture of child safety in transport and the prevention of road traffic injuries, some aspects of which were revealed by us earlier (Kamerilova et al., 2016; Kartavykh & Kamerilova, 2018). It should be noted the activity of the authors (V.P. Bespalko, M.N. Gorchakova-Sibirskaya, V.V. Kraevsky, I.A. Kolesnikova, V.A. Slastenin, V.I. Slobodchikov, A.P. Tryapitsyna, E.N. Shiyanov) in the development of general theoretical problems of pedagogical design (Kolesnikova, 2007). Our study is built in the context of the developed scientific approaches from the point of view of informatization processes of advanced training on a project basis, taking into account transfer integration.

The purpose of this work: the development and implementation in the electronic educational environment MOOC of a practice-oriented project for the advanced training of teachers in the field of developing a safety culture for children in transport.

2 MATERIALS AND METHOD

Theoretical understanding and practical implementation of the problem was carried out on the basis of the design methodology associated with the solution of the urgent problem of child safety in transport, based on new ideas of technological software. The logic of pedagogical design included methods of analysis, conceptualization, programming and construction of new educational practice in additional education of pedagogical staff. Using the potential of the interface of mass open online courses (MOOC), which is most suitable for web projects, allowed us to create a transfer-integrative software and methodological product that is widely in demand by users of various regions of the country.

3 RESULTS

Creation of a practice-oriented project to improve the qualifications of teaching staff in the field of developing a safety culture for children in transport, hosted at the MOOC Nizhny Novgorod State Pedagogical University named after K. Minin (University of Minin), was carried out on the basis of the following fundamental provisions:

- the presence of a new idea—the idea of informatization of additional education, when a pedagogical project is considered as a transfer-integrative field, combining the subject content of the safety culture for children in transport with information and communication methods of its development;
- orientation towards the future, corresponding to the meaning of teachers advanced training in advanced training courses, with a vector on their tomorrow's information needs and expectations;
- activation of the axiological direction within the framework of a single humanistic system of values, developing through the inclusion of information aspects; personal values and attitudes of students to preserve the life and health for children and teenagers; interactive dialogue and collaboration;
- the prospect of mass use of the innovative project as a way to promote informatization in the continuing education system for teaching staff.

The conceptual, substantive, technological, procedural levels of design are highlighted.

The product of activity at the conceptual level is represented by the concept of a practice-oriented project as a transfer-integrative field of education, which has a competence-based format and fulfills an orienting and guiding role. The core of integration is the results-target component, combining the competencies provided for the development of trainees: 1) social and legal, providing the ability to teachers consciously perceive social and regulatory requirements of safe behavior on roads in accordance with the dominant vector of educational policy and in the future development of legislative relations; 2) general professional— assuming the ability to assess the role of informatization and intelligent machines as a shock factor in the development of its humanistic traditions, the use of their opportunities, including the expansion of communications, in the development of a safety culture in transport, specialized competence means the ability to work effectively with electronic educational resources in the electronic educational environment MOOC, to apply modern technological solutions (ICT).

The product of activity at the substantive level is expressed in a set of programs and corresponding electronic educational-methodological complexes (EUMK) created for different target audiences for teachers:

regional institutes for continuing education and development of education, general educational organizations, organizations of additional and preschool education. The core of integration is EUMK as a specially designed system of electronic educational resources, which forms special content for students to work with. The modular principle of its construction provides a unified character and a general structure, including modules: (1) "Safe road of childhood: values and meanings"; (2) "Safe road of childhood: a vector for interactivity as information communication for joint action"; (3) "Safe road of childhood: from a monologue to dialogue"; (4) Final certification. The following are highlighted as additional: an introductory module containing navigation for the successful development of the content, and a module " Forming skills of safe behavior on the roads for students with disabilities". Moreover, the tasks and content of each of the modules are aimed at the development of relevant competencies.

For this reason, the product of activity at the technological level includes technological tools and methodological support for student activities. The core of integration is the mechanism ICT at different stages of training. Multimedia technology based on a combination of information transmission channels provides high-quality visualization of transport threats and examples of a culture of safe behavior on roads. A visual image affects the emotional state, forms real representations and abstract concepts. A large role is played by simulation or modeling, including the game situation, which allows reproducing dynamic patterns of behavior that are discussed interactively: online and offline (chats, forums). The electronic educational environment for advanced training is an effective open training ground for smart learning, characterized by the use of communication technologies of collective activity. During the course preparation, discussion and consultations on current issues are constantly ongoing, regardless of the place of residence of students (for example, in 2019 teachers of the federal districts (North Caucasus—Vladikavkaz, Central—Voronezh, North-West) took part in further training—St. Petersburg, Ural—Chelyabinsk, Volga region—Nizhny Novgorod, Far East—Vladivostok). Electronic presentations were widely used. Webinars were systematically held (installation, final, current webinars—"Prevention of childhood road traffic injuries. Fundamentals of first aid for victims", etc.), an open exchange of views and answers to questions on the forum.

The product of the activity at the procedural level represents the sequential phasing of project activities. The core of integration is its general logic, which is reflected in the following generalized stages: theoretical and methodological (pre-project), substantive-active (project implementation), and reflective-evaluative (post-project).

The theoretical and methodological stage is devoted to assessing the relevance of the project and its problematization, based on an analysis of the current situation in the field of informatization of additional professional and pedagogical education in the field of creating a safety culture for children in transport. Based on the identified trends and determinants of social development and the requirements of federal standards, a targeted competency-based orientation of all project activities is formed, conceptual foundations are developed, including its general strategy, ideas, approaches and principles, assessment criteria. In accordance with the leading methodological provisions (cultural, competency-based, informational, modular approaches; principles of systematicity, innovation, continuity, continuity, accessibility, management efficiency), the design of the EUMK is built on conditions and pedagogical support of students, as well as options for their effective assessment. As a result, the internal and external evaluation of the project is given.

Then the substantive-active stage begins with the installation webinar "Road safety: the design of the educational program, the trajectory of mastering the course", which proposes the general concept of the project, in order to achieve planned learning outcomes. All teachers involved in the implementation of the project have free access to the EUMK. They know the schedule of the educational process, the rating plan and are free to choose tasks and the order of their implementation. In case of difficulties, they easily get in touch with the heads of individual EUMKs and solve the problems that have arisen. So, the availability of feedback which includes the analysis and evaluation of intermediate results evaluated by qualitative (essay) and quantitative methods (test tasks, rating). As a final attestation it is proposed to perform an individual electronic educational product. The presentation of which is posted on the website "Dynamic formation system" cross-platform electronic educational resources".

Reflexive-evaluation (post-project) stage is devoted to the analysis and assessment of the general idea in the information-oriented project, and the process of its implementation and obtained results. It is carried out in the process of diagnosing the success of completed tasks and includes filling in a journal of reflection and questionnaire; customer expertise. We consider it fundamentally important that we reflect on the self-reflection of the participants and organizers of the project activity, which provides both a retrospective (analysis of successes and difficulties in completing the course preparation within the framework of the project) and a perspective (comprehension of the new acquired competencies in the field of creating a safety culture for children in transport, based on information-communication resources -"digital teacher assistants.") As a result of the overall, new options for the continuation of the project are put forward.

4 Conclusion

Therefore, the progress of professional teacher education is associated with the need for active development of ideas and practices of the era of intelligent machines. Created project on the basis of transfer-integration approaches and implemented in educational practice, is a project to improve the qualifications of teachers in the field of creating a safety culture in transport. This is evidence of movement in right direction. As a result, the fundamental informational principles and the main design levels on the MOOC platform of the Nizhny Novgorod State Pedagogical University named after K. Minin, with the allocation of integration cores for each of them. This made it possible to obtain a systematic idea of the staged nature of project activities and the relationship between the theoretical and methodological, substantive-active, reflective-evaluative stages. In the context of innovation, the remote form of continuing education courses ensured their accessibility for the entire interested pedagogical community, regardless of a residence place. The proposed technologies and techniques allowed to simultaneously educate teachers of different areas, including those who is working with children with disabilities, at a relatively short time. The development of new competencies, updating knowledge and methods of activity in the field of safety culture in transport was carried out with the active understanding of increased requirements for the level of professional competence and the need to master modern information methods and intelligent systems to solve professional problems.

Acknowledgements The work was carried out within the framework of the State contract of the Ministry of Education from 03.06.2019. №07.Z27.11.0005 on the project "Professional development (including modular courses) of teaching staff of general education organizations, organizations of additional

432 G. S. KAMERILOVA ET AL.

education and preschool educational organizations in the field of formation of children's skills of safe participation in road traffic"

REFERENCES

Asmolov, A. G., Shekhter, E. D., & Chernorizov, A. M. (2017). Preadaptation to uncertainty as a navigation strategy for developing systems: Evolutionary routes. *Psychology Issues, 4*, 3–26.

Dochkin, S. A. (2010). *Informatization of additional professional education of professional teaching staff: Organizational and pedagogical aspect* (p. 226). Arden.

Federal Law "On Education in the Russian Federation" dated 29.12.2012 N 273-FL. http://www.consultant.ru

Gosudarev, I. B. (2014). Deployment and integration of innovative learning environments: Boardcasting, cloud hosting and edX. *Computer Tools in Education, 1*, 26–35.

Kamerilova, G. S., Kartavykh, M. A., Ageeva, E. L., Veryaskina, M. A., & Ruban, E. M. (2016). Electronic informational and educational environment as a factor of competence-oriented higher pedagogical education in the sphere of health, safety and environment. *International Journal of Environmental & Science Education, 11*, 13. http://www.ijese.net/makale/786

Kartavykh, M. A., & Kamerilova, G. S. (2018). *Scientific and methodological support of additional professional training programs of teaching staff in the field of formation of safe skills among children participation in road traffic*. Vestnik of Minin University. https://vestnik.mininuniver.ru/jour/article/view/752/643

Khangeldieva, I. G. (2018). Digital age: Is advanced education possible? *Series 20: Teacher Education, 3*, 48–61.

Kolesnikova, I. A. (2007). *Pedagogical design: Textbook* (I. A. Kolesnikova, M. P. Gorchakova-Sibirskaya under the editorship of V. A. Slastenina, I. A. Kolesnikova; p. 288). Publishing Center "Academy".

Novikov, A. M. (2009). The educational process in a post-industrial society: Why should a person be prepared in conditions of high dynamics of the labor market? *Municipal Education: Innovation and Experiment, 4*, 6–11.

Robert, I. V. (2012). The forecast of the development of informatization of education as a transfer-integrative field of scientific knowledge. In *Modern Problems of the Informatization of Vocational Education: Materials of the International Scientific and Practical Internet Conference*. FGBOU VPO MGAU, pp. 5–17.

Toffler, E. (2002). *Shock of the future: Translated from English* (p. 557). ACT Publishing House LLC.

Zemlyakov, D. V., Korotkov, A. M., & Shtyrkov, A. V. (2016). Informatization of education: Advanced training of teachers in a cluster-network environment. *Azimuth of Scientific Research: Pedagogy and Psychology, 5*(4), 140–144.

The Methodology for Calculating the Productivity of Office Personnel at the Stage of Intelligent Machines Implementation

Vladimir A. Polyakov🄳, *Irina V. Fomicheva*🄳,
*Natalia E. Efremova, Svetlana V. Nefedova,
and Tatyana V. Medvedeva*

1 Introduction

Improving the efficiency of the domestic economy is one of the oldest problems that both business and the government are trying to solve. According to performance indicators, they assess not only the level of organization of production and the level of economic development, but also the socio-political system of the country. After a protracted innovation pause that arose as a result of a reduction in financing of the real sector of the economy, today the issues and problems of stimulating economic growth based on the achievements of the fourth industrial revolution, which are based on information and digital technologies, are especially acute. If the third industrial revolution was characterized as the process of transferring from person to machine the functions of

---

V. A. Polyakov (✉) · I. V. Fomicheva · N. E. Efremova · S. V. Nefedova ·
T. V. Medvedeva
Tula Branch of the University of Finance, Tula, Russia

© The Author(s), under exclusive license to Springer Nature
Switzerland AG 2021
E. G. Popkova and B. S. Sergi (eds.), *Economic Issues of Social
Entrepreneurship*,
https://doi.org/10.1007/978-3-030-77291-8_40

435

controlling the production process according to a given algorithm while maintaining the dominant role of man, then the fourth industrial revolution is based on the capabilities of computer technology to independently determine the most effective algorithm for solving not only production, but also many social problems.

According to the report of the World Economic Forum "The Future of Jobs, 2018", to date, not a single work task has been completely completed by a machine or algorithm. However, the increase in the proportion of machine working time spent on working tasks is steadily increasing. If in 2018 the level of automation during the performance of work tasks reached only 29%, then by 2022 in 12 studied industries it should be 42%, and by 2025, the share of machine time can reach more than half—52% (The Future of Jobs, 2018). Thus, changes in the organization of labor caused by digitalization will require the adaptation of well-known approaches to assessing and identifying reserves for increasing productivity in the new conditions for almost all countries and Russia in particular.

2   Materials and Method

Productivity as an economic category has been an object of research since the New Age period. In the works of W. Petty and A. Smith revealed a connection between productivity and the "wealth of peoples", which subsequently developed at the macroeconomic level in theories of economic growth of Keynesian, neoclassical, and institutional directions. At the micro level, theorists and practitioners made a significant contribution to the modern theory of productivity in industry:

- the second industrial revolution F. Taylor G. Gantt, F. Gilbreth, A. K. Gastev, O. A. Yermansky et al., Who studied productivity from the standpoint of the scientific organization of labor when performing operations and designing production processes. They introduced the basic principle of Taylorism: everything should be calculated up to a second (Emerson, 1992);
- the third industrial revolution Childs, N. O. Olesten, R. B. Thornhill, G. A. Shaumyan, N. I. Kapustin, V. F. Preis, L. I. Koshkin (Shaumyan, 1973), who studied the productivity of working machine tools and the identification of reserves to increase them,

as well as the issues and problems of replacing "living" labor with machines;
- the fourth industrial revolution A. I. Anchishkin, O. T. Bogomolov, D. S. Lvov, L. G. Sokolova and many other researchers (Golovanov, 2013; Sokolova, 2016).

At present, theories and concepts have been developed to optimize production processes not only at the enterprise or workshop level, but also to find reserves for increasing productivity at the level of workplaces in offices and administrations, such as "lean management" (LDMS), "continuous improvement"(Kaizen) and "improving jobs and processes" (Gemba Kaizen) (Imai, 2015). In particular, Gemba Kaizen is based on three rules: (1) maintaining order; (2) elimination of losses (muda); (3) standardization. Moreover, it is the elimination of losses (muda) "... that may become the most cost-effective way to increase productivity and reduce production costs" (Imai, 2013). The elimination of actions that do not add value is possible both in the workplace, in the service sector and in public administration. The main types of losses in the field of mental labor, according to M. Imai can be classified into four main groups: (1) loss of working time; (2) loss of an employee; (3) loss of the work system and (4) loss of business processes, and their total value can reach 27–38% of the work of white-collar workers (Imai, 2015). Methodological recommendations for increasing the productivity of these concepts are generally universal in nature and make it possible to identify problems at the level of jobs, but do not allow for a quantitative assessment of the reserves for increasing productivity, as well as for evaluating productivity growth as a result of eliminating losses.

Most managers believe that in practice it is impossible to objectively evaluate the time spent on the duties of office employees. The main argument put forward in this case is that work requires decision-making, reflection, and often creative, non-standard thinking (Bushmin, 2020). Thus, the development of tools to assess the reserves of increasing the productivity of an individual employee or a group of office workers, interconnected by a technological process and computer tools in the context of digitalization, is still without attention of specialists.

3 Results

It is known that labor productivity is the ratio of labor results to time spent on its execution $Pt = N / T$ (Gaifutdinova, 2018). With regard to office or administrative work, the result of labor can be the volume of document flow N, and T is the time spent in the reporting period (minutes, hours, days, etc.) during which this document is processed. If we denote the average time spent processing a document flow unit ($t = T / N$) through t, then productivity can be written as $Pt = 1 / t$. Based on this formula, it is possible to increase labor productivity in the office if t is minimized, i.e. $t \rightarrow$ min.

Consider the reserves for increasing the productivity of an office worker performing certain actions and releasing an intellectual product or a copy of a document. The time to complete a unit of work of an office worker can be represented in the form of two terms: $t = t_n + t_p$, where t_p is the time of losses per unit of workflow; t_p—working time for processing a unit of workflow. In turn, working time t_p can also be represented as the sum: $t_p = t_{rp} + t_{pp}$, where t_{rp} is the time to work that does not add value (loss of time); t_{pp}—time for work creating value.

We first consider the design and evaluation of the effects of eliminating waste time t_n. The main reasons for the loss of time for the period T that need to be minimized include: T_o—late and early time of leaving work; T_{pz}—preparatory and final time (loss of time at the beginning of the working day to bring itself into the appropriate form, time to adapt to the working environment, turning on the computer, server, etc., and similar time losses in the end of the working day); T_{org}—losses due to organizational reasons (employee's absence of job assignments, meetings, and meetings during working hours); T_{ln}—losses on natural and personal needs; T_n—losses for unreasonable reasons; T—losses independent of the employee (breakage or freezes of the computer, office equipment, etc.); T_b—losses due to sickness or time off. Then the loss time per document unit will be $t_p = (T_o + T_{pz} + T_{org} + T_{ln} + T_n + T_k + T_b) / N$.

In order, to assess the proportion of time loss t_p in the value of t, we introduce the coefficient of time loss q_1, which is calculated as follows: $q_1 = t_p / t$. According to the results of expert observational data and the timing of the work of office employees obtained by the authors, the average value of the coefficient q_1 averages $0.18 \div 0.19$. This means that up to 20% of the time t is spent unproductive.

THE METHODOLOGY FOR CALCULATING THE PRODUCTIVITY ...   439

Let us consider possible solutions capable of minimizing these losses, i.e. $t_p \to 0$:

- establish the requirement to come to work some time earlier than the beginning of the working day (as agreed with the staff) for personal preparatory procedures;
- hold all meetings after completion of the main time;
- oblige the heads of structural divisions to plan the activities of their employees on the next working day before leaving work to avoid staff downtime;
- to eliminate time losses due to personal needs and unreasonable reasons, it is necessary to introduce regulated breaks, the duration of which is not included in working hours;
- prevention of office automation equipment should be carried out daily, and before the starting time of office employees.

Implementation of the organizational decisions listed above is possible if the office has strict regulations for the distribution of total time for working hours and time losses. Such regulation will require changes in the labor agreement (labor contract) and the total time spent by the employee at work will inevitably increase. This can provoke conflicts if management does not apply countervailing measures.

If these organizational decisions can be implemented, then the possible productivity will be $Pt1 = 1 / t_p$. The value of the reserve of possible labor productivity $\Delta P1$ will be $\Delta P1 = Pt1 - Pt = t_p / (t_p \cdot t)$. The estimated factor for the reserve of possible performance w_1 is calculated as follows: $w_1 = Pt1 / Pt = t / t_p$; and shows how many times it is possible to increase productivity after the loss of t_n.

Now consider the structure and assessment of the consequences of eliminating the loss of time t_{rp}. The structure of working time that does not create value includes: T_{rop}—loss of time to correct errors; T_{ph}—losses due to a misunderstanding of the requirements for the task to be performed; T_{rnz}—losses due to a not clear task by the management; T_{rnz}—losses due to insufficient level of knowledge (low qualification); T_{pop}—losses due to improper organization of the process of doing task; T_{pod}—losses due to lack of data on performed work; T_{pon}—improper distribution of the load, etc. Then the losses of time t_p can be calculated from the formula $t_{pn} = (T_{rop} + T_{rh} + T_{pnz} + T_{pop} + T_{pod}) / N$. To assess the proportion of time loss t_{rp} in the value of t_p we introduce the coefficient of time loss q_2, which is calculated as follows: $q_2 = t_{rp} / t_p$. Its value according to the results of expert evaluations is 25% on average.

Basically, all of these losses are associated with the qualifications of the staff, therefore, the tasks of the management are, first of all, the following: introduction of mentoring, training, organization of a quality school (outside working hours); widespread adoption of modern computers and professional software; recruitment and selection of highly qualified personnel with a high learning potential; referral to additional training in leading centers, participation in thematic conferences, foreign internships; Installing employee time tracking software on a computer.

Activities for the development and implementation of recommendations aimed at reducing t_{rp}, as a result of which $t_{rp} \rightarrow 0$, will allow to achieve maximum labor productivity $Pt2 = 1 / t_{pp}$; and will be determined by the qualifications of workers and the rationality of labor organization.

The reserve value of possible maximum labor productivity $\Delta P2$ will be $\Delta P2 = Pt2 - Pt1$. The coefficient of the reserve of productivity can be calculated as follows: $w_2 = Pt1 / Pt2 = t_p / t_{pp}$. It shows how many times it is possible to increase labor productivity using qualified personnel with the rational organization of labor. The total productivity reserve ratio is calculated by the formula: $w_3 = Pt1 / Pt2 = t / t_p = w_1 w_2$.

Thus, the total coefficient of time loss can be calculated $\sum q = q_1 \cdot q_2$, and according to the authors, it can reach more than 35% of T.

We perform the following transformation in the performance formula:

$$Pt = \frac{1}{t} = \frac{t_n}{t} \cdot \frac{t_{pn}}{t_p} \cdot \frac{t_p}{t_n} \cdot \frac{1}{t_{pn}} = q_1 q_2 a_1 a_2,$$

where: a_1—coefficient of efficiency of the organization of the office worker ($a_1 = t_r / t_p$); and a_2—loss of productivity due to the low qualification of the employee ($a_2 = 1 / t_{rp}$). This expression of labor productivity allows us to estimate its value through the values of the time loss coefficients.

However, in the context of digitalization, part of the office work begins to be transmitted to artificial intelligence. This circumstance will increase labor productivity by reducing the time that creates value. A further increase in labor productivity is possible if the condition $t_{pp} \rightarrow 0$ is fulfilled. This is due to the introduction of advisory and control software systems for human–computer interaction. In the era of the digital revolution, an employee through a sensor system connects to a computer and its software and thereby becomes a bio-cyber machine, which not only minimizes the time loss analyzed above, but also finds solutions to the problem $t_{pp} \to 0$. In the human–machine system, the working time t_{ppm} for processing a workflow unit includes: t_{pph}—time spent by a human, t_{rm}—time spent by a machine to help a person. Then $t_{ppm} = t_{pph} \, t_{rm}$. With increasing productivity of computers and software, $t_{rm} \to 0$, and t_{pph} will remain unchanged determined by psycho-physiology. Thus, the productivity of the bio-cybermachine Tp3 with the complete replacement of human labor by artificial intelligence will be limited only by the performance of computers: $Tp3 = 1/\,(t_{rrm} \to 0) \to \infty$.

The methodological recommendations discussed above for assessing and improving labor productivity in the workplace should be supplemented with recommendations to evaluate and improve the performance of the office, administration or state body as a whole. Depending on the scale of their activities and the complexity of the decisions made, the process of creating value in them can be organized sequentially, in parallel or sequentially in parallel (combined).

Consider the performance of organizational structures of office activity provided that the characteristics of components of the structure elements $\{\pi_i(t): i = 1, 2,... k\}$ are known.

1. Structure S_1 consisting of sequential action elements, i.e. $S_1 = \pi_1 \wedge \pi_2 \wedge ... \wedge \pi_k$, where $\wedge$ is the sign conjunctions, k is the number of elements (jobs) in the structure. Employees, machines, or a combination of them may be elements of the structure. Element π_i of the structure is characterized by a specific time t_i of the operation under the job instruction.

If the execution time of operations by all elements of the structure S_1 at workplaces $\pi\,(t)$ are equal ($t_1 = t_2 = ... = t_k$), then structure performance is maximum and equal to $Pts_1 = 1\,/\,t_i$, $i = 1, 2,... k$. However, such an ideal state is never found in practice. If in the structure S_1 the time of operations is not equal ($t_1 \neq t_2 \neq ... \neq t_k$). This is due to the value—building technology itself and the different functional responsibilities of structure components S_1, the performance of such structure can be calculated as: $Pts_1 = 1\,/\,t_i$, where $t_i = \max\,(\{t_i: i = 1, 2,..., k\})$.

In this case, "value creation" and productivity will depend on the duration of operations at the workplace, characterized by t_{max}. Thus, the performance of the structure S_1 is determined by the weakest element with characteristic:

$Pts_I \leq \min (\{Pts_1: i = 1, 2,..., k\})$. The weak link $\pi(t_{max})$ inhibits performance growth of the entire S_1 structure, while the rest of the subsystem is idle. Therefore, this workplace should be reorganized to the performance of the element, characterized by a minimum execution time t_{min}. As organizational measures can be offered: advanced training or retraining, organization of a parallel workplace (compensating link), in extreme cases, the search for a new, more productive employee. To synchronize the process, the required number n_i of parallel links for the i-th element is determined from the expression: $n_i = t_{max} / t_i$. As a result, the maximum possible performance of the structure Pts_1 will depend on element Pts_1 whose $t_j = \min (\{t_i: i = 1, 2,..., k\})$, i.e. $Pts_1 = \max (\{P_i: i = 1, 2,..., k\})$. The reserve for increasing labor productivity will be in the range: $Pts_1 \min < \Delta Pts_1 < Pts_1 \max$.

All of this reasoning and calculations will be fair, provided that the period τ between assignments to structure S_1 belongs to the interval $t_{min} < \tau < t_{max}$, i.e., the frequency of "inputs" provides partial or full workload. If the input of tasks to the structure occurs rarely i.e. $\tau > t_{max}$, then the performance of the structure depends on the frequency of inputs and is calculated based on the duration of this period τ: $Pts_1 = 1 / \tau_{av}$, where τ_{av} is the average time interval of work. If the input of tasks to the structure occurs more often, i.e. $\tau > t_{max}$, then there is a need for a different location of jobs in the space, which will be discussed hereinafter.

2. Structure S_2 parallel working elements $\{\pi_i\}$, $S_2 = \pi_1 \vee \pi_2 \vee ... \vee$, where $\vee$ is the disjunction sign, k is the number of parallel elements. If the execution time of all elements of the structure S_2 at the workplaces $\pi (t)$ is equal to $(t_1 = t_2 = ... = t_k)$, then the productivity of the structure Pts_2 is calculated as follows: $Pts_2 = kt_i$, where $i = 1, 2,..., k$. If t_i tends to a minimum $(t_i \rightarrow t_{min})$, then the structure reaches maximum productivity: $Pts_{2max} = k / t_{min}$. Achieving maximum performance is possible under the following conditions: artificial intelligence controls the performance of work, and under the control of artificial intelligence is carried out and synchronization, and minimizing the execution time of operations.

If in structure S_2 the time of operations in the workplace is not equal $(t_1 \neq t_2 \neq ... \neq t_k)$, the performance of such a structure can vary from minimum to maximum value depending on the time difference operations in these fields. The minimum performance of the structure will depend on the workplace with the longest execution time $t_j = \max (\{t_i: i = 1, 2,$

THE METHODOLOGY FOR CALCULATING THE PRODUCTIVITY ... 443

..., k}) and is calculated as: $Pts_{2min} = k \ / \ t_j$. Therefore, the performance of the parallel structure cannot be lower than the performance of each of the elements separately. Maximum performance is calculated according to the formula $Pts_{2max} = k \ / \ t_i$, where $i = 1, 2,..., k$. The working range ΔP of the productivity of the investigated structure $\Delta Pt_2 = Pts_{2min} \div Pts_{2max}$.

3. The combined structure of S_3 (parallel-series working elements) can be written as $S_3 = \pi_1 \wedge \pi_2 \vee \pi_3 \wedge ...$. In this case, the performance calculation procedure is broken down into two steps. First, the structure undergoes the analysis of workplaces, the results of which select and then aggregate successive and/or parallel groups of elements $(\pi_i, \pi_j, \pi_k) \subset S_3$. Aggregation of jobs is carried out until the structure takes the form of either sequential or parallel working elements. At the final stage, depending on the type of final generalizing structure obtained, the calculations of productivity and reserves of its increase are carried out according to the methods presented in clause 1 or clause 2.

4 Conclusion

The change in the format of office activities due to digitalization has increased the share of work carried out by cyber machines and increased productivity in management and service delivery. The value of performance reserves in these conditions depends on the requirements of the environment, and may be limited by the level of technology and the physical characteristics of structural elements.

The presented methodological approaches to assessing productivity and identifying reserves for its increase in individual jobs or their aggregates, and the result of which are documents, administrative acts, instructions or regulatory legal acts, that allow not only reengineering of commercial organizations and government institutions but also significantly improve the quality of provided services.

Acknowledgements The article was prepared as part of the implementation of research work under the contract No. 32 of research work of September 17, 2018 with Consult Audit LLC.

REFERENCES

Bushmin, S. V. (2020). *Rating of office and management personnel*. http://bus hminsergey.blogspot.com/2018/06/Normirovanieofisnihrabotnikov.html. Accessed 20 March 2020.

Emerson, G. (1992). *Twelve principles of productivity* (217 p). Economics.

Gaifutdinova, S. V. (2018). *Enterprise economics: Textbook* (507 p). INFRA-M.

Golovanov, A. I. (2013). From productivity to labor efficiency. *Bulletin of Tomsk State University, 376*, 137–141.

Imai, M. (2013). *Kaizen: The key to the success of Japanese companies* (274 p). Alpina Publisher.

Imai, M. (2015). *Gemba Kaizen: The way to reduce costs and improve quality* (324 p). Alpina Publisher.

Laro, U. (2009). *Office-Kaizen: Transforming office operations into a strategic competitive advantage* (224 p). Grevtsov Publisher.

Shaumyan, G. A. (1973). *Complex automation of production processes* (640 p). Mashinostroenie.

Sokolova, L. G. (2016). Methodology for calculating the productivity of managerial labor. Izvestiya Irkutsk State Economic Academy, 26(2), 213–219. https://doi.org/10.17150/1993-3541

The Future of Jobs 2018. (2020). http://reports.weforum.org/future-of-jobs-2018/key-findings/. Accessed 20 March 2020.

Philosophical and Methodological Aspects of Labor Quality Management in the Era of Intelligent Machines

Sofya S. Stukanova[ID], *Irina P. Stukanova*[ID], *Alexander V. Agafonov, and Igor A. Murog*

1 INTRODUCTION

The current stage of development of the world economy, characterized by the increasing prevalence and applicability of digital technologies and intelligent machines, necessitates the adaptation of labor resources to requirements of the time. Development of qualitative characteristics of workers becomes the most important task. This is ensuring the possibility of achieving competitive advantages both at the level of individual companies and at the level of regions and the country as a whole.

S. S. Stukanova (✉)
Moscow Polytechnic University, Moscow, Russia

I. P. Stukanova · A. V. Agafonov
Cheboksary Institute (Branch) of Moscow Polytechnic University, Cheboksary, Russia
e-mail: rektorat@polytech21.ru

I. A. Murog
Ryazan Institute (Branch) of Moscow Polytechnic University, Ryazan, Russia
e-mail: dir@rimsou.ru

© The Author(s), under exclusive license to Springer Nature Switzerland AG 2021
E. G. Popkova and B. S. Sergi (eds.), *Economic Issues of Social Entrepreneurship*,
https://doi.org/10.1007/978-3-030-77291-8_41

445

The quality of a human resource is subject to constant changes of an endogenous and exogenous nature. As well as any transformational process, the process of improving the quality of labor resources requires managerial influence. The main problem in this case is related to the presence, on the one hand, of a significant combination of management objects (people as carriers of the qualitative characteristics of the labor resource) and the multiplicity of management entities, on the other. Quality management of labor resources is carried out by individuals; management of enterprises and organizations through the implementation of personnel policies; by the government through development and implementation of programs for socio-economic development.

Polysubjectivity of labor resources quality management and various patterns of behavior in relation to quality formation and development cause a management process different orientation and often reduce its effectiveness. However, in the era of intelligent machines, in order to ensure socio-economic development, implementation of unidirectional management is especially important. This ensures stable improvement of quality and, first of all, such its elements as educational, professional, motivational and cultural components. In this connection, management methodological foundations development, which is based on scientific evidence, takes into account an object characteristics and the subjects of management structure, become of current interest.

2 Methodology

Methodological approaches to managing the quality of labor resources at the level of enterprises, regions, and country are developed by many researchers and include tools and methods of economic, sociological, psychological, medical and other sciences. However, on the one hand, the components, which characterize human resources quality are bulk. On the other,—marked variety of individuals patterns of behaviour determine interdisciplinary approach to study the problems of labour resources quality control. Interdisciplinary studies, which are a fairly young direction in the philosophy of science (Mac Leod & Nersessian, 2016), allow to integrate conceptual and methodological approaches of various sciences and spheres of knowledge. But they are often characterized by a certain complexity of their implementation in specific areas of practical activity (Politi, 2019) as well as by a complexity of applied concepts and theories attributability and, finally, by a complexity of their explanation and validation. Nevertheless, researchers agree that modern science needs a methodological basis for interdisciplinary research (Mac Leod & Nersessian, 2016).

This study is based on the application of conceptual and methodological approaches to philosophy, systems theory, labor economics, behavioral economics; methods of critical analysis, synthesis, descriptive formalization, analytical and bibliographic research, as well as on the principles of determinism and dualism.

Theoretical and methodological provisions and conclusions regarding approaches to labour resources quality management in socio-economic systems of various hierarchical levels are substantiated by the results of statistical data analysis. These data was collected and submitted by official statistics bodies, research centers and agencies.

Based on the foregoing, on modern conditions of socio-economic development, and on intellectual machines implementation intensification, it is suggested to investigate the principles of management from the standpoint of labour resources quality multi-levelness, interconnectedness and dynamism.

3 RESULTS

The most important condition for choosing a methodology of management is the fundamental properties of labour resources quality identification. Philosophical approach to labour resoures understanding as well as interdisciplinary approach application allows to compare the quality of labor resources with the cumatoid. This approach seems to be valid, since separate quality features of an individual (e.g., urgency of his knowledge) may appear and disappear; develop or disintegrate (for example, ones motivation to master innovations, to labor productivity improvement, etc.); be presented in all elements of the considered set (all employees of the enterprise, the labor resources of the region, etc.) or only in its definite part (Zhuk, 2015a). All this is inherent to cumatoid as well.

Thus, dynamism of cumatoid, on the one hand, and reproductability of its most typical qualities and characteristics, on the other, explains the importance for the philosophy of science and management methodology a particular scientific approach justification. This approach should take into consideration both features of labor resources quality and uni-oreintation of management in socio-economic systems of various levels availability.

In this case, fundamental principles of quality management determination is considered to become a logical step. Among these principles, in addition to the classical principles of structural unity; obvious and natural change of the state of the managed object; objectivity and scientific confirmation, it is appropriate to focus on the principle of determinism and the influence of dissipation.

Conceptual foundations of determinism prove a set of relations existence between different phenomena and results of management activities realization. Concerning labour resources quality research and management, various determinism concepts could be chosen, which, nevertheless, would be more or less effective from the position of their implementation into the methodological basis of management.

Thus, trying to identify the reasons that caused a certain level of labour resources definite qualitative characteristics development, it is possible to use definitive determinism. In the era of intelligent machines, when a high level of knowledge and professionalism become the most important indicators of labor resources quality, definite determinism finer points application allows to explain the low level of employers' satisfaction with the current workers' level and depth of knowledge (Table 1).

Employers' opinions are a subject to several reasons. These reasons include low motivation of current day workers to their qualification improvement, professional skills and competencies development. This

Table 1 Managers' satisfaction with the level of knowledge of their subordinates, belonging to different age groups, % (Zhuk. S., 2015b)

Characteristics of knowledge	Age groups				
	under 25 years old	26–35 years old	36–45 years old	46–55 years old	56 years and more
General knowledge	14	16	19	23	28
Special knowledge	8	24	31	20	17
Depth of knowledge	5	21	27	32	15
Knowledge width	9	19	32	34	6
Relevance of knowledge	18	27	30	14	11

could be approved by the following data. In Russia only 27% of the population (25–64 years old) is involved in the long-life education process, whereas in EU amount of such people achieves on average 53.9% of the overall population. At the same time in Russia only 24% of population is engaged in self-education process (Bondarenko, 2018) and very often main educational motives are far from the desire to achieve a high level of proficiency.

This, only 4 out of 10 people choose an educational program in accordance with their propensities and talents. The opportunity of new knowledge acquisition attracts only one third of students studying at master programs; each 10th student enters a master program to get a right to live in a dormitory or to avoid conscription. At the same time every second student's desire for professional development is replaced by motivation for career growth. It was also found that the majority of graduates (more than 60%) do not plan to work in accordance with their specialization but are going to look for managerial positions (each 5th graduate) (Stukanova & Stukanova, 2020).

Identified trends could be analyzed further. And in this case an analysis based on Laplace determinism principles is supposed to be effective. Thus, considering that any phenomenon can be a consequence of several previous and a cause of some future phenomena, it is possible to explain a low labour productivity in Russia (Table 2).

However, it is obvious that the process of labor resources quality development cannot always be described by linear function. In the vast majority of cases, while forecasting future results from managerial activities realization, we have to consider a statistical probability of these activities effect. Therefore the principles of probabilistic determinism are

Table 2 Labour productivity in selected countries, dollars/hour (Ilyina & Starostina, 2019)

Country	Indicator value
Ireland	99.5
Luxembourg	98.5
Norway	83.1
Belgium	76.8
Denmark	76.4
Germany	72.2
Chile	27.6
Russia	26.5

methodologically approved. The effect from these principles integration is especially relevant when managing labor resources quality in socio-economic systems of micro- and individual levels. Basically this happens because of managerial activities results dissipation.

The evidence of the probabililistic determinism and managerial activities dissipation influence on the results of labour resources quality development is illustrated on an example of such indicator as the state of health. A variety of policies and programs aimed at healthy lifestyle promotion, disease prevention, life expectancy increase realized on both federal and regional levels. These programs contribute to the predominant number of Russians prefer to buy quality products, without GMO; to the increasing number of citizens who have refused from alcohol and tobacco consumption (about 40% versus 31% in 2016); to the 2.6 times increase (in comparison to 2016) in the amount of people involved in sports and fitness (Stukanova & Stukanova, 2018).

As it is illustrated, there are positive results from managerial activities realization, nevertheless, these activities succeeded not in all cases, showing the results probabilistic determinism.

Probabilistic determinism of outcomes is caused by many factors, and not the least importance among them belongs to values and behavioral orientations of certain individuals.

Thus, on the one hand, the vast majority of Russians proclaim health as the main value in life (99 points out of maximum 100) (Stukanova & Stukanova, 2020). On the other hand, Russia has been already for quite a long period of time mentioned among the top 10 most "drinking" countries in the world and among countries where the fast food consumption is extremely popular among the population (Stukanova, 2018). Despite of the authorities efforts the relevant health care programs realization, only 1 out of 4 residents undergo medical examination regularly; at the same time 56% of Russians diagnose themselves by their own and look for cures and methods of treatment via Internet, and 80% of them follow the information and tips they have found (Zubarev, 2018). It is not surprising that with such attitude of Russians to their health, annually in the country it is resisted an increasing amount of diseases incidence and prevalence (in all major classes of diseases) (Table 3).

Labour resources quality aspects and individuals or their groups patterns of behavior concerning the quality improvement can be analyzed from philosophical and methodological positions of holism and individualism.

PHILOSOPHICAL AND METHODOLOGICAL ASPECTS ... 451

Table 3 The population incidence by certain classes of diseases (with a diagnosis established for the first time in life), thousand (Malkov et al., 2019)

	2000	2010	2018
All diseases	106,328	115,187	114,847
Of which:			
Neoplasms	1,226	1,540	1,705
Endocrine, nutritional and metabolic diseases	1,234	1,461	1,927
Circulatory system diseases	2,483	3,734	4,784
Respiratory diseases	46,170	46,281	52,833
Injuries, poisoning and some other consequences of external causes	12,544	13,096	13,072

Holism, which is based on the priority of the whole over the particular, institutions over individuals, formed scientific views and methodological approaches of Institutionalism and Keynesianism representatives. At the same time, some researchers (German economists) argue that the institutional economy is functioning independently and is not influenced by the behavior of individuals. The other group of scientists (American institutionalists) underline that each individual's behavior is the result of dual factors effect: biological nature and institutional interactions (Blaug, 1994).

Thus, methodology of holism seems to be reasonable in working under the concepts of socio-economic development and under federal and regional programs of labor resources quality improvement. In these cases management bodies of socio-economic systems of macro-level predominantly use quantitative aggregated data, which allows them to identify the labor resources quality macro-dependencies and to forecast and to build trends of its development. However, this data doesn't allow revealing neither the labor resources quality determinants, nor behavioral aspects of its formation. Macro-level management bodies in these situations use such methodological tools as regression analysis, analysis of trends, comparisons, etc. And this allows them to work out forecasts and benchmarks which are further included into the respective programs of socio-economic development.

According to the results of the mentioned above methodological principles and tools application, it is recognized that in the near future in Russia there will be no significant positive changes in the workforce structure (Table 4); and that it is improbable (due to significant gaps in

Table 4 Forecasted values of selected indicators of labor resources structure in Russia (Denisenko, 2010)

Indicator	2025		2030	
	Rosstat	UN population division	Rosstat	UN population division
Population, mln. of people (projections)	140.9	139.0	139.4	136.4
Population in working ages, mln. of people (projections)	93.0	89.6	91.1	86.6
Life expectancy, years				
Men	67.5	66.7	...	...
Women	78.4	76.9	...	...
	NRU HSE		NRU HSE	
Number of employed, mln. of people (projections)	69.6		68.1	
Number of unemployed, mln. of people (projections)	2.5		2.5	

indicators value) to reach the world leaders Human Development Index results (Table 5). And these factors are very unfavorable for national economy development in the era of intelligent machines.

Table 5 Human Development Index for selected countries, 2018 (Conseysao et al., 2019)

Ranking place	Country	Indicator value
1	Norway	0.954
2	Switzerland	0.946
3	Ireland	0.942
4	Germany	0.939
4	Hong Kong, China (ATS)	0.939
6	Australia	0.938
6	Iceland	0.938
8	Sweden	0.937
9	Singapore	0.935
10	Netherlands	0.933
49	Russia	0.824

It is quite difficult to predict an individual person conduct regard to his certain qualitative characteristics development, as well as to forecast possible changes in motives, which determine his definite pattern of behavior. It is common knowledge that any individual has a dynamic set of motives and assesses the level of his human capital development subjectively, which results in volatility of his labor resource quality characteristics. To overcome these constraints and to be able to analyze and to forecast trajectories of individual's workforce quality development a methodology of individualism can be used.

As a scientific methodology, individualism is opposite to holism in its basic principles. Individualism rests on postulates and assumptions that society consists of separate individuals, is characterized by their behavior and actions, and that there are no supra-individual factors that could be significant for research (Kincaid, 1998). Based on these assumptions, scientists (in particular, representatives of Neoclassical school) explain social phenomena through the behavior demonstrated by a single individual and through the actions expected from him. Scientific developments of neoclassics are widely used in researches of Behavioral school of representatives. In their works behaviorists develop models, of an individual social and economic behavior, in which individual's characteristics and certain conditions of his decision—making are taken into account.

Socio-economic phenomena and socio-economic processes research through analysis of a single individual actions and behavior forms the foundation for various 'man-models' development. These models, based on a combination of internal and external determinants of conduct and on particular model basic assumptions and limitations provide the ability to forecast an individual's behavior (including behavior in regard his individual qualitative characteristics development).

An individual's motivation to his human resource qualitative characteristics improvement is heavily formed on the basis of expectations, values, and satisfaction from the already achieved results. It is important to consider the fact that financial situation and stability is the main value of modern Russians (90 points out of 100). At the same time such values as professionalism; desire to be a useful member of society; interesting work; the opportunity to one's creativity realization, etc., which are the most significant for a qualitative development of an individual, do not occupy leading positions in this values ranking (Russian Newspaper, 2017). Based on the above, it could be concluded that with the current approaches to managing the labor resources quality and human capital development are not effective in individual's motivation for creative, productive work improvement, for stimulation of innovations implementation and for self-development revitalization.

4 Conclusion

Therefore, in the era of intelligent machines, when it is required that both human capital and labor resources quality of in socio-economic systems of all levels should develop constantly (in all their components: education, qualification, motivation, innovations orientation, labor and personal mobility, readiness for long-life development, professions of the future acquisition, etc.), close attention should be paid to the labor resources quality prosperities, its determinants and holism and individualism methodological principles synthesis in order to succeed in managing rhis quality under new conditions development and economic growth provision.

References

Blaug, M. (1994). *Not difficult lesson of economic methodology* (Thesis), 4, Volume 2.

Bondarenko, N. V. (2018). *Continuous education of adult population of Russia: Involvement, funding sources and major effects of participation* (Information Bulletin of National Research University Higher School of Economics, Monitoring the Economics of Education, No 12).

Conseysao, P., et al. (2019). *Report on Human Development 2019*. United Nations Development Program.

Denisenko, M. (2010). Population of Russia till 2030: Demographic and functional forecasts. In A. Vishnevskiy (Ed.), *Russia's population 2009: The 17th Annual Demographic Report* (pp. 295–329). Moscow.

Ilyina, N., & Starostina, Y. (2019). *Russia is behind Ireland in 3.8 times in regards to labor productivity*. https://www.rbc.ru/economics/05/02/2019/5c5872889a794725eb8d815e. Accessed 4 February 2020.

Kincaid, H. (1998). *Methodological individualism/atomism: The handbook of economic methodology*. London.

Mac Leod, M., & Nersessian, N. J. (2016). Interdisciplinary problem-solving: Emerging models of integrative system biology. *European Journal for Philosophy of Science, 6*, 401–416.

Malkov, P., et al. (2019). *Russian statistical yearbook 2019: Stat. book* (708p). Rosstat.

Politi, V. (2019). Specialisation and the incommensurability among scientific specialists. *Journal for General Philosophy of Science, 50*, 129–144.

Russian Newspaper. (2017, June 7). *Russians listed their main values in life*. https://rg.ru/2017/06/07/opros-rossiiane-nazvali-glavnye-cennosti-v-zhizni.html. Accessed 2 February 2020.

Stukanova, I. (2018). *Consumers' behaviour on the food market under environmental socio-cultural changes* (pp. 143–145). Bulletin of Chuvash State Institute of Culture and Arts.

Stukanova, S., & Stukanova, I. (2018). Health of Russians as a characteristic of human resources quality. *Standards and Quality, 8*(974), 86–89.

Stukanova, S., & Stukanova, I. (2020). The quality of education as an indicator and a tool for improving the quality of life. *Standards and Quality, 1*(991), 94–97.

Zhuk, S. (2015a). *Human resources quality management: Theory and practice* (232p). Dushkov & Co.

Zhuk, S. (2015b). *Institutional and methodological aspects of managing human resources quality* (239p). Dashkov & Co.

Zubarev, D. (2018, March 14). Russian opinion public center described the changes in Russians' attitude towards their health, opinion. *Business Newspaper*. https://vz.ru/news/2018/3/14/912373.html. Accessed 1 February 2020.

Contemporary Information Society and Higher Legal Education: Formation of a Professional and a Personality of Prospective Lawyer

Alexandra M. Drozdova, *Tatyana V. Vorotilina*, *and Igor V. Zhuzhgov*

1 INTRODUCTION

It is common knowledge that "social institution of education is an organization of activities and social interactions, implemented through a mutually agreed system of expedient norms of behavior, the occurrence and classification of which in the system are determined by the need to develop competences and to socialize the individuals, to transfer accumulated knowledge and skills to them with a view to augmenting them in order to preserve society, maintain its development, improvement and harmonization (Riterman, 2009). Furthermore, education is represented by a fairly complex social process, being one of the core, fundamental institutions of contemporary society, which generally determines the pace of scientific-technological progress, spiritual and cultural development,

---

A. M. Drozdova (✉) · T. V. Vorotilina · I. V. Zhuzhgov
North-Caucasian Federal University, Stavropol, Russia

I. V. Zhuzhgov
e-mail: zhuzhgov@bk.ru

© The Author(s), under exclusive license to Springer Nature Switzerland AG 2021
E. G. Popkova and B. S. Sergi (eds.), *Economic Issues of Social Entrepreneurship*,
https://doi.org/10.1007/978-3-030-77291-8_42

political well-being of the State, as well as morality, legal awareness and culture of people.

If we may be permitted this reminder, since March 16, 2020, the Ministry of Education and Science of the Russian Federation have recommended to organize distance education of students of higher education institutions to prevent the spread of coronavirus, and this project was widely implemented. Furthermore, today, the entire higher education system in the country prepares for the potential conversion of some part of State Final Examination in higher education institutions to online mode, as well as to the enrollment campaign of 2020 with potential use of distance technologies.

Moreover, the Minister of Science and Higher Education of the Russian Federation Valery Falkov, pointed out in his recent interview that the pandemic have revealed the problems of higher educational institutions that had not previously been apparent. "It is also a question of the efficient work of the Director and the management teams, a question of the financial and economic model which was used by the higher education institution, and whether economic indicators as such were considered at all in the activities of a higher education institution",—he explained (Web Portal "Nauchnaya Rossiya", 2020).

There are already scientific papers and research on the current state of problems in the field of higher education during the pandemic and after it (Dozhdikov, 2020), and new methodological solutions are offered, such as: "Distance education as a modern teaching format"; in addition, training programs for the teachers themselves are offered; moreover, provision is made for the possibility of accelerated training according to personalized schedule.

Since the development of science, technology, and ICT generate the need for improving the efficiency of education, including legal education, it is obvious that further interpretation of the modern period is required with due account for the pandemic, as well as the research on the problems of contemporary education in the Russian Federation along with possible solutions to the latter.

2   Materials and Method

We proceed from the premise that, when it comes to the place and importance of legal education, we should keep in mind its mission, namely to train and organize the teams of highly professional experts for different branches of jurisprudence, so that they, in turn, could function in a high-quality and efficient manner for the benefit of an individual, society, and the State, protecting their interests.

We should point out that development of the modern Russian educational system has served as the basis for the increasingly wide use of new educational technologies and methods, information telecommunication technologies and distance education; they might perfectly be used to explore and identify certain further development trends. And the current methodological methods and techniques will allow to explore the present and the future of legal education in Russia with account of complexities of modernity.

In our research, we proceed from the fact that the strategy for the development of education is defined by the government programs and concept until 2025 based on the National Doctrine of Education approved by the Government Regulation of the Russian Federation No. 751 of October 4, 2000, which defines the goals and ways of achieving them through State Policy in education, as well as the results of education until 2025 (Website of the President of Russia, 2011). Further, we are guided by the Basic Principles of State Policy of the Russian Federation for the development of legal literacy and legal awareness among citizens, approved on May 4, 2011 (Basic Principles of State Policy of the Russian Federation for the development of legal literacy and legal awareness among citizens (approved by the President of the Russian Federation on 28.04.2011 under No. PR-1168).

The methodology of research on information society and its impact on the development of the higher legal education system perfectly allows for the use of both the principles of scientific knowledge and the research studies based on certain approaches of the systematic, comparative, regulatory, formal logical, social-psychological, historical and logical methods, content analysis taking into account the principles of objectivity and comprehensiveness, modernity and actual state of things in the perception of phenomena under analysis.

3 RESULTS

Many problems, defined as objective and subjective, have been existing, and still exist, in the Russian education system. The practical aspect of the formation of a professional lawyer, graduate should still be acknowledged, though the theoretical aspect of the training undergoes significant changes, and these changes are by no means always for the better.

There is no well-established relationship between a school and a higher education institution, since the applicant who enters the first year of study at the university after passing the USE has little to no knowledge to be able to immerse himself or herself in the academic activity of a higher education institution.

Another challenging problem is the way in which students are selected and recruited for law schools, without taking into account the fact that the lawyer is a specialist who is intended to struggle for the effectiveness of public order, legal order and stable development of the State as a whole, while demonstrating high level of legal awareness, legal culture, managerial abilities, high moral qualities, discipline and responsibility. Russian researchers point out that "a society with high level of legal culture will have the appropriate level of legal order" (Drozdova et al., 2019).

56 second-year students in the training program 40.03.01 "Jurisprudence" (Bachelor's Degree) in the North Caucasus Federal University were surveyed within the scope of the research on the problems in the legal education system, at the premises of the Law Institute of the North Caucasus Federal University, in the course of implementation of the project grant of the Russian Foundation for Basic Research. Some survey findings were highly unexpected to the research team. For example, with the overwhelming majority of respondents reporting the need for compliance with law under any circumstances (87.5%), just a little more than half of respondents reported that "they wouldn't buy the item at a low price, knowing it is stolen"—57.1%, and that "given the chance to commit theft unnoticed", only 51% of respondents replied that "they would not do it themselves and would prevent their friends from doing it", i.e. there is a general negative trend in Russian society, indicating a low level of legal awareness and culture in general.

3.1 Problems in Education Due to Changes in Conventional Forms (Violation) of the Process of Education

The response of most of the world's States to coronavirus has directly affected education throughout the world, and foreign universities are already loudly considering the need for financial adaptation because they anticipate a sharp drop in income. However, the development of digital education platforms almost in all places is predicted. Like any phenomenon, the crisis has two aspects. Problem: will it be possible to remotely transfer the entirety of affiliation with the school of sciences, to build social ties?

An unexpected problem was the complete unpreparedness of parents for distance education of pupils and students due to their level of education and material security. Yet most of all they resent the need to educate, to train and to control their own children. Probably after a long period of self-isolation society will start a discussion about the personality of a teacher is, his or her role and mission in society, which will raise the teacher's profile everywhere!

Another problem is the lack of the necessary number of Internet-capable technical devices in many Russian families, where parents work and children study from home at the same time. We cannot ignore problem of the loss of the student body; there is an imminent task to bring all pupils and students back to the normal process of education in the following.

Distance education form has a variety of advantages, which does not exclude certain problems that have definitely become apparent due to its universal application.

Social isolation and the continuing loss of social activity and the constant interaction of individuals give cause for concern, as they may cause a wide range of negative effects, especially among adolescents and young people who are devoid of social development, education, and communication with their peers for a long time.

What is reassuring is that Russian students who have studied abroad will come back to higher educational institutions in their home country, and will bring financial flows with them, which is important for economists. We would like to believe that the patriots of their country who will come back to invest their knowledge and skills in the development of the national economy of Russia will be able to fulfill their career opportunities for the benefit of their State.

In the circumstances, we cannot disregard professors and teachers, who must adapt quickly to new conditions, to become engaged in the preparation and creation of a new national education platform.

3.2 Whether Higher Education Should Be Fee-Based or Tuition-Free

Proceeding from the fact that at some point every person is faced with the question of the choice of study, the acquisition of a profession for further activity, for life, for successful functioning and adaptation in society, the applicant faces a choice of the form of education—fee-based or tuition-free. Fee-based or tuition-free education, who benefits from it: a parent, a student, a higher education institution, or State?

Considering that the main regulatory legal act which regulates the social relations in education is the Constitution of the Russian Federation, Part 1 of Article 43 in which determines the right of all people to education, the Federal Law of the Russian Federation "On Education" No. 273-FZ (Consultant Plus Legal Reference System, 2020) was adopted in Russia in 2012, which specifies constitutional provisions in the field of education.

A certain population group, when reasoning about education, believes that when studying, accumulating knowledge and skills in a particular field, a student cannot quickly see and assess the results of his or her efforts or inactivity. One can agree that it is necessary to find a solution to such fundamental problem in the Russian legal system as finding, developing, and educating the fundamentals (ideas, principles, feelings, etc.) of the spiritual-cultural type of legal awareness (when a particular component of the content of principles of law will in any case determine the fundamental ideas, core values, conditions of application of legal remedies, ensuring achievement of the spiritual-moral component in the mechanism of law-making and law-enforcement activities (Tereshchenko et al., 2017).

We have ventured to suggest that those who believe that education will become more interesting, that professors and teachers will become more competent and students and pupils will learn with greater awareness and commitment have a point there.

3.3 Relationship Between an individual—Student—higher education Institution—State

All participants of the educational process—students, their parents, higher education institutions and the State—interpret the process of education as such and the outcome of it from their own perspective and with different

CONTEMPORARY INFORMATION SOCIETY ... 463

interest since there is no direct relationship between a student and the State, though it should be there.

Objectively, there should be a State order for an applicant, a prospective student from the State, to prioritize a student who will directly receive compensation (or a contract for compensation) of costs of his or her studies upon admission, and, having acquired a certain amount of knowledge and skills, will prove that the learning had made him or her become a carrier of the necessary knowledge, and that he or she can carry out professional activities, which will increase the responsibility of the student and will serve as a motivation for diligent learning. There are no problems if the goals of a higher education institution, a student and a parent as a participant of the process of education match, and a significant result can be achieved in that case.

In ordinary life, it was clear that distance education is needed by certain individuals and in a particular situation; we were slowly preparing and introducing distance education forms in the academic activity with great incredulity. It will be recalled that at the end of November 2019, the State Duma of the Russian Federation proposed to consider introducing the concept of "Internet education" in federal legislation, which could only be implemented if it was properly licensed (Prokshin, 2019).

Intrinsically, the violated process of education in schools and higher education institutions throughout the world affected millions of students, and UNESCO immediately provided the educational system with relevant recommendations. As our researchers have pointed out, one cannot ignore the development of social ties between students, their families, teachers and the higher education institution with a view to taking into account and preventing the arising psychosocial problems.

The authors of the research conclude that there is a need for trainings or orientation sessions for teachers and students, assistance and support in the use of mobile tools and online lessons, while limiting the use of same-type platforms and applications, and applying tools available to most students, without making things more complicated for students and teachers, but providing for controls of the process of education.

For students, especially those who lost their jobs due to the pandemic, some higher education institutions of the country have already developed the programs for their employment in various sectors depending on acquired profession or currently necessary areas of activity; besides, while working, they develop certain skills that may be required in the future.

It happened that suddenly, during the pandemic, we were faced with a choice: nothing or distant. Some people believe that everything will resume its natural course, but Kuzminov (HSE) claims with confidence that there will be no return to the past.

In this case, integratory higher education institutions should be established, which will develop appropriate educational paths for students. Still, a computer will not be able to replace a higher education institution, and higher education institutions will have to change their educational space with new labs by creating new modern campuses. However, these are all our assumptions, and soon we'll see whether they will or will not come true.

Today, legal education, like the entire society, goes through dark times, when new problems have been added to the previously existing problems, which can be eradicated not by immediate opportunistic decisions of government agencies, but by methodical, focused activity, which will involve various actors in the educational process.

In our opinion, this complex work can consist of several interrelated stages: (1) a fundamental study of accumulated problems, especially amid the coronavirus pandemic; (2) elaboration of the scientific concept, (3) introduction of new innovative technologies, methods and methodologies in the academic activity in law schools. We are trying to define the methodology for the analysis of the implementation of mechanisms of formation of an array of applicants, taking into account the psychological and worldview characteristics of prospective lawyers, since all activities of universities, especially law schools, in contemporary information society, become important, visible and significant for the legal life of the entire region, as was noted in the Resolution of the 15th General Conference of the International Association of Universities.

Digitalization, quarantine and forced self-isolation have caused a number of problems that are challenging for all of us: children and adults; pupils and students, parents and teachers.

The fact of the matter is that the forced transition occurs rapidly, in a force majeure mode, rather than gradually, as has repeatedly been the case; social behavior is changing under the impact of epidemic and economic crises.

Today, we don't have a single place to communicate with students; all of us have left the classroom, but time is still a common thing, and it unites us. In such a psychologically and economically challenging environment, it is important not to lose human dignity, "whereas the recognition of the inherent dignity and of the equal and inalienable rights of all members of the human family is the foundation of freedom, justice and peace in the world" (UN, 1948).

4 Conclusion

Considering the fact that legal education is not only a system of a set of knowledge of a particular individual, this is not only a system of knowledge created and preserved by human civilization, but also a result of perception of state-legal phenomena while learning the grammar of legal profession.

Today, when the world experiences such global changes resulting from the pandemic, legal education requires not just another modernization, but a research study.

The educational system requires the special attention of scholars and practicing educators in terms of the prompt study and analysis of various problems that are related not only to the teaching process and not so much to it as to the state of education in the country and the training of professional legal advisers.

Based on the completed theoretical and empirical research, considering the fact that legal education trains legal professionals for various fields of activity who should treat particular circumstances from the perspective of law while realizing their potential and serving their Motherland, country, and the State, we point out that currently it has many problems, which have never been characteristic either of legal education or practicing lawyers before.

We cannot conceal another Russian problem in education: highly qualified practitioners are constantly invited to law schools of the country by creation of necessary conditions for them in order to ensure the practical focus in the study of industry-specific legal disciplines. This is because, as is rightly pointed out by Russian researchers, "the new digital format of the professional legal environment should be based solely on the balance of fundamental knowledge and practical knowledge and skills" (Smirnov et al., 2020).

When we examine legal education as an element, factor, component of the system of development of human society at any stage of its development, it is impossible not to note such important functions of legal education as sustainment, cultural development, humanization and democratization of society in the formation of legal awareness and culture of each individual in society.

We venture to suggest that the process of education will remain a remarkable and exciting process. Well, only those who will learn and want to learn, who will transmit positive thinking on the process of education as such, will be able to survive and adapt to the new conditions. If the student will have to change, the teacher must become a mentor, a designer, an adviser. It is important to maintain inextricable high-level connection of legal awareness and culture, knowledge and skills in professional activity for law students, for graduates and young professionals, as well as for the entire legal education in general; it largely determines the fates of people and industries, as well as the future of the country.

Acknowledgements The paper has been prepared with financial support from the Russian Foundation for Basic Research (grant No. 20-011-00344 A).

References

Consultant Plus Legal Reference System. (2020). *Federal Law "On education in the Russian Federation" No. 273-FZ of December 29, 2012* (As amended on February 6, 2020). http://www.consultant.ru/document/cons_doc_LAW_140174/. Accessed 12 May 2020.

Dozhdikov, A.V. (2020). On measures taken in the world education systems in response to the COVID-19 pandemic and the edutech used. *Monitoring of the Economic Climate in Russia: Trends and Challenges in Socioeconomic Development, 10*(112). http://www.iep.ru/files/text/crisis_monitoring/2020_10-112_April.pdf. Accessed 12 May 2020.

Drozdova, A. M., Balakireva, L. M., Vorotilina, T. V., Makarova, E. V., & Meleshkin, V. V. (2019). Legal awareness and legal culture as elements and means for the implementation of a mechanism for ensuring the legal impact. *Opcion, Año, 35*(19), 2922–2934.

Prokshin, N. (2019). *Mironova, K. The State Duma has started addressing the issue of online education.* https://www.kommersant.ru/doc/4171490. Accessed 12 May 2020.

Riterman, T. P. (2009). *Social Science: Full-time course.* AST.

Smirnov, D. A., Tereshchenko, E. A., Botasheva, L. E., Trofimov, M. S., Melnikova, V. A., & Dolgopolov, K. A. (2020). Digital jurisprudence. *Revista Inclusiones, 7*(1), 273–283.

Tereshchenko, E. A., Kovalev, V. V., Balakireva, L. M., Savchenko, E. V., & Solovtsova, E. A. (2017). Characteristics of legal culture study in Russian and foreign legal literature. *Journal of Advanced Research in Law and Economics,* *8*(27), 1619–1628.

UN. (1948). *Universal Declaration of Human Rights* (Adopted by the UN General Assembly on 10.12.1948). https://www.un.org/ru/documents/decl_conv/declarations/declhr.shtml. Accessed 12 May 2020.

Web Portal "Nauchnaya Rossiya". (2020). *The Minister of Science and Higher Education Valery Falkov on the TV program of "Rossiya-24"—Russian Academy of Sciences.* https://scientificrussia.ru/articles/rossiya-24-ran-uchenye-o-kor onaviruse-ministr-nauki-i-vysshego-obrazovaniya-valerij-falkov. Accessed 12 May 2020.

Website of the President of Russia. (2011). *Basic principles of state policy of the Russian Federation for the development of legal literacy and legal awareness among citizens* (Approved by the President of the Russian Federation on 28.04.2011 under No. PR-1168). http://kremlin.ru/events/president/news/11139. Accessed 12 May 2020.

Problems of the Formation of Legal Awareness of Youth in the Process of Digitalization in Russian Education

Rustam Z. Abdulgaziev, Magomed R. Alsultanov, Albert S. Arshinov, Viktor N. Mamichev, and Dmitry I. Sostin

1 Introduction

The training of highly qualified personnel for the modern economy is the most important task in the education sector. The digital economy, which is currently a globalization trend, requires high-quality specialists, and in this regard, the education sector should optimize this process and provide new approaches to their training.

On the one hand, digitalization opens up broad prospects for obtaining education, raises problematic issues of the formation of digital skills and competencies, and on the other hand, contributes to the development of an appropriate level of legal awareness of young people in educational establishments.

R. Z. Abdulgaziev (✉) · M. R. Alsultanov · A. S. Arshinov · V. N. Mamichev · D. I. Sostin
Stavropol Branch MIREA-Russian Technological University, Stavropol, Russia
e-mail: abdulov126@mail.ru

© The Author(s), under exclusive license to Springer Nature Switzerland AG 2021
E. G. Popkova and B. S. Sergi (eds.), *Economic Issues of Social Entrepreneurship*,
https://doi.org/10.1007/978-3-030-77291-8_43

The relevance of the topic under study is due to the theoretical crudity in reality of the problems of legal consciousness of student youth in the process of digitalization, which are analyzed by the authors of the article.

2 Materials and Method

Currently, the total digitalization is an important trend that determines the digital transformation of the economy (Smirnov, 2020).

The digital economy assumes that digital data is a key factor of production in the socio-economic sphere, where digital technologies provide effective interaction between business, government and citizens (Khalin & Chernova, 2018; Rachinger, 2019; Solovyova, 2019).

The transformation of education plays an important role in the development of the digital economy. The transformation of education and, accordingly, an increase in the level of legal awareness should be based on two criteria: preparing young people for life and activities in the context of digitalization and using the potential of digitalization to improve the effectiveness of the educational process. These criteria are aimed at achieving the required educational results and the all-round development of student youth.

The educational process should be accompanied by the necessary teaching material for students of the relevant specialties.

During the research, a general scientific method was used, and as a result the essence of the "legal awareness" and "digitalization" concepts were distinguished. Historical and comparative methods were widely used, which made it possible to identify the emergence and development of the main normative acts in the field of digitalization, their comparison based on emerging problems and implementation in the educational process. The comparative legal and analogy methods were also used, which made it possible to study the views of foreign and Russian scientists on the process of digitalization in education.

3 Results

The modern world is subject to constant changes in all spheres of life and in all areas of social consciousness. It is in the public consciousness that the essence and the status of a particular society are manifested.

Modern science distinguishes forms of social consciousness, including life, the structure of social institutions, the organization of the process of cognition, and these forms include ideology, science, morality, art, religion and legal awareness.

Let's consider the theoretical aspects of legal awareness.

The concept of "legal awareness" is interpreted in the legal literature based on the subjective approach of the authors. So, Matuzov and Malko (2004) believe: "The concept of legal awareness directly answers the question: how the law is perceived, realized, evaluated, interpreted by the person, how he relates to it."

According to Safronov (2008), legal awareness is "one of the forms of social consciousness, represented in the aggregate of psychological, ideological and behavioral components, expressing the attitude of individuals, social groups, and society as a whole to the current or desired law, to the behavior of people in the sphere of legal regulation".

A new definition of legal awareness was introduced by Tikhomirov (2020): "Legal awareness is a reflection of the state of understanding the role of law in society, assessment of real and possible legal phenomena, potential ability to act or in one way or another reflect the interests of people, their will and actions."

Legal awareness is an objective and permanent phenomenon. It characterize the legal system, the political structure of society and the prospects for the development of the state depend on the level of ordinary, professional and scientific legal consciousness (Friedman, 1975).

The basic features of legal awareness, which determines the social and legal behavior of a person, include knowledge of legal regulations and attitude to law and legal regulations and social and legal behavior: subjects of social and legal behavior, social values, public authorities, fulfillment of civic duty in maintaining law and order, social legal expectations.

Legal awareness as a form of social consciousness has a structure consisting of legal ideology and legal psychology.

The basis of legal ideology is the knowledge of law, which provides a person with rights and obligations, deals with prescriptions, permissions and prohibitions. If a person strives for legal knowledge, then he must understand their content and understand it as an objective need for the progressive development of the state and society. This knowledge will significantly increase the level of perception of the legal realities of the Russian state in the process of exercising individual rights and freedoms, separation of powers, political pluralism and judicial practice. Ideological preparation of a person allows controlling affections, emotions, feelings, etc., that is, what constitutes the content of legal psychology.

Legal psychology reflects knowledge of the law, social norms and self-esteem—the criteria for assessing behavior in accordance with the principles and norms of law.

In this regard, legal awareness contains mental processes that manifest themselves in real legal behavior. A person should be aware of the content of the instructions addressed to him, respond appropriately and choose the required behavior. Ultimately, the recognition and non-recognition of law depends on legal psychology, and the latter, unfortunately, dominates the mass legal awareness (Abdulgaziev, 2019a).

Modern society lives in a digital reality caused by information technologies that have taken root in human life. Digitalization is becoming an objective reality.

Professor Rachinger (2018) in the article "Digitalization and its impact on the innovation of business models" digitalization means "the use of digital opportunities in various fields."

The essence of digitalization lies in the automation of processes, namely, in the transition of information to a more accessible digital environment, where it is easier to analyze it, and then, using data analysis, find out exactly what the market wants to get at a particular moment and introduce the most priority areas of digitalization into everyday life—the economy, business, management, healthcare, education.

Digitalization is considered as an effective global development trend if:

- it covers production, business, science, the social sphere and the life of citizens;
- accompanied by the effective use of the results;
- the results are available to users of the converted information;
- the results are used not only by specialists, but also by citizens;
- users of digital information have work skills (Khalin & Chernova, 2018).

Thus, new technologies, means of communication, opportunities provided by new standards of service—all this predisposes to a change in the traditional system of values of Russians.

This study allows us to identify the peculiarities of the legal consciousness of modern youth in the educational process in the course of mastering the necessary knowledge in the field of digitalization.

The priority in the field of the formation of legal consciousness, of course, is youth, as the most promising, socially and politically creative part of Russian society; at the same time, it should be remembered that the legal consciousness of youth is one of the basic conditions that determine the political culture of society, the prospects for the development of the law-governed state.

Currently, almost 24.3 million people live in Russia within the ages of 15 and 29, i.e. 16.5% of the total population of the country, according to the message of the Organizing Committee of the 2020 all-Russian Population Census. More than 88% of young people aged 15–19 gain knowledge in educational institutions of various levels (Rambler News, 2019). At present, the exact data on the student population in Russia is not known. The all-Russian Population Census in the country was planned from October 1 to October 30, 2020, and using modern digital technologies. And if the situation in the country changes due to the pandemic, then next year we will receive these data.

The fundamental documents of the digital transformation of the Russian society and economy and the achievement of an appropriate level of legal awareness are the Strategy for the Information Society Development in the Russian Federation for 2017–2030 and the Digital Economy of the Russian Federation.

Awareness of the importance and necessity of digitalization of the Russian society, the education system in the information society, enhances the use of this, of course, an extraordinary resource in the framework of the implementation of tasks to form the legal awareness of youth. This trend in Russian education has been gradually implemented since 2005 within the framework of the national project "Modernization of Russian education" within the framework of the completion of this project by the end of 2024.

In the "Fundamentals of the state policy of the Russian Federation in the development of legal literacy and legal awareness of citizens of April 28, 2011 No. Pr-1168, it is emphasized that "... the quality level of education and training in educational institutions of various types and kinds, including the assignment and development of students legal awareness; outspreading and use of information materials accessible for perception by an individual that form legal literacy and legal awareness, in print, electronic, audiovisual and other forms, as well as with the help of the media...".

At present, the Ministry of Science and Higher Education of the Russian Federation has taken a course towards digitalization of educational activities. This, according to the ministry, corresponds to the global trend, the program for the development of a "digital society". In education, digitalization will be associated with the transition from traditional education to digital management in the formats of Samsung, IBM, Microsoft and other electronic digital products.

At different times, scientists and practitioners have conducted numerous empirical studies of the quality and effectiveness of educational standards in higher education, including legal education. The result of this work was the selection of educational programs, which were then used as a tool for the formation of the foundations of the legal awareness of students. However, in the conditions of rapid development of socio-communicative transformations of the late XX—early XXI centuries, the crisis of the traditional institutions of younger generation socialization, this is clearly not enough. It is already obvious that both the school and the university should form young people knowledge, competencies, as well as skills that are in demand in the context of digitalization, the economy, social sphere, and culture.

The formation of the legal awareness of young people at an early stage is associated with digital technologies and, to a lesser extent, with traditional agents of socialization, for example, the family, the institution of which has recently been in crisis.

The most important institution that took part in the formation of the legal awareness of society was the state. For decades, if not more, the state and society have been managing the process of communicative influence on the legal awareness of young people and have been responsible for this. The digitalization of public life with its unlimited communicative capabilities, if they are uncontrolled, can not only give a quick informational effect, but can also carry negative one when the consciousness of the younger generation is influenced by anti-social, criminal ideas and views (Abdulgaziev, 2019b).

Much in such conditions depends on the organization of legal and moral education. In the context of digitalization, teachers need not only skills and abilities to work with a digital-type information environment, but also a different mentality, a completely different perception of the picture of the world, different approaches and forms of work with students.

In connection with the optimization of the educational process with the use of digitalization, the role of the legal awareness of young people is increasing.

The legal awareness of young people has its own specifics, characterizing it as a special socio-demographic group.

At different times, scientists and practitioners have conducted numerous empirical studies of the quality and effectiveness of educational standards in higher education, including legal education. The result of this work was the selection of educational programs, which were then used as a tool for the formation of the foundations of the legal awareness of students. However, in the conditions of rapid development of socio-communicative transformations of the late XX—early XXI centuries, the crisis of the traditional institutions of socialization of the younger generation, this is clearly not enough. It is already obvious that both the school and the university should form young people knowledge, competencies, as well as skills that are in demand in the context of digitalization, the economy, social sphere, and culture.

It should be borne in mind that the genesis of the legal awareness of youth takes place in the process of socialization and social development. The impact of the Internet, computer-based media and telecommunication technologies leads to the fact that young people are developing a new, so-called "mosaic" type of culture. In general, it corresponds to the trend of the global information society.

In the process of forming the legal awareness of the younger generation with the help of digital technologies, certain problems are also identified. The renowned expert in the field of educational technologies Khagurov (2010) noted that "today schoolchildren and students read much less than their peers 20 years ago. The average student spends time in a never-ending stream of audiovisual information. It is often possible to observe simultaneous absorption in several media channels.

Thus, the formation of the legal awareness of young people at an early stage is associated with digital technologies and, to a lesser extent, with traditional agents of socialization, for example, a family, the institution of which has recently been in crisis. This reality is very destructive, because the role of those who first formed a positive attitude towards law among young people was most often played by parents with ordinary legal awareness.

To train qualified personnel, it is necessary to make appropriate changes in educational programs. Moreover, the development of these programs requires the fastest possible solution. It is believed that for specialties closely related to information and communication technologies, it is necessary to introduce the course "Legal Foundations of Digitalization", and in the future to develop and start studying the "Digital Law" industry.

Recently, articles on digital law have appeared in the media, which should find a place in the system of objects of civil rights and provide individuals and legal entities with protection in transactions with digital rights. According to the Chairman of the Constitutional Court of the Russian Federation Zorkin "A new law is emerging that regulates relations in the context of the world of numbers and artificial intelligence" (Rossiyskaya Gazeta, 2018).

The Federal Law "On Amendments to Parts One, Two and Article 1124 of Part Three of the Civil Code of the Russian Federation" dated March 18, 2019 No. 34-FZ was adopted, which introduced Article 141.1 into the Civil Code of the Russian Federation the concept of "digital law", in which digital rights are "obligations and other rights, the content and conditions of implementation of which are determined in accordance with the rules of the information system" (Reference and legal system ConsultantPlus, 2019).

An important role in the formation of legal awareness in the process of digitalization is assigned to the teaching of relevant disciplines. In this regard, it is necessary to accelerate the process of training teachers in this area, and to introduce an appropriate direction in refresher courses.

According to Solovyova (2019), "The formation of the digital economy and the invasion of digital processes into all spheres of life pose a number of tasks for the educational system of Russia, among which the most important are: improving the educational infrastructure, developing digital literacy among teachers and students, increasing the level of development of digital skills of the population in general, which will help narrow the digital gap between different generations and categories of people."

The state supports digital technologies in the field of education, which will allow introducing effective methods of teaching and building a new educational environment.

4 Conclusion

The theoretical crudity in modern science of the problems of legal awareness of student youth in the field of digitalization leads to the substitution of empiricism for the conceptual approach. To solve the problems that arise in the formation of legal awareness in the field of digitalization among young people, it is necessary, in our opinion, to pay attention to the following.

At the federal and regional levels, develop an appropriate strategy and regulatory framework for the development of digital skills in youth, basing on the recommendations of the International Telecommunication Union and the International Labor Organization, which drew attention to the classification of digital skills, including:

- basic digital skills, which include basic skills in working with information and communication technologies, which are necessary both at work and in the educational process. These are search and communication on the Internet, the use of professional online platforms;
- medium digital skills requiring preparation of publications and social media management, graphic design and marketing, which are necessary both in the learning process, in the workplace and in business;
- developing interpersonal skills necessary for effective cooperation in the digital economy - teamwork, leadership, communication skills, etc.;
- advanced digital skills, which include the development, testing and analysis of information and communication technologies and their management.

The main changes in education related to digitalization will lead to changes in the labor market and the emergence of new competencies, which will be the basis for the further reorganization of the educational process using artificial intelligence technologies.

In the process of digitalization, the structure of training and the organization of the educational process will fundamentally change, requiring material for creating courses, organizing them, as well as improving the methods and style of managing an educational institution.

A mechanism for creating educational materials is required, an effective delivery of an information resource to students for effective teaching. Currently, Russian universities use a two-component information and educational environment. It accumulates the resources of international educational platforms and the content of its own developments.

It is important to optimize the information and educational environment, the implementation of which will be the basis for the development of any university. It is necessary to improve the qualification requirements for the teaching staff in the process of digitalization of higher education.

It is necessary to update the content of educational programs aimed at increasing the digital legal literacy of students, which will increase the level of legal awareness of young people.

REFERENCES

Abdulgaziev, R. Z., Mamichev, V. N., Sostin D. I., Sukhorukova A. N., Alsultanov, M. R. (2019a). Legal consciousness as a factor in the formation of the rule of law. *Revista Dilemas Contemporáneos: Educación, Política y Valores, 37*, 1–12.

Abdulgaziev, R. Z., Alsultanov, M. R., Mamichev, V. N., Sukhorukova, A. N., Sarukhanyan, A. R., & Sostin, D. I. (2019b). Social causation of criminalization of cyber crime committed with the use of information technology. *International Journal of Advanced Trends in Computer Science and Engineering, 8*(5), 2459–2463.

Electronic reference legal system "ConsultantPlus". (2019). Federal Law of 18.03.2019 No. 34-FZ on Amendments to Parts One, Two, and Article 1124 of Part Three of the Civil Code of the Russian Federation. http://www.con sultant.ru/document/cons_doc_LAW_320398. Accessed 20 April 2020.

Friedman, L. M. (1975). *The legal system: A social science perspective*. Russell Sage Foundation.

Khagurov, T. A. (2010). Education in the "Pepsi" style (polemical notes). *Sociological Research, 7*, 96–103.

Khalin, V. G., & Chernova, G. V. (2018). Digitalization and its impact on the Russian economy and society: Advantages, challenges, threats and risks. *Administrative Consulting, 10*, 46–63. https://doi.org/10.22394/1726-1139-2018-10-46-63.

Matuzov, N. I., & Malko, A. V. (2004). *Theory of state and law*.

Rachinger, M., Rauter, R., Müller, C., Vorraber, W., & Schirgi, E. (2019). Digitalization and its influence on business model innovation. *Journal of Manufacturing Technology Management, 30*(8), 1143–1160. https://doi.org/10.1108/JMTM-01-2018-0020.

Rambler News. (2019). In Russia, the number of boys and girls was counted https://news.rambler.ru/community/43142790/?utm_content=news_m

edia&utm_medium=read_more&utm_source=copylink. Accessed 20 April 2020.

Rossiyskaya Gazeta. (2018). *Law in the digital world.* https://rg.ru/2018/05/29/zorkin-zadacha-gosudarstva-priznavat-i-zashchishchat-cifrovye-prava-gra zhdan.html. Accessed 20 April 2020.

Safronov, V. V. (2008). *Legal awareness of the citizen.*

Smirnov, D. A., Tereshchenko, E. A., Botasheva, L. E., Trofimov, M. S., Melnikova, V. A., & Dolgopolov, K. A. (2020). Digital jurisprudence. *Revista Inclusiones, 7*(1), 273–283.

Solovyova, T. S. (2019). Russian education in the context of digitalization: Trends and prospects. *Moscow International Higher Business School Bulletin, 3*(19).

Tikhomirov, Yu. A. (2020). Legal consciousness in the context of social dynamics. *State and law, 3.*

CONCLUSION

Rethinking of the Essence and Prospects for the Development of Social Entrepreneurship in the Post-pandemic Period

The COVID-19 pandemic has made its adjustments to the development of social entrepreneurship around the world. Business entities do not have sufficient resources to use them within the framework of corporate social responsibility initiatives. Employees, being afraid of a new wave of layoffs, hold on to their jobs and place low demands on the corporate responsibility of employers in terms of providing public goods and providing socially significant services. Consumers, faced with the reduction of incomes, are not willing to pay high prices for the products of social enterprises.

At the same time, the need for public goods and socially significant services has increased sharply and is greater than ever. The acute deficit of the national budgets of the countries of the world does not allow full-scale financing of the provision of public goods and socially significant services, and their receiving on commercial terms (as economic benefits) is inaccessible to the great masses of the population in the context of falling incomes. Growing social inequality and a critical drop in the standard and quality of life require the intervention of social entrepreneurship.

This causes a contradiction between the capabilities of the business environment and the needs of the state and society, the resolution

© The Editor(s) (if applicable) and The Author(s), under exclusive license to Springer Nature Switzerland AG 2021
E. G. Popkova and B. S. Sergi (eds.), *Economic Issues of Social Entrepreneurship*,
https://doi.org/10.1007/978-3-030-77291-8

481

482 CONCLUSION

of which requires the development of new mechanisms for the functioning and development of social entrepreneurship. Pandemic is a period when society must rally and support a common idea to overcome the viral threat. But how can it be done against the background of social distancing? These questions are yet to be answered by the social and economic sciences in the post-pandemic period.

Many workers consider corporate vaccination as an important measure of corporate social responsibility - it is beneficial for enterprises as well, as it reduces employee morbidity and operations downtime. There is also a need for an inflow of private investment in health care. Medical services should be available for the whole society, which implies the development of a system for the provision of preferential medical services for socially unprotected categories of the population.

Private investment in new medicines and vaccines is a fundamental condition of their creation. It is obvious that the prospects for health care development are associated with the use of special mechanisms of public–private partnership in it. The training of medical personnel is also an urgent issue. Medical workers must be highly qualified and aware of their responsibility before the whole society. Probably, it is only through funding from social enterprises public health services can achieve high quality due to the effective incentives for health personnel.

In this regard, we can expect that in the coming years the new aspects of social entrepreneurship will be mainstream, previously unclaimed or inaccessible, but activated by the pandemic. It may happen that thanks to the progress of social entrepreneurship, modern society and economy will be much better at coping with the viral threat, and this will avoid future epidemics and pandemics.

Social entrepreneurship is designed to become a particular social institution, which, based on its socially significant activities, will unite society even in disconnecting conditions and allow the world to become resistant to future threats. We hope that this book will serve as a reliable basis for continuing the study of social entrepreneurship as a market economy phenomenon that requires a multidisciplinary interpretation at the intersection of social and economic sciences.

INDEX

A
additional professional pedagogical education, 425, 430

B
blockchain, 165–169, 385
business ethics, viii, 290, 291, 296

C
commercialization of rights, 259
communication platform, 63, 64, 66
competencies, viii, 15, 40, 42, 370, 371, 373, 383–385, 387, 391, 392, 395, 396, 400–403, 410, 426, 428–431, 448, 469, 474, 475, 477
compliance, 39, 40, 43, 44, 221, 260, 264, 291, 297, 299–303, 305, 306, 308, 309, 324, 370, 377, 392, 412, 460
compliance management, 300–310
compliance risks, 299, 302, 303, 305–309

Coronavirus, 148, 167, 205, 211, 289–292, 295, 458, 460, 464
corporate data network, 48
corporate governance, 163–166, 168, 170
corporate law, 163, 164, 166, 169, 170
corporate social responsibility, vii, viii, 1, 2, 291, 300, 317, 323–325, 327, 328, 332–339, 481, 482
the COVID-19, viii, 1, 146, 165, 170, 293, 294, 296, 297, 328, 481
creative industries, 259–264

D
data transmission risk, 48, 58
developed countries/developing countries, 146, 155, 254, 325–328, 333, 337, 338, 346, 349
digital age, 88, 260
digital competencies model, 396, 403
digital economy, vii, viii, 15–17, 19–21, 88, 152, 154, 155, 158,

© The Editor(s) (if applicable) and The Author(s), under exclusive license to Springer Nature Switzerland AG 2021
E. G. Popkova and B. S. Sergi (eds.), *Economic Issues of Social Entrepreneurship*,
https://doi.org/10.1007/978-3-030-77291-8

483

484 INDEX

162, 163, 170, 206, 207, 217,
257, 381, 395–401, 406, 469,
470, 473, 476, 477
digitalization, 15, 21, 38, 62, 64,
88, 91, 96, 151, 152, 161–164,
168, 170, 185, 186, 192, 205,
207, 236, 237, 243, 252, 254,
285, 381–384, 386–391, 393,
395–397, 399, 402, 405, 406,
412, 436, 437, 440, 443, 464,
469, 470, 472–478
digitalization of education, 405
digital technologies, 20, 21, 38–40,
42–45, 87, 91, 161, 162, 164–
167, 169, 186, 205, 209, 210,
236, 239, 245–247, 249–251,
253, 254, 258, 265, 382, 385,
396, 405–408, 412, 425, 426,
435, 445, 470, 473–476
digital transformation, 38, 39, 162,
206, 282, 283, 285, 382–385,
388, 390–392, 403, 470, 473
distance technologies, 458

E
e-Commerce, 206, 208, 209, 212,
213, 218–224, 258
economic freedom, 358–362
electronic educational environment,
406, 408, 426–429
electronic services, 407–413
export, v, 142, 143, 155, 175, 180,
181, 258

F
flexible methodologies, 11

G
government support, vii, 154

H
higher education, vi, 113–118,
120–122, 131, 260, 276, 370,
373, 406, 458, 460, 462–464,
474, 475, 478

I
industrial cooperation, 62, 63
industrial enterprises, 4, 75, 284
industrial parks, 62–65
informatization, 236, 237, 243, 247,
251, 426–428, 430
infrastructure support, 174, 175,
178–182
innovative activities, 63, 114–117,
152, 154, 155, 157, 158, 174,
285
innovative transformation, 118
institutional modernization, 113–115,
117, 120, 122
intellectual property, 257–260,
262–265
international cooperation, 173–175,
177–182
international integration, 174–176,
181
internet, 88, 90, 91, 94, 98, 178, 186,
188–192, 207, 213, 217–224,
237, 239, 246, 250, 252,
261, 381, 382, 397, 398, 402,
406–409, 412, 450, 461, 463,
475, 477
investments, 2, 28, 29, 33–35, 62–64,
78, 81–83, 103, 105, 107, 140,
141, 145, 154, 155, 180, 181,
262, 265, 285, 343, 344, 400,
482

L

legal awareness, 197, 202, 218–223, 236–243, 458–460, 462, 466, 469–478

legal culture, 218–224, 236–238, 460

legal education, 223, 238, 458–460, 464–466, 474, 475

legal regulation, 162, 164, 170, 185, 186, 196, 198, 199, 206, 208, 213, 218, 220, 224, 227, 228, 238, 247, 320, 471

M

malicious influence, 48, 49, 58

market economy, v–viii, 2, 137, 138, 143, 145–147, 264, 316, 324–328, 331–333, 337, 339, 344, 345, 355–362, 398, 482

modernization, 26–29, 35, 48, 81, 88, 116, 120–122, 163, 170, 174–176, 180, 181, 236, 237, 239, 243, 285, 416–422, 465, 473

N

national economic system, 138, 146

non-commercial business, 357–359

non-commercial organizations, 343–350

P

the pandemic, 2, 137, 138, 144–147, 197, 290–293, 296, 328, 458, 463–465, 473, 482

partners, 21, 62, 63, 70, 72, 73, 91, 98, 121, 221, 283, 296, 306, 382, 396

personnel management, viii, 20, 382–386, 388, 391, 393, 400

project, vi, vii, 3, 4, 6–9, 11, 26–29, 32, 35, 38, 39, 42, 45, 62–65, 72, 74, 79, 80, 91, 98, 103–110, 113–122, 139, 142, 143, 146, 154, 163, 175, 177, 180, 181, 211, 227, 233, 236, 270, 273, 274, 276, 283, 286, 308, 317, 343, 344, 369–379, 382, 396, 407, 410, 411, 426–428, 430, 431, 458, 460, 473

R

risk assessment, 43

S

safety culture in transport, 426, 428, 431

securities, 40, 48, 50, 163, 165, 168–170, 186, 188, 191, 192, 195–202, 230, 237, 249, 277, 293, 295, 314–317, 319–321, 370, 412, 415–422, 461

small and medium-sized businesses, viii, 65, 66, 137–140, 143–146, 174–176, 180–182, 317

social entrepreneurship, v–viii, 1, 2, 314, 316–321, 323–328, 331–333, 335–339, 344, 345, 350, 355–362, 481, 482

socially responsible business, 357–359

stakeholder, 66, 81, 177, 296, 299–303, 305–309, 333

students, 369–379, 406–413, 425, 426, 428–430, 449, 458, 460–464, 466, 470, 473–478

systemic scientific vision, 358, 359

T

transfer-integrative field, 428

CPSIA information can be obtained
at www.ICGtesting.com
Printed in the USA
LVHW081525091021
700007LV00002B/29